Trainee Guide

Sheet Metal

Level 2

National Center for Construction Education and Research

*Wheels of Learning
Standardized Craft Training*

Upper Saddle River, New Jersey

Prentice Hall
Columbus, Ohio

© 1992 by National Center for Construction Education and Research

Prentice-Hall, Inc.
Upper Saddle River, New Jersey 07458

All rights reserved. No part of this book may be reproduced, in any form or by any means, without permission in writing from the publisher.

This information is general in nature and intended for training purposes only. Actual performance of activities described in this manual requires compliance with all applicable operations procedures under the direction of qualified personnel. References in this manual to patented or proprietary devices do not constitute a recommendation for their use.

Printed in the United States of America

10 9 8 7 6

ISBN: 0-13-462763-6

Prentice-Hall International (UK) Limited, *London*
Prentice-Hall of Australia Pty. Limited, *Sydney*
Prentice-Hall of Canada, Inc., *Toronto*
Prentice-Hall Hispanoamericana, S. A., *Mexico*
Prentice-Hall of India Private Limited, *New Delhi*
Prentice-Hall of Japan, Inc., *Tokyo*
Pearson Education Asia, *Singapore*
Editora Prentice-Hall do Brasil, Ltda., *Rio de Janeiro*

Preface

This volume is one of many in the *Wheels of Learning* craft training program. This program, covering more than 20 standardized craft areas, including all major construction skills, was developed over a period of years by industry and education specialists. Sixteen of the largest construction and maintenance firms in the U.S. committed financial and human resources to the teams that wrote the curricula and planned the national accredited training process. These materials are industry-proven and consist of competency-based textbooks and instructor guides.

The *Wheels of Learning* was developed by the National Center for Construction Education and Research in response to the training needs of the construction and maintenance industries. The NCCER is a nonprofit educational entity affiliated with the University of Florida and supported by the following industry and craft associations:

Partnering Associations
- ABC Texas Gulf Coast Chapter
- American Fire Sprinkler Association
- American Society for Training and Development
- American Vocational Association
- American Welding Society
- Associated Builders and Contractors, Inc.
- Associated General Contractors of America
- Carolinas AGC, Inc.
- Carolinas Electrical Contractors Association
- Construction Industry Institute
- Design-Build Institute of America
- Merit Contractors Association of Canada
- Metal Building Manufacturers Association
- National Association of Minority Contractors
- National Association of Women in Construction
- National Insulation Association
- National Ready Mixed Concrete Association
- National Utility Contractors Association
- National Vocational Technical Honor Society
- Painting and Decorating Contractors of America
- Portland Cement Association
- Steel Erectors Association of America
- University of Florida
- Women Construction Owners and Executives, USA

Some of the features of the *Wheels of Learning* program include:
- A proven record of success over many years of use by industry companies.
- National standardization providing "portability" of learned job skills and educational credits that will be of tremendous value to trainees.
- Recognition: upon successful completion of training with an accredited sponsor, trainees receive an industry-recognized certificate and transcript from NCCER.
- Each level meets or exceeds Bureau of Apprenticeship and Training (BAT) requirements for related classroom training (CFR 29:29).
- Well illustrated, up-to-date, and practical information. All standardized manuals are reviewed annually in a continuous improvement process.

Acknowledgments

This manual would not exist were it not for the dedication and unselfish energy of those volunteers who served on the Technical Review Committees. A sincere thanks is extended to the:

1993 Technical Review Committee
- Mike Bergen
- Dallas Gamache
- Bob Haley
- Maynard Kettner
- Dave Price
- Bobby Shelton

1997 Technical Review Committee
- Steve Dooley
- Ellie Hein
- Maynard Kettner
- Curtis McMullen
- Walt Mills
- Mike Van Zeeland

Contents

Trade Math II	**Module 04106**
Basic Piping Practices	**Module 04110**
Fabrication II – Radial Line Development	**Module 04303**
Bend Allowances	**Module 04304**
Soldering	**Module 04312**
Blueprints and Specifications	**Module 04403**
The SMACNA Manuals	**Module 04405**
Sheet Metal Duct Fabrication Standards	**Module 04406**
Insulation	**Module 04409**
Gutters and Downspouts	**Module 04502**
Roof Flashing	**Module 04503**

Trade Math II
Module 04106

NATIONAL
CENTER FOR
CONSTRUCTION
EDUCATION AND
RESEARCH

Task Module 04106

TRADE MATH II

Objectives

Upon completion of this task module, the trainee will be able to:

1. Perform addition, subtraction, multiplication, and division tasks necessary for solving linear, area, volume, and angular measurement problems.

2. Correctly apply mathematical symbols in the solution of mathematical problems.

3. Solve percentage problems.

4. Understand, define, and solve ratio and proportion problems and equations.

5. Sequentially solve problems with the use of simple equations.

6. Understand how to use protractors, vernier calipers, and micrometers for angle and tolerance measurement problems.

7. Calculate the number of fitting blanks which can be cut from a given dimension of sheet metal stock.

8. Calculate stretchouts of square fittings, rectangular fittings, rectangular box fittings, circular, and cone fittings.

The exercises and practice drills in this module are designed to assist beginning sheet metal workers in developing proficiency in solving mathematical problems related to their field. The productive worker must first master the "how" of applied mathematics prior to developing production skills.

Copyright © 1992 National Center for Construction Education and Research, Gainesville, FL. All rights reserved. No part of this work may be reproduced in any form or by any means, including photocopying, without written permission of the publisher. Updated: 1998.

LINEAR MEASUREMENT

The measure of any length by workers is usually in terms of inches, fractions, or decimals of inches. In countries using the metric system, the common linear dimension is the millimeter (mm).

The SI (metric system) is based upon the use of the meter for linear measurement. The meter is subdivided into 100 equal parts called centimeters. Centimeters are further divided into ten equal parts called millimeters. There are 1000 millimeters in one meter. One meter is equal to 39.37 inches. When this inch length is divided by 100, the conversion factor of 0.3937 inch equals 1 centimeter (cm). One millimeter will then equal .03937 inch.

Knowing that 1 centimeter equals .3937 inch, we can get the value of 1 inch in terms of centimeters by dividing 1 centimeter by .3937 and arrive at the value of 1 inch as being 2.54 centimeters or 25.4 millimeters.

For construction purposes, the conversion of shop drawing dimensions and other technical information sources from the English system to the metric system must be made with extreme accuracy. Dual dimension procedures are now used for shop drawings and in labeling construction parts and supplies. Simple measuring tools can be obtained with both the inch/foot and metric scales imprinted on their faces.

LINEAR CONVERSION FACTORS

Construction workers commonly practice the use of meters and centimeters. The following comparisons of English and metric units should help workers to "think metric."

1. One millimeter is slightly more than 1/32 inch.
2. One centimeter is approximately 2/5 inch.
3. One meter is about 1-1/10 yards.
4. One kilometer is about 5/8 mile.

Industrial designers and architects have begun placing both metric and English dimensions on blueprints. All dimensions, no matter how large, will be in millimeters.

1. One millimeter equals .0394 inch.
2. 1/10 millimeter equals .00394 inch.
3. 1/100 millimeter equals .00039 inch.
4. 1/1000 millimeter equals .00004 inch.

Conversion charts or metrication aids will become increasingly common in construction trade areas. However, there will be times when workers will need to make on-the-spot conversions from English to metric measurements. When this occurs, rules are available which can be used in such circumstances. In order to convert from English to metric measurements multiply the English unit by its desired metric counterpart.

Study Examples

1. 1 in = 2.54 cm = 25.4 mm.
2. 5 in = 5 × 2.54 cm or 12.7 cm = 5 × 25.4 mm or 127 mm.
3. 3/4 in = .75 × 2.54 cm or 1.905 cm = .75 × 25.4 mm or 19.050 mm.

Study Problems

1. Convert each measurement to millimeters (1 inch = 25.4 millimeters).
   a. .25 inch
   b. 5/8 inch
   c. 25/32 inch
   d. 7.375 inches
   e. 3-3/4 inches
2. Convert each measurement to centimeters (1 inch = 2.54 centimeters).
   a. 1-5/8 inches
   b. 39.37 inches
   c. 12 inches
   d. 30 inches
   e. 18 inches

3. Convert each measurement to centimeters (1 foot = 30.48 centimeters).

   a. 1-1/2 feet
   b. 8-1/2 feet
   c. 6/23 foot
   d. 5-1/2 feet
   e. 2 feet 6 inches

4. Convert each measurement to meters (1 foot = .3048 meters).

   a. 2.5 feet
   b. 100 yards
   c. 16-1/2 feet
   d. 660 feet
   e. 5,280 feet

Two additional forms of linear measurement that are important to sheet metal workers are calculating circumferences of circles and lengths of arcs. These two facets of measurement are often used when performing sheet metal layout and development tasks.

The formulas for performing these types of calculations are:

Circumference of a circle: $C = \pi d$

Length of an arc: $L = \dfrac{n}{360}(\pi d)$

Study Problems

1. Calculate the circumference of a round duct seven inches in diameter (*Figure 1*).

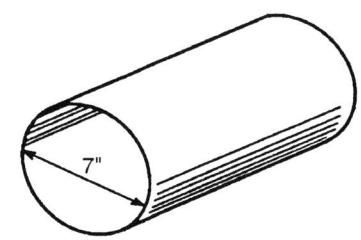

Figure 1 - Round Duct

2. Calculate the length of the stretchout of the throat on the 90 degree rectangular elbow (*Figure 2*).

3. Calculate the length of the heel stretchout on the 90° rectangular elbow in number 2.

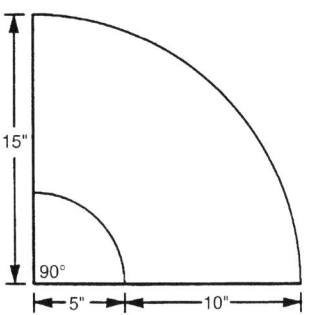

Figure 2 - 90-Degree Elbow

Area

Area measurement pertains to two-dimensional surface measurement. Area is always designated as some unit squared. For example the area of a rectangle is calculated by multiplying the length times the width. The resultant product will be expressed in terms of the unit of measurement squared. If, for example, the length of the rectangle is found to be 8 feet, and the width of the rectangle is measured to be 4 feet, the resultant product of 8 feet times 4 feet (A = LW) would be 32 square feet.

Sheet metal workers often use formulas for solving many practical problems concerning geometric shapes and figures. These workers should be able to know how to apply formulas in both direct measurement (using a measuring instrument to obtain information) and indirect measurement (using equations and elementary mathematical processes). This portion of the module should help the trainees become more proficient in formula manipulation and assist them in calculating the area of rectangles, squares, parallelograms, triangles, circles, and other geometric shapes. *Table 1* gives some of the common formulas used by sheet metal workers for calculating area measurement.

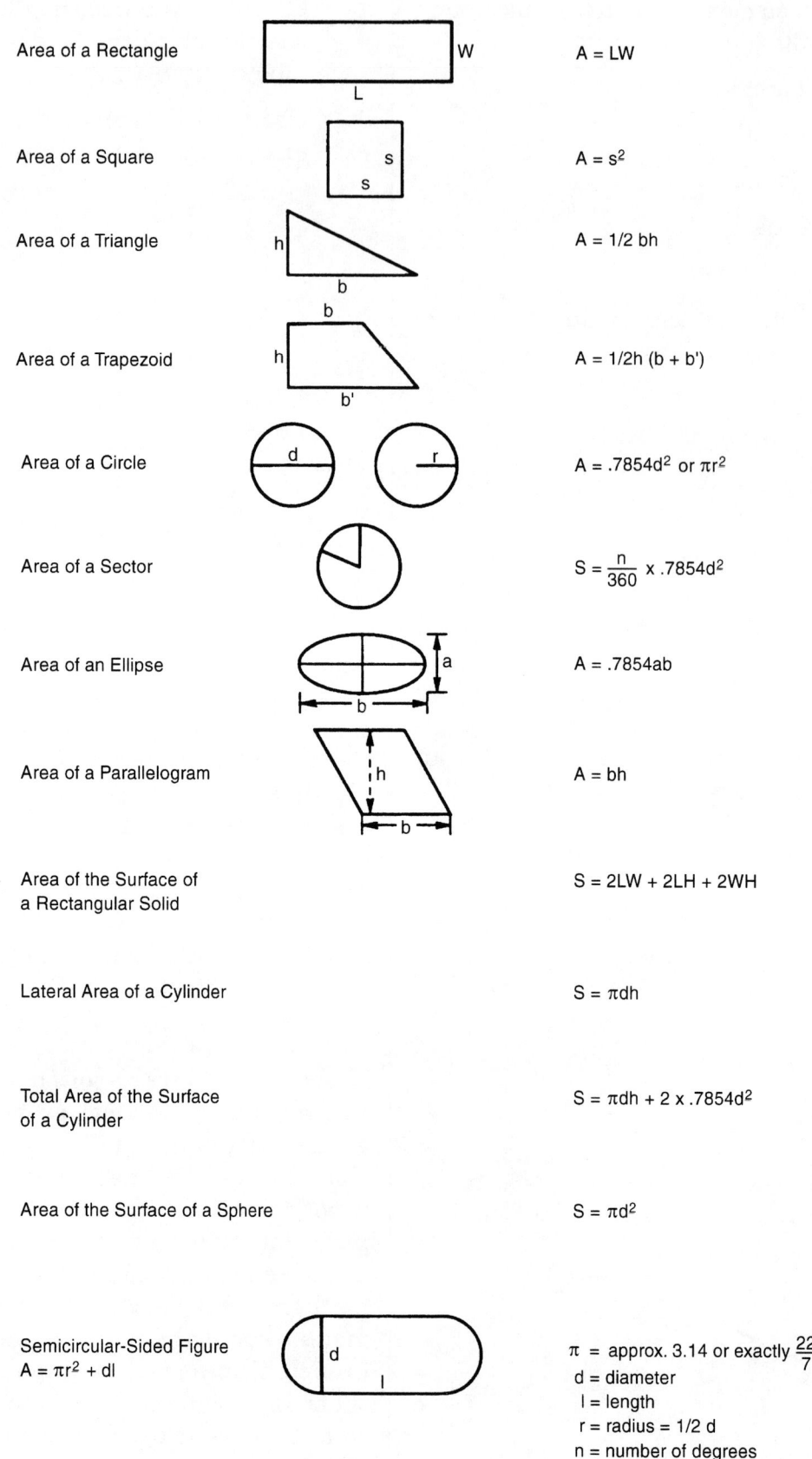

Area of a Rectangle	$A = LW$
Area of a Square	$A = s^2$
Area of a Triangle	$A = 1/2\, bh$
Area of a Trapezoid	$A = 1/2 h\, (b + b')$
Area of a Circle	$A = .7854 d^2$ or πr^2
Area of a Sector	$S = \dfrac{n}{360} \times .7854 d^2$
Area of an Ellipse	$A = .7854 ab$
Area of a Parallelogram	$A = bh$
Area of the Surface of a Rectangular Solid	$S = 2LW + 2LH + 2WH$
Lateral Area of a Cylinder	$S = \pi dh$
Total Area of the Surface of a Cylinder	$S = \pi dh + 2 \times .7854 d^2$
Area of the Surface of a Sphere	$S = \pi d^2$
Semicircular-Sided Figure $A = \pi r^2 + dl$	

π = approx. 3.14 or exactly $\dfrac{22}{7}$
d = diameter
l = length
r = radius = 1/2 d
n = number of degrees in angle of arc
h = height

Table 1 - Geometric Formulas

Study Problems

1. Calculate the area of a rectangle if L (Length) equals 15' and W (Width) equals 10'.
2. Calculate the area of a square if S = 14'.
3. Calculate the area of a triangle if the base (B) = 8 cm and the altitude or height (H) = 10 cm.

In a case where the altitude of a triangle (*Figure 3*) is not given, the area can still be calculated if the lengths of its three sides are known. The procedure is as follows:

Step 1. Find half the sum of the sides and find the difference between this sum and each side.

Step 2. Multiply the difference by half the sum.

Step 3. Extract the square root of the resulting product.

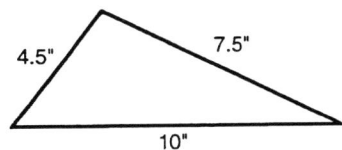

Figure 3

The formula for this type of calculation is:

Area = $\sqrt{s(s-a)(s-b)(s-c)}$, where

$s = \frac{a+b+c}{2}$ and a, b, and c are the lengths of the sides.

Thus,

$s = \frac{4.5 + 7.5 + 10}{2} = \frac{22}{2} = 11$

Now plugging 11 into the formula, we have:

$A = \sqrt{11(11-4.5)(11-7.5)(11-10)}$

$A = \sqrt{11(6.5)(3.5)(1)}$

$A = \sqrt{250.25}$

A = 15.81 square inches

4. Calculate the area of the triangle (*Figure 4*).

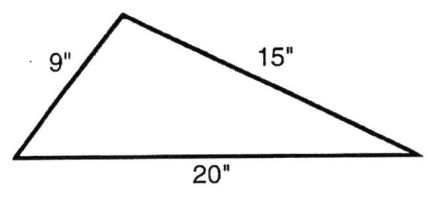

Figure 4

5. Calculate the area of a parallelogram (*Figure 5*) with a base of 7 m and an altitude or height of 4 m.

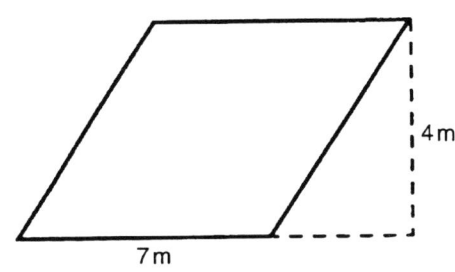

Figure 5

6. Calculate the area of a trapezoid (*Figure 6*).

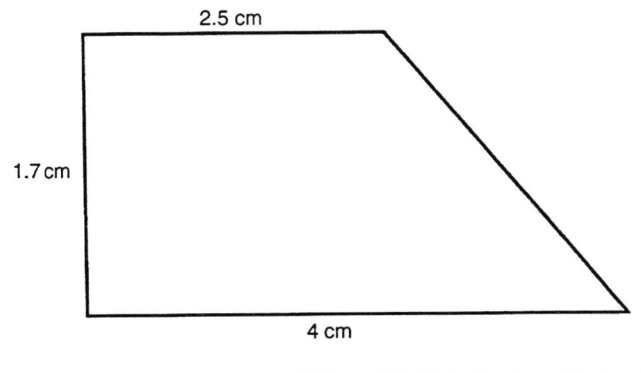

Figure 6

7. Calculate the area of round duct 7 inches in diameter.

TRADE MATH II — TRAINEE TASK MODULE 04106

8. Calculate the area of a circle sector diameter of 30 cm (*Figure 7*).

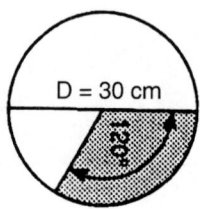

Figure 7

9. Calculate the area of an ellipse (*Figure 8*).

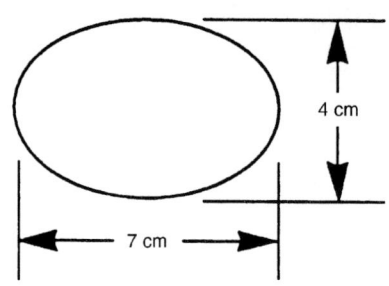

Figure 8

10. Calculate the area of a rectangular solid (*Figure 9*). Note the area of a rectangular solid is the sum of the area of its six rectangular faces. Dimensions: L = 4 yds, W = 5 yds, H = 6 yds.

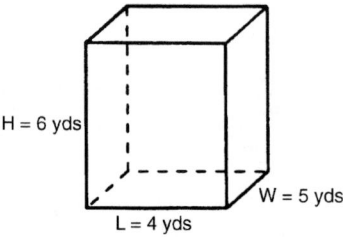

Figure 9

11. Calculate the area of a 10' cube (*Figure 10*).

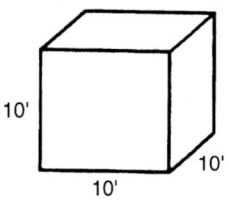

Figure 10

12. Calculate the lateral area of a cylinder (*Figure 11*).

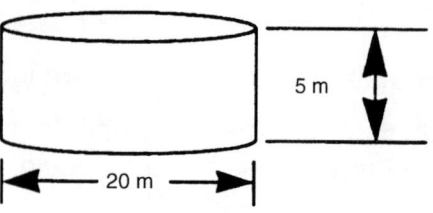

Figure 11

13. Calculate the total area of the surface of the cylinder in number 12.

14. Calculate the total area of the surface of a sphere 20 cm in diameter.

15. Calculate the total area of the semicircular-sided figure (*Figure 12*).

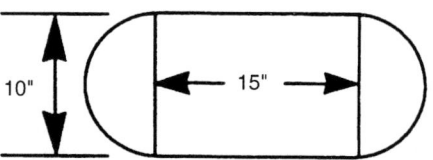

Figure 12

VOLUME MEASURE

Volume measure is expressed in cubic units, such as cubic inches, cubic feet, or cubic yards. When computing the volume of a rectangular solid, the volume in cubic units is the product of its length, width, and height. Bodies such as cones, cylinders, pyramids, spheres, etc., require special formulas to calculate volume. These calculations can be arrived at by using standard formulas for the specified shapes and configurations. As with square measure the dimensions must have the same units.

Study Examples

1. A box is 1 meter long, 75 centimeters wide, and 50 centimeters high. How many cubic meters/cubic feet are contained in its volume?

SHEET METAL — TRAINEE TASK MODULE 04106

(1 m) (.75) (.50 m) = .375 m³

To convert an English unit to its metric equivalent, multiply the English unit by its desired metric counterpart.

1 ft³ = (1 m³)(35.315)

Thus,

(35.315)(.375) = 13.243 ft³

Study Problems

1. A tank holds 1.57 cubic feet of fuel. How many cubic centimeters and cubic meters are contained in the tank?

2. A diesel engine on a generator has a piston displacement of 425 cubic inches. How many liters of displacement is this equal to? (Refer to *Appendix A*.)

3. An end loader has a capacity of 3 cubic yards. How many cubic meters is this equivalent to?

The following figures illustrate some of the standard formulas that can be used by sheet metal workers for calculating volumes of specified shapes.

Volume of a rectangular-shaped solid (prism) (*Figure 13*).

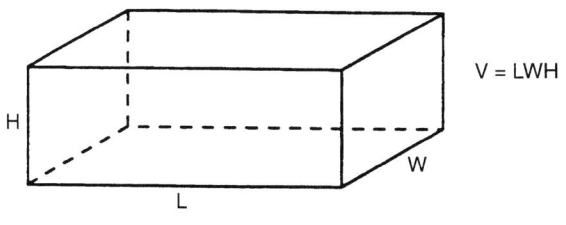

Figure 13

Volume of a cube equals the cube (*Figure 14*) of an edge.

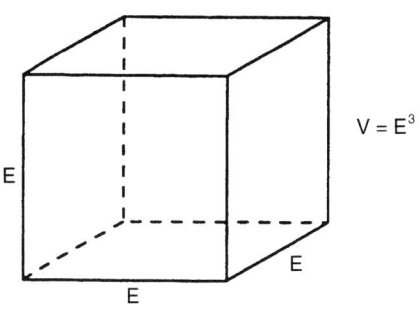

Figure 14

Volume of a prism (*Figure 15*) equals the product of the area of the base and the height. (B is the measure of the area of the base of the prism.)

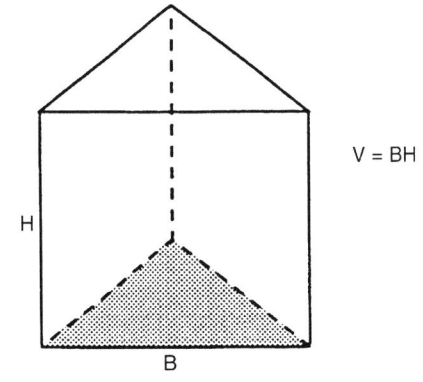

Figure 15

Volume of a pyramid (*Figure 16*) equals one-third the product of the area of the base and the height.

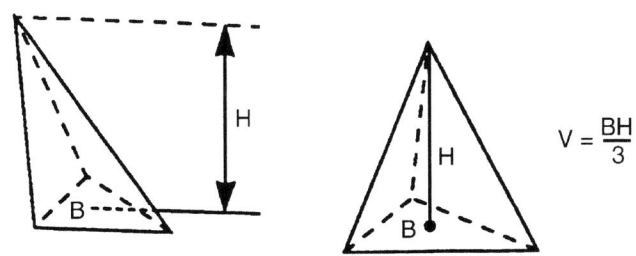

Figure 16

Volume of a sphere (*Figure 17*) is equal to four-thirds the product of pi (π) and the cube of the radius.

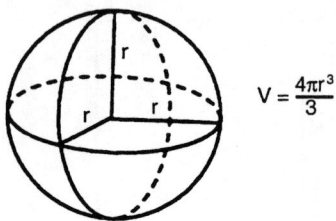

Figure 17

Volume of a cylinder (*Figure 18*) equals the product of the area of the base and the height.

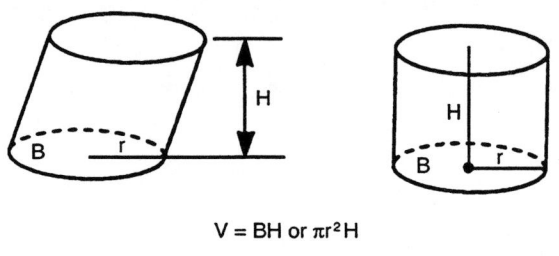

$V = BH$ or $\pi r^2 H$

Figure 18

Volume of a cone (*Figure 19*) equals one-third the product of the area of the base and the height.

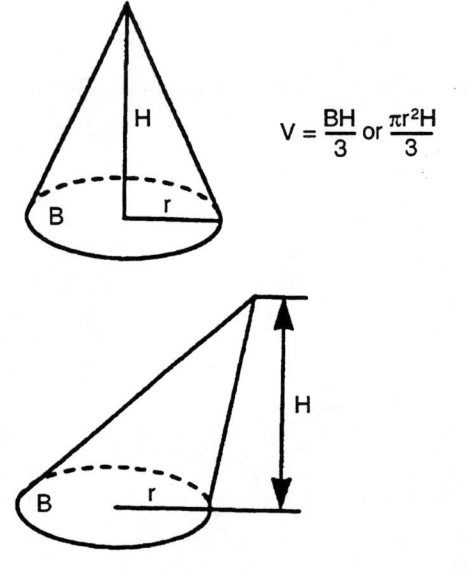

$V = \dfrac{BH}{3}$ or $\dfrac{\pi r^2 H}{3}$

Figure 19

Study Problems

Round off to the nearest tenth (0.1).

1. Calculate the volume of a rectangular-shaped prism 5 feet long (L), 4 feet high (H), and 3 feet wide (W).

2. Calculate the volume of a cube whose edge is 5 feet.

3. Calculate the volume of a prism whose base area equals 40 square inches and is 24 inches in height.

4. Calculate the volume of a pyramid whose base area equals 40 square inches and whose height is 24 inches.

5. Calculate the volume of a sphere whose radius is 6 inches.

6. Calculate the volume of a cylinder whose radius is 6 feet and height is 4 feet.

7. Calculate the volume of a cone with a 6 foot radius base and 4 foot height.

ANGLE MEASUREMENT

An angle is an inclination of one line with respect to another line or one surface with respect to another surface.

Angle Measures

The Task Module from Sheet Metal Level 1, *Trade Math I*, particularly the section entitled "Geometry," should be used as a basis for review prior to studying this section of the module.

Right Triangle

A right triangle is one of the most important shapes in design and construction work. It is the basis for rectangular coordinates (*Figure 20*) which is a system for precision hole location in fabrication work.

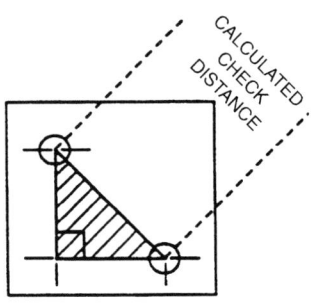

Figure 20

A right triangle (*Figure 21*) contains one 90° angle. The side opposite the right angle is called the **hypotenuse** and is the longest side. Side CB is the altitude or height and side AB is the base. If CB is the base, then AB becomes the altitude or height.

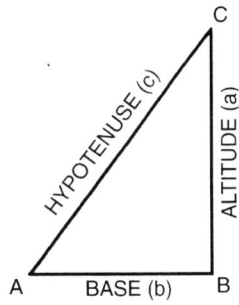

Figure 21

The sum of two acute angles (interior angles less than 90°) of a right triangle (*Figure 22*) equals 90°.

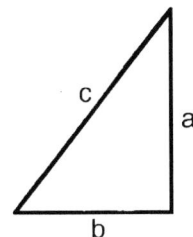

Figure 22

Therefore, if one acute angle of a given right triangle equals 50°, the other angle must equal 40°. Each angle, therefore, is the complement of the other angle. The Pythagorean Theorem states the relationship between the three sides of a right triangle. The rule is as follows:

The square of the hypotenuse is equal to the sum of the squares of the other two sides.

As a formula, this rule can be stated in the following form:

$$c^2 = a^2 + b^2$$

Algebraic variations of the basic formula are:

$$a^2 = c^2 - b^2$$

$$b^2 = c^2 - a^2$$

Study Example

1. Use the basic formula with

    $a = 3"$

    $b = 4"$

    Insert the dimensions into the formula:

    $$c^2 = a^2 + b^2$$

    $$c^2 = 9 + 16$$

    $$c^2 = 25$$

2. Use the variation to solve for a^2 with $c = 5$ and $b = 4$.

    $$a^2 = c^2 - b^2$$

    $$a^2 = 25 - 16$$

    $$a^2 = 9$$

3. Use the variation to solve for b^2 with $c = 5$ and $a = 3$.

    $$b^2 = c^2 - a^2$$

    $$b^2 = 25 - 9$$

    $$b^2 = 16$$

The squares of all the sides of the triangle in the above figure are perfect squares, but not all solutions are as simple as the example. Construction workers are not interested in the square of a side as much as the side itself. The above formulas render the square of the sides; thus, in order to find the side, the square root of both sides of each formula must be taken and:

$$c^2 = a^2 + b^2$$
becomes $c = \sqrt{a^2 + b^2}$

$$a^2 = c^2 - b^2$$
becomes $a = \sqrt{c^2 - b^2}$

$$b^2 = c^2 - a^2$$
becomes $b = \sqrt{c^2 - a^2}$

Square root extractions can be accomplished by arithmetic processes, the use of tables, or by hand-held calculators.

Study Problems

Round off to nearest tenth (0.1).

1. Solve for C (*Figure 23*).

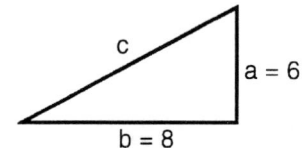

Figure 23

2. Solve for B (*Figure 24*).

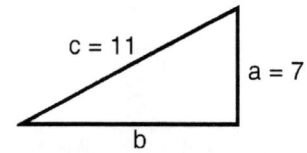

Figure 24

3. Solve for A (*Figure 25*).

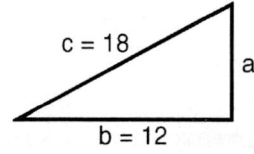

Figure 25

4. Solve for X (*Figure 26*).

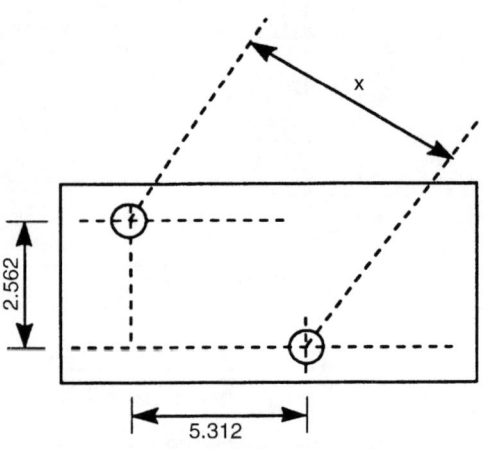

Figure 26

5. How long is the ladder (*Figure 27*)?

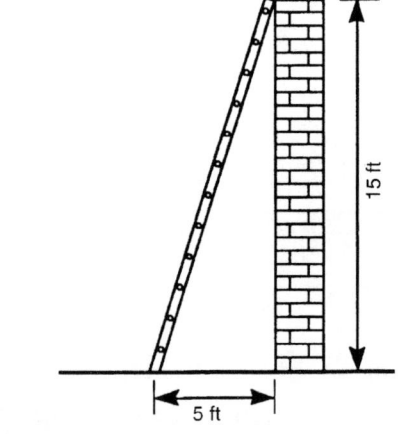

Figure 27

Using the Steel Square

Sheet metal workers in the field may encounter instances where it may be advisable to calculate right angles with the use of a steel carpenter's square. The steel square has a combination of numbers or "sets" (*Figure 28*) that can be used as a basis for calculating right angles.

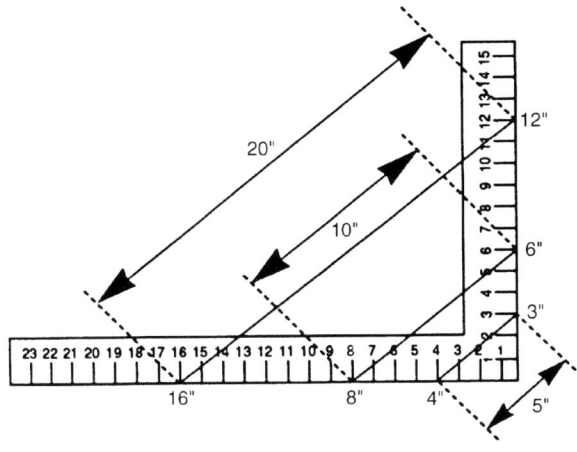

Figure 28

The combination of numbers illustrated in the above figure may be used to represent inches or feet, depending upon the size of the right angle to be formed.

Study Example

To form a right angle use one of the three combinations of numbers in *Figure 29*. Draw a base line equal to 4 inches, adjust the dividers to span 3 inches and scribe an arc at position C using A as center. Next adjust the dividers to span 5 inches and use position B as a center to scribe an arc to cross the previously scribed arc at position C. This obtains the right angle (*Figure 29*).

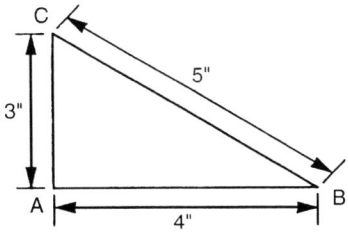

Figure 29

This combination of numbers is referred to as 3, 4, 5, with 5 being the hypotenuse of the right triangle. The remaining combinations are 6, 8, 10, and 12, 16, 20. The combination of each set will form a 90° angle. The combination "sets" can be used with almost any type of measurement unit (inches, feet, centimeters, meters, etc.) for solving field layout problems and as a method of checking perpendicularity.

MATHEMATICAL SYMBOLS

Many construction specification problems are solved by the use of formulas. Applicable handbooks provide many formulas which are used to calculate volumes, strength of materials, and other technical data. Many practical problems can be solved by using an appropriate formula which can be located in a reference manual. Formulas are algebraic equations, and the solution of equations requires many procedures that must be understood and properly applied.

Shop formulas used by construction and craft workers represent general statements. Letters and symbols used in the formulas have definite values assigned to them in order to solve the formula. Known values are substituted for related literal terms in the solution of working formulas. Formulas can be solved when the values of the constants and the letter (literal) terms are known. For example, when using the formula for calculating the area of a circle,

$$Area = \pi r^2$$

the values of pi (π) and "r" (radius) are known. Therefore, the area of a 4-inch circle would be:

$$A = (3.14)(2^2)$$

$$A = (3.14)(4)$$

$$A = 12.5664 \text{ square inches}$$

Note that the radius of the circle (2) is half its diameter (4).

When a shop formula is evaluated, the formula becomes an arithmetic problem and the rules of the sequence of operations must be followed. The answers to solved formula problems must always have the proper unit of measure attached; otherwise, the numerical value is incorrect.

Grouping Symbols

Symbols are needed in the science of mathematics to indicate grouping of terms and expressions. These symbols may be compared to punctuation in writing.

Symbols used for mathematical grouping include:

Parentheses ( )

Brackets [ ]

Braces { }

Another grouping symbol is the vinculum. This is a line placed above terms or digits ‾. An example of the vinculum is the line at the top of the long division sign: ‾) and at the top of the square root "radical" √‾. It is also used as the bar in a fraction:

$$\frac{1}{2}$$

Grouping symbols are important to the solution of mathematical problems because they indicate the specific relationships between numbers and groups of numbers.

Operational Symbols

Operational symbols are the shorthand of mathematics whereby the following symbols are used to express a thought relating to an operation. They are:

Equals or is equal to =

Does not equal ≠

Approximately equal to ≈ or ≅

Plus or minus ±

Is greater than >

Is less than <

Is similar to ~

SEQUENCE OF OPERATIONS

Equations can become confusing to solve when they contain combinations of terms in parentheses ( ), brackets [ ] or braces { }. Coefficients are often placed before these grouping symbols and can be either plus or minus. Complicated equations must be solved by doing the indicated arithmetic in a prescribed sequence. This sequence is:

MULTIPLY, **D**IVIDE, **A**DD, and **S**UBTRACT (**MDAS**).

For example, the arithmetical statement

$$3 + 3 \times 2 - 6 \div 3 + 6 =$$

can result in a number of different answers if the MDAS sequence is not followed. The expression above must be solved in the order as follows:

Step 1   **Multiplying:**

3 + **3 x 2** − 6 ÷ 3 + 6

Giving:

3 + **6** − 6 ÷ 3 + 6

Step 2   **Dividing:**

3 + 6 − **6 ÷ 3** + 6

Giving:

3 + 6 − **2** + 6

Step 3   **Adding:**

3 + 6 + 6 − 2

Step 4   **Subtracting:**

15 − 2

Result:

13

When an algebraic expression appears in an equation such as

$$x = 5a[2(a + b)(b)]$$

the MDAS sequence also applies. The grouping symbols represent multiplication so they are worked on first. It is suggested that the innermost symbol is removed first. Thus, in the above equation, the parentheses (a+b) with the coefficient 2b are multiplied first, giving:

$$x = 5a[2ab + 2b^2]$$

Then the terms within the bracket are multiplied by a, giving:

$$x = 5[2a^2b + 2ab^2]$$

Finally the terms in the brackets are multiplied by the coefficient 5, giving:

$$x = 10a^2b + 10ab^2$$

Coefficients

Algebraic expressions are often within the grouping symbols that have a plus (+) or minus (−) coefficient. If there is no numerical coefficient outside of the grouping symbol, it means that +1 or −1 is the coefficient. The following rules apply in the removal of grouping symbols (parentheses, brackets, and braces):

1. *Removal of a plus coefficient of +1:* When the symbol is preceded by a plus (+) sign and no other coefficient, drop the grouping symbol:

    $$3x + (2b − d) = 3x + 2b − d$$

    This is the same as multiplying each term within the grouping symbol by +1.

2. *Removal of a minus coefficient from −1:* When the symbol is preceded by a minus (−) sign and no other coefficient, multiply each term within the symbol by (−1), then drop the symbol:

    $$3x − (2b − d) = 3x − 2b + d$$

3. *Removal of a plus numerical or literal coefficient:* When the grouping symbol is preceded by a plus numerical or literal coefficient, multiply each term within the symbol ( ) by the coefficient and drop the symbol:

    $$3x + 2a(2b − d) = 3x + 4ab − 2ad$$

4. *Removal of a minus numerical or literal coefficient:* When the grouping symbol is preceded by a minus numerical or literal coefficient, the grouping symbol may be removed by one of two methods:

    a. Multiply each term within the symbol by the coefficient and its sign and drop the symbol:

    $$3x − 6a(2b − d) = 3x − 12ab + 6ad$$

    b. Multiply each term within the symbol by only the coefficient:

    $$3x − 6a(2b − d) = 3x − (12ab − 6ad)$$

Then proceed as in rule 2:

$$3x − (12ab − 6ad) = 3x − 12ab + 6ad$$

Study Examples

Simplify by removing parentheses:

$$3a + 2(3b) − 3(4c − 5d)$$
$$3a + 6b − 12c + 15d$$

Study Problems

Simplify by removing grouping symbols and combining like terms:

1. $(5 + 3)(4 − 2 \div 4) =$
2. $3a − (2b + c) + 3a =$
3. $(3x + 4y) − (x − 3) =$
4. $(5a − 3b + c) − a(3 + 4) =$
5. $12 + 5(6 + 7) − 8(2 − 4)(5 + 2) − 2 =$

SOLVING SIMPLE EQUATIONS

Simple equations are usually solved for the value of the unknown by performing a series of sequential operations, the order of which are:

1. Eliminate fractions.
2. Remove grouping symbols.
3. Simplify and combine.
4. Transpose terms, unknowns to left, knowns to the right side of the equal sign.
5. Divide both sides by the coefficient and sign of the unknown.

Study Examples

Solve for x in the following.

$$\frac{3(2x-4)}{2} - \frac{6(3x+5)}{3} = 0$$

1. Remove parentheses by multiplying:

    $$\frac{6x-12}{2} - \frac{18x+30}{3} = 0$$

2. Divide each term by its denominator:

    $$3x - 6 - 6x - 10 = 0$$

3. Group like terms:

    $$3x - 6x - 6 - 10 = 0$$

4. Add like terms:

    $$-3x - 16 = 0$$

5. Transpose:

    $$-3x = 16$$

6. Divide both sides by the coefficient of the unknown:

    $$x = -5\ 1/3$$

Study Problems

Solve for x:

1. $(3x - 7) - (x - 4) = 0$
2. $2(5x - 5) - 5(3x + 10) = 0$
3. $x - 3(x + 2) + 2(x + 1) = x - 4$
4. $\dfrac{4(x-2)}{2} = \dfrac{3(6-x)}{2}$
5. $3x(4 + 3) + \dfrac{9(x-2)}{3} = 0$

PERCENTAGE

Percentage is a method of expressing a fractional part of something. The term percentage means per hundred. There are one hundred pennies or "cents" in one dollar. One half of a dollar would be fifty pennies or 50 percent of a dollar. As a decimal 50 percent becomes .50. One hundred pennies then is 100 percent of a dollar. Thus, fractional parts of that hundred would be written or expressed as if pennies were being recorded.

Study Examples

10% = .10

25% = .25

7% = .07

75% = .75

1% = .01

Percentage signs (%) represent two decimal places in a number. Therefore they are not used with the decimal point unless a fractional part of 1% is being expressed. Thus, 1% = .01, but .1% = .001.

Working with Percentages

1. *Fractional percentages:*

   In order to properly express fractional parts of 1% in decimal form, the decimal point and the sign are added.

Study Examples

10% = .10, but 1/10 of 1% = .001

25% = .25, but 1/4 of 1% = .0025

50% = .50, but 1/2 of l% = .005

75% = .75, but 3/4 of 1% = .0075

Common percentages can also be expressed as common fractions:

1% = 1/100

5% = 1/20

20% = 1/5

25% = 1/4

33-1/3% = 1/3

50% = 1/2

66-2/3% = 2/3

75% = 3/4

Percentage Formula

In order to calculate the percentage of an integer, the formula $P = b \times r$ is used. To solve for P (percent), b equals the base and r equals the rate or percent written as a decimal.

Study Examples

1. What is 18% of 600?

   P = br

   P = (600)(.18) = 108

2. What is 60% of 600?

   P = (600)(.60) = 360

Study Problems

1. 38% of 490 =
2. 7-1/2% of 425 =
3. 33-1/3% of 425 =
4. 8% of 96 =
5. 30% of 5-1/2 =

If you know the whole quantity of what you have, and if you know a portion of what you have, you can find the percentage using this formula:

$$r = \frac{P}{b}$$

where:

   r = rate of percentage

   P = portion

   b = base quantity

Or, if you know the percentage rate and the base quantity, you can calculate the portion you need to know by rewriting the formula:

   P = rb

Study Examples

1. What percentage of 1200 is 240?

   $$r = \frac{240}{1200} = \frac{20}{100} = 20\%$$

2. What percentage of 480 is 120?

   $$r = \frac{120}{480} = \frac{1}{4} = 25\%$$

Study Problems

1. What percentage of 40 is 36?
2. What percentage of 500 is 96?
3. What percentage of 12 inches is 1/8 inch?
4. What is 15 percent of 125 times $14.00?
5. What is 3-1/2 percent of 2080?

RATIO AND PROPORTION

Ratio is defined as the relation between two similar magnitudes in respect to the number of times the first contains the second. For example, the ratio of 3 to 4 may be written 3:4 or 3/4.

Proportion is defined as the relative amount of ingredients, that is, the ratio of one ingredient to another, or to the whole with respect to magnitude, quantity or degree.

A ratio, therefore, is a mathematical way of making a comparison. The rule of ratios is: the ratio of one quantity to another like quantity is the quotient obtained by dividing the first quantity by the second quantity. Ratios can express "greater than," "less than," or "equal to" statements. Ratios express relationships in multiples of one another, such as "twice as heavy," or in percentages such as "100 percent heavier." Unlike quantities or units cannot be compared. For example, yards to pounds or rpm's to dollars cannot be compared. Also note that the ratio has no unit value. For example, the ratio of 3" to 4" is not 3:4 inches.

A ratio is a fraction. All the rules applying to fractions apply to ratios. A ratio can be expressed as a fraction, such as 2/3, or as an improper fraction, such as 4/3. A ratio is always written in the same sequence as the relationship in a verbal statement. For example, the statement, "Engine A is running at twice the rpm's of Engine B," is written as the statement 2:1 or 2/1. In the case of an axle ratio, the statement may be: "The rear axle ratio is 3.08." This means that the ratio is 3.08 to 1 or 3.08:1, or 3.08/1, and the input rpm is 3.08 rpm faster than the output rpm of the rear wheels.

Direct and Indirect Proportion

Proportion is an expression of equality between two ratios. If two ratios are numerically equal they can be written as an equality. For example, the ratios of 2/3 and 4/6 are numerically equal and can be written: 2/3 = 4/6. Proportions are valuable when calculating costs, speeds, quantities, cycles, etc., when a known ratio can be equated to a second ratio, one of whose terms is known.

For example, if the diameter of a pulley in a belt transmission system is three times the diameter of the second (*Figure 30*), this gives us the first ratio, 3:1.

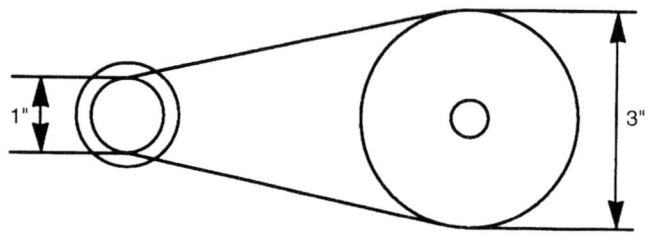

Figure 30

If the diameter of the second pulley is known, the first pulley's diameter will be three times the diameter of the second pulley. The proportion is:

$$3/1 = \frac{\text{Diameter of first pulley}}{\text{Diameter of second pulley}}$$

If the second pulley is 5 inches in diameter, the proportion will read:

$$3/1 = \frac{\text{Diameter of first pulley}}{5}$$

SHEET METAL — TRAINEE TASK MODULE 04106

This proportion can be solved by cross-multiplying the figures:

$$\frac{3}{1} = \frac{a}{5} = 1 \times a = 15$$

Another example of proportion can be found in the ratio for a duct-fitting transition change such as a 20° angle, which may yield a ratio of 1 to 3 (approximately) (*Figure 31*).

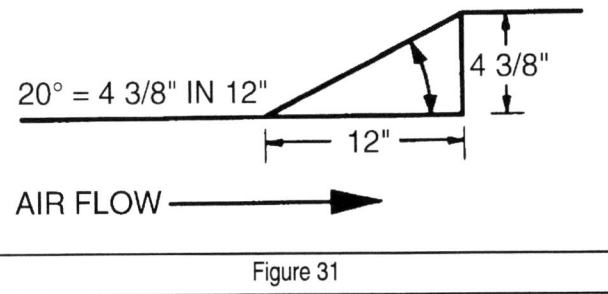

Figure 31

Figure 32 shows some common slope angles with their degrees that are used in figuring sheet metal fittings.

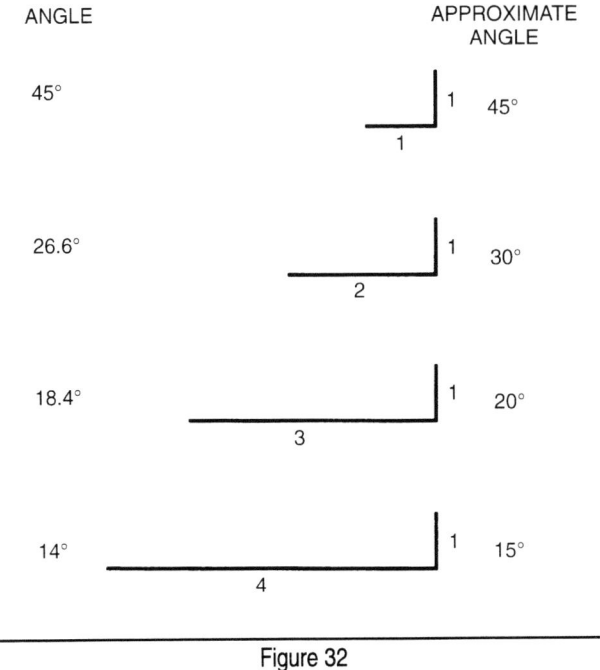

Figure 32

Direct Proportion

In the following example, the ratios are direct and the proportion is likewise direct and written in the order of the terms (feet : inches = feet : inches). Ratios are directly proportional when an increase in one denomination causes an increase in the other.

One foot equals 12 inches. How many inches are in 6 feet? Let x = the unknown number of inches in 6 feet. State the unknown ratio of feet to inches:

$$1 \text{ ft.} : 12 \text{ in.} = \frac{1 \text{ ft.}}{12 \text{ in.}}$$

$$6 \text{ ft.} : x \text{ in.} = \frac{6 \text{ ft.}}{x \text{ in.}}$$

Then equate the ratios:

$$1/12 = 6/x$$

Finally, cross-multiply:

$$1x = 72$$

$$x = 72$$

Indirect Proportion

Ratios are indirectly or inversely proportional when an increase in one ratio causes a decrease in the other. Problems pertaining to the pulley and gears use inverse ratios in the solution of speed and diameter problems.

Study Examples

An electric motor running at 1750 rpm has a 2.5 inch diameter pulley. What size pulley is required on the driven shaft to turn it at 875 rpm?

The ratio speed is:

$$\frac{1750 \text{ (motor speed)}}{875 \text{ (shaft speed)}}$$

TRADE MATH II — TRAINEE TASK MODULE 04106

Pulley diameter ratio:

$$\frac{2.5 \text{ (motor shaft pulley)}}{x \text{ (shaft pulley)}}$$

Cross-multiply:

$$(875)(x) = (2.5)(1750)$$

$$(875)(x) = 4375$$

$$x = 5$$

Study Problems

1. What is the ratio of 40 to 10? What is the inverse ratio?

2. Solve for x in.:

$$\frac{3}{1/2} = \frac{18}{x}$$

3. The ratio of teeth in gears A and B is 2.5 to 1. How many teeth has gear B if A has 15?

4. Grades or slopes are measured as the number of feet of rise per 100 feet horizontally. A ten-foot rise in a distance of 100 feet is designated as a 10 percent grade. If there is a 400 ft. hill and a road rises 8 ft. for every 100 ft., what is the percent of grade?

5. The volume of a quantity of gas is inversely proportional to the pressure exerted upon it. If the volume of a quantity of gas is 720 cubic feet when under a pressure of 16 psia, how many cubic feet will there be when the pressure rises to 28 psia?

Mean Proportional

In calculating common proportion, when three of the four terms are known, the fourth term can be calculated by cross-multiplication. A special type of problem arises when the second and third terms are equal. When this occurs, the second and third terms are referred to as the *mean proportional*.

Study Example

1. What is the mean proportional between 32 and 2?

   a. Write the proportions with the second and third terms designated by x (the mean proportional):

   $$\frac{32}{x} = \frac{x}{2}$$

   b. Cross-multiply:

   $$(x)(x) = (32)(2)$$

   $$x^2 = 64$$

   c. Extract the square root from each side:

   $$x^2 = 64$$

   $$x = \pm 8$$

   d. Therefore +8 or −8 is the mean proportional.

Study Problems

1. What is the mean proportional between 98 and 2?

2. If the mean proportional between 16 and x is 11, what is the value of x?

3. Two engines have equal ratios of horsepower to cubic inch displacement. One has a displacement of 424 cubic inches while the second has a rated horsepower of 200. If the horsepower of the first engine equals the displacement of the second engine, what is the displacement of the second engine?

Compound Ratios and Proportions

Compound ratios are the product of two or more simple ratios. In many calculations, more than one condition exists which affects their solutions. Two conditions which exist can change the value of a number:

1. When a number is multiplied by a ratio which is less than one, the value of that number is decreased. For example:

   (25) (3/5) = 15 (a decrease)

2. When a number is multiplied by a ratio whose value is greater than one, the value of the number is increased. For example:

   (25) (5/3) = 41.67 (an increase)

In solving proportions with a series of ratios (compounding), it becomes necessary to put down the individual ratios in the proper order stated in the problem.

Study Example

1. A load of 6 steel bars, 8 feet long by 4 inches wide and 1 inch thick weighs 652.8 pounds. How much will a load of 8 steel bars, 7 feet long by 3 inches wide and 2 inches thick weigh?

   a. Write the ratio of the unknown quantity to the known quantity (weight of second load to weight of first load):

   $$\frac{x \text{ lbs.}}{652.8}$$

   b. Write the ratio of the number of bars in load two to the number of bars in load one.

   $$\frac{8 \text{ bars}}{6 \text{ bars}}$$

   c. Write the ratio of the width of the bars in load one to the width of the bars in the second load to the thickness of bars in load one.

   $$\frac{7 \text{ ft.}}{8 \text{ ft.}}$$

   d. Write the ratio of the width of the bars in load two to the width of the bars in load one.

   $$\frac{3 \text{ in.}}{4 \text{ in.}}$$

   e. Write the ratio of the thickness of the bars in load two to the thickness of the bars in load one.

   $$\frac{2 \text{ in.}}{1 \text{ in.}}$$

   f. Write the proportion as the ratio of the weights equated to the bar description ratios. Note that the second load terms are the numerators of each ratio and the first load terms are the denominators.

   $$\frac{x}{652.8} = \frac{8}{6} \times \frac{7}{8} \times \frac{3}{4} \times \frac{2}{1}$$

   g. Cancel terms:

   $$\frac{x}{652.8} = \frac{\cancel{8}\ 7\ \cancel{3}\ \cancel{2}}{\underset{2}{\cancel{6}}\ \cancel{8}\ \underset{2}{\cancel{4}}\ 1}$$

   h. Multiply factors:

   $$\frac{x}{652.8} = \frac{7}{4}$$

   i. Cross-multiply:

   $$4x = (7)(652.8)$$

   j. Solve for x:

   $$4x = 4569.6 \text{ lbs.}$$

   $$x = 1142.4 \text{ lbs.}$$

Study Problems

1. Ten boxcars can be unloaded by two men using fork lifts in 8 hours. How many boxcars can be unloaded by four men using fork lifts in 6 hours?

2. Two pumps running at 360 gpm can empty a pond in 6 hours. How long will it take three pumps running at 250 gpm to pump the pond 75 percent dry?

3. An excavation project can be completed by 7 workers in five 8-hour days. How many 10-hour days would be required to complete 60 percent of the work with a 5-man crew?

Mixture Proportions

Mixtures present a special type of problem involving ratio and proportion. Many alloys, for example, are composed of two or more metals, the proportions of which determine the physical characteristics of the alloy. Therefore, care must be used to insure that an exact amount of each alloy metal be added to the mixture. Alloy quantities are either expressed as percentages of the whole or as parts. When percentages are used the separate percentages must add up to the whole (100 percent).

Study Example

1. An alloy is composed of five parts lead, three parts copper, and one part tin. How many pounds of each base metal will be needed to cast a 250-pound bar?

    a. Add the parts to obtain the whole:

    $5 + 3 + 1 = 9$

    b. Form the proportions:

    $5/9 = x/250$ (lead)

    $3/9 = x/250$ (copper)

    $1/9 = x/250$ (tin)

    c. Cross-multiply and solve for each proportion.

    d. Add the weights of each metal proportion:

    138.889 lead

    83.333 copper

    + 27.778 tin
    _____

    250 lbs. of alloy

Study Problems

1. A piece of solder is composed of 40 percent tin and 60 percent lead. How many pounds of solder can be made from 40 pounds of tin and how many pounds of lead will be used?

2. A casting has 6 parts copper, 4 parts lead, and 1 part tin. How many pounds of each are required to form the 185-pound casting?

3. How many pounds of lead must be added to change 849 pounds of solder which is 40 percent tin and 60 percent lead, to a mixture which is 30 percent tin and 70 percent lead?

THE PROTRACTOR

The device used to construct and measure angles is the **protractor**. The **swing blade protractor** is not designed to lay out angles but is primarily used to check angles. The protractor is shaped like a semicircle with two rows of numbers marked off from 0 degrees to 180 degrees. One row usually moves from left to right and the other row moves from right to left. The numbers are usually marked off in 10 degree graduations. *Figure 33* illustrates a typical swing blade protractor.

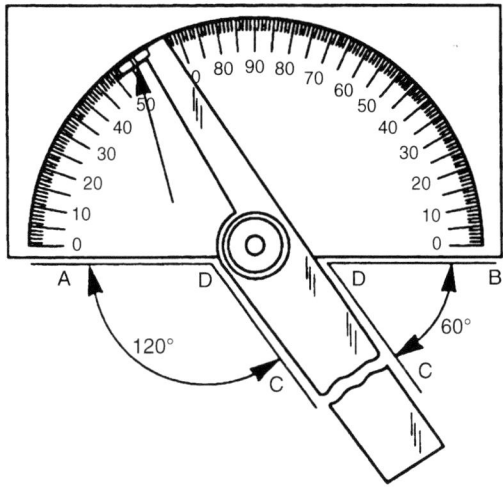

Figure 33 - Swing Blade Protractor

Measuring with a Protractor

Before measuring angles with a protractor, it is necessary to understand the different parts of an angle and the different kinds of angles. An angle is the opening between two intersecting lines. The lines themselves are called the "sides" of the angle. The actual point where the lines converge, or touch, is called the "vertex" of the angle.

There are basically five types of angles which will be encountered in direct measurement (*Figure 34*). They are:

The straight angle. This angle is formed by a straight line. A straight angle contains 180 degrees.

The right angle. This angle is 90 degrees. There are two right angles in a straight angle, and four right angles in a circle.

The acute angle. This angle is any angle less than 90 degrees.

The obtuse angle. This angle is more than 90 degrees but less than 180 degrees.

The reflex angle. This angle is seldom encountered. It is an angle which is more than 180 degrees but less than 360 degrees.

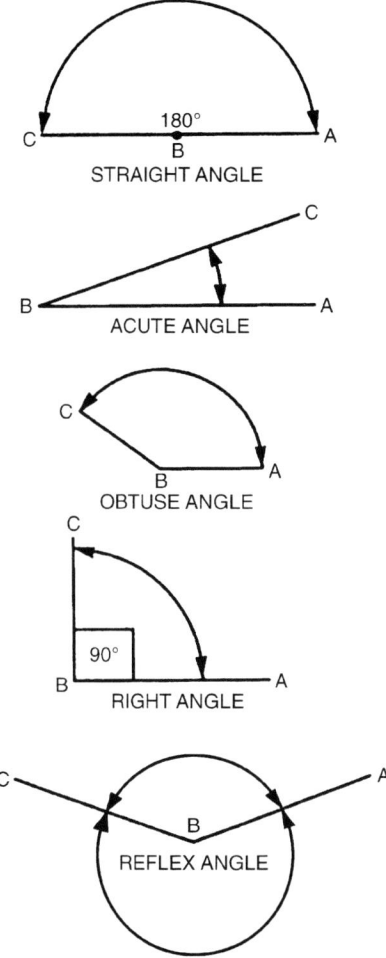

Figure 34 - Types of Angles

To measure an angle with a protractor, place the vertex of the angle at the bottom center of the protractor so that one side of the angle passes through the 0 degree mark. If the sides of the angle are too short to pass through this mark, carefully extend the sides so that they are long enough. When the vertex of the angle is centered at the bottom of the protractor and one side of the angle passes through the 0 degree mark, the other side of the angle will pass through the semicircle of the protractor.

The angle is measured by reading the number of degrees at the point where the side of the angle passes through the protractor.

Now that you know one method of reading angles, refer back to *Figure 33* for another method of reading angles with a protractor.

TRADE MATH II — TRAINEE TASK MODULE 04106

Here, the sides of the angles have been placed at various readings on the protractor. The measurement of the angle is arrived at by subtracting the differences between the numbers on the protractor. In *Figure 33*, angle BDC is found to be 60°. Angle ADC is 120°.

Study Problem

1. With a protractor measure the angles in *Figure 35*.

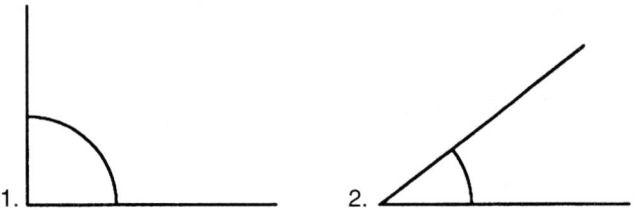

Figure 35

Constructing Angles

The protractor is also used for constructing angles. This is done in nearly the same way in which an angle is read from a protractor. To construct an angle, first draw one of the sides of the angle. Place the bottom center of the protractor at that point where the vertex of the angle will be and make sure that the side passes through the 0 degree mark of the protractor. Make a mark at that point on the semicircle of the protractor which yields the desired angle. Remove the protractor from the work surface and connect the mark with the end of the line which was placed at the bottom center of the protractor.

Study Problem

1. Practice constructing the following angles on a sheet of paper with a swing blade protractor.

    a. 90 degrees
    b. 45 degrees
    c. 37 degrees
    d. 115 degrees
    e. 135 degrees

THE MICROMETER

Of all of the precision measuring tools available to the sheet metal worker, the micrometer is one of the most used. The basic micrometer caliper (*Figure 36*) or *mike* as it is called in shop language can best be understood by engaging in actual practice with test pieces of fixed sizes.

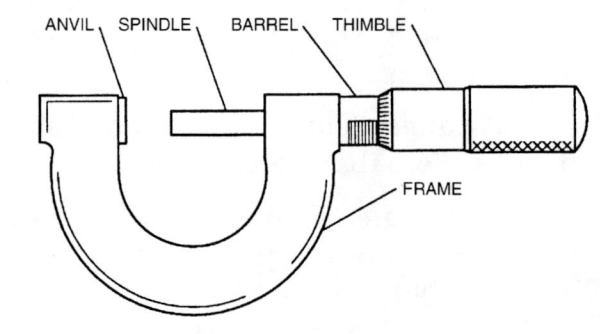

Figure 36 - Micrometer

SHEET METAL — TRAINEE TASK MODULE 04106

A worker does not have to be a mathematician to read the micrometer once the divisions on the spindle and the thimble are understood. The heart of this tool is the spindle with its forty threads per inch. One turn of the thimble advances the spindle one fortieth of an inch or .025". To read an English micrometer, the total number of .025 inch graduations uncovered by the thimble is noted. To this total is added the number on the thimble closest to the index line on the barrel. In order to take a micrometer reading, the following steps should be taken:

1. The micrometer is held in the right hand (provided the user is right-handed) across the palm and fingers, with the little finger curled around the frame. The thimble is revolved by using the thumb and the forefinger. The spindle revolves with the thimble.

2. The article to be measured is placed between the anvil and the spindle and the spindle is carefully tightened, using light pressure between the thumb and the forefinger.

3. The measurement of the opening between the spindle and the anvil is indicated by lines and figures on the barrel and the thimble. For example, one complete turn of the thimble changes the opening between the spindle and the anvil .025". Each line on the barrel also represents .025". Four complete turns of the thimble change the opening between the spindle and the anvil .100". Each number, therefore, represents .100", resulting in readings of .100", .200", .300", etc. The beveled edge of the thimble is divided into twenty-five equal parts, each division representing .001". These divisions are marked every five spaces by 0, 5, 10, 15, and 20. When 25 of these divisions have passed the horizontal line of the barrel, the spindle has moved .025" and the first line of the barrel is visible, indicating .025". The final reading is obtained by adding the three figures.

Study Examples

Final reading can be obtained by adding the three figures illustrated by the following examples in A, B, C, and D (*Figure 37*).

In A, the number of:

10ths on the barrel (1)	.100"
.025 spaces on barrel (2)	.050"
Divisions on thimble (0)	.000"
Total	.150"

In B, the number of:

10ths on the barrel (0)	.000"
.025 spaces on barrel (1)	.025"
Divisions on thimble (0)	.000"
Total	.025"

In C, the number of:

10ths on the barrel (3)	.300"
.025 spaces on barrel (0)	.000"
Divisions on thimble (5)	.005"
Total	.305"

In D, the number of:

10ths on the barrel (2)	.200"
.025 spaces on barrel (3)	.075"
Divisions on thimble (7)	.007"
Total	.282"

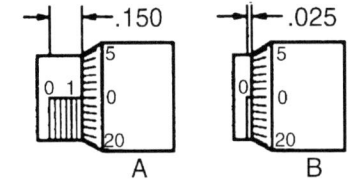

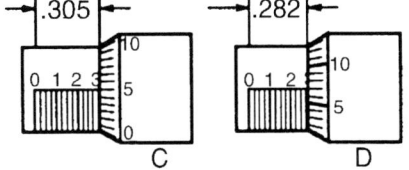

Figure 37

TRADE MATH II — TRAINEE TASK MODULE 04106

Study Problems

Record the micrometer readings illustrated in the following modules (*Figure 38*).

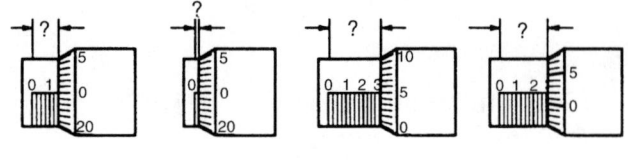

Figure 38

Micrometers are available in various sizes: 0-1", 1"-2", etc. Therefore, the original opening between the anvil and the spindle must be added into the readings indicated by the barrel and thimble. For example, if the micrometer used for taking the measurements in the above illustrations was a 2"-3" one, the above readings would have been:

A = 2.150", B = 2.025", C = 2.305", D = 2.282".

If the line on the thimble does not align with the datum line, use the value which comes closest to it, or estimate the fraction of a thousandth over the line on the thimble below the datum line. If more accurate readings are desired, a vernier micrometer (*Figure 39*) may be used.

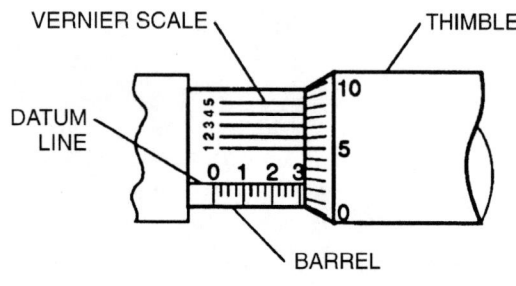

Figure 39 - Vernier Micrometer

This type of micrometer has a vernier scale on the barrel which divides thousandths on the thimble into tenths making it possible to make a measurement to one ten-thousandth inch (.0001"). To make this measurement, take the value of the line on the thimble which falls below the datum line and add to this the value of the vernier scale reading. To locate the vernier scale reading, look along the edge of the thimble and find any vernier line and thimble line which coincide. If, for example, the vernier line number 2 is found to coincide with a line on the thimble, the vernier value is .0002".

Study Example

Consider the following readings where the number of:

10ths on the barrel (2)	.200"
.025 spaces on the barrel (3)	.075"
.001 lines on the thimble	.011"
Vernier line coinciding with line on thimble	.0002"
Total	.2862"

THE VERNIER CALIPER

A **vernier caliper** (*Figure 40*) is used for measurements to 12 inches with an accuracy of one thousandth of an inch. The principle of the vernier on a caliper is identical to that of a ten-thousandths micrometer. There are twenty-five spaces on the vernier scale, which are separated by twenty-six graduations. There are twenty-four spaces in the same distance on the main scale. Each division on the main scale equals .025" and each division on the vernier equals .024".

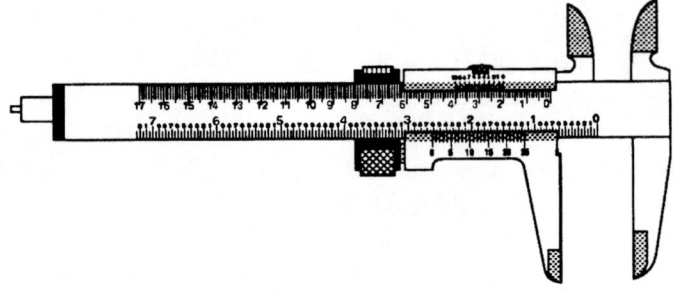

Figure 40 - Vernier Caliper

To find the value of the vernier (*Figure 41*), divide one division on the main scale by the number of divisions on the vernier. Read the inches, tenths of an inch, and .025" marks up to the zero on the vernier; then add the graduation on the vernier closest to a graduation on the main scale to these readings.

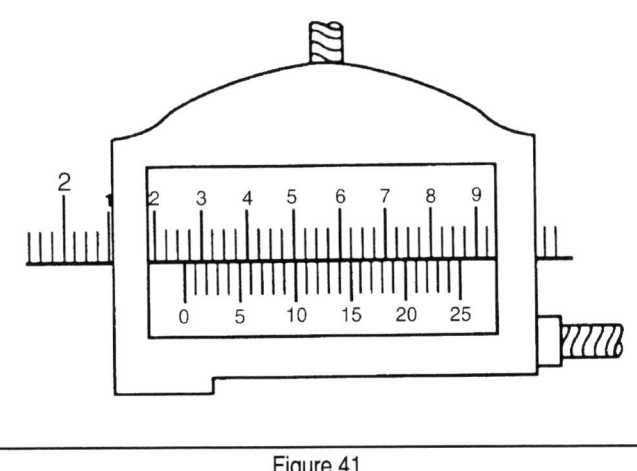

Figure 41

Study Example

Inches (2)	2.000"
Tenths of an inch (2)	.200"
.025 of an inch	.050"
Vernier 13 coincides	.013"
Total	2.263"

Study Problems

Read the scales illustrated in *Figure 42*.

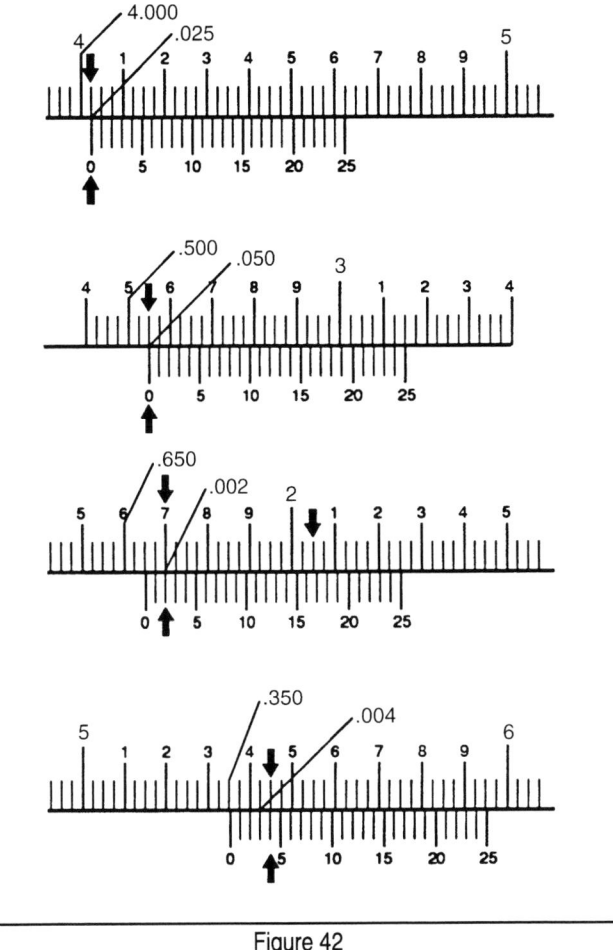

Figure 42

TOLERANCES

Tolerance is defined as the total permissible variation of a size. It is the difference between the maximum and minimum limits of a size. Tolerances on a blueprint or shop drawing may be general (specified with a note) or they may be specific (specified with a dimension). Whenever tolerances are not indicated on the applicable drawing, general tolerances apply. When no tolerance is specified, the tolerance generally is assumed to be ± 1/64" (± 1/2 mm) for fractional dimensions, ± 1/2 degree for angular dimensions, and ± .005" for decimal dimensions. This means that a shaft which is nominally 1-7/8" in diameter can be as large as 1-57/64" or as small as 1-55/64" in diameter without being rejected as a bad part.

Every tolerance has three parts: nominal size, upper limit, and lower limit. Sometimes the nominal size is also the upper or lower limit of the tolerance. For example, the opening of an open-end wrench must be a minimum size or it will not slip onto the bolt heads for which it was designed. If the opening is too large, the wrench will not fit snugly and will cause the bolt head to round off. The nominal size of the wrench opening is also the lower limit of the tolerance; therefore, the tolerance runs in a plus direction. The lower limit may be .562" and the tolerance listed as +.005" or –.000". The lower limit or nominal size is .562 inch and the upper limit is .567". This is an example of "unilateral" tolerance.

If a hole that is to be bored in a workpiece is specified to be

$$1.625 \pm .005"$$

this is called "bilateral" tolerance. Bilateral means running in both directions. The complete tolerance allowed is the sum of both plus and minus limits or .005" + .005", which equals .010". Therefore, the hole could vary in size from 1.630" to 1.620", but 1.625 is considered the nominal size which the worker attempts to bore.

Study Problems

Convert each of the following finished dimensions to (a) nominal dimension, (b) upper limit, (c) lower limit, and (d) total clearance.

1. 2.150 (+.004, –.000)

2. 1.875 (+.001, –.002)

3. 2.500 (+.0015, –.0000)

4. 3/4 (± 1/64)

SEAM ALLOWANCE

Seams and edges of various kinds are needed to eliminate raw edges on sheet metal jobs and to add strength to the fabrication. The addition of these seams and edges to a job requires that additional metal be allowed to accommodate them when laying out the pattern. These allowances will vary with the thickness (gage) of the metal and with the type of seam or edge. The allowances quoted in this section of the module pertain to 24 gage or lighter metal unless otherwise indicated.

Edge Allowances

The allowance for a single hem edge (*Figure 43*) is equal to the width of the seam. The formula A = W (allowance = width of the seam) is used for this calculation.

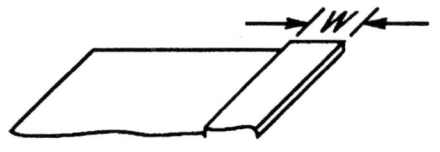

Figure 43

Study Example

Calculate the allowance of a single hem that is 3/16" wide.

$$A = W$$

$$A = 3/16"$$

Study Problems

Calculate the width of the following hems:

1. Hem 3/16", one edge
2. Hem 1/4", one edge
3. Hem 5/32", two edges

The allowance for a double hem (*Figure 44*) is twice the width of the intended seam. The formula A = 2W can be used for this type of calculation.

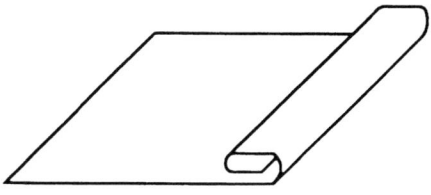

Figure 44

Study Example

Calculate the allowance for a double-edge seam 5/32" wide.

$$A = 2W$$
$$A = 2 \times 5/32"$$
$$A = 5/16"$$

Study Problems

Calculate the width of the following edge seams:

1. Hem 3/32", one edge
2. Hem 5/32", two edges

The allowance for a wired edge (*Figure 45*) is 2-1/2 times the wire diameter. The formula A = 2-1/2D can be used for this type of calculation.

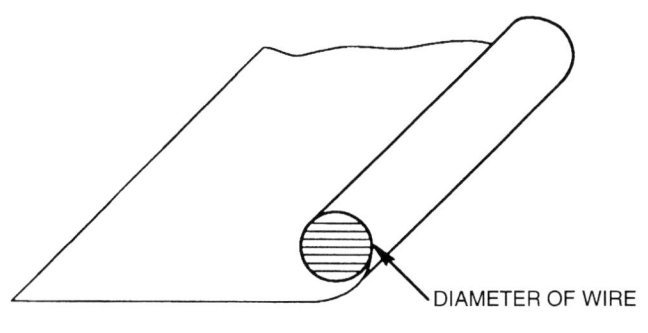

Figure 45

Study Example

Calculate the allowance for a wire edge using 5/32" diameter wire:

$$A = (2\ 1/2)\ (5/32)$$
$$A = \frac{5}{2} \times \frac{5}{32}$$
$$A = 25/64"$$

Study Problems

Calculate the allowance for the following wired edges:

1. Wire 1/8", one edge
2. Wire 5/32", two edges
3. Wire 3/32", two edges

The allowance for lap seams (*Figure 46*) is equal to the seam width. The formula A = W can be used for this type of calculation.

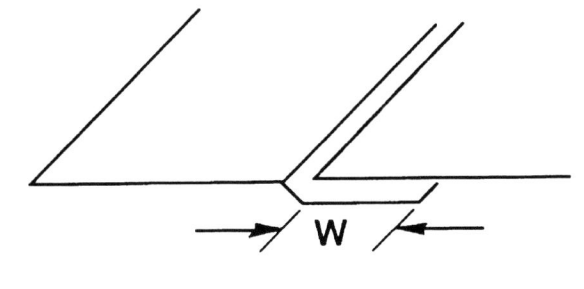

Figure 46

Study Example

Calculate the allowance for a lap seam 3/16" wide.

$$A = W$$
$$A = 3/16"$$

TRADE MATH II — TRAINEE TASK MODULE 04106

The allowance for a grooved lock seam (*Figure 47*) is usually three times the width of the seam, one half of which is added to each edge of the pattern. If the metal is 22 gage or heavier the allowance is 3 times the width of the seam plus 5 times the thickness of the metal. The formula A = 3W can be used for this type of calculation assuming the metal is 24 gage or lighter.

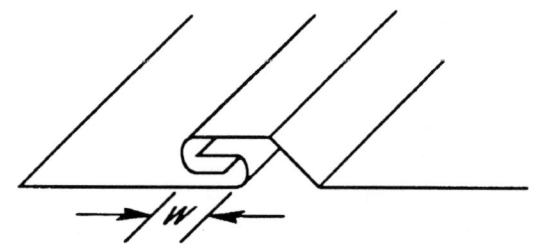

Figure 47

Study Example

Calculate the allowance for a grooved lock seam 3/16" wide.

A = 3W

A = 3 × 3/16

A = 9/16" (allowance for total)

The allowance for each edge is 1/2 total W or 9/32".

Study Problems

Calculate the allowance for the following grooved lock seams:

1. Lock 1/8", each edge
2. Lock 5/16", both edges (total)
3. Lock 3/16", each edge, 22 gage (0.0336")

The allowance for a lap seam that is riveted (*Figure 48*) is considered to be two times the diameter of the rivet for each edge of the seam. The formula A = 2D (D = rivet diameter) can be used for this type of calculation.

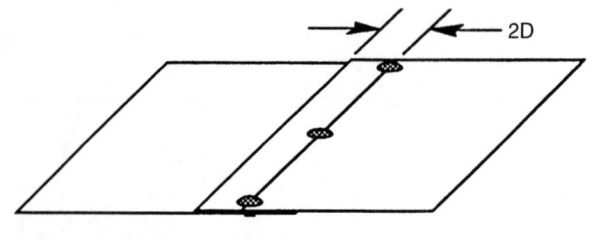

Figure 48

Study Example

Calculate the allowance for one edge of a riveted seam if the rivet size is 14 ounces with a diameter of 7/64" (0.109"):

A = 2D

A = 2 × 0.109"

A = 0.218" (7/32")

Study Problems

Calculate the allowance for the following riveted seams:

1. Rivet size 0.120", one edge
2. Rivet size 0.160", two edges

The allowance for a dovetailed seam (*Figure 49*) is equal to the seam width. The formula A = W (W = seam width) can be used for this type of calculation.

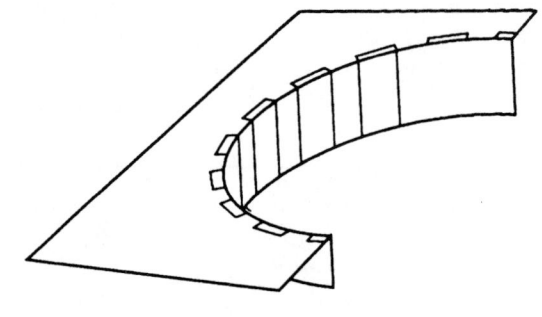

Figure 49

Study Example

Calculate the allowance for a 1/4" dovetailed seam:

$$A = W$$
$$A = 1/4"$$

The allowance for one side of a burred bottom seam (*Figure 50*) job is equal to the width of the lap (burr). The formula A = W can be used for this type of calculation.

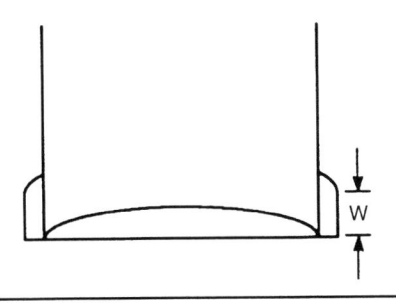

Figure 50

Study Example

Calculate the allowance for a 3/16" burred bottom seam:

$$A = W$$
$$A = 3/16"$$

The allowance for the body of a set-in bottom seam is equal to two times the width of the seam. The allowance for the bottom of a set-in bottom seam (*Figure 51*) is equal to the width of the seam. The formula A = 2W can be used for calculating the allowance for the body of a set-in bottom seam.

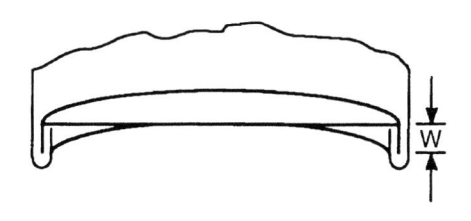

Figure 51

Study Example

Calculate the allowance for a 3/16" set-in bottom seam on the body portion of the pattern:

$$A = 2W$$
$$A = 2 \times 3/16"$$
$$A = 3/8"$$

Allowances on the body and the bottom of jobs with single and double seams are calculated in two steps or processes. The allowance on one side of the bottom for either the single seam or the double seam is equal to two times the width of the flange on the body. However, it must be distributed so that the outer allowance is equal to the width minus 1/32", and the inner allowance is equal to the width plus 1/32". The process for calculating allowances for this type of seam consists of three steps (*Figure 52*): calculating the allowance for one side of the body; calculating the allowance for one side of the bottom; and calculating the distribution or **bend allowances** for the bottom.

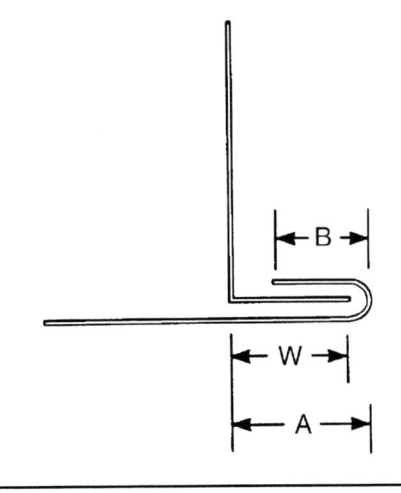

Figure 52

TRADE MATH II — TRAINEE TASK MODULE 04106

Thus, the formulas for this calculation process are: Allowance for one side of the body = W; allowance for one side of the bottom = 2W; the distribution of the bottom (two parts/2W) allowance for one part "A" = W + 1/32" and the allowance for the other part of the bottom "B" = W − 1/32".

Study Example

Calculate the allowances for one side of the body, the bottom and the bottom distribution of a fabrication job with a single seam with a flange width of 3/16":

$$A \text{ (one side of body)} = W$$

$$A = 3/16"$$

$$A \text{ (one side of bottom)} = 2W$$

$$A = 3/8"$$

Distribution for the bottom:

$$B = 3/16" + 1/32"$$

$$B = 7/32"$$

$$B = 3/16" - 1/32"$$

$$B = 5/32"$$

Study Problem

Calculate the allowances for one side (body and bottom) of a single seam. The allowance for the pocket part of one side of a Pittsburgh Lock Seam (*Figure 53*) can generally be determined by multiplying the width of the lower bending leaf of the brake by 2-1/2. Machine-formed Pittsburgh Lock **seam allowance** will vary with metal gage and type of machine.

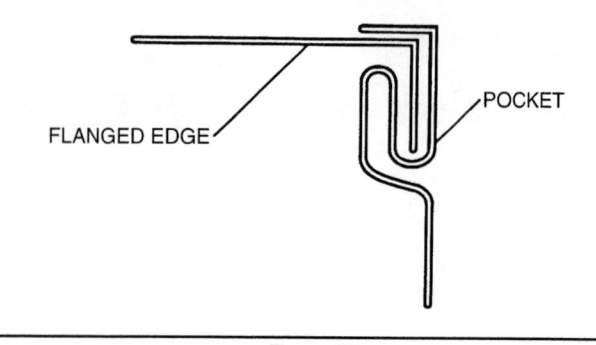

Figure 53

Study Example

Calculate the allowance for the pocket of one side of a Pittsburgh Lock seam job with a leaf width of 1/2" (*Figure 54*):

$$A = (2\text{-}1/2)(W)$$

$$A = (2\text{-}1/2)(1/2)$$

$$A = 1\text{-}1/4"$$

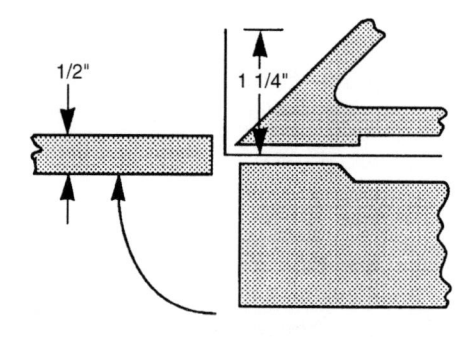

Figure 54

Study Problem

Calculate the allowance for a Pittsburgh Lock seam with a bending leaf equal to:

1. 5/8" bending leaf
2. 3/4" bending leaf

Bend allowances for various thicknesses of metal depend upon the thickness of that metal (*Figure 55*). For inside bend dimensions 20% of the thickness of the metal should be added on each side of the bend lines. For outside dimensions 80% of the thickness of the metal should be subtracted on each side of the bend lines.

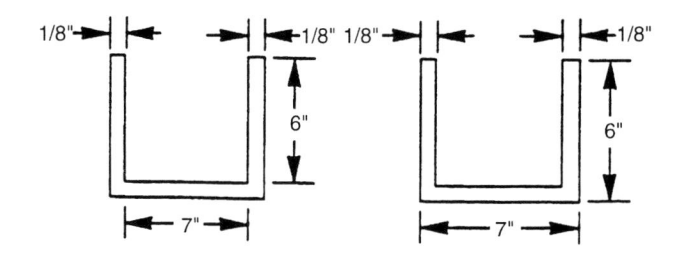

Figure 55

Study Example

Calculate the stretchout dimensions for a channel 6" deep by 7" wide (interior dimensions) that is to be constructed out of 1/8" thick metal. The stretchout will equal the dimensions listed below.

1. The sum of:

    6" + .20t (thickness)

    7" + (.20 × 2t)

    6" + .20t

2. Substitute for t:

    6" + (.20 × .125)

    7" + (.20 × .250)

    6" + (.20 × .125)

3. Multiply and add:

    6" + .025 = 6.025"

    7" + .050 = 7.050"

    6" + .025 = 6.025"

Study Problem

Calculate the stretchout of a 1/4" piece of metal to be formed into a channel 7" wide and 6" deep, exterior dimensions.

CALCULATION OF BLANK SIZES

Although many sizes are available, standard sheet metal stock for duct ware is usually available in widths of either 36", 48", or 60" and in lengths of 8' (96"), 10' (120"), or longer coils, and any number of blanks or layouts must be calculated accordingly in order to minimize waste. One of the more appropriate ways to become familiar with the "calculation for minimum waste" process is to practice some of the following problems.

Study Problems

Find the number of pieces of the shape and size indicated that can be obtained from the size of material listed below.

1. Four-inch square from a piece of 20" by 28" stock.
2. Six-inch diameter circle from a piece of 14" by 20" stock.
3. Six-inch by five-inch rectangle from a piece of 20" by 28" stock.
4. Ten-inch by eight-inch semicircle from a piece of 36" by 120" stock.
5. A rectangle, 12.5" by 10.5", from a piece of 36" by 120" stock.

Note: Overall dimensions and geometric shapes are more important than area in square inches when calculating the number of pieces per sheet of stock.

COMPUTATION OF STRETCHOUTS

When layout work is done directly on the metal, it is necessary to calculate the size of the **stretchout** to eliminate any unnecessary waste of material. Allowances must be added for edges, seams, or notches that are to be included on the finished pattern. Rules have been established for these calculations.

Square Duct

The rule for calculating the stretchout of a square job is: the stretchout of a job of this type is equal to the sum of the sides or four times the length of one side. The length of the stretchout (LS) is therefore found by using the formula for the perimeter and adding the allowance for the seam. The width of the stretchout (WS) is equal to the length of the duct or fitting plus the allowance for the edge or seam. The effect of the thickness of metal is usually disregarded for square duct.

Study Example

Calculate the length and width of a stretchout with an end dimension (s) of 6.5" and a length (L) of 12 inches.

$$LS = 4s$$

$$LS = (4)(6.5)$$

$$LS = 26"$$

$$WS = L$$

$$WS = 12 \text{ inches}$$

Study Problems

Calculate the length and width of a stretchout with the following dimensions (square duct):

1. S = 10-1/2", L = 18"
2. S = 3' 3", L = 2' 6"

The formula for calculating the stretchout of a square job with a lap seam is:

$$LS = 4s + W$$

S = length of the end

W = width of the seam

WS = L (length of the job)

Study Problems

Calculate the length and width of a stretchout with the following dimensions (square duct, lap seam):

1. S = 4-1/4", L = 9", W = 3/16"
2. S = 3-7/8", L = 12", W = 5/32"

The formula for calculating the stretchout of a square job (*Figure 56*) with a grooved seam is as follows, where S is the length of the end, W is the width of the lock, and L is the length of the job.

$$LS = 4s + 3W$$

$$WS = L$$

Note: One-half of the total W dimension is allowed at each end of the LS dimension.

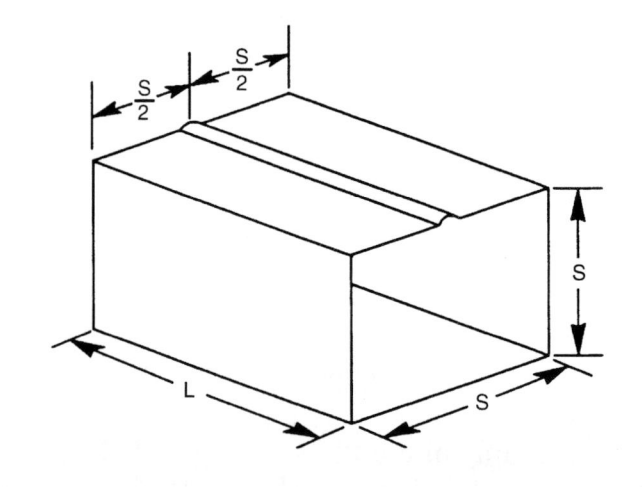

Figure 56

Study Problems

Calculate the length and width of a stretchout with the following dimensions (square duct, grooved seam):

1. S = 10", L = 12", W = 1/4"
2. S = 20", L = 18", W = 5/16"

Rectangular Ducts

The rule for calculating the stretchout of a rectangular job is: the stretchout of a job of this type is equal to the sum of all four sides or twice the width of the job plus twice its height. The formula used for this type of calculation is:

LS = 2H + 2W

H = height of end

W = width of end

WS = L

L = length of job

In order to calculate the stretchout for a rectangular duct job (*Figure 57*) with a grooved seam, the formula will include the addition of the width of the grooved lock seam or Pittsburgh Lock seam. This type of job will necessitate the use of the formula:

LS = 2H + 2W + 3W (width of seam)

WS = L

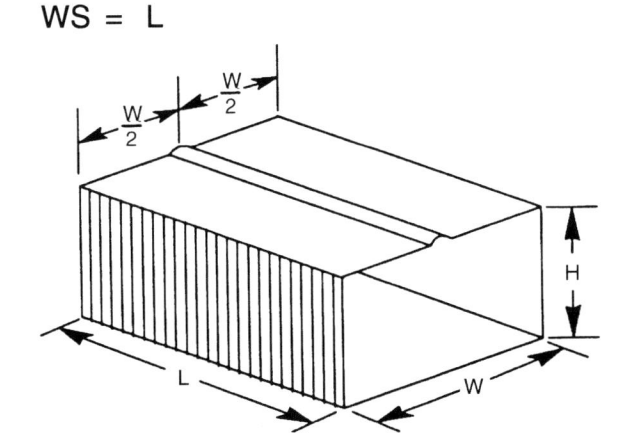

Figure 57

Study Problem

Calculate the stretchout for a job with the following dimensions (rectangular duct, grooved seam):

1. H = 5", W = 20", L = 18", W = 1/4"

Square or Rectangular Boxes

Boxes of this type are usually riveted and/or soldered, and allowance must be made for the tabs that are necessary for riveting or soldering when the layout is being accomplished. The formula for stretchout of boxes without edges or hems is:

LS = L + 2H

L = length

H = height

WS = W + 2H

W = width

H = height

The formula for stretchout of boxes with single hem (*Figure 58*) edges is:

LS = L + 2H + 2W

WS = W + 2H + 2W

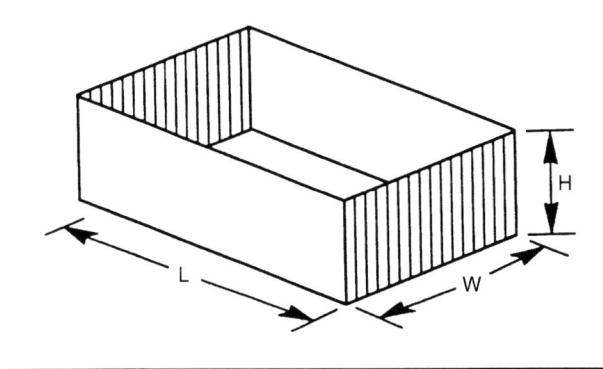

Figure 58

The formula for stretchout of boxes with double hem edges is:

LS = L + 2H + 4W

WS = W + 2H + 4W

The formula for stretchout of boxes with wired edges is:

LS = L + 2H + 2-1/2D + 2-1/2D

WS = W + 2H + 2-1/2 D + 2-1/2D

D = diameter of wire

TRADE MATH II — TRAINEE TASK MODULE 04106

Study Problems

Calculate the stretchout dimensions for the following boxes:

1. L = 12", W = 9-3/4", H = 2", W (single hem) = 3/16"
2. L = 11-1/2", W = 8", H = 2-7/8", W (double hem) = 1/4"
3. L = 12", W = 8", H = 2-1/2", D (wire) = 7/32"

Note: Solve for LS and WS.

Circular Stretchouts

The stretchout of a cylindrical fitting (*Figure 59*) will be rectangular in shape. One dimension of the rectangle will be the height of the cylinder, and the other dimension will be the circumference of the cylinder. When measurements are stated for a cylindrical fitting, the diameter rather than the circumference is usually stated. To calculate the length of the stretchout of a cylinder, it is necessary to find the circumference of the cylinder and add the allowance for the seam.

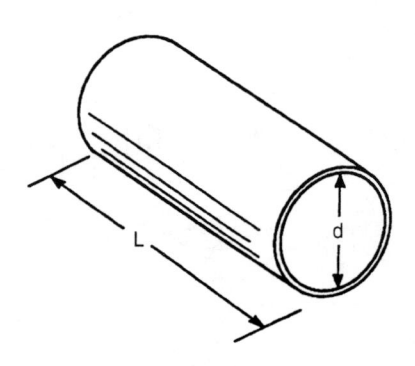

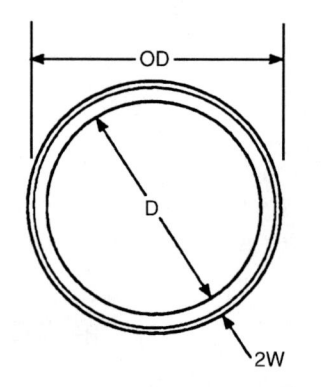

Figure 59

The formula for calculating the stretchout of a cylinder is:

LS = πd

WS = L

The formula for calculating the stretchout of a cylinder with a grooved seam is:

LS = c (πd) + 3W

W = width of the seam

WS = L

The formula for a riveted seam is:

LS = c (πd) + 4d

D = rivet diameter

WS = L

The formula for circular jobs with edges and seams is:

1. Body: LS = πd + 3W, D = diameter of cylinder, W = width of grooved seam.
2. Bottom: OD = D + 4W, OD = diameter of cylinder bottom overall, D = diameter of cylinder, W = width of double seam.

Study Problems

Calculate the stretchout dimensions for the following cylinders:

1. D = 10-1/2", L = 24", W (grooved seam) = 3/16"
2. Bottom for above fitting: D = 10-1/2"

Cone-Shaped Stretchouts

The material needed for the stretchout pattern of a right cone is equal to the slant height of the cone, which produces the radius of the disc, minus the computed angle of the cut out portion of the disc. The length of the slant height (H) (*Figure 60*) is obtained by using the Pythagorean

Theorem discussed in this module pertaining to right triangles. Thus,

$$H^2 = a^2 + b^2$$

where:

a = altitude or height of the cone and
b = 1/2 the diameter of the cone.

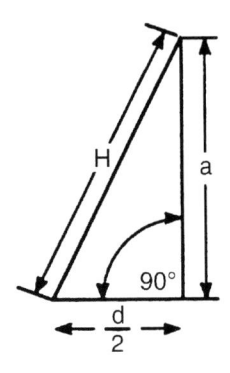

Figure 60

Study Example

Calculate the radius of the stretchout for a cone with a diameter of 4 inches and an altitude or height of 3-3/4":

$$H^2 = (3.75)^2 + (2)^2$$

$$H^2 = 14.0625 + 4$$

$$H^2 = 18.0625$$

$$H = 4.25"$$

The included angle of the stretchout is equal to the ratio of the circumference of the diameter of the cone (base) to the circumference of the stretchout circle times 360 degrees. The formula for the stretchout cone pattern (*Figure 61*) is:

$$N = \frac{\pi d}{2\pi H} \times 360 \text{ or}$$

$$\frac{180d}{H}$$

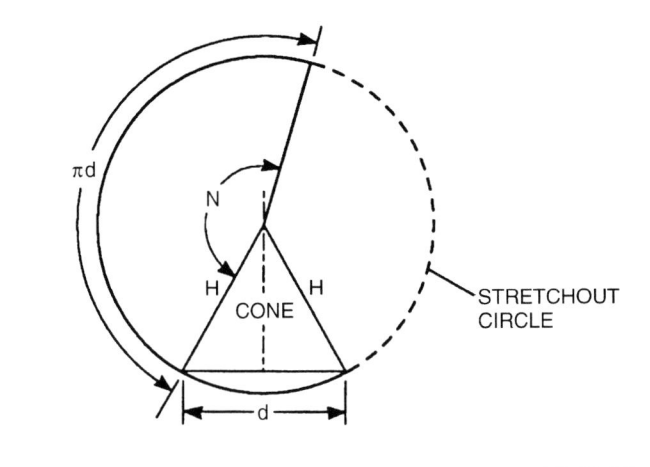

Figure 61

Study Example

Calculate the included angle of the stretchout (n) where d = 4" and H = 4.25":

$$N = \frac{180d}{H}$$

$$N = \frac{180 \times 4}{4.25}$$

$$N = \frac{720}{4.25}$$

$$N = 169.4 \text{ degrees}$$

Study Problems

Calculate the radius and the included angle of the stretchout for the following problems:

1. d = 4-7/8", altitude = 1-1/4"
2. d = 4", altitude = 3"

TRADE MATH II — TRAINEE TASK MODULE 04106

REVIEW QUESTIONS

Answer the following questions to review your knowledge of this module and to prepare for the Module Examination.

1. What is the purpose of formulas in sheet metal work?

2. What is the term basic to area measurement?

3. What term is used to denote volume measurement?

4. Where can the Pythagorean Theorem be used in sheet metal work?

5. What is the number set 3, 4, 5 or 6, 8, 10 applicable to?

6. Define LS, WS, and W, as they pertain to stretchout calculations.

SUMMARY

Applied mathematics is a necessary tool for the sheet metal worker. It can be used in almost every facet of the trade. It may be utilized in reading blueprints and detail drawings and for calculating stretchout material needs and fitting tolerances. Workers may be called upon to work in fractions, decimals, and metric dimensions and to construct or fabricate fittings for special, one-of-a-kind applications. Thus, the science of mathematics may not be stored in every worker's tool box, but the mathematical practices and procedures necessary for trade competency will be used almost every working day by skilled workers.

TRADE TERMS

Bend allowance
Hypotenuse
Protractor
Ratio
Seam allowance
Square prism
Stretchout
Swing blade protractor
Trapezoid
Vernier caliper

APPENDIX A

Resource for Trade Math II Module

ENGLISH-METRIC EQUIVALENTS

Length Measures

1 inch (in)	=	25.4 millimeters (mm)
1 inch (in)	=	2.54 centimeters (cm)
1 foot (ft)	=	0.3048 meters (m)
1 yard (yd)	=	0.9144 meters (m)
1 mile (mi)	=	1.609 kilometers (km)
1 millimeter (mm)	=	0.03937 inch (in)
1 centimeter (cm)	=	0.39370 inch (in)
1 meter (m)	=	3.28084 feet (ft)
1 meter (m)	=	1.09361 yards (yd)
1 kilometer (km)	=	0.62137 miles (mi)

Area Measures

1 square inch (sq.in.)	=	645.16 square millimeters (mm^2)
1 square inch (sq.in.)	=	6.4516 square centimeters (cm^2)
1 square foot (sq.ft.)	=	0.092903 square meters (m^2)
1 square yard (sq.yd.)	=	0.836127 square meters (m^2)
1 square millimeter (mm^2)	=	0.001550 square inch (sq.in.)
1 square centimeter (cm^2)	=	0.15500 square inch (sq.in.)
1 square meter (m^2)	=	10.763910 square feet (sq.ft.)
1 square meter (m^2)	=	1.19599 square yards (sq.yd.)

Angle Measures

1 degree (°)	=	60 minutes (')
1 minute (')	=	60 seconds (")

Resource for Trade Math II Module

APPENDIX A

Volume Measures for Solids

1 cubic inch (cu.in.)	=	16.387064 cubic centimeters (cm³)
1 cubic foot (cu.ft.)	=	0.028317 cubic meter (m³)
1 cubic yard (cu.yd.)	=	0.764555 cubic meter (m³)
1 cubic centimeter (cm³)	=	0.061024 cubic inch (cu.in.)
1 cubic meter (m³)	=	35.314667 cubic feet (cu.ft.)
1 cubic meter (m³)	=	1.307951 cubic yards (cu.yd.)

Volume Measures for Fluids

1 gallon (gal.)	=	3785.411 cubic centimeters (cm³)
1 gallon (gal.)	=	3.785411 liters (L)
1 quart (qt.)	=	0.946353 liter (L)
1 ounce (oz.)	=	29.573530 cubic centimeters (cm³)
1 cubic centimeter (cm³)	=	0.000264 gallon (gal.)
1 liter (L)	=	0.264172 gallon (gal.)
1 liter (L)	=	1.056688 quarts (qt.)
1 cubic centimeter (cm³)	=	0.033814 ounce (oz.)

Math Measures

1 pound (lb.)	=	0.453592 kilogram (kg)
1 pound (lb.)	=	453.59237 grams (g)
1 ounce (oz.)	=	28.349523 grams (g)
1 ounce (oz.)	=	0.028350 kilogram (kg)
1 kilogram (kg)	=	2.204623 pounds (lb.)
1 gram (g)	=	0.002205 pound (lb.)
1 kilogram (kg)	=	35.273962 ounces (oz.)
1 gram (g)	=	0.035274 ounce (oz.)

APPENDIX B

Site plans use a survey scale which is in feet and one hundredths of a foot. The building trades work in feet, inches, and fractions of an inch, down to 1/8 of an inch. A craftsperson should be able to convert dimensions from hundredths of a foot to inches and eighths almost automatically.

By remembering certain bench marks and applying simple addition and subtraction, the craftsperson can easily approximate the dimensions.

There are ninety-six 1/8s in one foot and one hundred 1/100s in one foot, so 1/8 of an inch equals approximately 1/100 of a foot.

Since .50 one hundredths of a foot is equal to 6 inches, then .59 is approximately 7-1/8 inches (add 9/8 to 6 inches). Since 9 inches is equal to .75 one hundredths of a foot, then 8 inches is equal to approximately .67 hundredths of a foot (subtract 8/100 from .75). These dimensions are approximate, but this is an easy way to convert hundredths of a foot to inches or inches to hundredths of a foot.

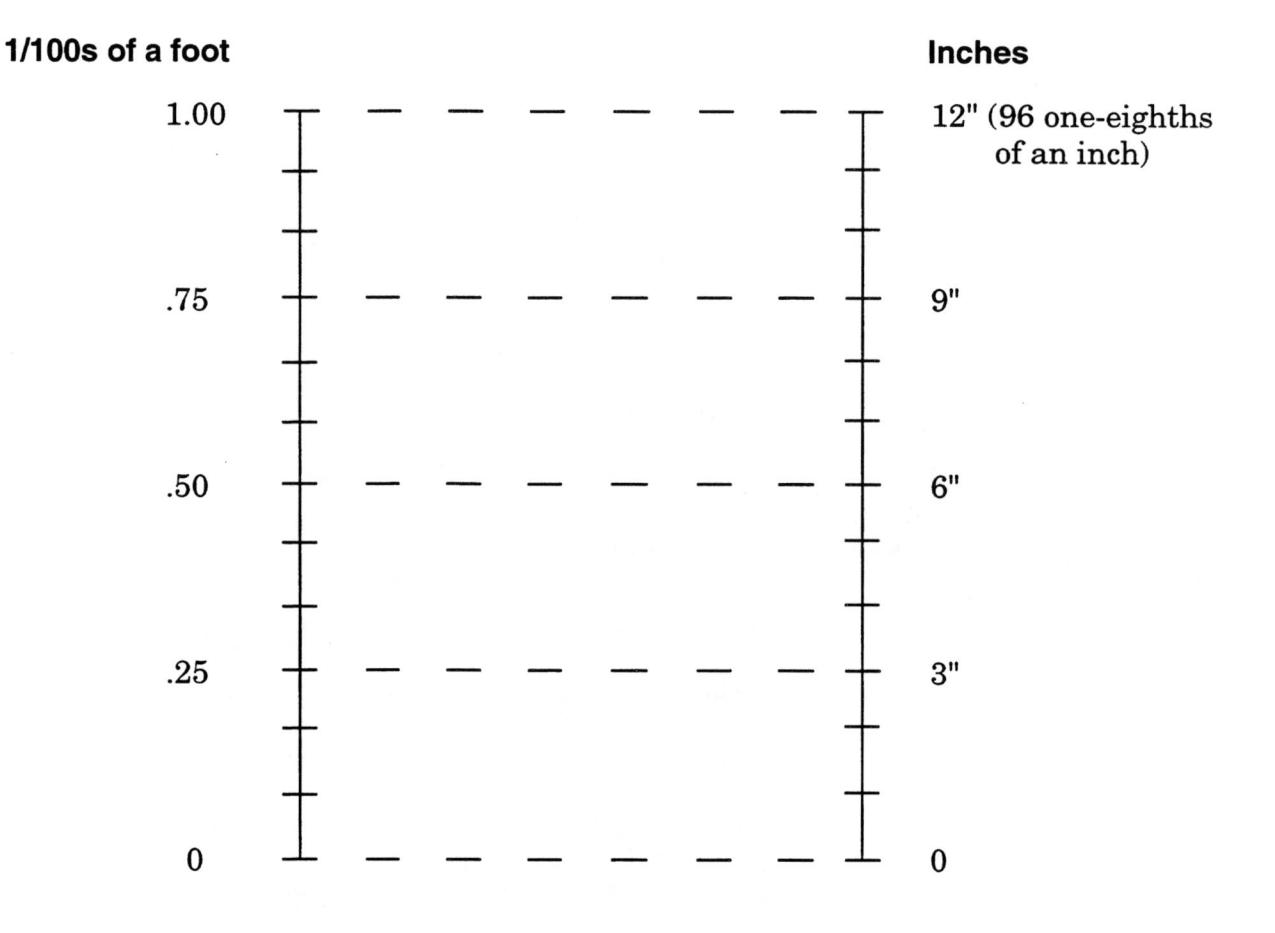

1/100s of a foot   **Inches**

1/100s of a foot	Inches
1.00	12" (96 one-eighths of an inch)
.75	9"
.50	6"
.25	3"
0	0

SHEET METAL — TRAINEE TASK MODULE 04106

NCCER CRAFT TRAINING USER UPDATES

The NCCER makes every effort to keep these manuals up-to-date and free of technical errors. We appreciate your help in this process. If you have an idea for improving this manual, or if you find an error, a typographical mistake, or an inaccuracy in the NCCER's Craft Training Manuals, please write us, using this form or a photocopy. Be sure to include the exact module number, page number, a description of the problem, and the correction, if possible. Your input will be brought to the attention of the Technical Review Committee. Thank you for your assistance.

Instructors – If you found that additional materials were necessary in order to teach this module effectively, please let us know so that we may include them in the Equipment/Materials list in the Instructor's Guide.

Write: Curriculum and Revision Department
National Center for Construction Education and Research
P.O. Box 141104
Gainesville, FL 32614-1104

Fax: 352-334-0932

Craft _____ Module Name _____

Module Number _____ Page Number(s) _____

Description of Problem
_____
_____
_____
_____

(Optional) Correction of Problem
_____
_____
_____

(Optional) Your Name and Address
_____
_____
_____

notes

Basic Piping Practices
Module 04110

National
Center for
Construction
Education and
Research

Task Module 04110

BASIC PIPING PRACTICES

Objectives

Upon completion of this module, the trainee will be able to:

1. State the various materials from which pipe is made.
2. List applications of various materials.
3. List the common methods employed for joining pipe.
4. List the common types of pipe hangers and supports.

THE CHOICE OF MATERIAL

Basically, materials are chosen in an attempt to balance economics with practicality. The cost of the materials must suit their application. Considerations such as maintenance, durability, and suitability must be considered along with the cost of the entire system. It would be wasteful, for example, to use an expensive, specialized **alloy** when carbon steel will do as well.

METHODS OF FITTING PIPE

Welding

Pipe can be "butt welded" or socket welded. Butt welding joins pipe of equal diameters. Socket welding is a special system in which a straight length of pipe is inserted into a fitting having a formed opening slightly larger than the outside diameter of the straight pipe. The circumference is then welded.

Welding lends itself well to prefabrication and is usually the best method for joining large diameter pipe. The joints, when properly made, are leakproof and stronger than the material from which the pipe is made.

Copyright © 1992 National Center for Construction Education and Research, Gainesville, FL. All rights reserved. No part of this work may be reproduced in any form or by any means, including photocopying, without written permission of the publisher. Updated: 1998.

However, because welding cannot be done in the presence of flammable materials, its use is limited to those areas that present no danger of fire. Another disadvantage of welded pipe is the formation of "icicles" on the inside of the pipe joint. Icicles are irregular bits of weld metal that decrease the inside diameter of the pipe and offer obstructions to the material flowing inside the line. In most cases, this is not an objectionable condition.

Three methods of welding are commonly used to join pipe. These are:

Shielded metal-arc welding. This is stick welding, the most common process used to weld pipe. It uses a consumable electrode whose composition must match the material being welded.

Gas tungsten-arc welding. This process is usually called "TIG" (tungsten inert gas). It uses a non-consumable tungsten electrode that is shielded by an inert gas, usually argon or helium. A filler metal is usually added to the joint. The TIG process produces a weld of high purity and is used to weld stainless steel pipe and other complex alloys.

Gas metal-arc welding. This process is usually called "MIG" (metal inert gas). It is a wire-fed system that also uses an inert gas to shield the weld metal. The rate of metal deposition using the MIG system is faster than that obtainable with the previous two methods.

Threading

Threaded pipe offers quick installation, is good for small lines and is easily adaptable to field use. The joints can be made leakproof by the use of sealants. A wide range of fittings is available for threaded systems, making this method versatile and practical. Most of the materials from which pipe is made can be threaded.

There are disadvantages, however, to threaded piping systems. The threading operation greatly reduces the outside diameter of the pipe which, in turn, decreases the strength of the pipe at the joint. In addition, threaded joints are the most prone to leaking.

Flanging

Flanges can be used to join pipe when welding is impractical or when the line needs to be accessible for easy removal.

Installation is easy. A gasket is placed between two flanges and they are then bolted together. Since the flange itself does not come into contact with the material in the line, the flange does not have to be made of the same material as the pipe itself.

The proper gaskets must be used in conjunction with flanges.

Solvent Coatings

Plastic and fiber glass reinforced pipe are usually joined by cementing with special adhesives. These joints are strong, leakproof and easy to make.

METAL PIPING SYSTEMS

Carbon Steel Pipe

Pipe is available in a wide variety of materials from the very common to the very specialized. Throughout the course of a career, you will likely encounter many different materials. Some of the most common are listed in this section.

A combination of iron ore and carbon make steel. The term "carbon steel" is often used to avoid confusion with stainless steel.

Steel pipe has many uses in the field. Some uses include hot and cold water distribution, steam and hot water heating systems, gas and air piping systems, drainage and vent systems, as well as many other special uses that are too numerous to list.

The two common types of carbon steel pipe are **black iron pipe** and **galvanized pipe**.

Black iron pipe gets its color from the carbon in the steel. It is most often used as gas or air-pressure pipe. Black iron pipe is used where corrosion will not affect its uncoated surfaces.

Galvanized steel pipe is dipped in molten zinc. This protects the surfaces from abrasive, corrosive materials and gives the pipe a dull, grayish color. Galvanized pipe is most often used when the specifications require steel pipe.

Weights and Sizes

Steel pipe for threading is manufactured in three weights or strengths: standard (schedule 40), extra strong (schedule 80) and double extra strong (schedule 120). Extra strong is referred to by some manufacturers as extra heavy and double extra strong is called double extra heavy. The cross-sections in *Figure 1* show the inside and outside diameters for 1-inch nominal-size steel pipe.

Because all weights have the same outside diameter, the same threading dies will fit all three weights of pipe.

The wall thickness and the inside diameter differ with each weight. The thicker the wall, the smaller the inside diameter, but the more pressure the pipe will withstand. Standard weight will prove adequate in most plumbing situations; however, the two stronger weights are available when pressure requires their use.

Nominal Size

Nominal size is based on the inside diameter (I.D.). Nominal size is measured in inches. Steel pipe is manufactured in the following nominal sizes: 1/8", 1/4", 1/2", 3/4", 1", 1-1/4", 1-1/2", 2", 2-1/2", 3", 4", 5", 6", 8", 10" and 12". Pipe greater than 12" are measured by their outside diameter (O.D.).

Lengths

Steel pipe is manufactured in lengths of 21 feet, threaded or unthreaded. Larger sizes (6" and above) come in random lengths of 18 to 22 feet. For ease of handling, pipe is shipped in bundles. The number of lengths per bundle is determined by the size of the pipe. A tag is attached to each bundle, labeling the number of feet within the bundle. Consult a manufacturer's catalog to determine the number of feet contained in specific sized bundles.

GROOVED PIPE

The concept of grooved piping dates back to World War I when it became necessary for armies in the field to join pipe quickly and efficiently. Since then, the concept has undergone continuous development such that it is considered as a primary means of joining pipe today. Steel pipe, cast iron pipe and ductile iron pipe may have grooved joints.

Standard (Schedule 40): I.D. 1.0499, O.D. 1.315"

Wall Thickness

Extra Strong (Schedule 80): I.D. .9577, O.D. 1.3155

Double Extra Strong (Schedule 120): I.D. .66

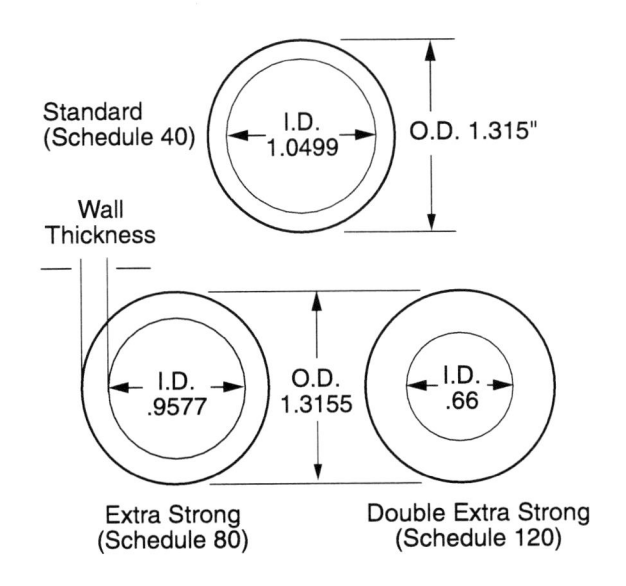

Figure 1 - Inside and outside diameters

BASIC PIPING PRACTICES — TRAINEE TASK MODULE 04110

Components

A grooved pipe joint consists of the following components:

1. Specially grooved pipe ends cut by special machines to exact manufacturer's standards.
2. A synthetic rubber gasket.
3. Lubricant.
4. A coupling consisting of two housings.

A wide variety of fittings and valves is available with grooved ends. Special gaskets are also available for various service conditions.

It is important to consult with the manufacturer's design specifications before using a grooved pipe system.

Joining Procedure

Carbon steel pipe can be joined using nearly all common joining methods.

The procedure used to join grooved pipe is as follows:

1. Check to insure that the gasket is suitable for the intended service. Some manufacturers color code their gaskets. Apply a thin coat of lubricant to the gasket lips and the outside of the gasket.
2. Check the pipe ends. To assure a leakproof seal, they must be free from indentations, projections, or roll marks.
3. Install the gasket over the pipe end. Be sure the gasket lip does not hang over the pipe end.
4. Align and bring the two pipe ends together. Slide the gasket into position and center it between the grooves on each pipe. Be sure that no part of the gasket extends into the groove on either pipe.
5. Assemble the housing segments loosely, leaving one nut and bolt off to allow the housing to swing over the joint.
6. Install the housing, swinging it over the gasket and into position into the grooves on both pipe.
7. Insert the remaining bolt and nut. Be sure that the bolt track head engages into the recess in the housing.
8. Tighten the nuts alternately and equally to maintain metal-to-metal contact at the angle bolt pads.

WORKING WITH STEEL PIPE

This section of the module discusses the major components of working with steel pipe. These are measuring, cutting, reaming, threading, and assembling.

Measuring

Threaded pipe may be measured by a variety of methods: end-to-end, end-to-center, face-to-end, face-to-face, or center-to-center. *Figure 2* shows the different measuring techniques. It is important to allow for fitting dimensions (end-to-end or end-to-center) and for length of thread engagement.

End-to-end measure is accomplished by measuring the full length of the pipe including both threads.

End-to-center measure is used for a length of pipe having a fitting screwed on one end only. The pipe length is equal to the measurement minus the end-to-center dimension of the fitting plus the length of the thread engagement.

Face-to-end measure is used for a length of pipe having a fitting screwed on one end only. It differs from end-to-center in that the length of pipe is equal to the measurement plus the length of the thread engagement.

Center-to-center measure is used to measure pipe that has a fitting screwed to both ends. The length is equal to the measurement minus the sum of the end-to-center dimensions of the fittings plus two times the length of the thread engagement.

SHEET METAL — TRAINEE TASK MODULE 04110

Face-to-face measure can be used under the same conditions as the center-to-center method. It is figured by measuring the length of pipe plus two times the length of the thread engagement.

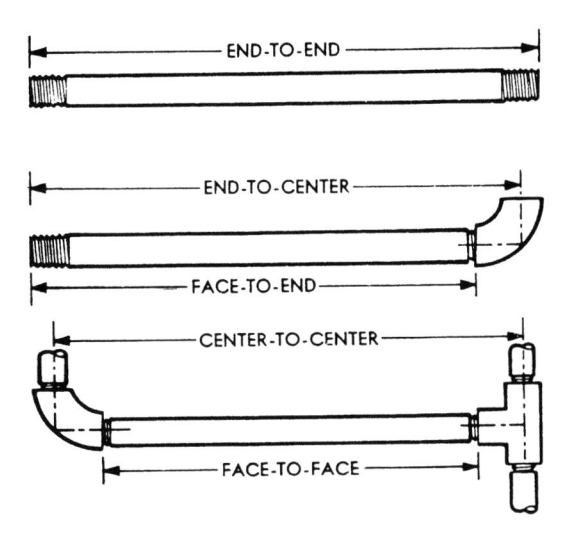

Figure 2 - Measuring methods

Cutting

The pipe cutter (*Figure 3*) is the best tool to use when cutting steel pipe. To operate, revolve the cutter around the pipe and tighten the cutting wheel 1/4 revolution with each turn. Avoid overtightening the cutting wheel. This could damage the wheel or cause it to break.

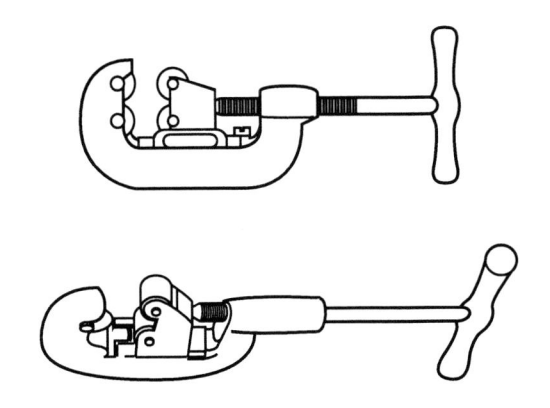

Figure 3 - Pipe cutters

Reaming

Once the pipe is cut, a reamer (*Figure 4*) removes the burr that forms on the inside of the pipe. Not removing the burr can cause blockage and restrict liquid flow.

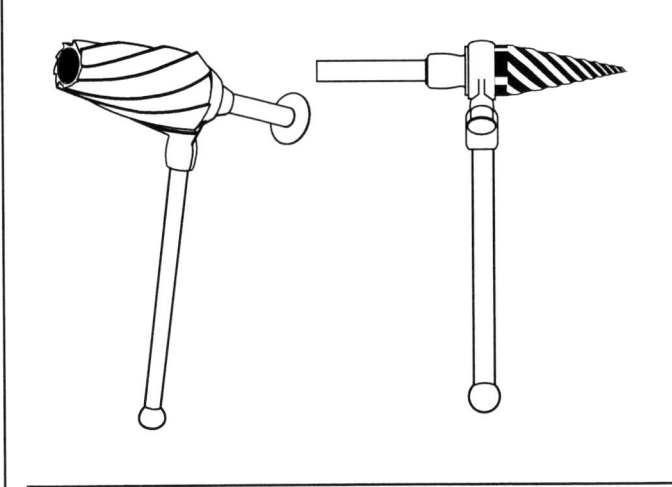

Figure 4 - Reamers

Threading

Threads may be cut by hand with a die and stock or with an electric pipe threading machine. See *Figure 5*.

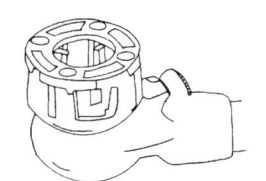

PIPE DIE AND STOCK

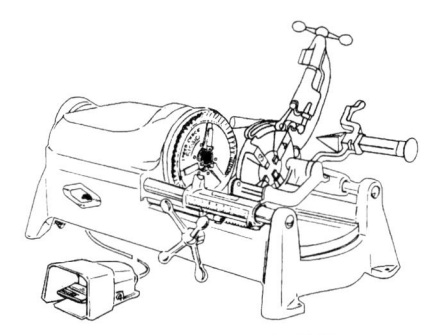

THREADING MACHINE

Figure 5 - Pipe threaders

BASIC PIPING PRACTICES — TRAINEE TASK MODULE 04110

To cut threads using a hand die and stock, proceed as follows:

1. Select the correct size die for the pipe being threaded.

2. Inspect the die to see if the cutters are free of nicks and wear.

3. Lock the pipe securely in vise.

4. Slide the die over the end of the pipe, guide end first.

5. Push the die against the pipe with the heel of one hand. Take three or four short, slow, clockwise turns. Be careful to keep the die pressed firmly against the pipe. When enough thread is cut to keep the die firmly against the pipe, apply some thread cutting oil. This oil prevents the pipe from overheating due to friction and it lubricates the die. Oil the threading die every two or three downward strokes.

6. Back off a 1/4 turn after each full turn forward to clear out the metal chips. Continue until the pipe projects one or two threads from the die end of the stock. Too few threads is as bad as too many threads.

7. To remove the die, rotate it counter-clockwise.

8. Wipe off excess oil and any chips. Use a rag, not your bare hand. The chips are sharp and could cause cuts.

To cut threads using a power threading machine, proceed as follows:

1. Select and install the correct size die and inspect it for nicks.

2. Mount pipe into chuck. Long pipe must have additional support.

3. Check the pipe and die alignment.

4. Cut threads until two threads appear at the other end of the die. Stop threading action. Apply cutting oil during threading operation.

5. Back off the die until it is clear of the pipe.

6. Remove the pipe from the machine chuck. Be careful not to mar the threads.

7. Wipe the pipe clean of oil and metal chips.

Each threading machine is slightly different. Become familiar with the manufacturer's operating procedures before attempting to operate the machine. Also, become thoroughly familiar with the maintenance and safety instructions for the machine. A poorly maintained machine can become a safety hazard.

Assembling

Apply pipe joint compound to the male threads before assembling a pipe connection. Do not apply the compound to the threads of the fitting. Either the paste compound or teflon tape may be used.

When using teflon tape, apply the tape in a clockwise direction, the same direction as the fitting turns. Be sure to check the local gas codes to see if the use of tape is permitted.

Start the fitting onto the threaded pipe by hand. Turn the fitting clockwise. Finish tightening the fitting with a pipe wrench, *Figure 6*.

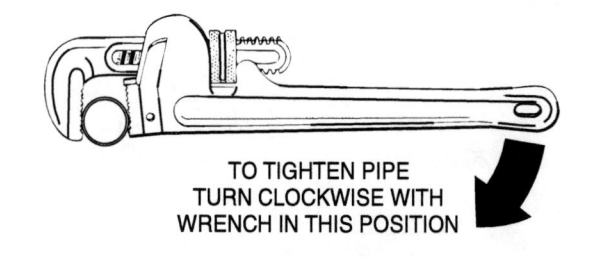

Figure 6 - Tightening the fitting

COPPER TUBING

Copper is divided into three classifications based on the wall thickness. Type K and type L, heavy and medium wall tubing are ACR approved for use in refrigeration pressurized lines. Type M, thin wall, is utilized on water lines, condensate drains and other associated system requirements.

Heavy-wall, type K, is meant for special use where abnormal conditions of corrosion might be expected. Type L is most frequently used for normal refrigeration applications. Both K and L copper tubing are available in soft or hard drawn types.

Soft copper tubing is commercially available in sizes from 1/8" OD to 1-5/8" OD. It is usually sold in 25, 50 or 100-foot coil lengths. This tubing may be soldered or used with flared or other mechanical fittings. It is easily bent or shaped, but it must be held in place by clamps or other hardware as it cannot support its own weight. More frequent applications use line sizes from 1/4" to 3/4" OD.

Hard-drawn tubing is also widely used in commercial refrigeration and air-conditioning systems. It comes in straight lengths of 20 feet and in sizes from 3/8" OD to over 6 inches OD. The lengths are charged with nitrogen and plugged at each end to maintain a clean, moisture-free, internal condition. It is intended for use with formed fittings to make the necessary bends or changes in directions. It is more self-supporting and therefore needs fewer supports than soft copper tubing.

Stainless Steel

Stainless steel is not a single material. Rather, it is the name given to a large group of "alloys." An alloy is a mixture of metals that produces a material having different characteristics than those of the metals used in the mixture. The metals used to make stainless steel "stainless" are varying amounts of chromium and nickel mixed with iron.

Although it is an expensive material, stainless steel offers high resistance to corrosion and is used in those situations where high purity is required. It is able to retain its strength at both high and low temperatures and is used where carbon steel would be impractical.

Stainless steel can be welded, threaded or flanged. Welding is the most common method used to join stainless steel pipe.

In order to preserve its corrosion-resistant qualities, it is important that stainless steel not come into contact with material other than stainless steel during its installation. It should be handled with special slings used only for stainless steel and should be supported by hangers that will not scratch the surface of the metal. Many times stainless steel "bearing plates" will be used between the pipe support and the pipe itself to protect the surface of the pipe.

Chromium-Molybdenum Pipe

The addition of molybdenum to chromium steels with a low carbon content increases the hardenability of the steel as well as its resistance to corrosion. This makes "chrome-moly" pipe suitable for high pressure/high temperature applications.

Chrome-moly pipe is joined by welding. Preheating of the joint is usually required and the pipe is stress-relieved after welding. The root pass is usually made using the TIG process of welding.

Aluminum Pipe

Like stainless steel, the word "aluminum" has come to stand for a large group of alloys, each having a particular application. Because of its ability to resist corrosion, aluminum is used to convey materials that are difficult to convey by steel pipe.

In addition to its corrosion-resistant qualities, aluminum retains its strength at very low temperatures and is well suited for these applications.

Aluminum pipe is most commonly joined by TIG welding, but it can also be threaded or flanged. To retain the corrosion-resistant qualities of the metal, welding is best.

As with stainless steel pipe, care must be taken when supporting aluminum pipe. Only aluminum or padded hangers should be used. Galvanized hangers may be used but they will be good only as long as the coating lasts.

OTHER ALLOYS

The use of specialized alloys is increasing to meet the demands of new developments in technology. While these alloys are too numerous to list, three have become common and will be briefly discussed in order to familiarize the trainee with them.

"Hastelloy"

This is a tradename of the Union Carbide Corporation used for its various nickel-based alloys. Hastelloy is particularly suited to the chemical processing industry in which it is used to convey highly corrosive materials, such as boiling sulfuric acid.

Pipe made of Hastelloy is available in sizes up to 30 inches. It can be welded, threaded or flanged.

"Monel"

This is a tradename of the International Nickel Corporation used for its various nickel-copper alloys. Monel shows good resistance to salt, lye and sulfuric acid and is used for handling salt water.

Pipe made of Monel is available in sizes up to 12 inches. It can be welded, threaded or flanged, but it is most commonly welded with the TIG process.

"Inconel"

This is a tradename of the International Nickel Corporation used for its various nickel-iron-chromium alloys. Inconel shows good resistance to acids in foods, such as fruit juices, and is used in the food processing industry. It also has applications in the pharmaceutical industry because it cannot contaminate the contents of the pipeline. Inconel is also good for conveying dry chlorine gas, which is highly corrosive.

Pipe made of Inconel can be welded or threaded. It is welded using the same procedures as those used to weld stainless steel.

PLASTIC PIPING SYSTEMS

There are several different types of plastic used in the manufacturing of plastic pipe. Each type is manufactured with special characteristics or properties. Matching the pipe's characteristics with the job requirements, allows the best plastic pipe to be selected. Be sure to consult the manufacturer's specified applications. Due to the large number of types of plastic pipe, only the seven most common types will be presented. These seven types (ABS, PVC, CPVC, PE, SR, PB, and PP) account for 95% of the plastic used.

PVC Pipe

Polyvinyl chloride (**PVC**) pipe is used widely in plumbing. Its uses include both pressure and drainage applications. The material itself is most often white. PVC offers high impact tensile strength, and resistance to most salt solutions, acids, and bases. It can be used above or below the ground.

PVC pipe is suitable for service up to 140° F. However, at a constant internal or external temperature of 110° F, PVC has a tendency to sag. Horizontal installation at this temperature or at higher temperatures requires continuous support along the length of the run.

Even though PVC's rate of thermal conductivity is lower than most of the other plastic piping materials, it responds rapidly to alternating flows of hot and cold temperature changes and continues expanding and contracting with each cycle. Therefore, expansion joints or offsets may be required in the system. A support system that accounts for movement must also be provided.

PVC is available in sizes from 1/4 inch to 16 inches in diameter. Schedule 40 DWV - PVC is the same as cast iron DWV.

PVC pipe and fittings can be joined by a number of methods, including solvent cement, threading, and flanges. Solvent cementing techniques are discussed later in the module.

Only Schedule 80 or greater PVC should be threaded. Threaded connections to Schedule 40 PVC pipe can be made with adaptor connections. Schedule 80 pipe can be threaded with conventional pipe dies, but the dies must be sharp and should only be used to thread plastic pipe.

PVC flanges are available for both Schedule 40 and Schedule 80 pipe. They may be joined with threaded or solvent cemented joints.

It is important to note that PVC piping systems should never be tested over rated pressures with compressed air. The pipe could shatter.

CPVC Pipe

Chlorinated polyvinyl chloride (**CPVC**) is a variation of PVC pipe that was developed to meet the needs of a corrosion-resistant pressure piping at higher temperatures. It was first introduced in 1960 and since then has gained wide acceptance.

CPVC is primarily used for piping hot water and chemicals. It is rated at 215° F. CPVC is self-insulating. This means that its thermal conductivity (ability to conduct heat) is a tiny fraction of that of copper tubing. Thus, heat remains inside the pipe and hot water is delivered more quickly. This reduces the danger of burns from touching hot water lines. The nuisance of condensation on cold water pipe is reduced. Also, sludge or scale build-ups within the water systems are reduced.

CPVC in copper tubing sizes may be purchased in diameters of 1/2" to 2" in rigid lengths of 10 feet. The product is generally tan in color and has the same outside diameter as copper tubing. The pipe is often manufactured to a standard dimension ratio, which insures that the pipe and fittings have the same pressure rating regardless of size.

Industrial iron pipe sizes range from 1/2" to 10" in Schedule 40 and Schedule 80. This type of CPVC pipe is gray in color and is used primarily with corrosive chemicals. CPVC has the same chemical resistance as PVC but is not recommended for use with certain solvents, acids and alcohols.

CPVC may be joined with the same methods as discussed for PVC.

ABS Pipe

Acrylonitrile-Butadiene-Styrene (ABS) plastic pipe and fittings are used primarily for drainage, waste, and vent systems, sewer mains, and some water distribution. Two grades of ABS are manufactured: DWV and service. DWV is usually required within a structure by the building code. The grade is identified by the label on the pipe. ABS pipe is black in color.

ABS pipe is non-toxic and resistant to household liquids. It retains its chemical properties over a temperature range of -40° to 200° F, but should not be used over 180° F.

ABS pipe has a low rate of thermal transfer. In a DWV system, this means that hot water going to the sewer line retains most of its heat, allowing greasy waste materials to flow through the pipe, and not stick to the sides.

ABS pipe may be joined with solvent cement or mechanical connections. Threading is not recommended but adaptors are available to make the transition to threaded materials.

When solvent cementing ABS pipe, no primer is required, but a special solvent must be used.

PE Pipe

Polyethylene (PE) pipe is a flexible plastic pipe that is often installed in coils underground. Some of its typical underground applications are sprinkler systems, wells, and portable ice skating rinks.

PE pipe is also used to pipe natural gas. It may also be used to irrigate and to distribute potable water. It is available in low, medium, and high density. Codes do not approve low density for pressure piping.

In sizes up to 2", PE pipe is available in coils. Sizes above 2" come in rigid lengths.

SR Pipe

Styrene-rubber (SR) is used for septic tank and leach field connections, storm drains, building sewers, and other drainage applications.

Polybutylene Pipe

Unlike other plastics used for pipe, polybutylene pipe (PB) is relatively soft when it is first extruded. After four days it attains about 90 percent of its final strength. The material sold in this cured condition.

PB pipe is used in four major areas:
- water distribution and services
- gas distribution and services
- hot and cold water lines
- industrial piping

PB pipe is resistant to chemicals, abrasion, and changes in temperature. It is used in chemical process piping, hot water lines, and slurry piping in chemical plants, pulp and paper mills, power plants, mining operations, and food processing plants.

Polypropylene Pipe

Polypropylene pipe (PP) is the lightest of the plastic pipe materials discussed in this module. PP pipe is often used in irrigation, water treatment, and water systems because of its resistance to soil conditions.

Even though the surface hardness of polypropylene is greater than other plastic piping materials, the surface tends to mar more easily than metal piping. PP's puncture resistance is also less than that of metal piping. Therefore, even though PP pipe requires no protection against soil corrosion, it should be protected from direct contact with hard materials during trenching operations.

Polypropylene pipe can be joined in a number of ways, including socket fusion and fillet welding. The socket fusion process uses a special 110 volt AC tool that provides the correct temperature for the fusion process to take place. The joint is heated by the tool for a specified amount of time at a temperature of 540° F. For 1/2" pipe, the time is about 10-15 seconds; for 4" pipe, the time is about 25-35 seconds. During this time a bead of melted material appears around the complete circumference of the pipe.

Polypropylene pipe can also be welded. The welding process is not recommended for pressure-rated systems. See *Appendix B*. The process uses a heated gas, not a burning gas as is common with soldering or brazing. Compressed air is usually used but it is also possible to use nitrogen equipment. The welding rod must be of the exact same material as the pipe being welded. The welding rod is held at a 75-degree angle to the joint while pressure is put upon the rod. The torch is moved in an arcing motion. For a full fillet weld, three passes are required:

- Pipe to fitting
- Pipe to bead
- Fitting to bead

Because the weakest part of any plastic welded bead is the beginning, the end of the bead should overlap the beginning by at least 3/8" to 1/2".

The Thermosets

Two common types of **thermosets** are the fiber glass reinforced polyester resins and the fiber glass epoxy resins. In either case, the methods of manufacture are similar.

Fiber glass pipe is built layer upon layer in a type of construction known as **laminate**

construction. Fiber glass serves as the bonding agent for the resin, its "skeleton".

Properties of the thermosets vary according to the material and method of construction. However, no thermoset can be reshaped or bent after it is cured.

STANDARDS AND MARKING OF PLASTIC PIPE

Marking

Labels indicate the quality of the product and the type of material (ABS, PVC, PP, or CPVC). The four-digit code on plastic pipe identifies the material, type, grade, and tensile strength of the pipe to the nearest 100 pounds. Refer to *Figure 7* for a labeling example.

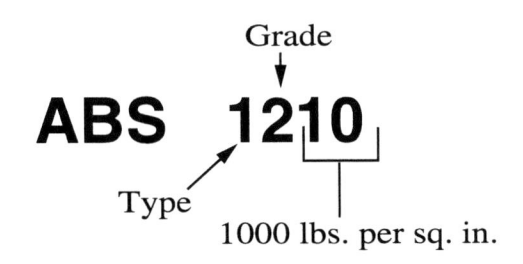

Grade
ABS 1210
Type
1000 lbs. per sq. in.

Figure 7 - Labeling

Standards

To ensure users that plastic piping products are of high quality and suitable for specified systems, the National Sanitation Foundation (NSF), a widely recognized laboratory, has a materials testing program. In order for manufacturers to use the NSF seal, *Figure 8*, on their products certain criteria must be met:

1. Each product line must pass the ASTM test for size and material performance.

2. The manufacturer must allow NSF to make random inspections of the production steps, inspection techniques, and warehouse facilities.

3. The manufacturer must show NSF the production records indicating the quality of the materials that were used.

Figure 8 - NSF seal

If, at any time, the manufacturer's products are found to be defective, the manufacturer must correct the problem and have proof that the defective products were removed from the market. Failure to do so means loss of the NSF seal.

The NSF seal guarantees that you have purchased and are installing a quality product.

Size and material standards for plastic pipe sizes are set by the American Society for Testing and Materials (ASTM). These standards are used by NSF as their reference.

Joining Methods

Plastic pipe may be glued with special solvents, threaded, flanged, and, in some cases, fusion welded.

Solvent Cementing

This is the most popular method for joining the **thermoplastics**, especially PVC and CPVC. However, not all types of plastics can be cemented and different types of plastics require special types of cement. Therefore, it is very important to know what type of plastic is being used so that the proper type of cement may be used.

Primer is required on PVC and CPVC joints. The primer has two purposes. First, it cleans the portion of the pipe and fitting to be connected. Secondly, it conditions the plastic for the solvent cement. Primer is often different in color from cement. Primers for different plastic should not be interchanged. Check the manufacturer's label.

BASIC PIPING PRACTICES — TRAINEE TASK MODULE 04110

Most cements are designed to be applied within a temperature range of 40° to 90° F, but there are special cements that permit application in temperatures as low as 10° F.

Some cements are designed to work on pipe up to 6" in diameter; others work on larger diameter pipes. Be sure to read the label carefully to determine the limits of the particular cement.

The purpose of a cleaner is to remove surface dirt, grease, and grime. Cleaners generally evaporate quickly, preparing the surface of the plastic for primer and/or cement.

Always dry fit the pipe before cementing. This procedure eliminates costly errors. Keep in mind that due to the close tolerances between pipe and fittings, a dry pipe may be prevented from going the full depth of the socket. The solvent cement will probably lubricate and soften the pipe permitting a full-depth fit. Dry fit is meant to insure that pipe does not wobble in the fitting socket. Finish assembly in the following order:

1. Apply a thin coat of cement to the inside of the fitting.
2. Apply a thick coat of cement to the outside of the pipe.
3. Insert and twist pipe 1/4 turn into socket. Hold for at least 30 seconds.
4. A bead of solvent cement should form around the completed joint.
5. Allow the cement to set up approximately one minute.
6. Wipe excess cement from the joint.

Allow one hour before testing or service.

Threading PVC Pipe

Only schedule 80 PVC pipe should be threaded. Standard pipe threading equipment can be used. Vise saws should be padded so that the pipe is not cut.

Fusion Welding

This is not an arc welding process. Rather, it uses a welding tool that is heated either electrically or by a fuel gas. A filler plastic of the same composition as the pipe itself is added and fused to the pipe and fitting. However, only certain types of thermoplastic pipe may be fusion welded. Fusion welding is not possible with the thermosets.

PIPE FITTINGS

Tees

Tees can be purchased in a great number of sizes and patterns. They are used to make a branch that is 90 degrees to the main pipe. If all three outlets are the same size, the fitting is called a regular Tee, shown in *Figure 9*. If outlet sizes vary, the fitting is called a reducing Tee, shown in *Figure 10*. Tees are specified by giving the straight-through (run) dimensions first, then the side-opening dimensions. For example, a T with a run outlet of 2 inches, a run outlet of 1 inch and a branch outlet of 3/4 inches is known as $2 \times 1 \times 3/4$ T (always state the large run size first, the small run size next and the branch size last). Tees are also available with male threads on a run or branch outlet.

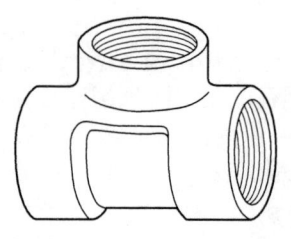

Figure 9 - Regular tee

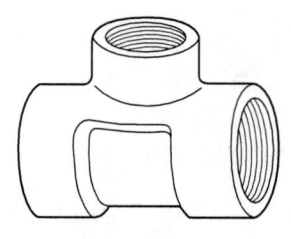

Figure 10 - Reducing tee

Elbows

Elbows, often called ells, are used to change the direction of the pipe. The most common ells, shown in *Figure 11*, are the 90-degree ell; the 45-degree ell; the street ell, which has a male thread on one end; and the reducing ell, which has outlets of different sizes. Ells are also available to make 11-1/4, 22-1/2 and 60-degree bends.

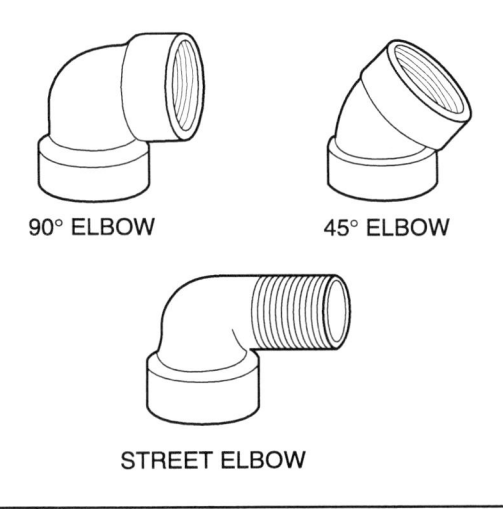

Figure 11 - Elbows

Unions

Unions make it possible to disassemble a threaded piping system. After disconnecting the union, it is possible to unscrew the length of pipe on either end of the union. There are various types of steel pipe unions. The two most common are the ground joint and the flange.

The ground joint union, *Figure 12*, connects two pipes by screwing the thread and shoulder pieces onto the pipe. Then both the shoulder and thread parts are drawn together by the collar. This union creates a gas-or water-tight joint.

The flange union, *Figure 13*, connects two separate pipe. The flanges screw to the pipe to be joined. Then the flanges are pulled together by nuts and bolts. A gasket between the flanges makes this connection gas- or water-tight.

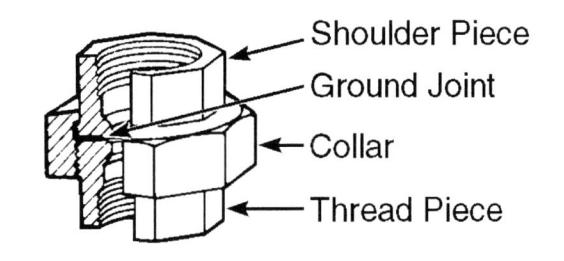

Figure 12 - Ground joint union

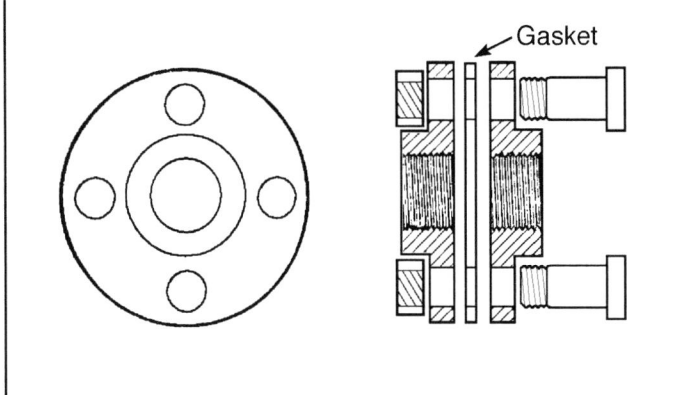

Figure 13 - Flange union

Couplings

Couplings, *Figure 14*, are short fittings with female threads in both openings. They are used to connect two lengths of pipe when making straight runs. Couplings cannot be used in place of unions because they cannot be disassembled.

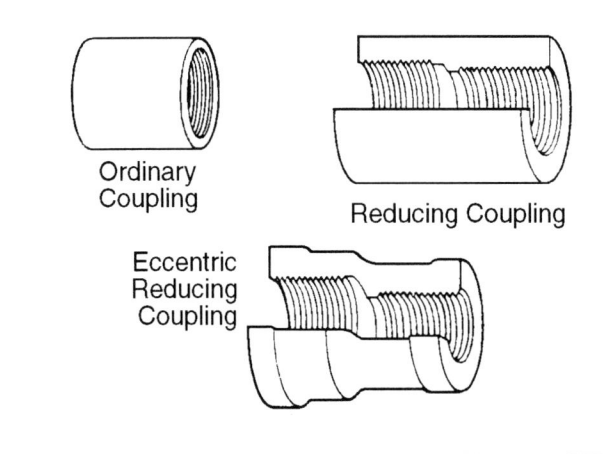

Figure 14 - Couplings

BASIC PIPING PRACTICES — TRAINEE TASK MODULE 04110

Other Common Fittings

Nipples, *Figure 15*, are pieces of pipe 12 inches or less in length, threaded on both ends and used to make extensions from a fitting or to join two fittings. Nipples are manufactured in many sizes beginning with the close or all-thread nipple.

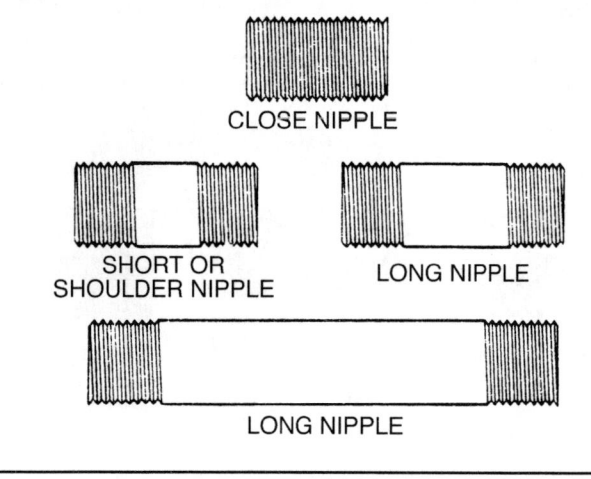

Figure 15 - Nipples

Crosses, *Figure 16*, are four-way distribution devices.

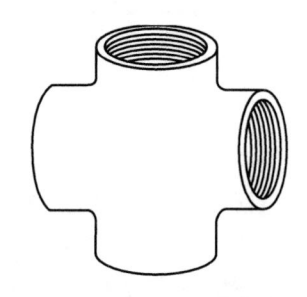

Figure 16 - Cross

Plugs are male-threaded fittings used to close openings in other fittings. There are a variety of heads (square, slotted and hexagon) found on plugs, as shown in *Figure 17*.

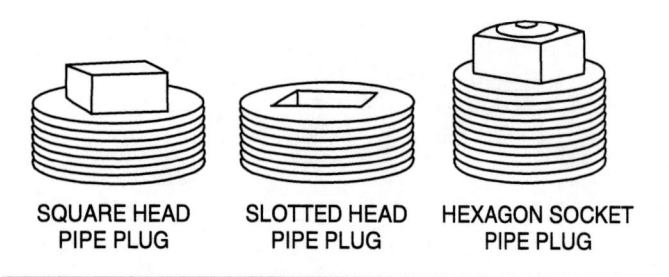

Figure 17 - Plugs

Caps, *Figure 18*, are fittings with a female thread used for the same purpose as plug except that the cap fits on the male end of a pipe or nipple.

Figure 18 - Cap

Bushings, *Figure 19*, are fittings with a male thread on the outside and a female thread on the inside. They are usually used to connect the male end of a pipe to a fitting of a larger size. The ordinary bushing has a hexagon nut at the female end.

Figure 19 - Bushing

PIPE HANGERS AND SUPPORTS

The proper support of a piping system is equally important as the proper joining of the pipe within the system. The words "hanger" and "support" technically refer to two different methods of bearing pipe. A "hanger" generally suspends a single line of pipe from structural steel or concrete. A "support" usually carries the weight or pipe and is made from structural steel or a combination of steel and concrete. In actual practice, however, the term "support" covers both methods.

There are basically two types of pipe supports, the standard hangers (as shown in *Figure 20*), and the spring or engineered hangers.

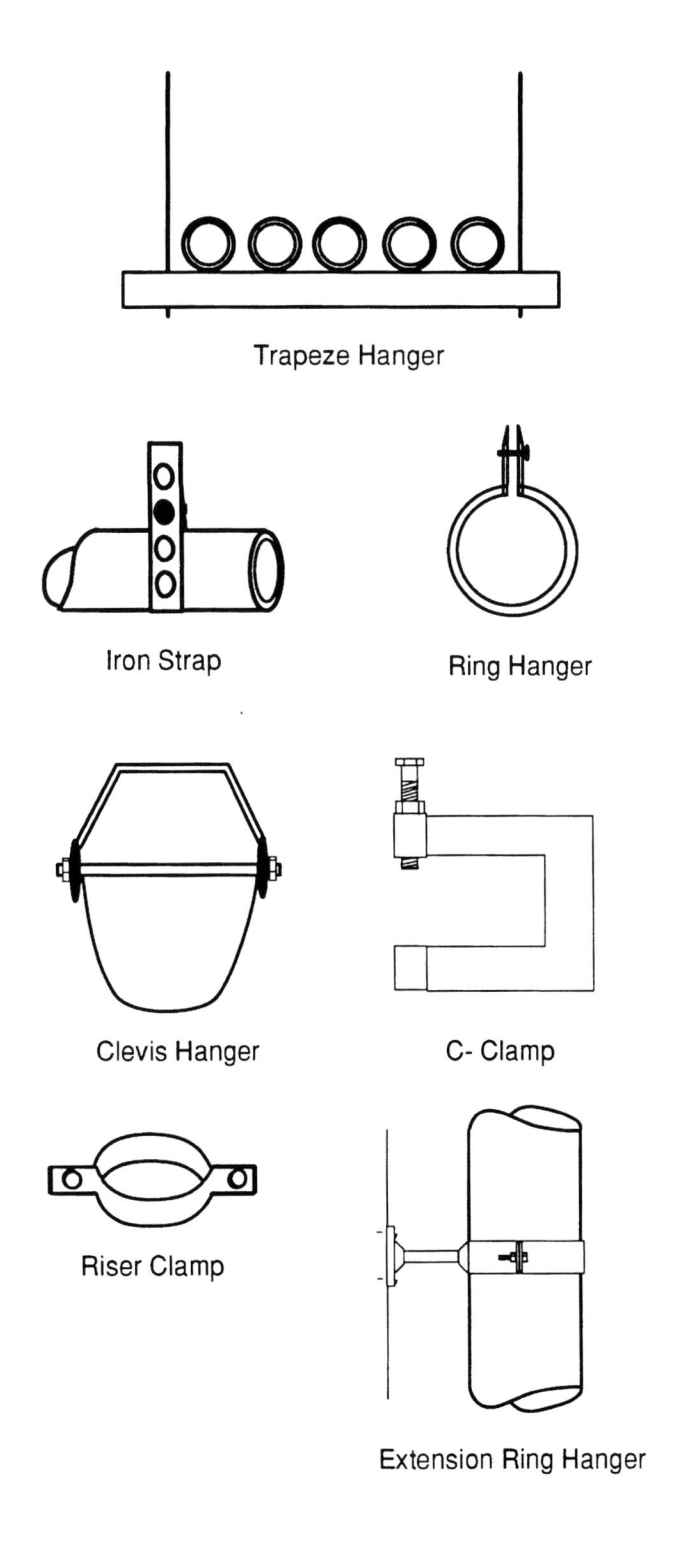

Figure 20 - Examples of pipe hangers and supports

There are two types of spring hangers, the "constant load" and the "variable load." Constant load hangers have a coil spring and a lever that rests inside a housing. Movements of the piping system, provided they are not excessive, do not change the force this spring exerts upon the pipe.

Variable spring hangers and supports operate on the same principle with the exception that the load exerted by the spring is not constant. This means that an external load may be put on the pipe by the support system itself. Where this condition would be objectionable, a constant load hanger should be used.

Any system of support must satisfy the following requirements:

1. It must be able to carry the total weight of the system with an adequate margin of safety. "Total weight" includes the weight of the liquid within the system, the weight of any insulation, as well as any external factors such as wind loads or ice build-up the system may encounter if it is outdoors.

2. It must be able to prevent stress. If the material from which the pipe is made is subject to more stress than it was designed for, structural damage may result.

3. It must allow for draining. A certain amount of sag between supports is acceptable. The amount of sag acceptable is usually determined by the liquid being conveyed and the process requirements of the system. Sag may be reduced by moving the supports closer.

4. It must allow for the thermal expansion and contraction within the system. Operating temperatures have an effect upon the material from which the pipe is made. With certain materials the amount of pipe which will expand or contract with temperature is considerable and must be taken into account within the support system.

5. It must be able to withstand the forces caused by the vibration of pumps or compressors within the system.

BASIC PIPING PRACTICES — TRAINEE TASK MODULE 04110

Inadequate spacing of supports can cause stresses to build up within the system which, in extreme cases, can cause structural failure of the pipe. Proper spacing is usually figured separately for each system and takes into account factors such as material, operating temperatures, rates of thermal expansion or contraction, the weights of valves, fittings or flanges.

Material Considerations

Certain materials require special supports. For example, any contact of carbon steel with stainless steel will cause the stainless steel to corrode. Therefore, **bearing plates** made of stainless steel are usually placed between the pipe and the hanger.

The same holds true for aluminum pipe. It is possible to support aluminum pipe with hangers made of galvanized steel, but these hangers protect the pipe only as long as the galvanized coating lasts.

Insulated systems require special supports that will not cut into the insulation.

Plastic piping systems require support at more frequent intervals than metal pipe, especially when the plastic piping system will encounter elevated temperatures. The hangers should have broad, smooth surfaces rather than narrow, sharp edges and no concentrated loads should ever be allowed to sit on a sharp or narrow surface.

In areas where a plastic piping system must be used at elevated temperatures, support can be supplied by using continuous lengths of angle iron or channel under the pipe.

With plastic pipe, it is important to supply supports with large bearing areas to avoid any concentrated loads being placed on the pipe.

Review Questions

1. What are the advantages of a welded piping system? The disadvantages?

2. What are the advantages of a threaded piping system? The disadvantages?

3. What are some applications of stainless steel pipe?

4. Name three special alloys used in piping systems.

5. What is the main difference between the thermoplastics and the thermosets?

6. Name the methods that plastic pipe may be joined by.

7. What are the requirements a support system for pipe must meet?

8. Why must carbon steel not come into contact with stainless steel?

SUMMARY

Pipefitters join many different types of pipe in many different ways. A knowledge of the basic properties and applications of each type of pipe is essential to ensure proper joining and supporting methods.

Trade Terms

Alloy
Bearing plate
Black iron pipe
Constant load spring hanger
CPVC
Galvanized pipe
Gas metal-arc welding
Gas tungsten-arc welding
Laminate construction
PVC
Shielded metal-arc welding
Thermoplastic
Thermoset
Variable load spring hanger

NCCER CRAFT TRAINING USER UPDATES

The NCCER makes every effort to keep these manuals up-to-date and free of technical errors. We appreciate your help in this process. If you have an idea for improving this manual, or if you find an error, a typographical mistake, or an inaccuracy in the NCCER's Craft Training Manuals, please write us, using this form or a photocopy. Be sure to include the exact module number, page number, a description of the problem, and the correction, if possible. Your input will be brought to the attention of the Technical Review Committee. Thank you for your assistance.

Instructors – If you found that additional materials were necessary in order to teach this module effectively, please let us know so that we may include them in the Equipment/Materials list in the Instructor's Guide.

Write: Curriculum and Revision Department
National Center for Construction Education and Research
P.O. Box 141104
Gainesville, FL 32614-1104
Fax: 352-334-0932

Craft _____ Module Name _____

Module Number _____ Page Number(s) _____

Description of Problem _____

_____

_____

_____

_____

(Optional) Correction of Problem _____

_____

_____

(Optional) Your Name and Address _____

_____

_____

notes

Fabrication II – Radial Line Development

Module 04303

Task Module 04303

FABRICATION II — RADIAL LINE DEVELOPMENT

Objectives

Upon completion of this task module, the trainee will be able to:

1. Describe the principles of radial line development used to determine layouts for sheet metal fittings.

2. Use the principles of radial line development for the layout of selected sheet metal fittings.

3. Demonstrate skill in the layout and fabrication of selected sheet metal fittings and related tasks.

INTRODUCTION

Radial line developments employ many of the procedures of parallel-line development and triangulation. Just as parallel-line development is used to create patterns for parallel forms, radial-line development is used for objects having straight lines or elements radiating from an apex (common center). Radial-line developments embrace a variety of forms of frequent occurrence in sheet metal work. The shapes of these forms have for their base the circle or any of the regular polygons, such as the square, hexagon, octagon, and figures of unequal sides that can be drawn within a circle, in which the lines drawn from the corners of the object terminate in a common center over the center of the base. Cones and pyramids are good examples of radial forms.

REVIEW OF PRINCIPLES

Patterns for radial forms of sheet metal fittings can be developed when the following two specifications have been determined:

1. The true length of the elements.
2. The circumference or the perimeter of the base.

The radial line development method is basically used for round tapering fittings, although it can be used for other shapes of tapering fittings. For radial line development to be practical, all the lines must be drawn from the same center point or apex and the amount of slant must be great enough that it does not intersect the center line at too great a distance. The basic process can be illustrated by unrolling a cone (*Figure 1*) on a flat plane. It should be noted that the apex or common center of the cone remains at one point and that the form unrolls in a circular path about that point (apex) as a center. A method of developing another shape of tapering fitting can be illustrated by the unfolding of the surfaces of a pyramid (*Figure 2*). In this type of development, the pyramid apex also remains fixed, while the surfaces of the pyramid unfold in a circular manner about the apex as a center. Thus, pyramids with sides that are equally tapered can be developed with the radial line method.

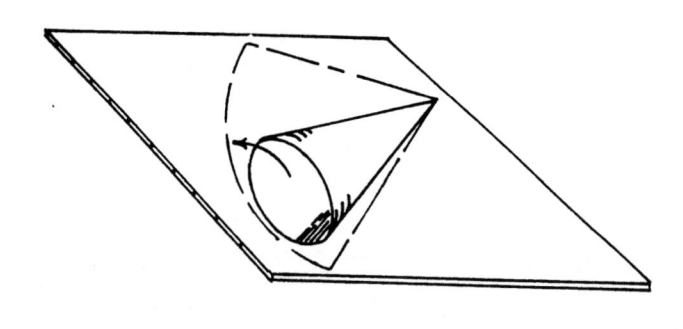

Figure 1 - Unrolling a Cone

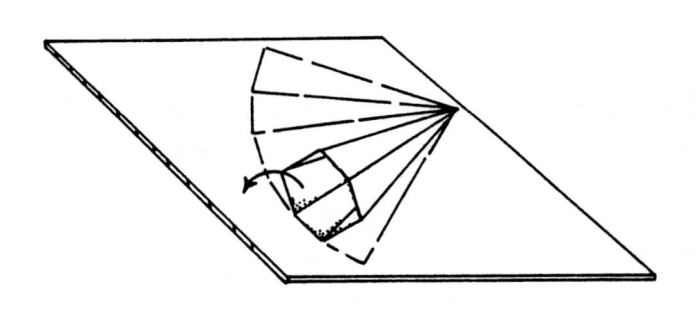

Figure 2 - Unfolding a Pyramid

When using the radial line method of pattern development, it is necessary to determine true lengths of various elements in the pattern being constructed. For example, the pattern for a cone can be developed in the following sequence as shown in *Figure 3*.

1. Draw the elevation view, showing the true height of the apex.

2. Draw the plan view. Use this view to determine the length of the stretchout.

3. Draw the stretchout arc with the radius equal to the true length of the edge of the object. The stretchout arc must be drawn of sufficient length to contain each space in the plan view and in the same order.

4. The true lengths of the elements are obtained from the elevation view. They are placed on the stretchout to complete the pattern development.

USES OF RADIAL LINE DEVELOPMENT

As previously indicated, the radial line development method is basically used for producing round tapering fittings, but it can also be used for other shapes of tapering fittings. In order for radial line methods to be effective, all lines must radiate from a common center (apex). Additionally, the amount of slant of those lines must be relatively large, since most radial line developments begin by drawing the side or elevation view and then extending the side lines until they meet at the peak. If the side taper is so slight that the peak is several feet from the fitting, it is impractical to use radial line development because the radius needed to swing the arc is long and, therefore, difficult to use. Some of the typical fittings that can be laid out using radial line development include cone-shaped objects, roof jacks, and various applications of these shapes (*Figure 4*).

SHEET METAL — TRAINEE TASK MODULE 04303

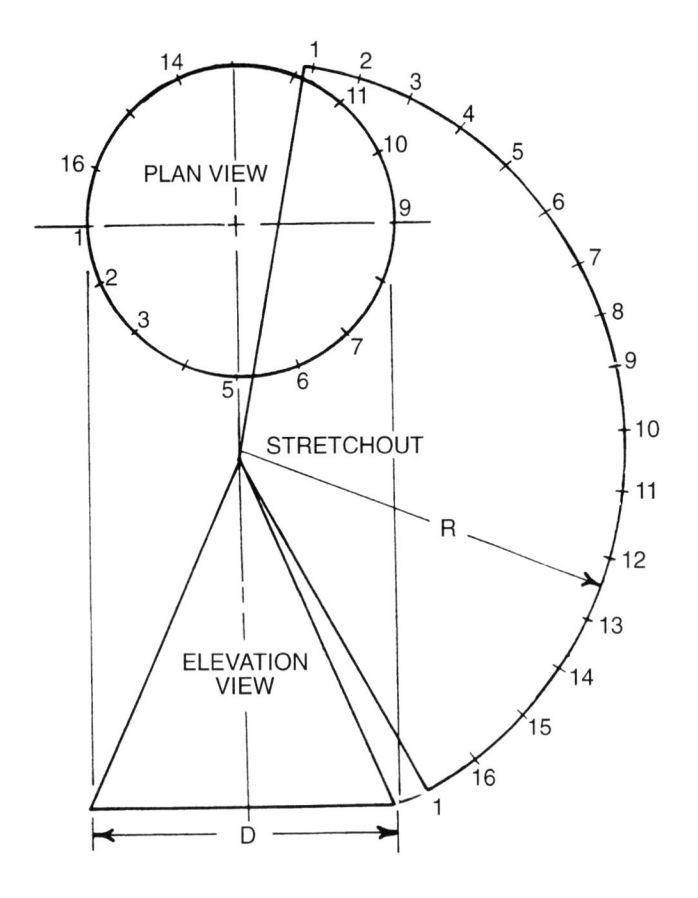

Figure 3 - Radial-Line Method

Figure 4 - Radial Method Shapes

FABRICATION II – RADIAL LINE DEVELOPMENT — TRAINEE TASK MODULE 04303

JOB SHEETS

Prior to beginning the procedures necessary for layout and fabrication of the identified fittings by the radial line method, the trainee should have the following tools and fabrication equipment available for use.

Layout Tools

1. Scratch awls
2. Pencils
3. Straight edges
4. Flat steel square
5. Combination square
6. Prick punch
7. Center punch
8. Dividers
9. Trammel points
10. Marking gage
11. Irregular curves
12. Circumference rule
13. Pee wee tape

Fabrication Equipment

1. Pliers
2. Hand seamer
3. C-clamps
4. Parallel clamps
5. Setting or riveting hammer and mallet
6. Bench plate and stakes
7. Sheet metal snips: combination, curved, hawk-bill, etc.
8. Chisel
9. Rivet set and hand groover
10. Drill bits and drills
11. Files
12. Hacksaw
13. Bar folder
14. Sheet metal brake
15. Slip roll former
16. Sheet metal shear
17. Beading, crimping, turning and burring machines
18. Ring and circle shears
19. Screwdrivers, wrenches and hand tool assortment
20. Electric spot welder
21. Gas welding equipment
22. Arc welder
23. Whitney hand (lever) punch

TASK 1

RECTANGULAR WEATHER CAP

Objective

Upon completion of this task, the trainee will be able to lay out and fabricate the illustrated rectangular weather cap (*Figure 5*).

Some vents in commercial buildings must be made either square or rectangular. Small caps are made in one piece, whereas larger ones are often made in four pieces with standing seams on the corners.

Tools and Materials

Tools and materials necessary for the layout and construction of the rectangular weather cap should be selected from the tools and equipment listed previously. The sheet metal and other fabrication materials can be as indicated by the instructor or at the discretion of the trainee in keeping with established sheet metal trade practices.

Procedure

1. Draw the elevation and plan view of the fitting as indicated in the working drawing.

2. Draw half the elevation or side view.

   a. Draw the base line A-B, square a line upward from point B to establish the center line of the drawing.

   b. From point A, draw a line at 30° or equal to the pitch of the fitting (usually 4-1/2" to 12") or as established by the instructor. Establish point C.

   c. From point C, draw a line perpendicular to line A-C. Measure outward on this line from point C a distance equal to one half the width of the weather cap (2"). Establish point D. The developed radius line (A-D) is the true-length corner line and thus the radius of the pattern development circle.

3. Draw the pattern stretchout.

   a. Use point O as center and distance A-D as radius and describe the circle for the pattern stretchout.

   b. Draw a straight line from point O to the circumference of the circle and establish point E.

   c. Hold a rule so that chords, equal to twice A-B, can be formed in the circle to establish point F.

   d. Using point F as center and distance equal to the width of the weather cap as radius, establish point G on the circumference.

   e. Repeat steps "c" and "d" to establish points H and J on the circumference of the circle.

   f. Draw straight lines between the established points on the circumference to locate the bend lines and the cutout section.

   g. Add allowances for seams or joints, locate the rivet holes for the stays. Note: some shops prefer the stays on the corners, whereas others prefer that they be located in the center of each side. The stays are normally made from 1" × 1/8" band iron. The edge of the rectangular weather cap is usually bent down vertically about 1/2", with a 1/4" hem.

4. Mark the pattern for cutting and bending. Cut and notch the pattern. Form the fitting and spot weld or rivet the seam.

5. Restore the work area.

Questions

1. What was the pitch of the rectangular weather cap?

2. How is the true length of the corner line established?

FABRICATION II – RADIAL LINE DEVELOPMENT — TRAINEE TASK MODULE 04303

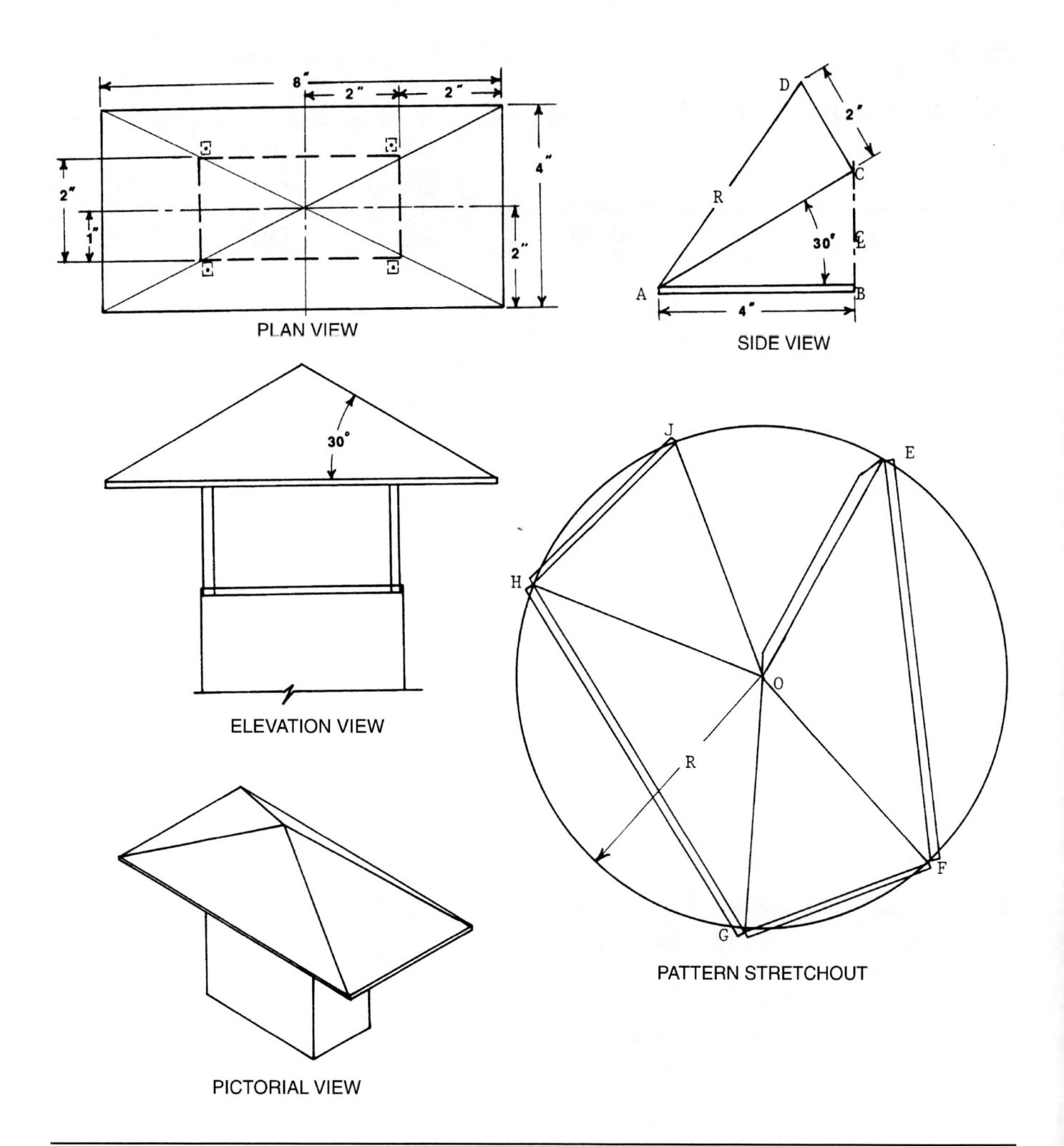

Figure 5 - Rectangular Weather Cap

TASK 2

SYMMETRICAL TAPERED DUCT

Objective

Upon completion of this task, the trainee will be able to lay out by radial line development and fabricate a symmetrical tapered duct.

The symmetrical tapered duct or round equal-taper joint (*Figure 6*), as it is often referred to, can be developed by the radial line method as well as by triangulation. Round tapers are a class of fittings that involve the same basic principles as square-to-rounds. They are basically triangulation problems, but like square-to-rounds, many shortcut layout methods have been developed for their production. This is the most frequently used type of taper fitting.

Tools and Materials

Equipment and supplies necessary for the layout and fabrication of the symmetrical tapered duct can be selected from any traditional sheet metal shop. The type and gage of the sheet metal can be determined by the instructor or by the trainee.

Procedure

1. Draw the plan view and elevation view as illustrated.

2. Draw the half-profile view.

   Note: Only a half-front profile is necessary to develop the full taper pattern.

   a. Draw a base line C-C' equal to one-half the diameter of the large end of the fitting. Square a line upward from point C' an undetermined distance to establish the center line of the half profile.

   b. From point C', measure up the distance equal to the height of the fitting and establish point B'.

   c. Square a line upward from point B' a distance equal to one-half of the diameter of the small end of the fitting and establish point B.

   d. Draw a straight line from point C through point B until it intersects with the center line and establish point A.

3. Draw the pattern stretchout.

   a. With distance A-C as radius and point A as center, draw an arc to establish the circumference of the large diameter of the fitting (circumference equal to 3.14 × diameter, or 3.14 × 4).

   b. With distance A-B as radius and A as center, scribe an arc to establish the circumference for the small diameter of the fitting.

   c. Draw straight lines from point C on the stretchout to point A. This establishes the circumference of the small diameter automatically.

   Note: The half-front profile can be included within the arc C and D (*Figure 6a*) without any wasted space.

4. Lay out the collars with the length of the stretchouts equal to the circumference of the large and small diameters of the arc. The width can be determined from the working drawing.

5. Make allowances for seams and edges on the patterns.

6. Cut out the patterns and form the shapes.

7. Rivet or spot weld the seams and edges as instructed.

8. Restore the work area.

Questions

1. What method of development is generally used for laying out this type of fitting?

2. Explain how to draw the half-profile without wasting space.

PLAN VIEW

ELEVATION VIEW

SMALL COLLAR
3.14 x D

LARGE COLLAR

PICTORIAL VIEW

FIGURE 6a

HALF PROFILE

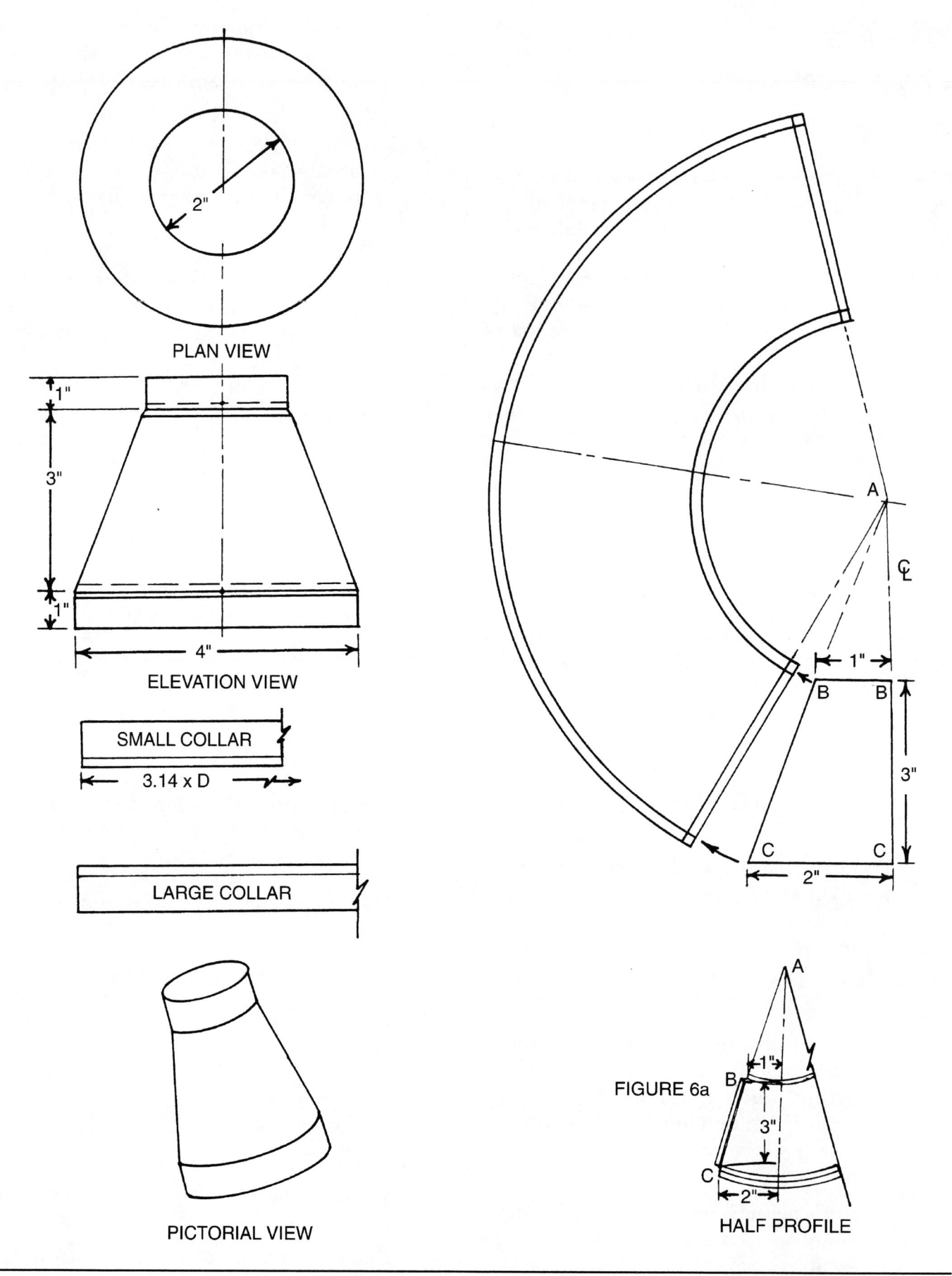

Figure 6 - Round Equal-Taper Joint

SHEET METAL — TRAINEE TASK MODULE 04303

TASK 3

ROOF SLOPE STACK FLANGE

Objective

Upon completion of this task, the trainee will be able to lay out by radial line development, and fabricate a stack flange for a roof slope (*Figure 7*).

This fitting is another object that is usually laid out by triangulation, but can also be developed by the radial line method. Other terms for this type of fitting include: round taper with mitered base, and roof jack on a pitch. Most fittings of this type are drawn according to pitch such as 7/12 (7" of rise in 12" of horizontal measurement), but they may also be identified in degrees.

Tools and Materials

Tools, equipment and supplies necessary for the layout and fabrication of the stack flange round taper fitting can be selected from any conventional sheet metal shop. The type and gage of the sheet metal may be specified by the instructor or left up to the trainee.

Procedure

1. Draw the elevation or side view.

   a. Draw a vertical line to establish the centerline of the fitting.

   b. At any distance on the center line, establish point 16. From point 16 measure up 5" and establish point O.

   c. Draw a horizontal line through point O extending to the right and left of the center line.

   d. Draw a 30° line through point 16 or the pitch angle as directed by the instructor, such as 7/12.

   e. With point O as center and one-half the diameter of the small end as radius, draw a half-circle below the diameter line of the small end.

   f. Divide the half-circle into 6 equal parts and mark the points of intersection 1, 2, 3, 4, 5, 6, and 7. Connect these points by vertical lines to line 1-7.

   g. Draw lines at 30° to the center line through points 1 and 7 to intersect at the apex.

   h. Draw lines from the apex through the intersection points of the perpendicular lines with small diameter line 1-7 to intersect the "pitch" line drawn through point 16 and establish points 13, 14, 15, 16, 17, 18, and 19.

   i. From points 14, 15, 16, 17, and 18 on the pitch line, draw horizontal lines to the left to intersect the line from the apex to point G and establish points F, E, D, C, B, and A.

   j. Add 1" below point 13 to establish point 20. Add 1" above point 19 to establish point 21. 1" is the size of the flange.

2. Draw the half-plan view.

   a. Draw vertical lines downward from points 20 and 21 on the pitch line to establish the length of the roof flange pattern, locate points H and J.

   b. Draw a horizontal line between points H and J. Measure down a distance equal to one-half the width of the roof flange and draw line I-K.

   c. Identify the intersection point of the vertical center line and line H-J as point O'. With O' as center and one-half the diameter of the small end as radius, draw a half circle.

   d. Divide the half circle into 6 equal parts and locate points 1', 2', 3', 4', 5', 6', and 7'. Extend lines through these points from O'.

FABRICATION II – RADIAL LINE DEVELOPMENT — TRAINEE TASK MODULE 04303

e. Project point 14 from the elevation downward to intersect line O'-14'. Mark this line as distance 12. Follow the same procedure for points 15, 17, 18, and 19. Mark each distance on the lines as indicated (11, 9, 8).

f. To find distance O'-16', set the dividers to distance 16-D in the elevation view; and with O' as center establish point 16', mark this line as 10.

g. Draw the developed curve outline by connecting points 13', 14', 15', 16', 17', 18', and 19'.

3. Draw the pattern stretchout.

   a. Draw a horizontal work line and locate a center (apex'), from which to develop radii, at any point near the center of the work line.

   b. With the dividers set at distance Apex-1 on the elevation view, use Apex' as center and locate point 1 on the work line. With this distance as radius and Apex' as center, strike an arc in a circular manner equal to the circumference of the small end of the roof stack.

   c. Divide the arc into 12 equal spaces, locate points 1, 2, 3, 4, 5, and 6 on each side of the arc center line (point 7). Extend lines from Apex' through each of the points just established.

   d. Working from the elevation view, transfer distance Apex-A to Apex'-A' on the stretchout pattern. Follow the same procedure for each of the other corresponding distances (Apex-B to Apex'-B', etc.).

   e. When this process is completed, draw the stretchout pattern outline through the developed points.

4. Lay out the flange pattern.

   a. Draw a rectangle equal to the dimensions as indicated in the working drawing.

   b. Find the center of the rectangle (bisect the center line) and draw a center line through the shape.

   c. Measure up 1" from the bottom horizontal line and establish point 13'.

   d. Transfer lengths 13-14, 14-15, 15-16, 16-17, 17-18, and 18-19 from the pitch line of the elevation view above point 13'.

   e. Use the half-plan view as reference and transfer distance 12 on each side of the center line at point 14'; distance 11 on each side of the center line at point 15'; distance 10 on each side at point 16'; distance 9 on each side at point 17'; distance 8 on each side at point 18'.

   f. Draw the pattern outline through the developed points.

Note: A more common method for locating the hole in the roof flange pattern is to form the roof stack pattern. Position it on the roof flange rectangle and mark the opening.

5. Lay out the collar pattern.

6. Recheck the dimensions and general pattern layout. Mark the pattern for fabrication, cut the sheet metal, form the seams and flange, form the pattern, set and lock the seam and spot weld, solder, or rivet the flange as directed by the instructor.

7. Restore the work area.

Questions

1. In your estimation, what method of layout is desired for this type of fitting?

2. Explain how to lay out the stretchout pattern.

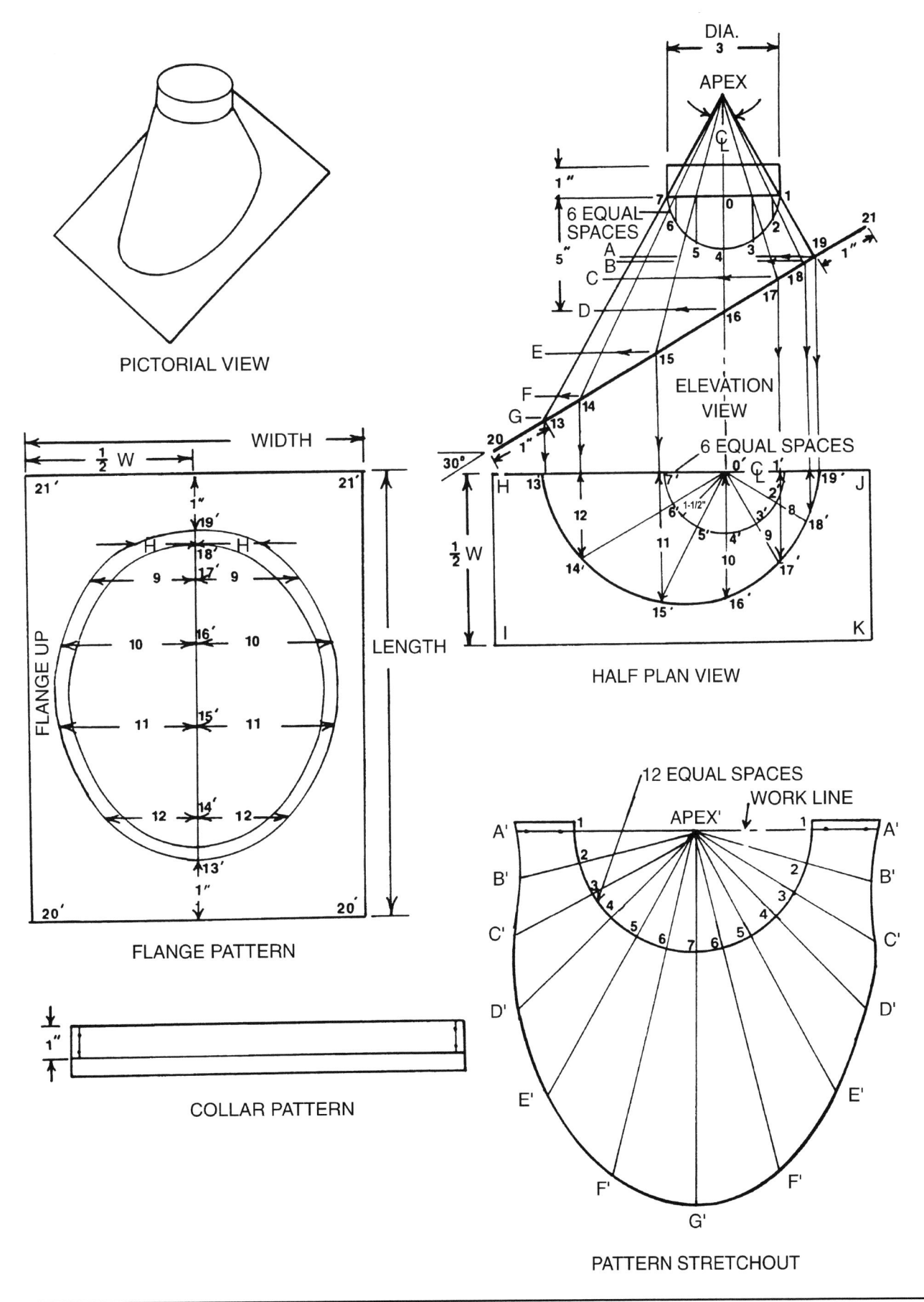

Figure 7 - Stack Flange

FABRICATION II – RADIAL LINE DEVELOPMENT — TRAINEE TASK MODULE 04303

TASK 4

CONE-SHAPED EXHAUST WEATHER CAP

Objective

Upon completion of this task, the trainee will be able to lay out by radial line development, and fabricate a selected cone-shaped exhaust weather cap (*Figure 8*).

When a cap is to be placed over an exhaust vent or discharge cap, it is generally accepted practice that the inside splitter cone should be equal to the diameter of the stack in order to properly deflect air. Depending on the size and gage of the metal, four to six band-iron brackets may be used to support the cap, but three brackets will probably support a medium-diameter cap.

Tools and Materials

Tools, equipment, and supplies necessary for the layout and fabrication of the cone-shaped exhaust weather cap can be selected from the list at the beginning of the module. The sheet metal stock may either be specified by the instructor or left to the discretion of the trainee.

Procedure

1. Draw the elevation or front view.

Note: The diameter of the cap should be twice the diameter of the stack. The distance from the top of the stack to the bottom of the cap line should be about one half of the stack diameter. The pitch of the cap is usually 30°. The diameter of the inside splitter cone should be equal to the diameter of the stack. The tip of the splitter cone should begin at the base of the hood line.

2. Draw the top or plan view.

3. Lay out the top cap pattern.

    a. Draw a vertical and horizontal center line and establish point A as center.

    b. With distance A-B as radius and A as center, scribe an arc to establish the circumference circle for the top cap.

    c. Draw a straight line to intersect the outer circumference line at point B.

    d. Set a divider at a radius equal to distance H on the elevation view. Multiply this distance by 2 pi (6.28) to find the cut out for a full pattern. Measure this distance along the circumference and establish point B'. Mark the cut out line, make a seam allowance.

    e. With distance A-D from the elevation view as radius and point A as center, scribe an arc to establish the location for the brackets to be fastened. Divide this line into three, four, or six parts and mark the positions for the holes to be drilled.

    f. With distance A-C as radius and point A as center, scribe another arc to establish the line for riveting the splitter cone. Divide this line and mark it in a similar manner.

4. Lay out the inside splitter cone.

    a. Use the distance C-E as radius and point E as center and scribe an arc to establish the circumference of the splitter cone circle.

    b. Draw a second arc 1/4" outward from the circumference circle to allow for riveting laps.

    c. Set the dividers at radius C to the center line A-E and strike an arc across line B-F-E to establish distance I. Use this distance times 6.28 to establish the cut out for the splitter cone pattern.

    d. Mark the riveting line for drilling.

5. Lay out the bracket pattern. This distance F-G is equal to F-G on the elevation view.

PLAN VIEW

CAP PATTERN
6.28 x H

ELEVATION VIEW

SPLITTER PATTERN
6.28 x I

BRACKET PATTERN

STACK PATTERN

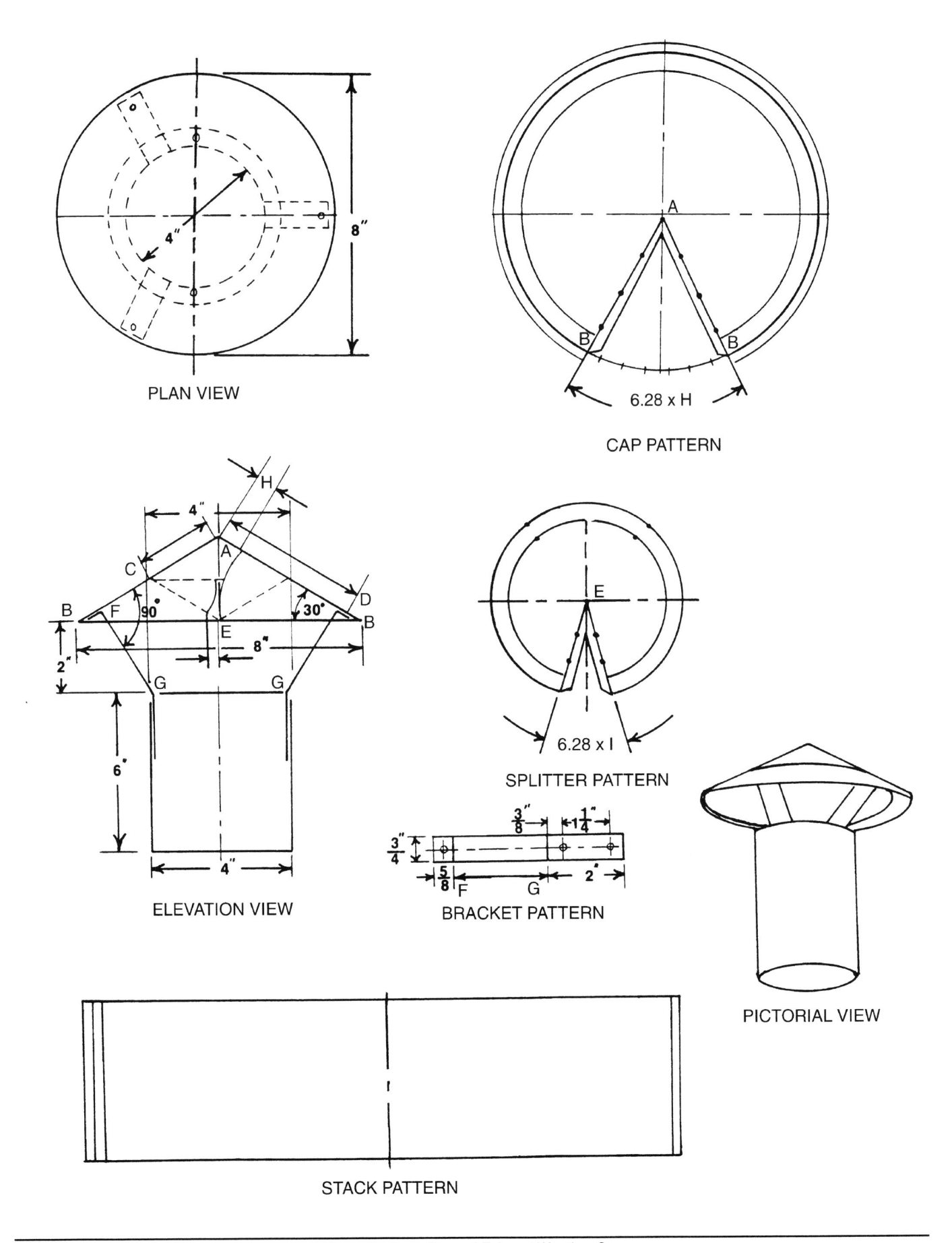

PICTORIAL VIEW

Figure 8 - Cone-Shaped Exhaust Weather Cap

FABRICATION II — RADIAL LINE DEVELOPMENT — TRAINEE TASK MODULE 04303

6. Lay out the stack pattern to equal the circumference of the stack (3.14 × 4) for the length of the stretchout. The width of the stretchout should equal the height of the stack.

7. Make seam allowances on each of the patterns that require them. Mark the brackets for bending.

8. Check the dimensions, cut out and notch the pattern. Form the patterns. Assemble the parts and rivet, spot weld, or solder into place.

9. Restore the work area.

Questions

1. How is the width of the cap determined? The width of the splitter cone?

2. Describe how to calculate the area of the metal to be removed in order to form the cone shapes.

TASK 5

ROOF PEAK GRAVITY VENTILATOR

Objective

Upon completion of this task, the trainee will be able to lay out by the radial line method, and fabricate a roof peak gravity ventilator (*Figure 9*).

Most roof gravity ventilators are mass-produced today, but the sheet metal worker may still be called upon to lay out and fabricate ventilators of special sizes or from special materials.

Tools and Materials

The tools, equipment, and supplies selected for this task may be chosen from the conventional inventory of a sheet metal shop. The type and gage of metal may be selected by the instructor or left to the discretion of the trainee. The choice should adhere to proper sheet metal techniques and specifications.

Procedure

1. Draw the elevation and plan view as indicated on the working drawing.

2. Lay out the stretchout for one half the taper stack section.

   a. Draw a vertical center line and label the very bottom of the line A.

   b. After point A is established, measure up the height of the stack (ridge to top = 5") and establish point 1'.

   c. Draw a horizontal line from point 1' to the right of the center line a distance of 2" (radius of the top of the stack), establish point 4.

   d. With the dividers set at radius 1'-4 and 1' as center, scribe a quarter circle; divide the circle into 3 equal parts; identify the spaces as 1, 2, 3, and 4.

   e. From points 2 and 3 on the quarter circle, draw vertical lines upward to intersect line 1'-4.

   f. Extend a 30° line downward and to the right from point 4 to represent the slant of the stack. From point A, draw a 30° line downward and to the right to intersect the line just drawn from point 4; establish point D/D'. This represents the pitch of the stack pattern. Extend the 30° line D-4 upward to intersect the center line at point X.

   g. Draw straight lines downward from point X through the points established by the vertical lines drawn upward from points 2 and 3 from the quarter circle to line 1'-4 and establish points B and C on the pitch line A-D. From points A, B, and C, draw horizontal lines to the right from the pitch line and establish points A', B', C' and D' on line 4-D.

   h. With distance X-4 as radius and point X as center, scribe a semi-circular arc around point X. Draw a "work line" downward and to the right of line X-D. Where this line intersects the arc just drawn, establish work line point 1'. Calculate the circumference of the small end of the stack pattern (3.14 × 4) and measure this product around the semi-circular arc; establish the end of this distance as point 1' on the work line. Divide the arc 1'-1' into 12 equal parts as indicated. Label the intersections of these parts with the X-4 arc as points 1', 2', 3', and 4' as shown. Extend straight lines through each of these points from point X to an undetermined length.

   i. With point X as center and distance X-A' as radius, scribe an arc across line 1'-1' to establish points A'. With point X as center and distance X-B' as radius, scribe an arc across lines X-2' as shown to establish points B'. Follow the same procedure for points X-C' and X-D'.

j. When all twelve of the points have been established on the outer perimeter of the stretchout, draw the pattern outline through the developed points.

3. Make a working drawing for the cap.

   a. On the elevation view, find points P, N, S, and H.

   b. With distance N-P as radius and point N as center, scribe an arc across the 30° line of the top of the cap and establish distance E.

4. Lay out the cap pattern.

   a. With distance H as radius and any point on the layout sheet as center, scribe an arc to establish the diameter of the cap.

   b. Find the segment for the cutout (6.28 times E) and establish points U and V on the cap pattern.

   c. Scribe an arc to locate the rivet or bolt holes for the brackets.

5. Recheck the dimensions of the layouts and measure out the seam and edge allowances.

6. Lay out the top collar pattern as indicated.

7. Cut and notch the pattern.

8. Form the pattern and edges and set and lock the seam. Attach the brackets.

9. Restore the work area.

Questions

1. Does this particular pattern, as shown, contain a splitter cone?

2. Describe the procedure necessary to find distance E.

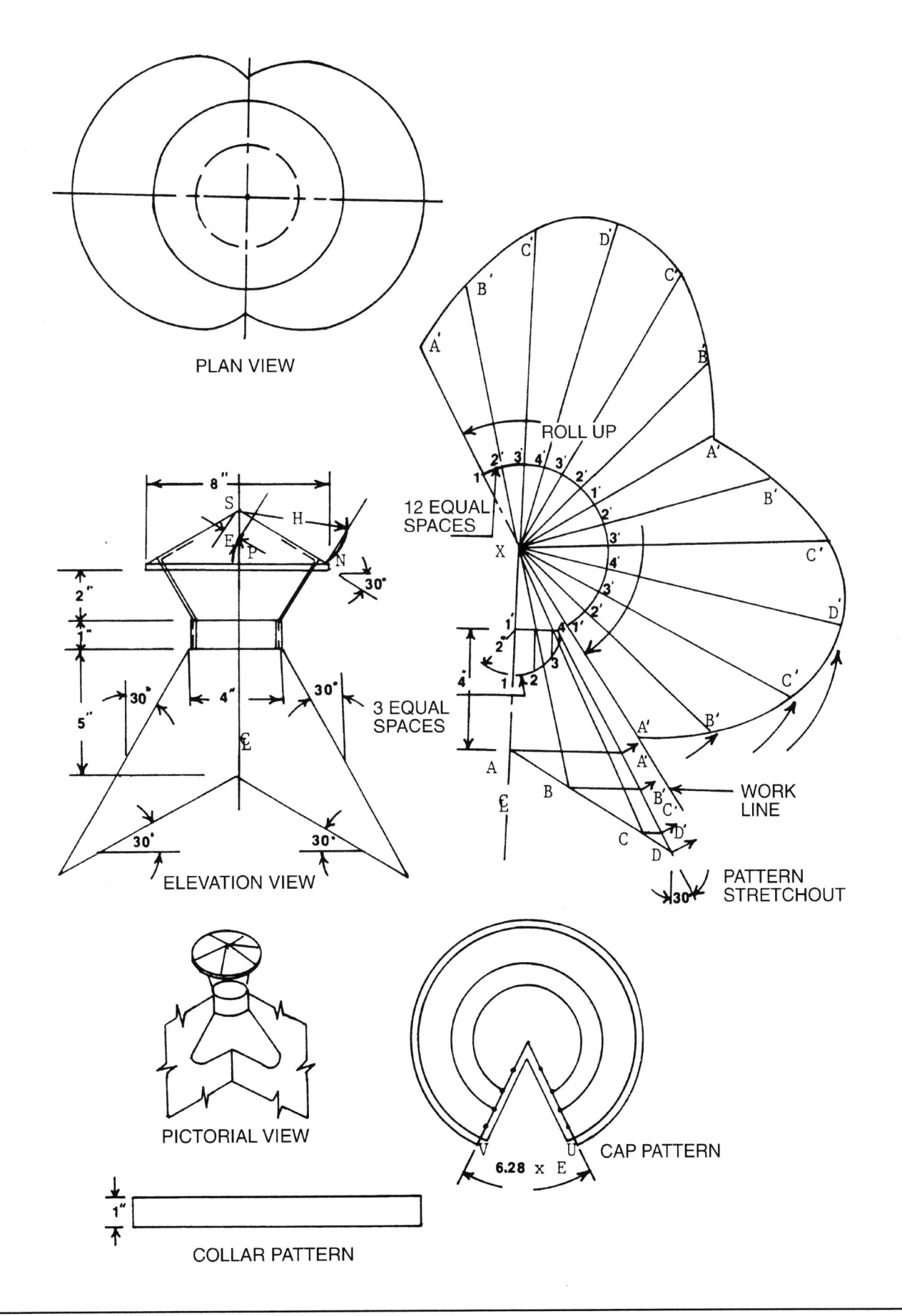

Figure 9 - Gravity Ventilator

FABRICATION II – RADIAL LINE DEVELOPMENT — TRAINEE TASK MODULE 04303

TASK 6

ROUND DUCT INTERSECTING A TAPER

Objective

Upon completion of this task, the trainee will be able to lay out by radial line development, and fabricate a round duct intersecting a taper at a given angle (*Figure 10*).

It may often become necessary for the sheet metal worker to connect two pipes of different diameters whose axes lie at angles to each other. When making a connection of this kind in blowpipe work, it is important to construct the fitting so that there is as little resistance to air flow through the pipes as possible. The fitting to be fabricated during this exercise may also be called a round tee intersecting a taper at a 45° angle.

Tools and Materials

Select the tools and materials necessary for this fitting as experience may dictate, or as indicated by the instructor.

Procedure

1. Draw the working view.

    a. Draw a horizontal center line and at the left end of the line establish point Q.

    b. Measure to the right from point Q a distance equal to the height of the taper (7") and establish point O.

    c. Draw lines perpendicular to and extending through points Q and O on the horizontal center line. Measure 3" above and below point Q and establish points S and T. Measure 1-1/2" above and below point O and establish points R and U.

    d. Draw straight lines between T and U, and between R and S.

    e. Measure to the right from point Q 2-1/4" to establish point 10, the point of intersection for the 45° center line.

    f. From the point of intersection of the 45° line and line T-U, measure out (on the 45° line) 2" and establish point W.

    g. Draw a line perpendicular to the 45° center line at point W and extending to the sides of point W. With the dividers set at the radius equal to one half the diameter of the round tee (1-1/4") and point W as center, scribe a half circle about point W and establish points Y and Z. Divide the half circle into six equal spaces as indicated and from the points draw lines parallel to the 45° center line. Label these lines B, C, D, E, F, and G as indicated.

    h. Draw a line, perpendicular to line Y-Z, downward to intersect line T-U, draw line H as shown. With the point where H intersects the horizontal line of the taper as center and distance 1/2 H as radius, scribe an arc to the left of the intersection of H with line T-U.

    i. With the intersection of lines Y-H and T-U as center and 1-1/4" as radius, strike a quarter arc to the left. Divide this 90° arc into 3 equal spaces. From these spaces, draw vertical lines to intersect the arc previously drawn. Draw horizontal lines from the intersecting points to intersect with line H.

    j. With point P as center and distance P-G as the radius, draw a long arc.

    k. With point P as center and 1-1/4" as the radius, draw a 90° arc; divide this arc into 3 equal spaces also. From each point draw a vertical line upward to intersect the arc P-G.

l. From the intersection points on the arc, draw horizontal lines to the left to intersect line P. Draw straight lines to connect the points on line H and line P. Where the 45° lines B, C, D, E, and F intersect with the straight lines from H to line P, mark the intersection line of the round tee and the taper.

m. Draw vertical lines downward from the intersection points just established to intersect line R-S and establish points H', J', K', L', M', N', and P'.

2. Draw the half end view.

Note: The half end view is needed to establish the opening in the taper. The more practical shop method requires fabrication of the taper and the round tee and then placing the tee on the taper and marking the cut out.

a. Extend lines R-S and T-U from the working view to the right to intersect with the horizontal center line at point X.

b. Project a horizontal line to the right from point W on the working view to intersect with the vertical center line of the half end view and establish point W'.

c. With W' as center and 1-1/4" as radius, draw a quarter circle and divide it into three equal parts. Draw vertical lines downward from the points just established.

d. With point X as center and distance Q-T and distance O-U as radii, draw the half circles to represent the large end and the small end of the taper respectively.

e. With point X as center and distances H, J, K, L, M, N, and P as radii, strike arcs within the half pattern as indicated. Mark the intersection points of the lines and the arcs as 1, 2, 3, 4, and 5 as shown.

3. Lay out the round tee pattern.

a. Calculate the circumference of the tee section (3.14×2) and draw a horizontal line equal to that distance. Divide the line into 12 equal parts.

b. Use the working view and transfer lengths A, B, C, D, E, F, and G as perpendicular lines upward from the horizontal line just drawn.

c. Draw the pattern outline through the developed points.

4. Lay out the half pattern for the taper and the opening for the intersecting tee.

a. With point X as center and X-S as radius, strike an arc to establish the length of the taper pattern S-S. Calculate the circumference of the large end (3.14 × 6) and establish one half this distance on line S-S for a half pattern.

Note: The half pattern is used to conserve space.

b. From the bottom point S on the half pattern, draw a straight line to point X.

c. With X as center and distance X-R as radius, strike an arc to establish the small end of the taper (half pattern). Draw straight lines between points S and R on the half pattern.

d. Bisect distance S-S and draw a straight line to point X to establish the center line of the half pattern stretchout.

e. With X as center and distances X-H, X-J, X-K, X-L, X-M, X-N, and X-P as radii, strike arcs from the working view across the center line of the half pattern stretchout as indicated.

f. From the half end view, transfer the arc length from the vertical center line to each of the points 1, 2, 3, 4, and 5 to each side of the center line on the half pattern taper stretchout to establish the outline for the tee opening.

FABRICATION II – RADIAL LINE DEVELOPMENT — TRAINEE TASK MODULE 04303

5. Make seam allowances and recheck the measurements for the taper stretchout and the intersecting tee.

6. Cut and form the patterns.

7. Bend and set the seams, connect the tee to the taper.

8. Restore the work area.

Questions

1. Where might fittings of this general shape be found?

2. What is the most convenient method for determining the size of the cut out for the intersecting tee?

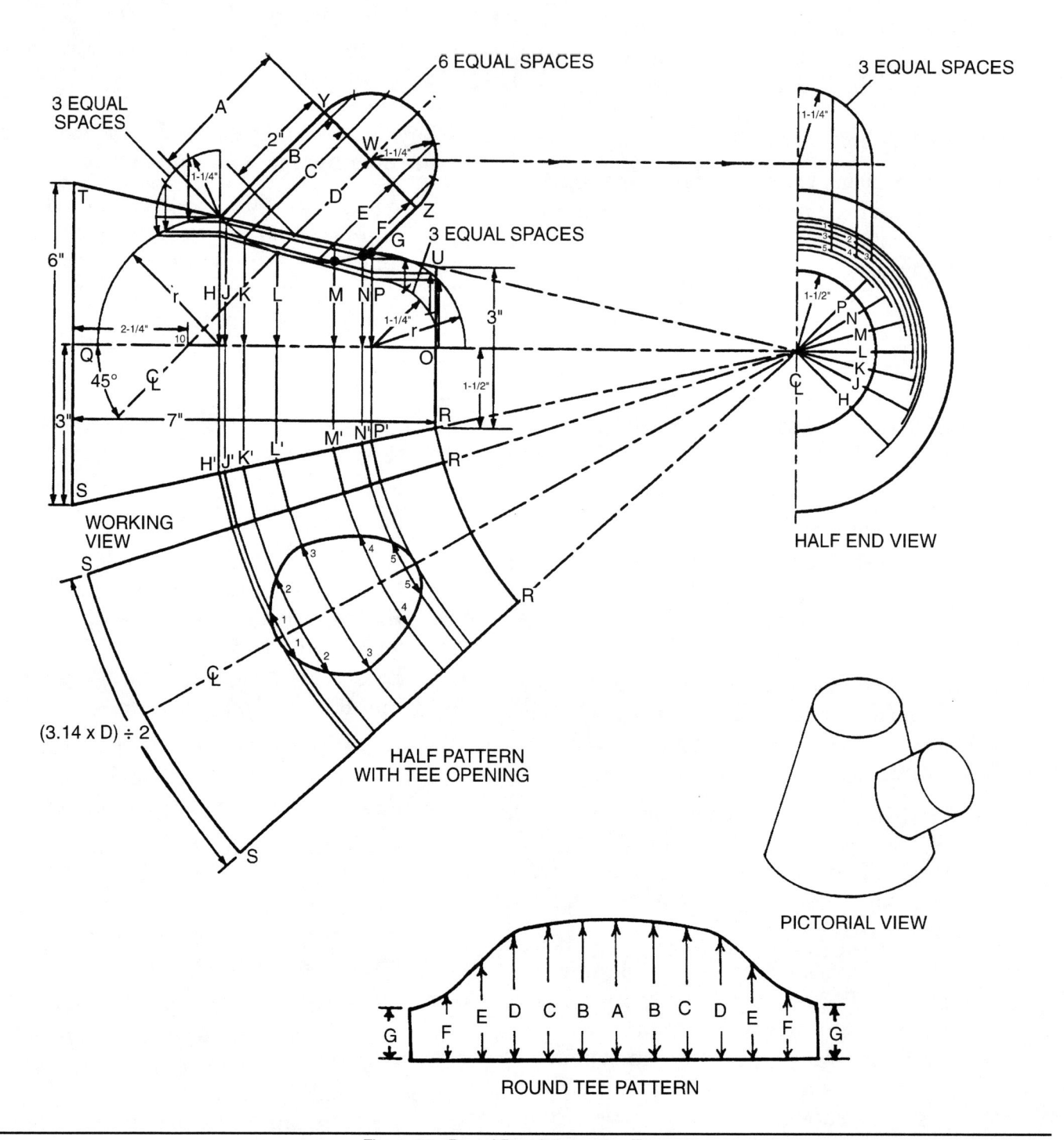

Figure 10 - Round Duct Intersecting Taper

TASK 7

TAPERED OFFSET DUCT

Objective

Upon completion of this task, the trainee will be able to lay out by the radial line method, and fabricate a tapered offset duct (*Figure 11*).

Triangulation is generally used for laying out these types of fittings, unless the diameters of the two ends vary considerably and the length of the fitting is limited. Collars are usually attached to the openings of a round offset taper joint. The collar should be wide enough for a secure connection with the connecting lengths of round pipe. Soldering or welding the collars on metal taper joints is considered to be a good practice even though the procedure may not be called for in the specifications. The seams on the body of the taper section should be riveted or soldered to prevent buckling when the collars are attached.

Tools and Equipment

The tools, equipment, and supplies necessary for the layout and fabrication of this fitting can be chosen from the general inventory of a conventional sheet metal shop. The type and gage of the metal may be at the discretion of the trainee or as directed by the instructor.

Procedure

1. Draw the elevation view first.
2. Draw the working view next.
   a. Draw a base line of undetermined length.
   b. Establish the height of the pattern as indicated.
   c. Establish the diameter of the small end (line A-B).
   d. Establish the distance for the offset (line C-D).
   e. Establish the diameter of the large end (line D-E).
   f. Extend lines A-D and B-E upward to establish point X.
   g. Draw a vertical line downward from point X to intersect the base line and establish point Y.
   h. Bisect line D-E and with the bisect point as center and one half the diameter of the large end as radius, draw a half circle below line D-E. Divide the half circle into 6 equal parts.
   i. With point Y as center and point 6 on the half circle as radius, draw an arc from point 6 to intersect line D-E. Draw an arc from each of the other points on the half circle in the same manner.
   j. Draw straight lines from each of the numbered points on line D-E to point X.
3. Lay out the collar patterns.
   a. Lay out the collar patterns as illustrated. The length of the collars are equal to the circumference of the openings for the large and small ends.
   b. Divide one fourth of the large collar pattern into equal spaces to use as reference in the layout of the taper pattern stretchout.
4. Lay out the taper stretchout pattern.
   a. With point X as center and each point of intersection on line A-B and line D-E as radius, draw arcs upward of undetermined length.
   b. Determine point 1 on the perimeter of the outer arc at any convenient location above line D-E.
   c. With the dividers set at a distance equal to one of the equal spaces on the large collar pattern, use point 1 as center and strike an arc on arc line 2 to establish point 2 on the taper pattern.

With point 2 as center and the dividers set the same, strike an arc across arc line 3 to establish point 3. Follow the same procedure to establish each numbered point on the taper pattern stretchout.

d. Draw the pattern outline through the developed points.

e. Draw straight lines from each of the established points on the pattern outline to point X. The intersection of these lines with the arcs drawn from line A-B automatically establish the corresponding points on the pattern stretchout for the small end of the taper.

f. Draw the pattern outline through these developed points.

5. Make seam allowances on each of the developed patterns. Recheck the measurements.

6. Cut and form the patterns.

7. Set and lock the seams. Crimp the small end of the fitting if required.

8. Restore the work area.

Questions

1. What precautions should or may be taken to insure strength and rigidity during fabrication of this fitting?

2. What is the purpose of laying out the collar pattern prior to the taper pattern?

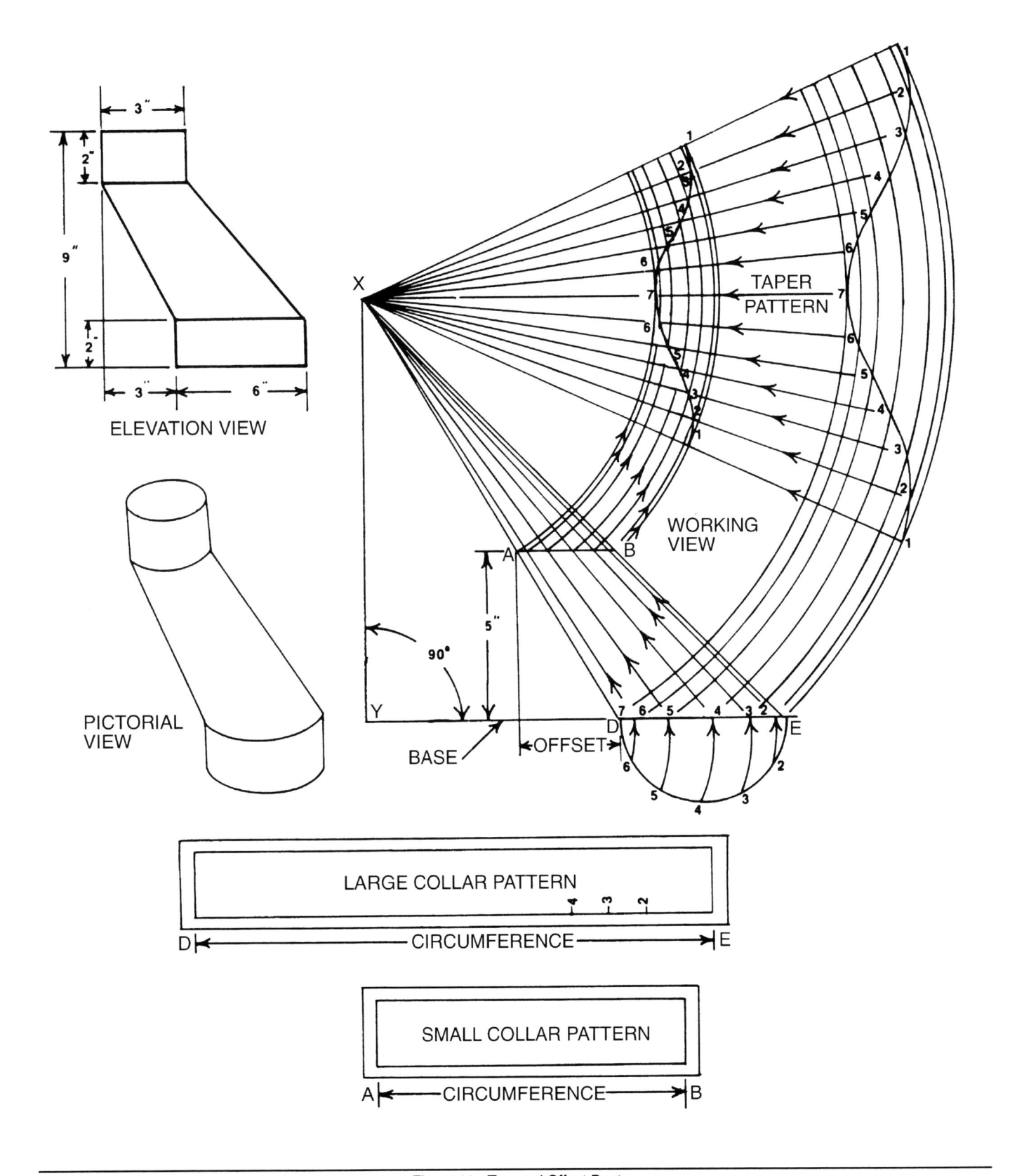

Figure 11 - Tapered Offset Duct

TASK 8

TWO-WAY Y-BRANCH

Objective

Upon completion of this task, the trainee will be able to lay out by the radial line method, and fabricate a two-branch Y-joint, round to round (*Figure 12*).

Y-branches are used extensively to complete the piping for blowpipe and exhaust systems. Welded or soldered seams and connections may be specified by the design engineer to help insure efficient operation of the system and to eliminate the possibility of noxious gases seeping back into the conditioned space. Exhaust and blowpipe systems are designed to entrain (transport) a product by means of a high-velocity airstream.

Tools and Materials

Tools, equipment, and supplies necessary for the layout and fabrication of this fitting may be selected from the conventional inventory of a sheet metal shop. The gage and type of metal may be specified by the instructor or left to the decision of the trainee.

Procedure

1. Construct the working drawing as illustrated.

2. Draw the half front view.

   a. Draw the horizontal base line equal to the diameter of the large end of the fitting. Establish points 1 and 7.

   b. Bisect line 1-7 and establish point 0. Draw a vertical line upward from point 0 equal to the height of the taper part of the fitting (8"). Draw a line parallel to line 1-7 and intersecting the vertical center line at point X. Measure to the right from point X one half the distance between the small ends of the Y-branch (2") and establish point A. Measure to the right from point A a distance equal to the small end of the Y-branch (3") and establish point G.

   c. Draw straight lines upward through points 7-A and points 1-G to intersect at point Y. Draw a vertical line downward from point Y to intersect the line extended through points 1-7 to establish point Y'.

   d. With point 0 as center and 3" as radius, draw a half circle below line 1-7. Divide the half circle into 6 equal parts. Mark points 2, 3, 4, 5, and 6 on the half circle arc.

   e. From point Y', draw lines to points 5 and 6 to intersect the vertical center line at points 11 and 12 when they are extended to points 5 and 6 on the half circle.

   f. With point Y' as center and distance Y'-2 as radius, draw the arc to establish point 2' on the horizontal line 1-7. Draw a straight line from point 2' to Y. Establish point F where the straight line intersects line A-G.

   g. Follow the same procedure to establish points 3', 4', 5' and 6' and, consequently, points E, D, C, and B on line A-G.

   h. With Y' as center and distance Y'-11 as radius, scribe an arc upward to intersect line 1-7. Draw a vertical line upward from this intersection point to intersect line Y-5' and establish point 8. Follow the same procedure to establish point 9 on line Y'-6. Establish point 10 where the vertical center line intersects line A-7.

3. Lay out the full pattern for one leg.

   a. Draw the work line downward from point Y at any convenient angle.

   b. Use point Y as center and radii Y-1', Y-2', Y-3', Y-4', Y-5', Y-6' and Y-7' and scribe long arcs to the upper left of the work line.

SHEET METAL — TRAINEE TASK MODULE 04303

c. Establish point 7' where the work line intersects arc Y-7. With point 7' as center and distance 1-2 on the half circle as radius, intersect arc line 6' to establish point 6'. Follow the same procedure to locate points 5', 4', 3', 2', and 1' as indicated.

d. With point Y as center and distance Y-10 as radius, scribe an arc to intersect lines Y-7' and establish point 10'.

e. With point Y as center and distance Y-9 as radius, strike arcs to establish points 9' on lines Y-6'.

f. With point Y as center and distance Y-8 as radius, strike arcs to establish points 8' on line Y-5'. Locate points 4' on the pattern stretchout in a similar manner.

g. With point Y as center and distance Y-A as radius, strike an arc to intersect lines Y-7' to establish point A'.

h. With point Y as center and distance Y-B as radius, strike an arc to intersect lines Y-6' to establish points B'. Follow a similar procedure to establish points C', D', E', F', and G'.

i. Draw the pattern outline through the developed points.

4. Lay out the collar patterns.

   a. Calculate the circumference of the large collar and the two small collars.

   b. Draw rectangles representing the stretchout measurements of the two collars.

   c. Allow for seams.

5. Recheck the measurements.

6. Cut out the patterns (2 leg patterns) after making seam allowances on all parts.

7. Form the patterns, bend and lock the seams. Solder, weld, or rivet, if required, for fabrication.

8. Restore the work area.

Questions

1. Where might these types of fittings be found?

2. What could be done to eliminate gas or dust leaks on the fittings?

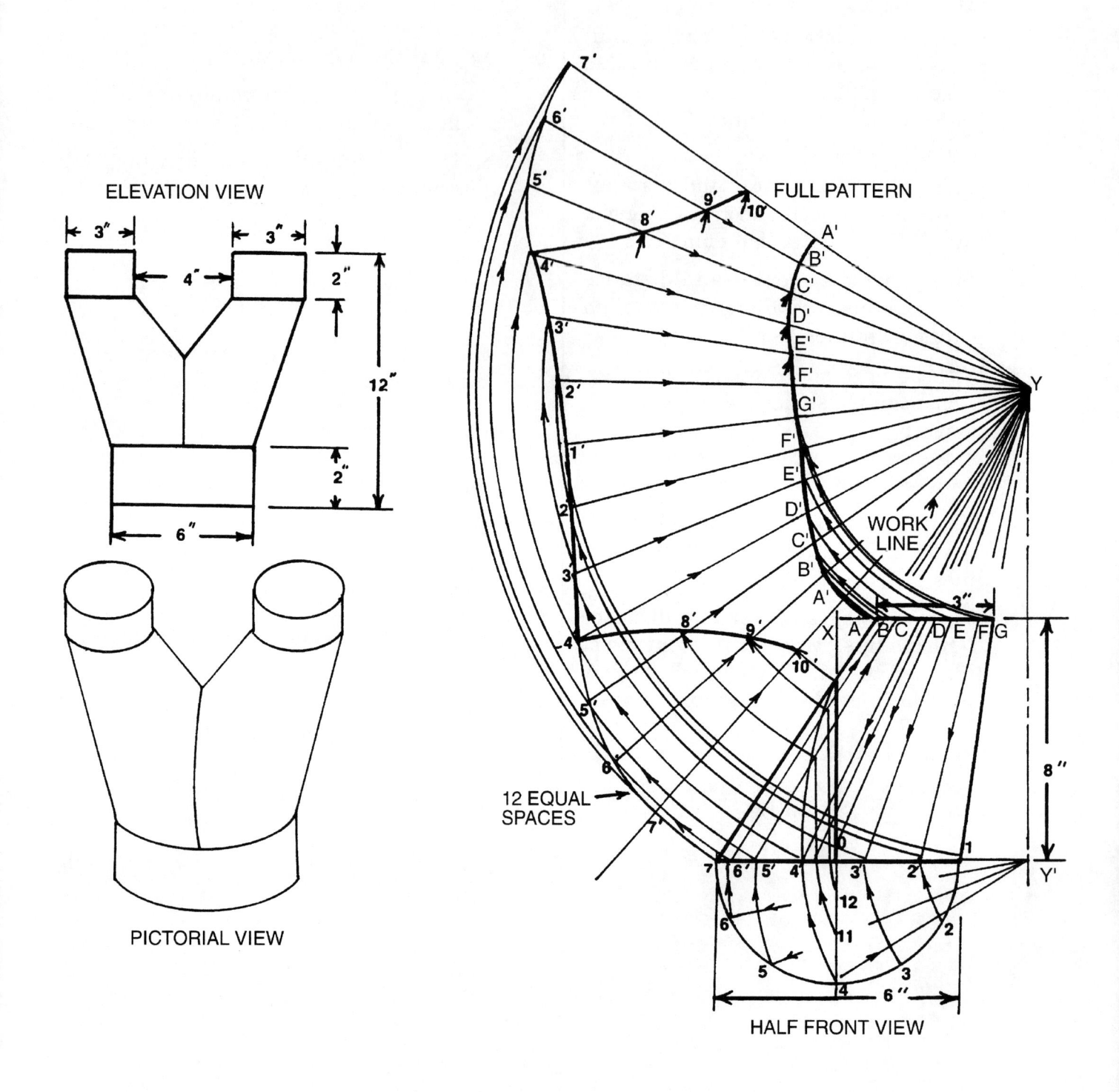

Figure 12 - Y-Joint

TASK 9

OFF-CENTER TAPERED DUCT

Objective

Upon completion of this task, the trainee will be able to lay out and fabricate an off-center tapered duct (*Figure 13*).

Patterns for round tapering fittings are considered to be cone sections and are usually laid out by radial line development. However, the triangulation method may also be used.

Tools and Materials

The tools, equipment, and supplies needed for this task should be minimal and may be selected from the regular supply of a sheet metal shop. The type and gage of the metal selected should adhere to general fabrication specifications.

Procedure

1. Draw the plan view to illustrate the amount of offset of the small end of the tapered fitting.

2. Draw the front or elevation view.

    a. Draw vertical lines downward from the plan view to locate the size of the small and large ends and the amount of offset of the opening.

    b. Establish horizontal line C-D equal to the diameter of the small end and line 1-7 equal to the diameter of the large end.

    c. Bisect line 1-7 and draw the half circle 1 to 7. Divide the half circle into equal parts as indicated.

    d. Draw a straight line from point 1 to C and another one from point 7 to D. Continue these two lines until they intersect at point X.

    e. Square a line upward from line 1-7 to intersect point X, establish point B at the base of this line on line 1-7.

    f. Use point B as center and draw arcs from points 1, 2, 3, 4, 5, and 6 to intersect line 1-7. Draw straight line from each of these intersecting points with line 1-7 to terminate at point X.

3. Develop the taper pattern stretchout.

    a. Use point X as center to scribe an arc from each intersecting point on line 1-7 an undetermined length to establish the approximate area for the taper pattern.

    b. At any convenient distance, draw a work line from point X toward the arc lines to establish point 1'.

    c. Set the dividers to span any one of the equal spaces on the half circle and with point 1' as center, strike an arc toward large arc 2' to establish point 2' on the arc.

    d. Continue swinging the dividers from one arc space to the next until the full circumference of the taper pattern stretchout is set out as 1' to 7' and 7' to 1' as illustrated.

    e. Draw the large end pattern outline through the established points.

    f. Use point X as center to strike arcs from each intersecting point on line C-D (points 1, 2, 3, 4, 5, 6, and 7) upward to establish the general outline for the small end of the taper.

    g. Mark each point of intersection with their respective lines as established from the large end layout.

    h. Draw the small end pattern outline through the established points.

4. Lay out the collar patterns.
   a. Calculate the circumference of the large collar and the small collar.
   b. Draw rectangles representing the stretchout measurements of the collars.
   c. Make seam allowances.
5. Recheck the developed patterns for proper size and make seam allowances.
6. Cut and form the patterns; form and lock the seams.
7. Restore the work area.

Questions

1. What is the most common method for laying out round tapered fittings?
2. Explain how to develop the small end of the taper stretchout.

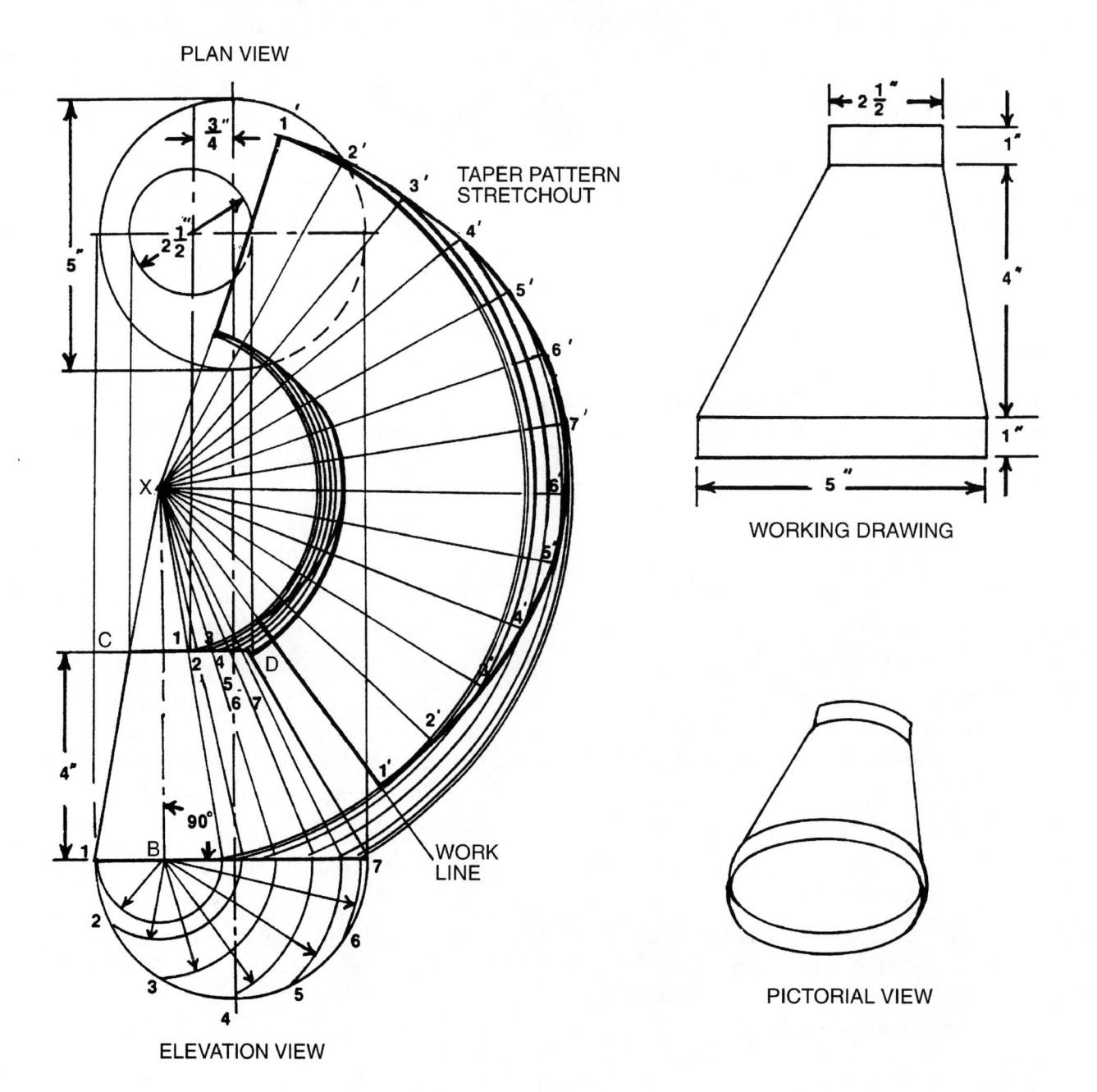

Figure 13 - Off-Center Tapered Duct

SHEET METAL — TRAINEE TASK MODULE 04303

TASK 10

SQUARE-TO-SQUARE TAPERED DUCT

Objective

Upon completion of this task, the trainee will be able to lay out and fabricate a square-to-square tapered duct (*Figure 14*).

This type of tapered component is considered to be a trunkline fitting designed to carry air to a branch of the ductrun. This type of fitting is usually made in two pieces because it can be cut from the sheet metal economically. However, these problems are generally made in one piece for practice by the trainee.

Tools and Materials

Equipment, supplies, and tools necessary for this task can be selected from the listing in the front of the module. The galvanized iron sheet metal selected should probably be 26 gage in thickness or as decided by the instructor.

Procedure

1. Draw the plan view as illustrated.
2. Draw the elevation view.
   a. Draw a horizontal base line and locate the diameter of the large end of the taper.
   b. Bisect the base line and establish point D.
   c. Square a line upward from point D to establish the center line.
   d. Measure upward on the center line and locate the height of the fitting.
   e. Draw the top line at the given height and set one half of the diameter of the small end of the taper on each side of the center line to establish points C and E.
   f. Draw a straight line upward from point G through point F and establish point A on the center line.
   g. Transfer the distance A-B (slant line) from the plan view to the base line point D to B to establish the true length of the corner on the taper pattern stretchout.
3. Lay out the taper pattern stretchout.
   a. With point A (at any convenient location for the stretchout) as center and distance A-B as radius, draw a large arc to establish the outer circumference of the stretchout.
   b. Adjust the dividers to any side, equal to the diameter of the large end of the taper from the plan view, and strike an arc across the outside arc on the taper pattern. Set this distance four times on arc B to depict the sides of the pattern.
   c. Draw straight lines connecting each point B on the pattern. Draw straight lines from each point B to point A to establish the sides of the pattern.
   d. With point A as center and distance A-C as radius, draw the arc at point C to establish the circumference of the small end of the taper.
   e. Draw straight lines connecting the intersecting points of arc C and the lines from A to B.
   f. Make allowances on the pattern for the S and drive clips.
4. Recheck the dimensions, make seam allowances.
5. Cut, notch, and form the pattern. Set and lock the seam. Complete the bends for the S and drive clips.
6. Restore the work area.

FABRICATION II – RADIAL LINE DEVELOPMENT — TRAINEE TASK MODULE 04303

Questions

1. Where might this type of fitting be located on a typical ductrun system?

2. How is the true length of the pattern radius established?

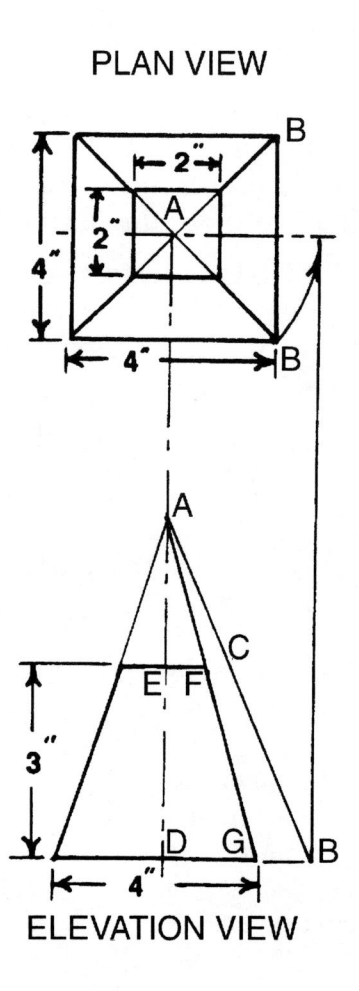

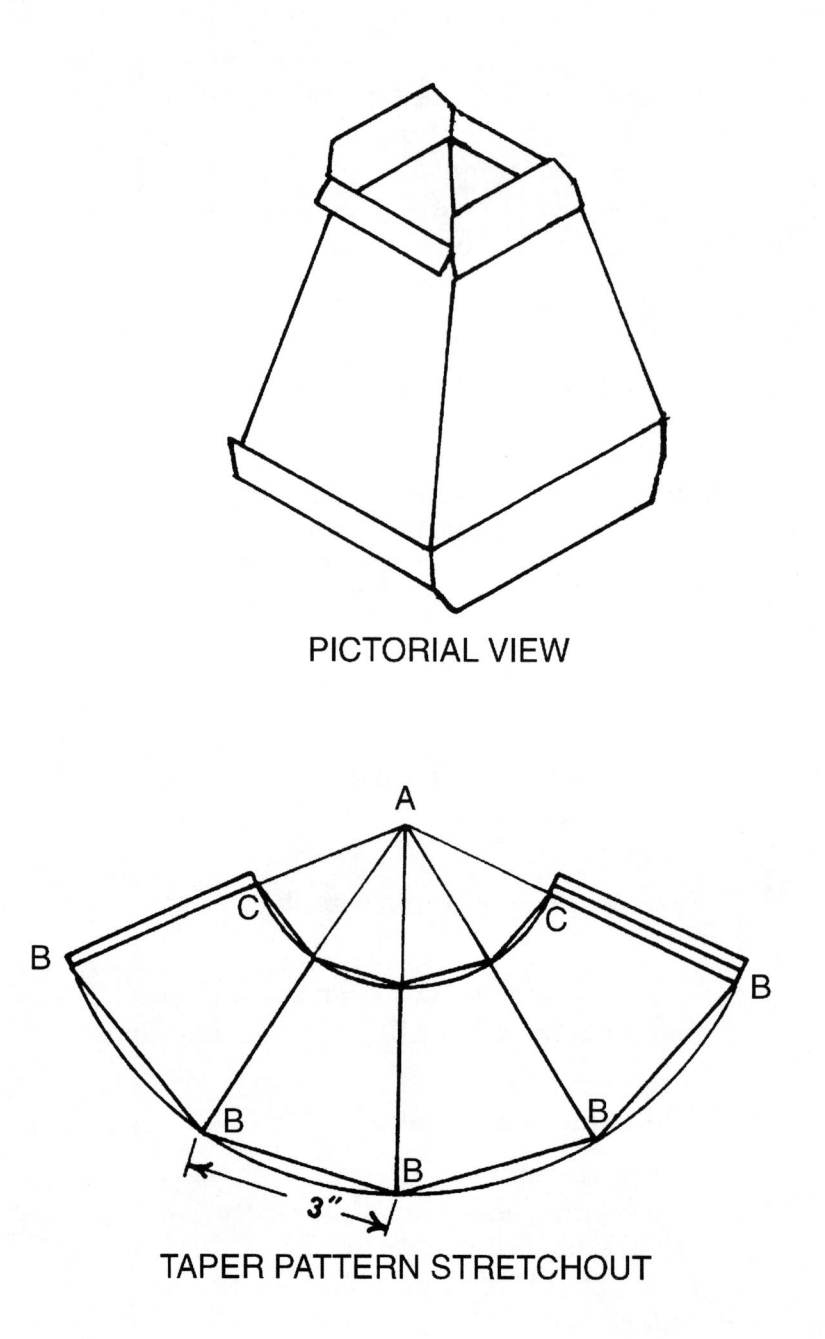

Figure 14 - Square-to-Square Tapered Duct

TASK 11

SHOE TEE INTERSECTING A TAPER ON CENTER

Objective

Upon completion of this task, the trainee will be able to lay out and fabricate a shoe or boot tee intersecting a taper on center (*Figure 15*).

Tools and Materials

The tools and materials selected for this task may be chosen from the inventory of a conventional sheet metal shop. The type and gage of metal may be left to the discretion of the trainee or as directed by the instructor.

Procedure

1. Draw the elevation or front view as illustrated.

2. Construct the working drawing.

    a. Using the elevation view as reference, draw a horizontal center line.

    b. Establish point E' at the left of the horizontal center line.

    c. Measure right from point E' on the center line a distance of 7", establish point A'.

    d. Measure left from point A' a distance of 2-5/8" and establish point O'.

    e. Draw lines perpendicular to the center line through points E' and A'.

    f. Measure one half the diameter of the large end and mark this distance above and below point E', establishing points E and Y'. Follow the same procedure for establishing points A and Z' above and below point A'.

    g. Draw straight lines through points E and A and through points Y' and Z' to intersect the center line, establishing the Apex.

    h. Square a line R upward from point O' the distance equal to the height of the shoe portion of the tee from the center of the fitting (5"). Establish point O.

    i. Draw a horizontal line through point O and establish points 1 and 7 (O-7 and O-1 equal one half the diameter of the tee, or 1").

    j. Draw a 45° line downward from point 1 to intersect line A-E to establish point T and line U. Square a line downward from point 7 to intersect line A-E to establish point J and line Q.

    k. With point O as center draw a half circle above line 1-7, divide the half circle into 6 equal spaces, number the spaces 1 through 7.

    l. Draw vertical lines downward from points 2, 3, and 4 on the half circle to intersect line 1-7. From these intersection points with line 1-7, draw 45° lines downward and to the left an undetermined distance establishing lines V, W, and X. Draw vertical lines downward through the taper pattern from points 5 and 6 on the half circle establishing lines Y and N.

    m. Square lines downward from points T and J where the shoe intersects the taper. Using the points in which these lines cross the center line as circle centers, and the dividers set at 1" or radius of shoe opening, swing quarter circle arcs and divide each arc into 3 equal spaces. Label these points E, F, G, and H on large end and A, B, C, and D on small end of taper. With the same center, swing an arc from T on left and from J on right down to where they cross the center line. Square lines upward from 1" divided quarter circle to intersect larger arc. Label these points the same. Square lines to the left and right to where they intersect line T and the centerline, and line J and the centerline. Connect and draw lines from B-F to cross N and V to establish points, from C-G to cross Y and W to establish points, and from D-H to cross R and X to establish points. Draw lines and curves through these established points to outline miter and show how it sits on taper.

n. Draw the line L'-P' at 90° to line 1-T (line L'-P' can be positioned at any point on line 1-T). Measure each distance from line 1-7 to points 4, 3, and 2 on the half circle and transfer this distance from line L'-P' to the corresponding 45° lines and establish points 1', 2', 3', and 4'. Draw the developed curved line 1'-4' through these developed points.

o. Label the 45° lines from line L'-P' to line 1-7 as U', V', W', and X'.

p. From the points where the shoe tee intersects with the taper pattern, draw vertical lines downward until they intersect with line Y'-Z' of the taper pattern. Label the points as (from right to left) J, K, L, M, N, P, S, and T.

3. Lay out the taper pattern stretchout.

   a. Draw a vertical line of undetermined length and establish the Apex for the development.

   b. With the Apex as center and distance Apex-Y' as radius, strike an extended arc to include the circumference of the large end of the taper. Locate this distance and label the arc line as E' and Y'.

   c. With Apex as center and distance Apex-Z' as radius, strike an arc to establish the circumference of the end of the taper. Draw straight lines from E' and Y' to intersect at the Apex, thereby, establishing points A' and Z'.

   d. Bisect arc E'-Y', establish the center line. Mark the intersection of arc A'-Z' and the center line as point A', and the intersection of arc E'-Y' as point E'.

   e. From the 3" arc on the working drawing, transfer arc chords F, G, and H to both sides of the center line on arc E'-Y'. Label the points F", G', and H'.

   f. From the 1-1/2" radius arc on the working drawing, transfer arc chords B, C, and D, on each side of the center line on arc A'-Z'. Label the points B', C', and D'. Draw straight lines connecting points B' and F", points C' and G', and points D' and H'.

   g. With Apex as center and distance Apex-J from the working view as radius, scribe an arc between the edges of the taper pattern stretchout. Follow the same procedure for each of the arcs Apex to K, L, M, N, P, S, and T. Mark the points of intersection with the corresponding chord lines previously determined.

   h. Draw the cutout outline through the developed points.

4. Lay out the shoe-tee pattern.

   a. Draw a horizontal line at any convenient location. Calculate the length of the line by multiplying the radius of the round portion of the tee by 3.14 (3.14 × 1). Establish points X and X on the horizontal line. Divide the line into 6 equal spaces. Square lines downward from each identified space division.

   b. Draw 45° lines downward and outward from points X on each end of the horizontal line.

   c. Transfer length X' from the working drawing to the 45° line on each side of the pattern. Square lines outward from this intersection with the 45° lines and establish lines L'-P' on each side of the stretchout as shown.

d. From the developed ellipse line on the working drawing, transfer chords 4'-3', 3'-2', and 2'-1' along line L'-P' outward from the 45° lines on each side of the pattern. At each point of intersection with line L'-P', draw lines perpendicular to, and extending on both sides of lines, L'-P'.

e. Transfer the vertical lines Q, N, Y, and R from the working drawing to the pattern stretchout as shown. Mark each line with a prime (').

f. Working from lines L'-P' on each side of the pattern transfer lengths U', V', W', and X' to the upper side of the line as indicated. Transfer lengths U, V, W, and X to the bottom of the lines also as shown.

g. Draw the pattern outline through the developed points.

h. Measure up from line X-X the height of the tee collar and draw lines to include the proper area within the rectangle.

5. Lay out the half collar pattern.

   a. Draw a rectangle equal to the included area as developed in part "h" above. Make seam allowance.

6. Lay out the collars for the small end and the large end of the taper.

7. Recheck all dimensions, make seam allowances on the patterns.

8. Cut and notch the patterns. Form the patterns.

9. Fabricate the fitting, set and lock the seams, rivet or solder as necessary.

Questions

1. What is another name for the shoe-tee type fitting?

2. What is the purpose of the working drawing?

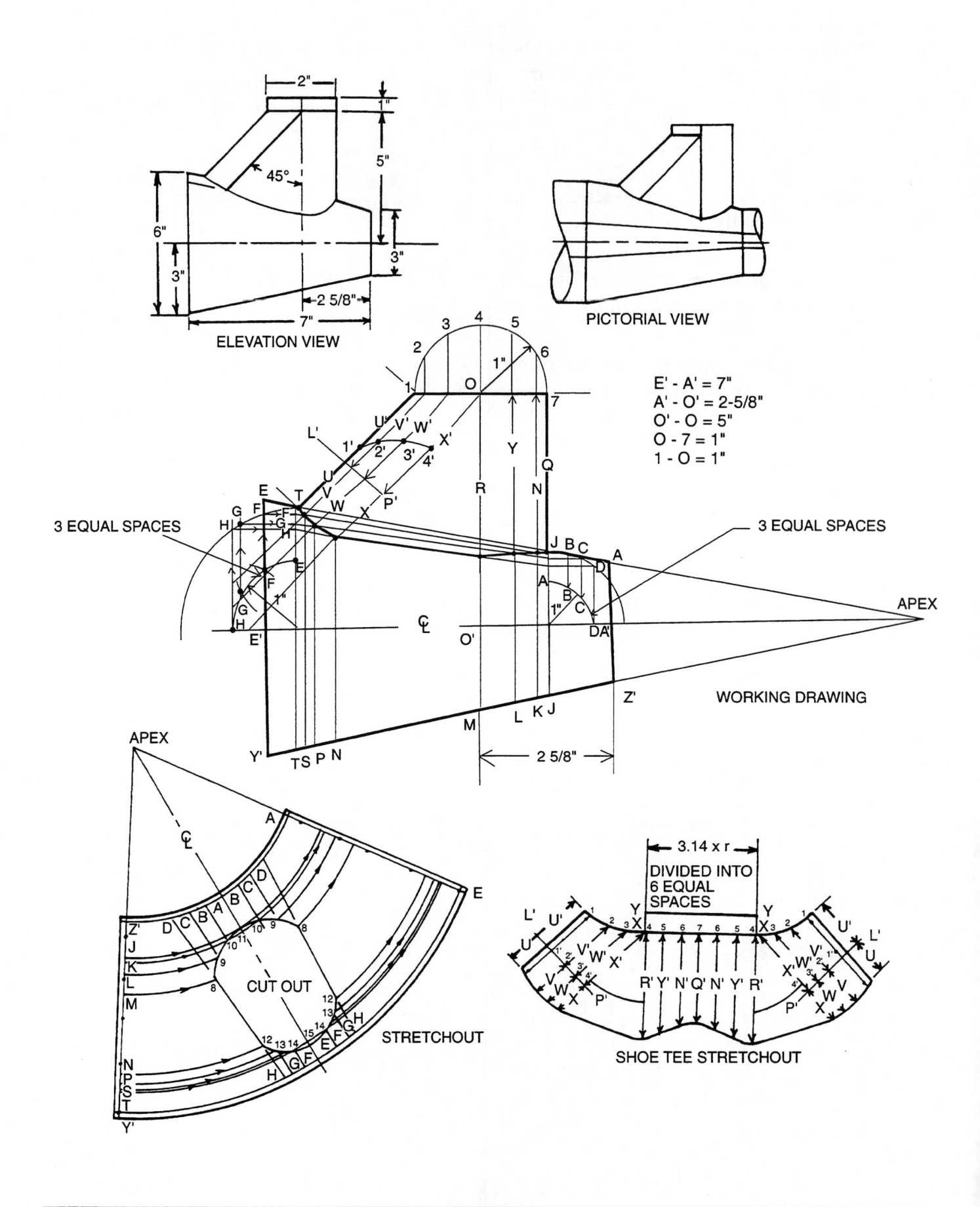

Figure 15 - Boot Tee Intersecting Taper

TASK 12

TAPERED ELBOWS – 90°

Objective

Upon completion of this task, the trainee will be able to lay out and fabricate a 90° tapered elbow (*Figure 16*).

Round elbows can be laid out by any of the three traditional methods. Each of them is practical if used in the proper circumstances. Generally speaking, however, all the methods for round-elbow layout, including shortcuts, are based upon parallel-line development. However, for this particular task, the radial line method will be used. Some general rules for the layout procedure for a round elbow are:

1. Seams should run along the center line of the elbow, or they should run on the heel or throat as the pattern is layed out.

2. Seams should be staggered. The seam of the first gore should be on the side opposite of the seam of the second gore and so on.

3. The gores should be run through the elbow rolls in the same position as they lie in the pattern.

4. When the edges are run through the elbow machine, they must be arranged so that the seams are properly staggered.

5. The seams on the elbow can be either riveted, grooved or spot welded. However, many workers prefer to use a groove seam because it is considered to be tighter and faster to fabricate.

6. When the pattern is developed, the lines on the side view and on the pattern should be numbered. This saves time by reducing the chances for error and having to recount the lines. Remember, gore patterns for an elbow should look like a fish.

Tools and Materials

The galvanized iron sheet metal used for this problem should be 24 gage or lighter to eliminate the possibility of fitting "growth." Other tools, equipment, and supplies can be chosen from the regular inventory of a conventional sheet metal shop.

Procedure

1. Draw the elevation view of the fitting as illustrated.

2. Construct the working drawing.

    a. Calculate the length of the center line 90° arc in the elevation view by multiplying the 6" radius by the constant 1.57 (1/2 pi), which equals 9.42" or approximately 9-7/16 inches. Construct this centerline in the working drawing. Establish point 1, measure upward from point 1 and establish point 9 (9-7/16" up from point 1).

    b. Draw lines perpendicular to and extending on both sides of the center line at points 1 and 9 equal to one-half the diameter of the large end and one-half the diameter of the small end, respectively. Establish points A and points K.

    c. Draw straight lines upward from points K through points A to intersect at point X.

    d. Measure 5" (large end diameter) to the left and right of point 1 and establish points P and S. Square lines upward from points P and S.

    e. Divide the centerline 1-9 into 8 equal spaces, label the points of intersection with line 1-9 as 2, 3, 4, 5, 6, 7, and 8.

    f. Draw a straight line from point S through point 2 to intersect the vertical line from point P and establish point T.

g. Draw a straight line from point T through point 4 to the right and establish point U. Draw a straight line from point U through point 6 to the left and establish point V.

h. Draw a straight line from point V through point 8 to the right and establish point W.

i. Label the points of intersection of these lines with line A-K on the right side of the working drawing as points B, E, F, and J. Label the corresponding points of intersection on the left side with line A-K as points C, D, G, and H.

j. With point 1 as center and 2-1/2" (radius of large end) as radius, draw a half circle below line K-K. Divide the half circle into 4 equal spaces. Label the points L, M, and N.

k. Draw vertical lines upward from each of these points to intersect line K-K and establish points 10 and 11.

l. Draw straight lines downward from point X to points 10 and 11.

m. Draw lines to the left from the intersecting points of lines X-10 and X-11 and the developed elbow sections lines B-C, D-E, F-G, and H-J, parallel to line K-K until they intersect line A-K on the left of the working drawing.

3. Lay out the gore sections.

   a. With X as center and distance X-K as radius, strike a long arc to the left and upward from point K.

   b. Calculate the circumference of the large end and establish this length on the long arc (3.14 × 5").

   c. Divide the circumference into 8 equal spaces. Label the spaces as L, M, N, and K as indicated.

   d. Draw straight lines from each of these established points to point X.

   e. With X as center and distances X-J, X-1, X-2, X-3, and X-H as radii as developed on line A-K (left side of the working drawing), strike arcs to the left to intersect lines X-K, X-L, X-M, and X-N on the pattern stretchout.

   f. With point X as center and the other developed points on line A-K as radii, strike arcs to the left again to intersect the corresponding lines.

   g. Draw the pattern outline through the developed points. Note: if the gore sections are to be welded, continue on to the next phase. If the sections are to be connected by seams make the proper allowances by extending the pattern (the proper amount) for each gore.

4. Recheck the measurements. Cut the sections on the developed lines. Roll each gore section to the required diameter.

5. Fasten the sections to form the tapered elbow.

6. Restore the work area.

Questions

1. What type(s) of development can be used to develop this kind of fitting?

2. What is the purpose of identifying each section?

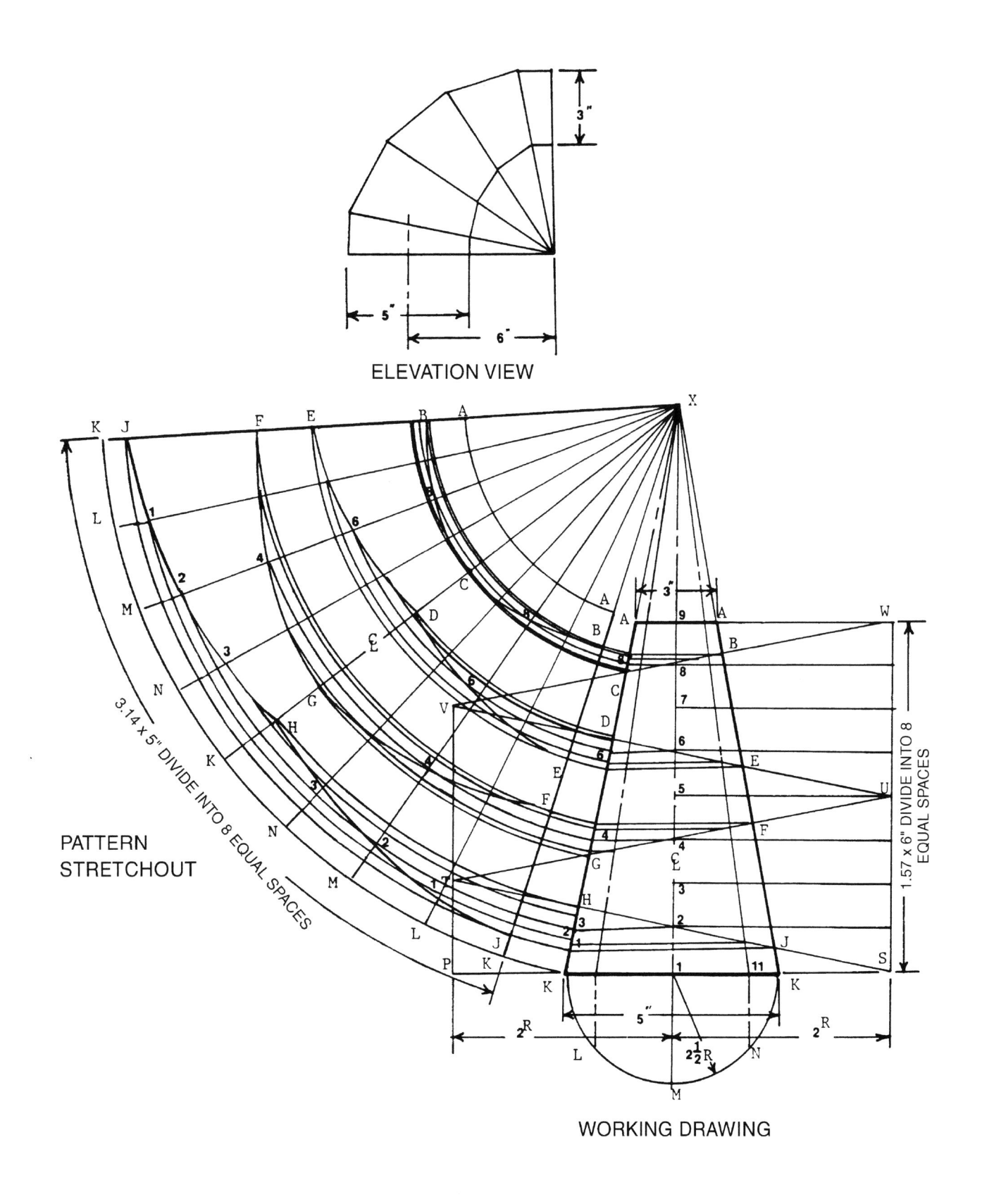

Figure 16 - 90° Tapered Elbow

FABRICATION II – RADIAL LINE DEVELOPMENT — TRAINEE TASK MODULE 04303

NCCER CRAFT TRAINING USER UPDATES

The NCCER makes every effort to keep these manuals up-to-date and free of technical errors. We appreciate your help in this process. If you have an idea for improving this manual, or if you find an error, a typographical mistake, or an inaccuracy in the NCCER's Craft Training Manuals, please write us, using this form or a photocopy. Be sure to include the exact module number, page number, a description of the problem, and the correction, if possible. Your input will be brought to the attention of the Technical Review Committee. Thank you for your assistance.

Instructors – If you found that additional materials were necessary in order to teach this module effectively, please let us know so that we may include them in the Equipment/Materials list in the Instructor's Guide.

Write: Curriculum and Revision Department
National Center for Construction Education and Research
P.O. Box 141104
Gainesville, FL 32614-1104
Fax: 352-334-0932

Craft _____ Module Name _____

Module Number _____ Page Number(s) _____

Description of Problem
_____
_____
_____
_____
_____

(Optional) Correction of Problem
_____
_____
_____

(Optional) Your Name and Address
_____
_____
_____

Bend Allowances
Module 04304

NATIONAL
CENTER FOR
CONSTRUCTION
EDUCATION AND
RESEARCH

Task Module 04304

BEND ALLOWANCES

Objectives

Upon completion of this task module, the trainee will be able to:

1. Describe the factors that influence bend allowances on sheet metal blanks.

2. Demonstrate an understanding of the calculations necessary for determining proper bend allowances on selected sheet metal problems.

3. Demonstrate skill in determining bend allowances on selected sheet metal problems.

INTRODUCTION

Bending is a forming operation that is used to fabricate parts for ductruns or other metal components. It is one of the easiest operations that is used for shaping metal. It is easy to accomplish with dies in presses, or by using hand tools in the sheet metal shop, or at the job site. Bending a section of sheet metal to some angular position is usually considered to be a rather straightforward operation at first. However, there are several stresses at work during the bending process that must be considered by the sheet metal worker. Unless the technician knows how to handle curves in bending metal, success in layout work cannot be achieved. One of the basic facts to be considered is that a curved corner requires less metal than a square corner. Therefore, the worker must decide how to cut the stock correctly before it is subjected to bending.

Copyright © 1992 National Center for Construction Education and Research, Gainesville, FL All rights reserved. No part of this work may be reproduced in any form or by any means, including photocopying, without written permission of the publisher. Updated: 1998.

BEND SHAPES

Bending a section of sheet metal to some angular position with respect to the remaining section depends on both the characteristics of the form and the use of it. Some of the more common bend shapes are depicted in *Figure 1*. The sharp break corner is normally used on very thin ductile (easily shaped) metal sheets. This kind of bend is not usually recommended because the bend line along the corner is weak. If the bend is formed in tempered metal, fracture lines will usually develop and the bent section will separate. The remaining four sections are considered to be much stronger and also to have a better appearance. These four shapes include a radius that forms the bend shape and that must be considered when laying out the sheet metal blank.

BENDING FACTORS

When a section of sheet metal is bent, there are at least two physical forces in action: tension and compression. These forces are in opposite directions, but are spread out over a wide area that results in plastic distortion of the metal without causing the metal to fracture or fail. Bending of sheet metal stresses the metal at localized areas only, and this stress occurs only at the bend radius (*Figure 2*). The remaining flat metal on each side of the bend radius is not stressed during bending, nor is it elongated. The metal on the outside of the bend radius, however, has been stretched and elongated, which indicates that a tensile stress has been applied on that side of the radius. The metal on the inside of the bend radius has been squeezed or placed under a compressive stress. As can be seen from the illustration, if fracture occurs during bending, it will occur at the outside of the bend surface where the metal is stretched. If any wrinkling occurs, it will take place on the inside surface of the bend where compression occurs.

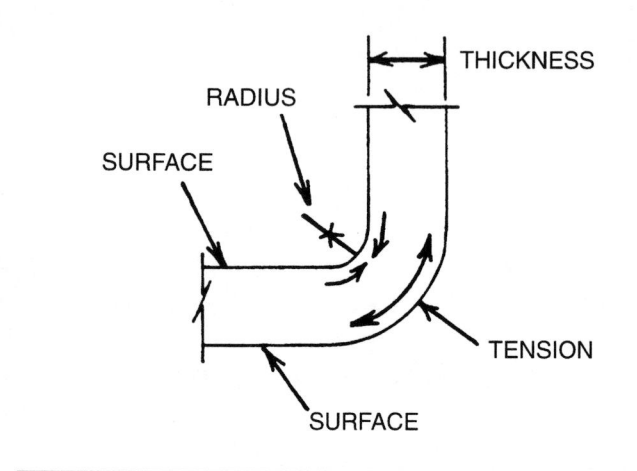

Figure 2 - Bend Forces

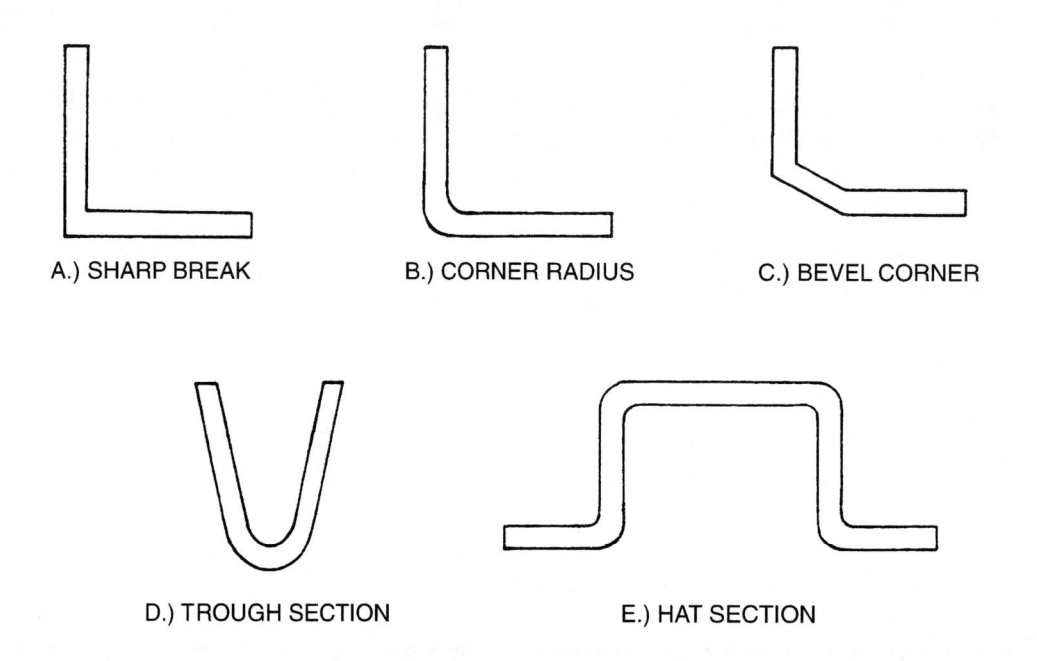

A.) SHARP BREAK

B.) CORNER RADIUS

C.) BEVEL CORNER

D.) TROUGH SECTION

E.) HAT SECTION

Figure 1 - Common Bend Sections

Neutral Axis

As can be noted from *Figure 2*, the sheet metal is stressed in tension on one surface (on the outside of the bend) and in compression on the other surface (on the inside of the bend). Therefore, at some point in the bend, a reversal of stresses must occur. This point at which the reversal of stresses occurs takes place at a certain line in the bend where the stresses are zero. This zero stress line is called the **neutral axis** (*Figure 3*). The neutral axis is near the center of the sheet metal thickness when the blank is first being bent, but as the bending progresses, the neutral axis shifts toward the inside of the bend, toward the compression side of the bend. This neutral axis, where the two forces of tension and compression meet within the metal, remains the same length after bending as its length before bending. Its thickness is considered to be about 44.5 percent of the metal measuring from the inside of the bend (*Figure 4*). The position of the neutral axis of the bend is dependent on the radius of the bend and the thickness of the metal. Therefore, the neutral axis position will shift for each variable, and precise blank size calculations (stretchout) may be difficult. As a result, some alteration of the blank dimensions may be necessary after making a few trial bends.

Metal Movement

During the process of production bending, one area of the sheet metal blank is usually held stationary, and the remaining free blank area is then bent to create the necessary change in contour. The metal that is forced up or down by the forming punch moves through space to occupy a new position. This movement through space (*Figure 5*) is called **swinging**. This swinging action of the metal blank must be predicted so that no obstacles are in the way.

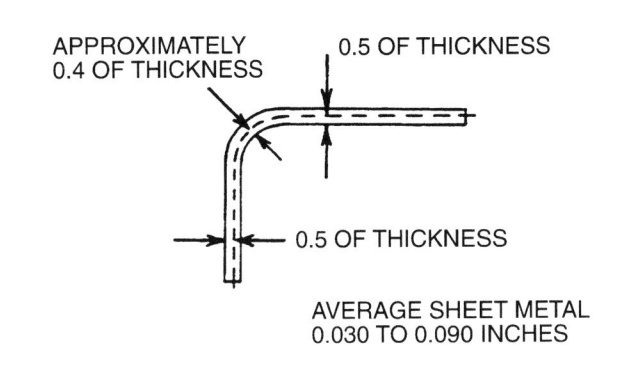

Figure 4 - t Constant

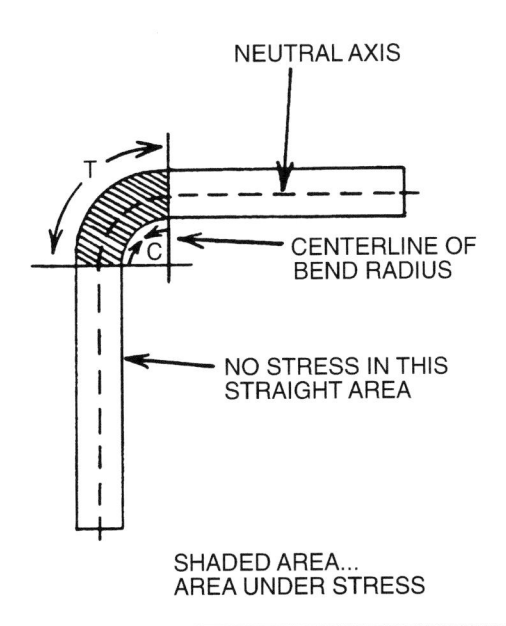

Figure 3 - Neutral Axis

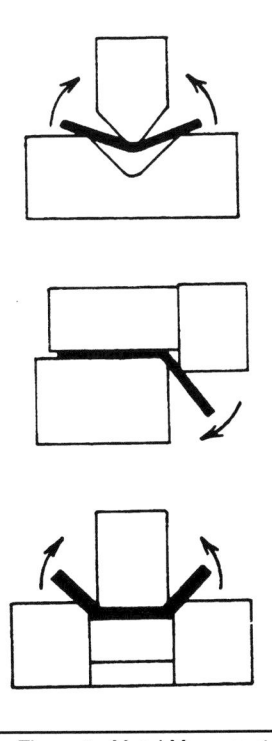

Figure 5 - Metal Movement

BEND ALLOWANCES — TRAINEE TASK MODULE 04304

Bending tonnage charts (*Table 1*) are available that indicate the approximate pressure in tons per linear foot required to make a 90° air bend on mild steel with various width die openings. The bold face figures indicate the pressures required using a punch with a radius equal to the metal thickness and a die opening approximately eight times the metal thickness. This combination will produce an air bend with an inside radius nearly equal to metal thickness.

Springback

The variation of bend stresses usually causes springback (*Figure 6*) after initial bending. This is due to the metal nearest the neutral axis being stressed to values below the elastic limit. This metal below the elastic limit creates a narrow elastic band on both sides of the neutral axis. When the die opens, the elastic band tries to return to the original flat shape, but cannot. However, some slight return does occur. This return is called **springback**. There are three methods of overcoming springback. They include the following:

1. Overbending
2. Bottoming or setting
3. Stretch bending

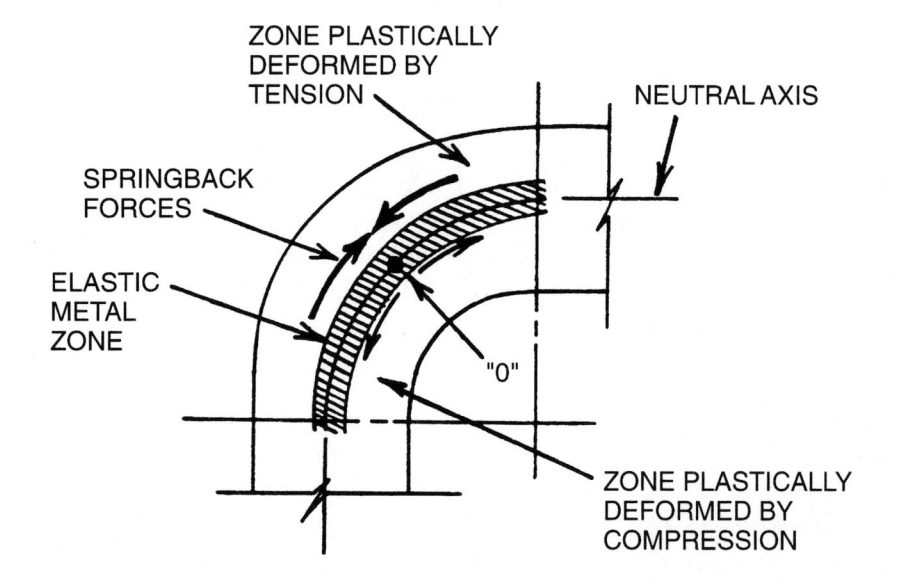

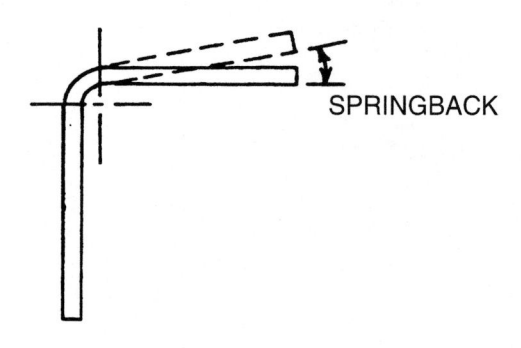

Figure 6 - Springback

THICKNESS OF METAL

Width of V-Die Opening	26 G. .018"	24 G. .024"	22 G. .030"	20 G. .036"	18 G. .048"	16 G. .064"	14 G. .075"	13 G. .090"	12 G. .105"	11 G. .120"	10 G. .135"	9 G. .149"	7 G. .187"	1/4" .250"	5/16" .313"	3/8" .375"	7/16" .437"	1/2" .500"	5/8" .625"	3/4" .750"	7/8" .875"	1" 1.00"
1/8"	1.2																					
3/16"	0.8	1.4	2.5																			
1/4"	0.5	1.1	1.8	2.9	5.4																	
5/16"		0.7	1.4	2.2	4.0	7.0																
3/8"			1.0	1.7	2.9	5.6	8.8															
1/2"				1.2	2.2	3.6	6.0	10.0														
5/8"					1.6	2.7	4.5	6.8	10.1													
3/4"					1.3	.2.	3.4	5.4	7.4	10.5												
7/8"						1.7	3.0	4.3	6.3	8.8	11.3											
1"						1.4	2.5	3.7	5.4	7.2	9.6	13.1										
1-1/8"							2.1	3.3	4.4	6.2	8.4	11.9	16.4									
1-1/4"							1.7	2.9	4.0	5.4	7.0	9.0	14.0									
1-1/2"									3.2	4.3	5.6	6.7	11.2	22.0								
2"										3.2	4.1	5.2	7.6	15.3	26.0	41.0						
2-1/2"											2.4	3.5	5.8	11.5	19.2	29.9	45.2					
3"												2.2	4.5	9.1	16.0	24.0	35.0	47.9				
3-1/2"														7.5	12.5	19.4	28.0	39.0	69.5			
4"														6.2	10.6	16.0	24.0	33.1	58.0	92.0		
5"															7.6	12.3	17.0	24.0	42.2	69.0	104.0	
6"																9.3	14.6	19.0	32.4	52.2	80.0	112.2
7"																	11.1	15.6	26.0	42.2	63.0	90.2
8"																		12.7	23.0	36.0	52.5	76.0
10"																			16.5	27.0	39.4	56.2
12"																				21.0	31.2	44.0

With these thicknesses it is usual practice to have die opening at least ten times metal thickness

Courtesy Dreis and Krump Manufacturing Company

Table 1 - Bending Tonnage

BEND ALLOWANCES — TRAINEE TASK MODULE 04304

Overbending (*Figure 7*) is produced by overbending the sheet an amount sufficient to produce the desired degree of bend angle after springback.

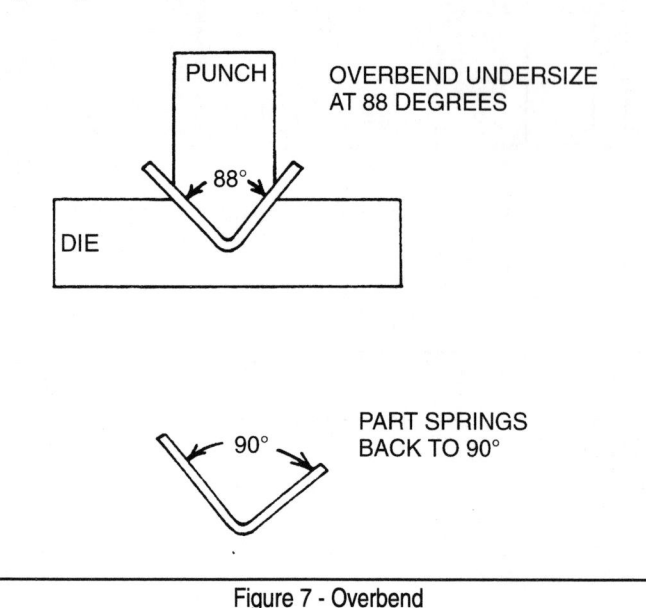

Figure 7 - Overbend

Bottoming or setting (*Figure 8*) results from striking the metal very hard at the radius area of the band. This places the metal under high compressive stresses that set the metal at the desired bend angle. Air bending relies on the bottoming process, but clearance ("air space") between the male and female sections of the punch and die occurs, and must be accounted for during the forming operation.

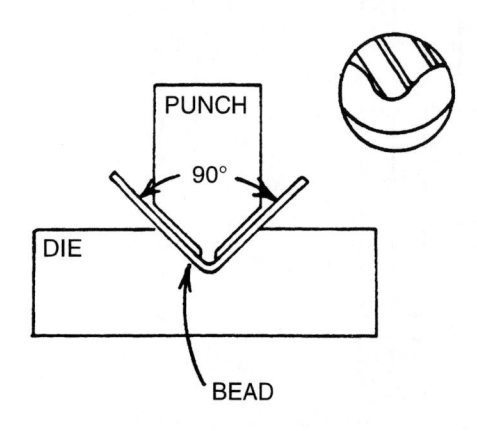

Figure 8 - Bottoming

Stretch bending (*Figure 9*) develops from stretching the metal blank so that all the metal is stressed beyond its yield strength. Due to this prestressing before bending, very little springback occurs. However, only relatively large radii can be bent by this method because a sharp-radius bend would prestress the metal beyond its ultimate tensile strength and fracture would occur. This practice is generally not used in the sheet metal trade but is more of a mill process.

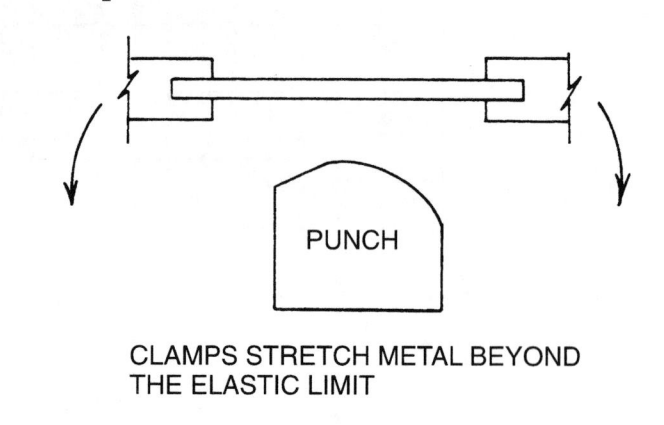

Figure 9 - Stretch Bending

APPROXIMATE BEND ALLOWANCE

There are several methods of calculating bend allowances for precision bending of metal sections. Some of them are somewhat complicated, but a simple method is also available. However, the simple method is only approximate and should not be used where precision bends must be formed. An approximate formula that can be used for finding bend allowances for relatively sharp bends in thin metal involves subtracting a percentage of the metal thickness from each bend (90° or so) from the outside dimension and adding a percentage of the metal thickness to the inside dimension.

For example, to calculate the bend allowance of 18 gage and lighter metal for the 90° section of metal shown in *Figure 10*, add one-half the metal thickness of the inside dimensions for

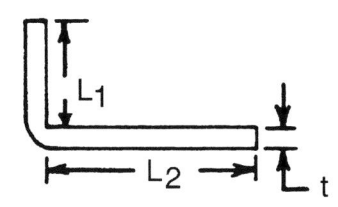

Figure 10 - Approximate Bend Allowance

the 90° bend to the summation of the lengths of the legs. The sum should be the amount of metal required for the section stretchout.

For example:

Set L_1 equal to 1.250"

Set L_2 equal to 2.50"

Set "t" equal to (0.050") (18 gage)

Solve for the stretchout:

s.o. = $L_1 + L_2 + 1/2(t)$

s.o. = $1.25 + 2.5 + \dfrac{(0.05)}{2} = 3.75 + 0.025$

s.o. = 3.775

To calculate the stretchout using outside dimensions (*Figure 10*) subtract 1/2t from the summation of the legs.

s.o = $L_1 + L_2 (-) 1/2t$

Solve for the stretchout:

L_1 = 1-1/2"

L_2 = 3"

t = 0.031" (22 ga.)

s.o. = 4.5 − 0.0155

s.o. = 4.4845"

PRECISION BEND ALLOWANCE

As previously stated, the procedures for calculating bend allowances are not as simple as it would seem at first. The bend allowance depends on the thickness of the metal, the type of metal, and the radius of the bend. In order to assist the sheet metal technician in calculating these allowances, several formulas have been made available by tool and manufacturing engineers. One of these equations is as follows:

$$B = \dfrac{A}{360} \times 2\pi (R + kt), \text{ or}$$

$$B = 0.017453A(R + kt)$$

Where: B = bend allowance, which is the arc length of the neutral axis in inches

A = angle of the bend in degrees

R = the bend radius of the part or section in inches

k = a constant pertaining to the location of the neutral axis

t = thickness of the metal in inches

All of the quantities in the formula are measurable except k, which can be calculated by another formula. The k factor depends on the location of the neutral axis, which in turn depends on the factors previously mentioned: the metal on the inside of the bend compresses, the metal on the outside of the bend stretches, and the plane along which no compression or stretching occurs is the neutral axis. The metal will usually stretch more than it compresses; therefore, the neutral axis will pull in from the center line of the piece toward the inside radius. The sharper the bend, the more the neutral axis will pull in to the inside surface. This constant, k, can be calculated, but due to much experimental evaluation, it has been found to range from values of 0.333 to 0.5, with usual values of 0.333, 0.40, or 0.5. The value of 0.5 for k places the neutral axis exactly in the center of the metal, and is a value that is generally used for some thicknesses of metal. This value

(0.50) is often used where the bend radius is greater than twice the thickness of the metal. For precision work, the k factor can be determined by experiment.

Some of the terms associated with the problems pertaining to bend allowance are indicated on *Figure 11*. As illustrated on the drawing, the bend begins and ends at the bend tangent lines. The distance between these bend tangent lines, measured on the neutral axis, is the bend allowance. The neutral axis does not change in length during bending; therefore, the bend allowance can be measured on the flat stock prior to bending.

Setback is not shown on *Figure 11*. It is the amount of metal saved by bending around a given radius. When the part is bent around a radius, the metal required for the radius is less than if it were a square bend. The metal required to make the part will be less in length than if it were a square bend; therefore, this dimension can be subtracted from the layout dimensions to determine the final blank size for the metal section. For further information, see Society of Manufacturing Engineers, 2nd Edition, *Die Design Handbook*, McGraw-Hill Book Co., 1965.

Formula

A common formula for determining bend allowance, based on observation and experimentation, is given as follows:

$$B = (A) \times (0.01743R) + (0.0078t)$$

Notice that this formula is very similar to the first one, with the exception that the k factor has already been calculated.

A geometrical process is also available for finding the bend allowance for a given bend. The length of the material in the bend (bend allowance) can be calculated by finding the circumference of a circle with a radius equal to the radius of the neutral axis in the bend. Therefore, the length of the material can be represented by the bend as if it were a part of the circle.

For example, the circumference of a circle is equal to $2\pi R$. With this in mind, the first step is to calculate the radius of the neutral axis that will be represented as part of the circumference; the second step is to calculate the length or distance on the circumference for each degree of circumference.

Step 1: To solve for the radius of the bend (neutral axis), use the formula:

$$R = R + kt$$

Step 2: To solve for the distance on the circumference for each degree of circumference, use the formula:

$$C = \frac{2\pi \times R}{360}$$

Where:

C = 1 degree of the circumference
pi = 3.1416
R = R + kt
k = K factor
   (0.333, 0.40, 0.455, or 0.50)
t = thickness of the metal

Bend allowance tables are available for the type of metal being used and can be employed to save calculation time. These tables are provided in the Appendices. *Appendix F* can be used for calculating bend allowances for thin sections of sheet metal and small radii. *Appendix G* has been developed on the basis of K factors varying from 1/3 or 1/2 combined with experimental data. *Appendix G* uses the identifiers D, E, G, and F, and thus bend allowances can be found directly from the table, where:

D = setback
E = bend allowance
G = bend allowance for 1 degree of bend angle
F = inside measurement of the legs

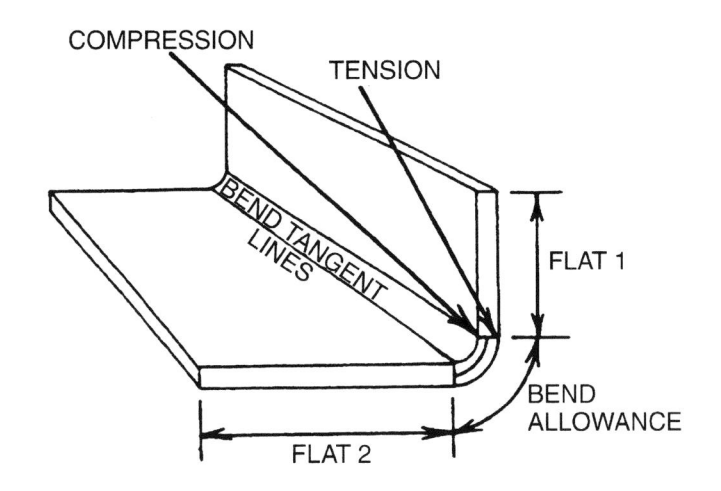

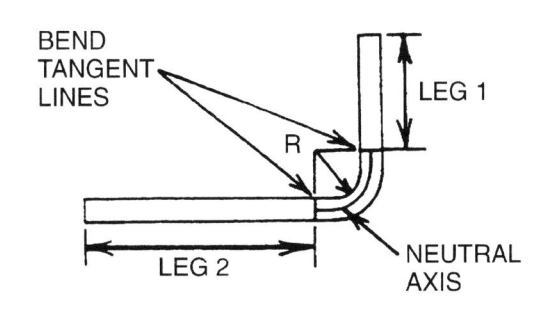

Figure 11 - Bend Nomenclature

To find the bend allowance using the common (empirical) formula, proceed as follows:

B = bend allowance
A = angle of the bend
R = bend radius
k = neutral axis constant
t = thickness

Refer to *Figure 12* for solving the illustrated problem by each of the three methods (empirical formula, geometric calculation, table).

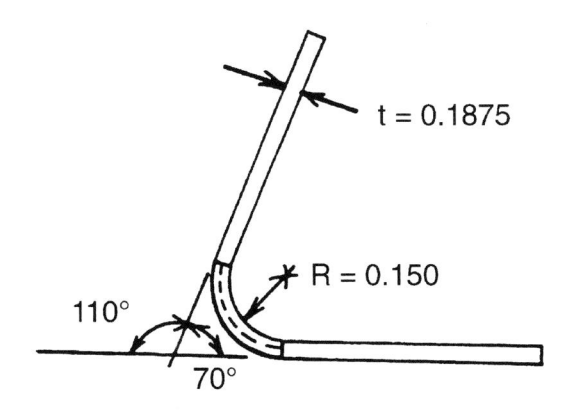

R = 1/2"
t = 3/16" = 0.1875
RADIUS TO NEUTRAL AXIS = 1/2 + Kt =
1/2 + (0.445 x 0.1875)

Figure 12 - Bend Allowance Problem A

BEND ALLOWANCES — TRAINEE TASK MODULE 04304

Example 1

Solve for the bend allowance (B) with the formula:

$$B = A(0.01743R) + (0.0078t)$$

Step 1: Place the values in the formula.

$B = 110(0.017438 \times 0.50) + (0.0078 \times 0.1875)$

Step 2: Solve for B:

$B = 110(0.008715) + (0.0014625)$
$B = 110(0.0101775)$
$B = 1.119525$ inches
$B = 1.120$ approximately

Example 2

Solve for the bend allowance (B) with the geometrical process.

One degree on the circumference of a given is:

$$C(1 \text{ degree}) = \frac{2 \pi \times R}{360}$$

Reminder: R is equal to R + kt.

Step 1: Place the values in the formula.

a) Solve for R:

$R = R + kt$
$R = 0.50 + (0.445 \times 0.1875)$
$R = 0.50 + 0.0853125$
$R = 0.5853125$

b) Place the values in the formula:

$$C = \frac{2 \times 3.1416 \times 0.5853125}{360}$$

Step 2: Solve for the inch value of 1 degree on the circumference:

$$C = \frac{6.2832 \times 0.5853125}{360}$$

$$C = \frac{3.6776355}{360}$$

$C = 0.0102$ (number in inches for 1 degree of circumference)

Step 3: Solve for B:

$B = A \times$ inches per degree on circumference
$B = 110 \times 0.0102$
$B = 1.122$ inches
$B = 1.120$ approximately

Example 3

Solve for the bend allowance with the illustrated tables.

Reminder: Terms used on the tables are as follows:

D = setback
E = bend allowance
G = bend allowance for 1 degree of angle
F = inside measurement of the section legs

Step 1: Locate the table with the proper values for the radius and metal thickness.

   a) Find the thickness column of 0.187 inches.

   b) Find the radius of 1/2 inch in the radius column.

Step 2: Locate the value of G.

   a) Find G in the allowance column to the right of 1/2 inch radius.

   b) Trace a horizontal line to the right from G until it intersects with the value given in the thickness column for 0.187 inches.

   c) Find G = 0.01035

Step 3: Solve for B:

$B = A$ (inches per degree) or $B = AG$
$B = 110(0.01035)$
$B = 1.1385$
$B = 1.139$ (to nearest 0.001)

Notice the discrepancy between the mathematical calculations and the values from the table.

Refer to *Figure 13* for values to use in solving for the bend allowance by each of the three methods.

Formula:
B = A(0.01743R) + (0.0078t)
B = 135(0.01743) + (0.0078 × 0.1875)
B = 135(0.0021787) + (0.0014625)
B = 135 × 0.0036412
B = 0.491562
B = 0.5 inches approximately

Geometric process:

B = A × inches per degree on circumference

Inches per degree on circumference is found by:

$$C \text{ (1 degree on C)} = \frac{2\pi R}{360}$$

R is found from R = R + kt

Step 1: Solve for R:
R = 0.125 + 0.445 × 0.1875
R = 0.125 + 0.0834
R = 0.2084

Step 2: Solve for C:

$$C = \frac{2 \times 3.1416(0.2084)}{360}$$

$$C = \frac{6.2832 \times 0.2084}{360}$$

$$C = \frac{1.3094188}{360}$$

C = 0.0036372

Step 3: Solve for B:
B = AC (inches per degree)
B = 135 × 0.0036372
B = 0.491022
B = 0.50 inches approximately

Use of tables:

Step 1: Locate the thickness column (0.187).

Step 2: Locate the radius column (1/8 inch– equal to 0.125).

Step 3: Locate the G reference to the right of the radius column.

Step 4: Locate the value of inches per degree of bend at the intersection of the G radius line and the thickness column. Find G (bend allowance for 1 degree) value to be 0.00364.

Step 5: Solve for B = AG
B = 135 × 0.00364
B = 0.4914
B = 0.50 approximately

Notice that the values for B are approximately equal for each of the three methods of calculation.

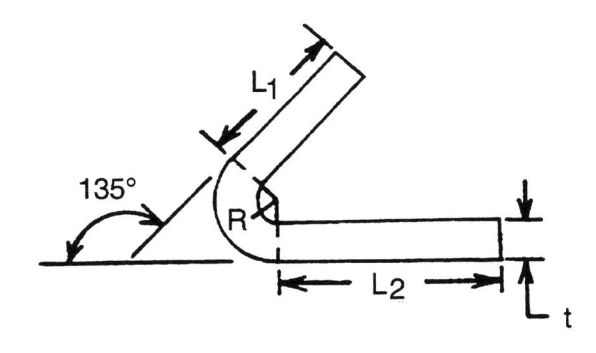

R = 1/8"
t = 3/16"
A = 135°
RADIUS TO NEUTRAL AXIS = 1/8 + Kt =
1/8 + (0.445 × 0.125)

Figure 13 - Bend Allowance Problem B

BEND ALLOWANCES — TRAINEE TASK MODULE 04304

Stretchout Development

The flat layout (development) for a section or drawing is simply one of determining the length and width of a flat sheet of metal that, when formed, will produce the required form of the specified dimensions.

The procedure may involve one or two steps. If the length of the unbent portion of each leg or flange is known, the bend allowance is added to those dimensions to derive the dimensions for the flat layout for the bend. If the dimensions that are given are outside dimensions, then the procedure requires two steps, one of addition and one of subtraction.

For the flat layout (stretchout) of either of the problems illustrated in *Figures 12* and *13*, the amount of flat stock necessary for the development of the problem can be found as follows:

1. Locate the bend tangent lines (*Figure 14*).

2. To locate the bend tangent lines, find the length of the unbent portion of each leg; add the bend allowance between the flat sections. The result is the final dimension for the stretchout of the form.

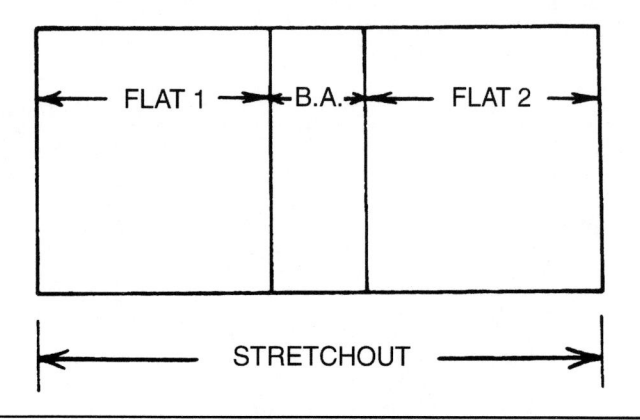

Figure 14 - Stretchout Development

If the problem involves more than one bend, and if the dimensions given are outside dimensions, the procedure requires the two steps above. To calculate the stretchout for a problem with more than one bend, proceed as follows:

1. See *Figures 15, 16,* and *17,* and note the number of bends and the radius of each bend.

2. Determine the thickness of the metal.

3. Calculate the bend allowance for each bend by any method you choose (formula, geometry, chart).

4. Add all the outside dimensions and note the final sum.

5. Subtract the setback of the bend allowances for each bend from the summation of the outside dimensions.

Note: The setback can be calculated through a mathematical process, which we will not cover, or it can be taken from the bend allowances in *Appendix G*.

6. The difference (summation of the sides, minus the setbacks) is the width of the stretchout.

For example, using *Figure 16* as a problem, calculate the width of the stretchout.

Step 1: Add the outside dimensions: 1/2 + 1 + 1/2 = 2.000 inches.

Step 2: Find the setback for the problem: R = 1/16, t = 0.065 (bend allowance *Appendix G*). Locate the radius in the lefthand column of the bend allowance table. Read to the right to the 0.064 inches column; locate the setback (D) as 0.110.

Step 3: Add the setback allowances for each two-blade bend; find total D = 0.036.

Step 4: Subtract the total setback summation from the outside dimensions summation:

2.000 inches minus 0.036 inches = 1.964 inches

Therefore, the width of the stretchout equals 1.964 inches.

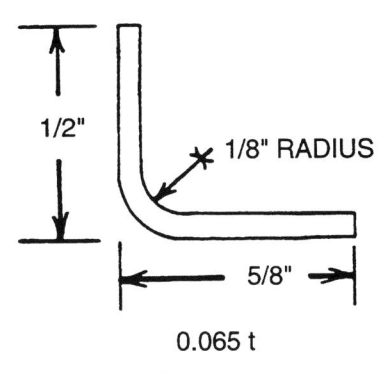

Figure 15 - Angle Problem

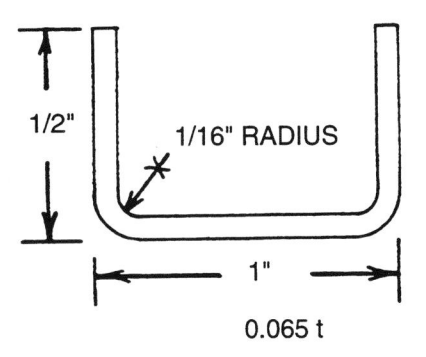

Figure 16 - Channel Problem

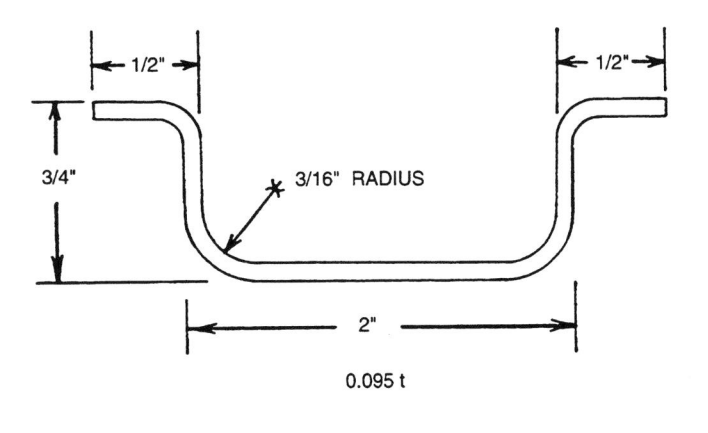

Figure 17 - Channel/Flange Problem

BENDING

Bending a sheet metal section to produce an accurate required bend necessitates the use of reference lines. The kind and location of these reference lines depends on the machine being used to perform the bends. One of the more common kinds of bending machines is the cornice brake. When a cornice brake is used, the bend must begin at the tangent line. When this is done, the tangent line is positioned directly below the radius bar on the brake (*Figure 18*) and will be out of sight of the operator. Therefore, another reference line must be established. This other reference line is called the **sight line**. It must be located at a distance equal to the radius of the bend from the tangent line. This sight line is placed directly below the "nose" of the radius bar when the stock is properly placed in the brake. The sight line is the only line required on flat layout. It may be used with a cornice brake, a bar folder, or a box and pan brake, because they all bend metal in a similar manner.

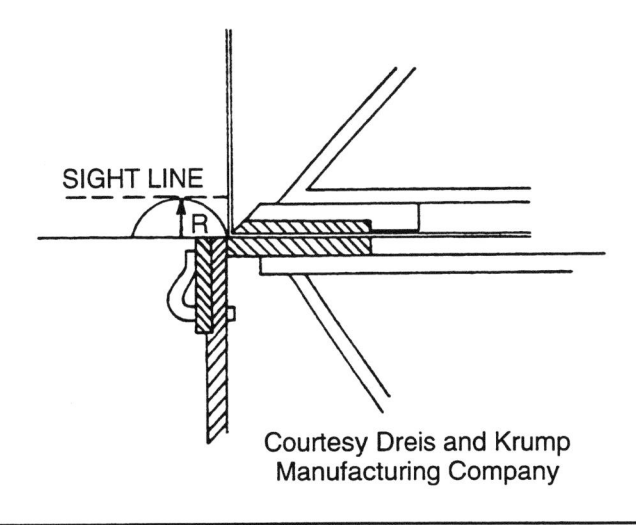

Figure 18 - Brake Setup

Great care must be exercised in order to produce an accurate bend. Therefore, the placing of the metal, the setting of the bending machine, and the actual bending all call for precise action to meet the close tolerances required for a given bend.

BEND ALLOWANCES — TRAINEE TASK MODULE 04304

TASK 1

CALCULATING BEND ALLOWANCES

Objective

Upon completion of this task, the trainee will be able to calculate bend allowances for selected sections of metal by one of several presented methods.

Bend allowance calculations depend on the thickness of the metal, the type of metal, and the radius of the bend. Calculation processes include an approximate method for right angle bends, precision methods of the "common" formula or the geometrical process, and the use of bend allowance charts. The sheet metal worker should be able to use all four methods for determining bend allowances for selected sections of metal.

Tools and Materials

The tools and materials necessary for the completion of this task include a copy of the task module and appendices A through E, paper and pencils, a pocket calculator, and a blackboard and chalk or an overhead projector with transparencies of the diagrams shown in this task section of the module.

Procedure

Part 1

1. Refer to the task module and allow the instructor to review the processes for approximate bend allowance calculations.

2. Using the approximate method for calculating bend allowances, refer to *Figure 19* and calculate the stretchout for each of the identified figures. Assume the metal to be either 24-gage galvanized steel or 22-gage aluminum.

3. Check your calculations for accuracy and check with the instructor for correctness.

4. When satisfied that your calculations are correct, proceed to the next part.

Part 2

1. Refer to the task module and allow the instructor to review the processes for bend allowance calculations using the formula, the geometric method, and tables.

2. Using any one, or all three, of the bend allowance calculation methods, calculate the stretchout for each of the sections shown in *Figure 20*. Assume the metal to be either 20- or 22-gage galvanized steel, or 24-gage or lighter stainless steel.

3. Using any one, or all three, of the calculation methods, determine the stretchout dimensions for each of the identified sections.

4. Check your calculations for accuracy; if satisfied, check with your instructor for correctness. Continue to the next part.

Part 3

1. Refer to the task module and allow the instructor to review the processes for approximate bend allowance calculations.

2. Using the approximate method for calculating bend allowances, refer to *Figure 19* and calculate the stretchout for each of the identified figures. Assume the metal to be either 24-gage galvanized steel or 22-gage aluminum.

3. Have the instructor set the dimensions of the flats for the stretchouts on the board or with a transparency, for example, to fit a 4 × 4 or 2 × 4.

4. Check your calculations for accuracy and check with the instructor for correctness.

5. When satisfied that your calculations are correct, proceed to the next part.

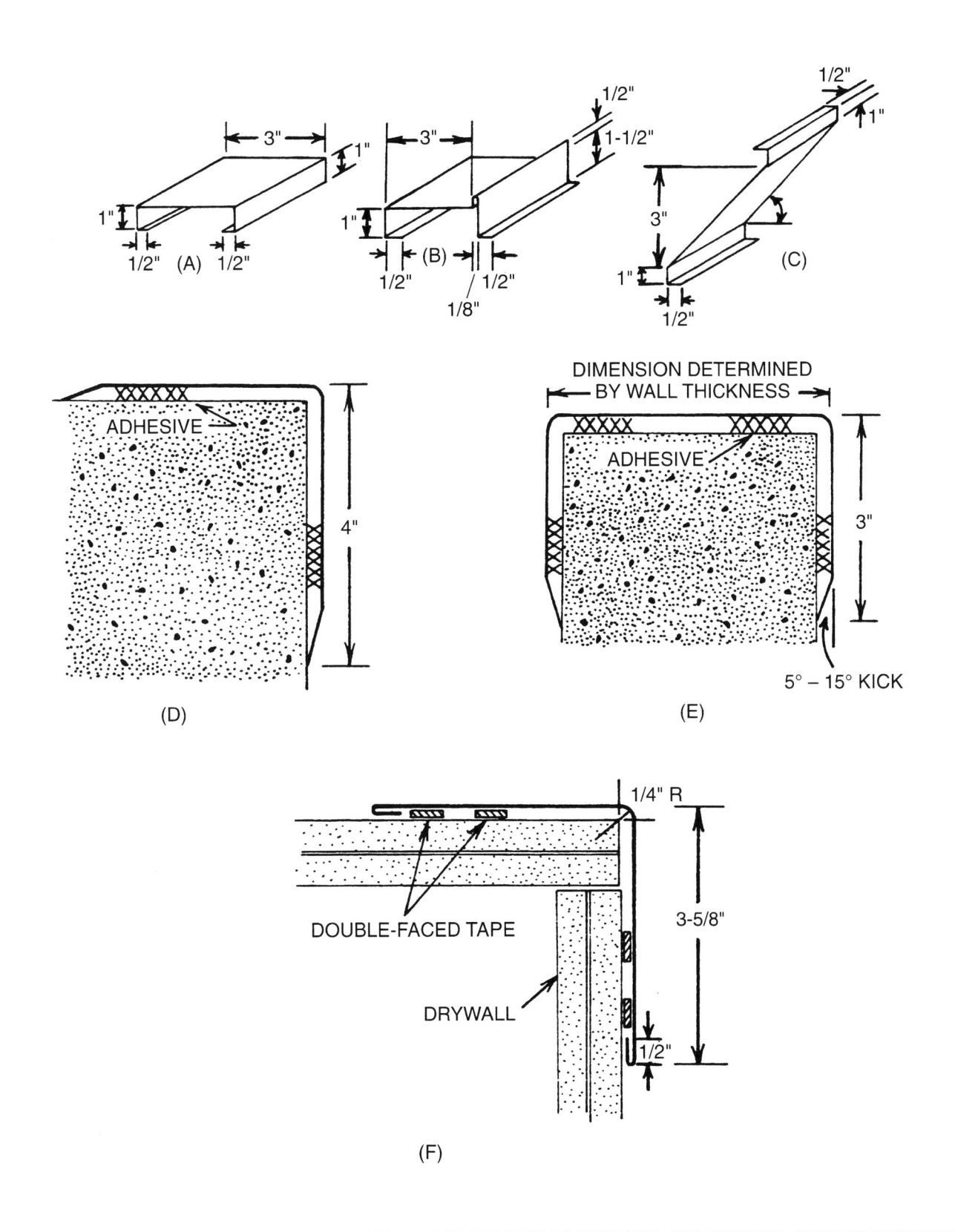

Figure 19 - Metal Sections

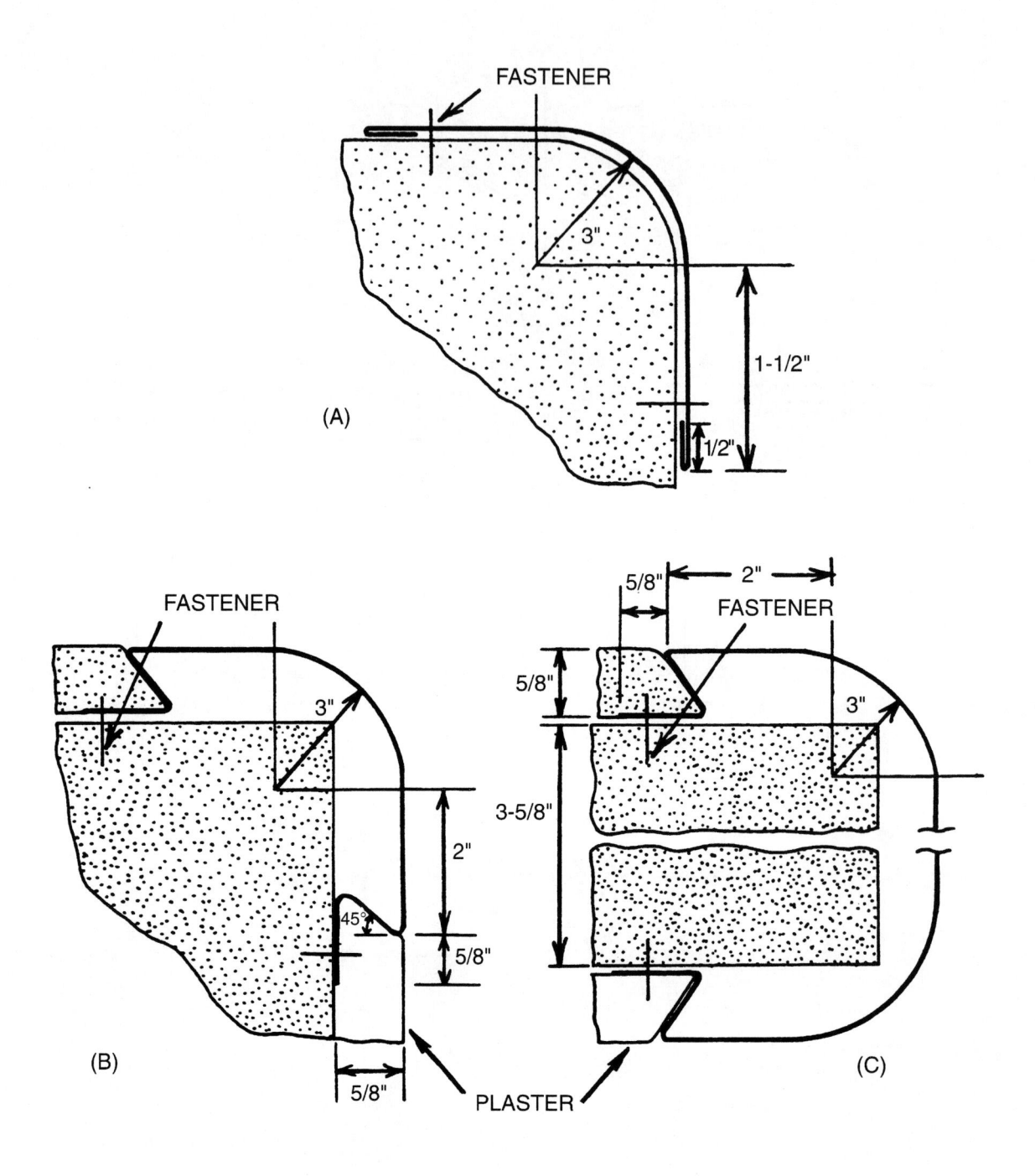

Figure 20 - Corner Guard Sections

Part 4

1. Refer to *Figure 21* and calculate the stretchout for the illustrated section (inside mating hat channel).
2. Use any method you prefer; perhaps you might want to compete with other class members for speed and accuracy.
3. When satisfied that your calculations are correct, check with your instructor.
4. If satisfied that you have mastered the various methods of calculating bend allowances, you may want to practice on "obvious" sections of ornamental or architectural sheet metal components around the room or shop.
5. If there is a method available for laminating the bend allowance charts in plastic, now may be the time to do it.
6. Prepare your work sequence for the next session.

Questions

1. Identify the steps necessary to calculate the bend allowances for the sections shown in *Figure 19*.
2. Describe the bend allowance process that you believe is most beneficial to the sheet metal worker.
3. Identify the steps you used in calculating the bend allowances for *Figure 21*.

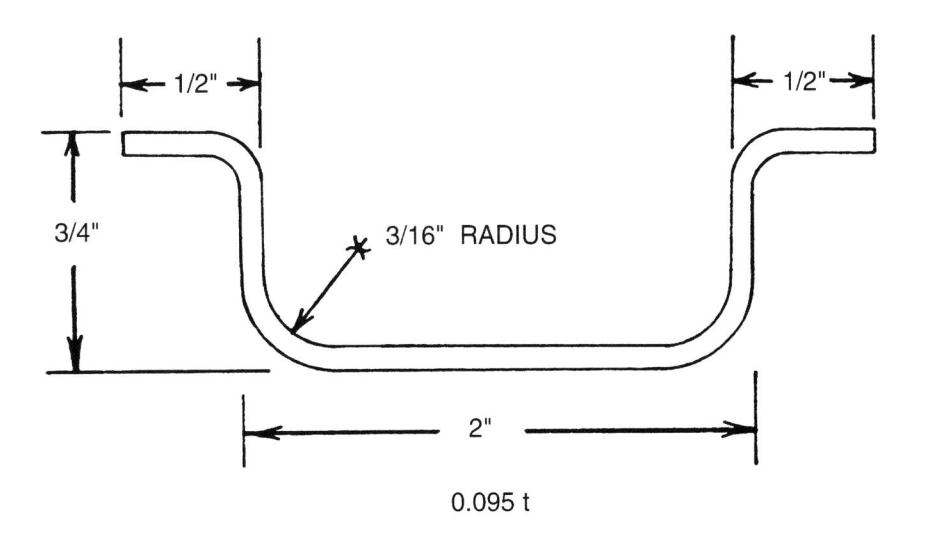

Figure 21 - Bend Allowance Problem C

TASK 2

MATING HAT CHANNEL

Objective

Upon completion of this task, the trainee will be able to calculate bend allowances for, lay out and develop, and form a hat section "mold" pattern and a mating hat channel. The purpose of this exercise is to carry bend allowance procedure to completion by calculating the bend allowances necessary for forming a hat section and a corresponding mating hat channel to fit inside the hat section mold pattern.

Tools and Materials

The tools and materials should include the general hand tool selection required by the sheet metal technician, plus bending and forming equipment that is usually located in the fabrication shop. In addition to the general sheet metal working tools and equipment, a supply of appropriate gage galvanized steel or aluminum sheet metal blanks must be supplied. It would also be helpful to have a copy of the task module for reference to the bend allowance chart or some other form of applicable bend allowance chart or table.

Procedure

1. Scrutinize *Figure 22*, especially Section A, to visualize the size and final shape of the "molded" hat section and the corresponding mating hat channel.

2. Calculate the bend allowance for the molded hat section (*Figure 23*), and enter the findings on a work sheet or scratch pad. Be sure to use the proper value for "t".

3. Select the appropriate gage and kind of metal (perhaps 22-gage galvanized steel) as decided upon in Step 2, and begin the layout procedure. Find the bend tangent lines and mark appropriately. Recheck your findings before cutting the proper size stretchout pattern from the sheet metal blank. Consult your instructor for tolerance limits.

4. When you are satisfied that the molded section has been properly laid out and the bend lines are accurately located, bend and form the hat mold section.

5. Present the section to your instructor, if necessary, before proceeding to the next part of the exercise.

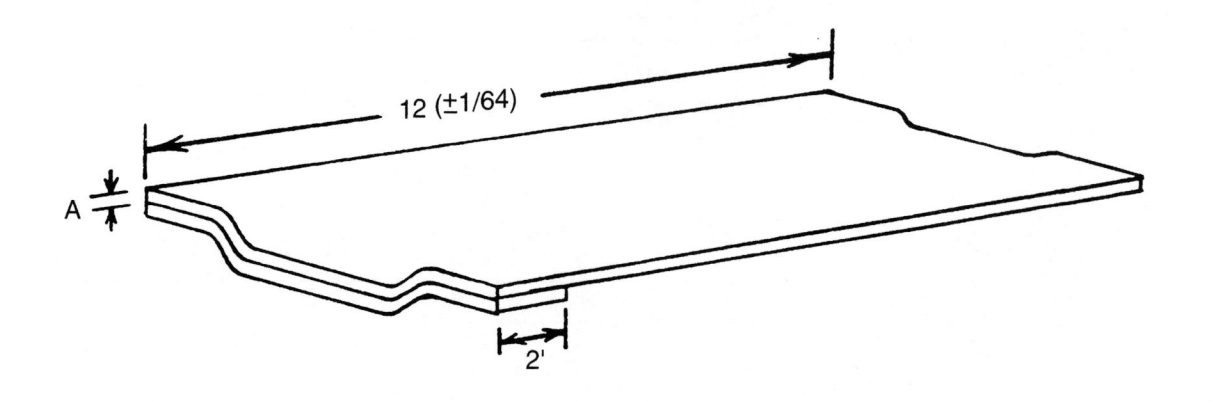

Figure 22 - Hat Section

SHEET METAL — TRAINEE TASK MODULE 04304

6. Consult your instructor for tolerance limits that will be required for the mating hat channel and record this information on your sheet.

7. Secure accurate measurements from the mold section you just completed and record this information on a sketch of the object. Use your worksheet for this information.

8. Using the sketch for reference, calculate the bend allowances necessary for the mating hat channel and place the proper dimensions on a sheet metal blank of appropriate size. Be sure to recheck your calculations before scribing the bend tangent lines, etc. It may also be advisable to use sheet metal of a lighter gage for this part of the exercise, such as 26-gage galvanized steel.

9. Carefully scribe the reference lines on the stretchout and recheck prior to forming.

10. At this time, your instructor may ask you to drill and ream a hole in the mold section for you to fit to. If this occurs, locate and lay out the hole in the mating hat channel. This dimension must be properly located so as to mate precisely with the hole in the mold section.

11. If the instructor requires that a hole must be located to match in each component of the exercise, drill and ream the hole prior to bending or forming the mating hat channel.

12. Bend and form the mating hat channel.

13. Check the mating hat channel for fit in the molded section, and if within tolerance limits, present both components to your instructor for evaluation.

14. Restore the work area.

Questions

1. What were the stretchout dimensions?

2. How well did your parts conform to the tolerance limits set by the instructor?

3. In your estimation, would this kind of task be more difficult if heavier gage metal were used?

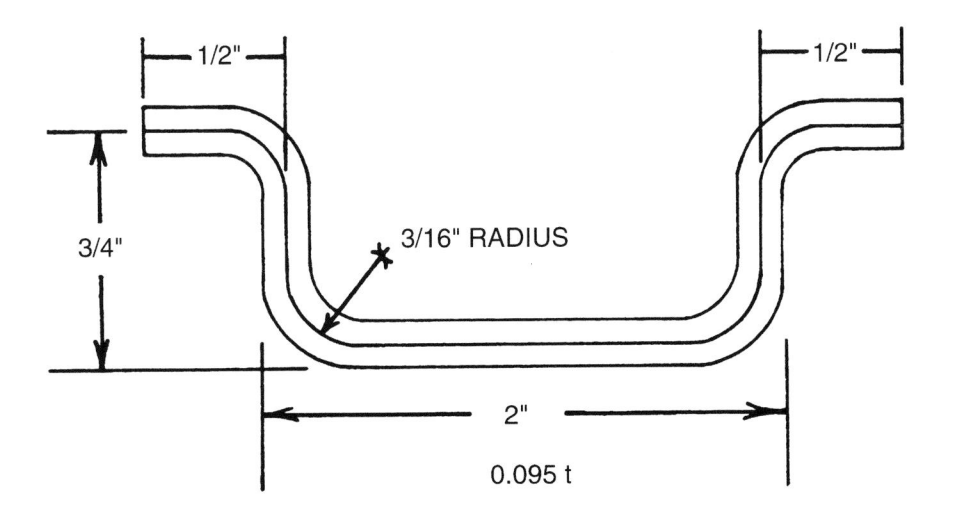

Figure 23 - Molded Hat Section

TASK 3

COLUMN GUARD

Objective

Upon completion of this task, the trainee will be able to fabricate a selected column guard.

Column guards are used to protect exposed columns or corners of support members or separation walls from damage by building traffic. They are very often formed in sections and then attached to steel plate or other wall covering. In other instances, they may be held in place with modified S-and-drive clips or with matching sheet metal procedures to produce a "common" finish.

Tools and Materials

Tools and materials necessary for this task should include the regular hand and power equipment and tools found in the conventional sheet metal fabrication shop. The sheet metal blank required for this task should probably also include a stainless steel sheet of an appropriate gage.

Procedure

1. Use *Figure 24* as a basis for determining how many sections the column guard will be made up of. Perhaps your instructor will suggest that various members of the class fabricate the guard from different numbers of components (one, two, three).

2. After you have made your selection for the number of pieces, consult the instructor for the kind of sheet metal to be used. Recommendations could include 16-gage galvanized steel or 16- to 18-gage (0.0500 to 0.0625 inch thick) stainless steel.

3. Ask your instructor for the finished dimensions for the column and the tolerance limit (such as plus or minus 1/6 inch thick) stainless steel.

4. Depending on the number of sections that are required for the task, sketch to scale the components, locate the bends, and calculate the bend allowance for each.

5. Check the steps for accuracy with your instructor and, if approved, begin the development of the stretchout.

6. Select your blank from the recommended material (of approximate thickness) and lay out the bend tangent lines after calculating the bend allowances again, or, after rechecking your previous findings, scribe the sight lines and check for accuracy.

7. Select the bending and forming equipment and adjust for proper angles. Make a trial run on scrap coupons to recheck for tolerance limits.

8. Bend and form your components after you are satisfied they will be within the tolerance limits set by your instructor.

9. When you are satisfied that you have correctly completed the task, present the column guard to your instructor for evaluation.

10. Restore the work area.

Question

1. What were the finished dimensions of your workpiece? Did it conform to the tolerance limits?

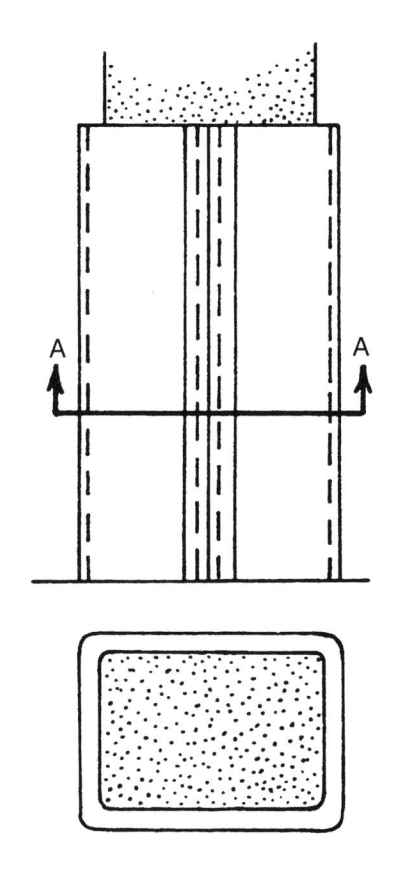

Figure 24 - Column Guard

BEND ALLOWANCES — TRAINEE TASK MODULE 04304

REVIEW QUESTIONS

Answer the following questions to review your knowledge of this module and to prepare for the Module Examination.

1. Define "neutral axis."

2. Identify the important factors that affect bend allowance calculations.

3. What is the k constant?

4. Describe how to use the bend allowance *Table 1-2*.

5. What are the three common methods, from the test, for calculating bend allowances for precision bends?

SUMMARY

Bending sheet metal sections is one of the easiest sheet metal forming operations to accomplish. It can be done in presses with dies, in the fabrication shop with bar folders, cornice brakes, or box-and-pan brakes, or it can be accomplished with hand tools at the job site. There are special physical forces that are in action during bending operations that must be considered when calculating bend allowances for precision forming of sheet metal sections. These forces—compression and tension—work in opposite directions that could ultimately result in harmful stress to the formed metal, even causing failure. In order to alleviate that possibility, bend allowances must be made prior to the bending activities. These bend allowances must take into consideration the thickness and type of metal, the radius of the bend, and the tolerances to which section must be formed. There are several methods of calculating bend allowances for stretchouts that can be used by sheet metal workers. In any event, there are many variables that must be considered when bending a sheet metal section to specifications.

TRADE TERMS

A	empirical formula
B	geometrical method
G	metal movement
k	neutral axis
R	radius
t	setback
	springback
	stretchout

APPENDIX A

THICKNESS OF GALVANIZED STEEL

GAGE (U.S. STANDARDS)	APPROXIMATE THICKNESS GALVANIZED (INCHES)
7	0.1793
8	0.1664
9	0.1494
10	0.1345
11	0.1196
12	0.1046
13	0.0897
14	0.0747
15	0.0673
16	0.0598
17	0.0538
18	0.0478
19	0.0418
20	0.0359
21	0.0329
22	0.0299
23	0.0269
24	0.0239
25	0.0209
26	0.0179
27	0.0164
28	0.0149
29	0.0135
30	0.0120

THICKNESS OF STAINLESS STEEL

GAGE (U.S. STANDARDS)	APPROXIMATE THICKNESS (INCHES)	
8		0.1719
9	5/32	0.1563
10	9/64	0.1406
11	1/8	0.1250
12	7/64	0.1094
13	3/32	0.0938
14	5/64	0.0781
15		0.0703
16	1/16	0.0625
17		0.0563
18		0.0500
19		0.0438
20		0.0375
21		0.0344
22	1/32	0.0313
23		0.0281
24		0.0250
25		0.0219
26		0.0188
27		0.0172
28	1/64	0.0156
29		0.0141
30		0.0125

APPENDIX C

THICKNESS OF ALUMINUM

GAGE (B & S)		APPROXIMATE THICKNESS (INCHES)
–		0.0403
9		0.0359
–		0.0320
10	1/32	0.0313
–		0.0285
11		0.0253
12		0.0226
–		0.0201
13		0.0179
14		0.0159
–	1/64	0.0156
15		0.0142
16		0.0126
–		0.0113
17		0.0100

APPENDIX D

THICKNESS OF COPPER

OUNCES (SQ. FT.)		APPROXIMATE THICKNESS
96		
88	1/8	0.1290
80		0.1190
72	7/64	0.1080
64	3/32	0.0972
56		0.0863
48	5/64	0.0755
44	1/16	0.0647
40		0.0593
36		0.0539
32	3/64	0.0485
28		0.0431
24		0.0377
20	1/32	0.0323
18		0.0270
16		0.0243
15		0.0216
14		0.0202
13		0.0189
12		0.0175
11	1/64	0.0162
10	1/64	0.0148
9		0.0135
8		0.0121
7		0.0108
6		0.0094
4		0.0081
2		0.0054
		0.0027

APPENDIX E

DECIMAL EQUIVALENTS IN INCHES

FRACTION	DECIMAL	FRACTION	DECIMAL	FRACTION	DECIMAL	FRACTION	DECIMAL
1/64	.015625	17/64	.265625	33/64	.515625	49/64	.765625
1/32	.03125	9/32	.28125	17/32	.53125	25/32	.78125
3/64	.046875	19/64	.296875	35/64	.546875	51/64	.796875
1/16	.0625	5/16	.3125	9/16	.5625	13/16	.8125
5/64	.078125	21/64	.328125	37/64	.578125	53/64	.828125
3/32	.09375	11/32	.34375	19/32	.59375	27/32	.84375
7/64	.109375	23/64	.359375	39/64	.609375	55/64	.859375
1/8	.125	3/8	.375	5/8	.625	7/8	.875
9/64	.140625	25/64	.390625	41/64	.640625	57/64	.890625
5/32	.15625	13/32	.40625	21/32	.65625	29/32	.90625
11/64	.171875	27/64	.421875	43/64	.671875	59/64	.921875
3/16	.1875	7/16	.4375	11/16	.6875	15/16	.9375
13/64	.203125	29/64	.453125	45/64	.703125	61/64	.953125
7/32	.21875	15/32	.46875	23/32	.71875	31/32	.96875
15/64	.234375	31/64	.484375	47/64	.734375	63/64	.984375
1/4	.250	1/2	.500	3/4	.750	1	1.000

SHEET METAL — TRAINEE TASK MODULE 04304

APPENDIX F

Approximate Lengths of Bend Allowances (Inches) For Small Radii in Thin Metal

Angle, deg	Inside Radius, in.																							
	0.000	0.007	0.010	0.015	0.020	0.025	0.000	0.007	0.010	0.015	0.020	0.025	0.000	0.007	0.010	0.015	0.020	0.025	0.000	0.007	0.010	0.015	0.020	0.025
	0.010-in. Metal Thickness						0.016-in. Metal Thickness						0.020-in. Metal Thickness						0.025-in. Metal Thickness					
1	......	......	......	......	......	0.001	......	......	......	......	......	0.001	......	......	......	......	......	0.001	......	......	......	......	......	0.001
2	......	......	......	0.001	0.001	0.001	......	......	0.001	0.001	0.001	0.001	......	......	0.001	0.001	0.001	0.001	......	......	0.001	0.001	0.001	0.001
3	......	0.001	0.001	0.001	0.001	0.002	......	0.001	0.001	0.001	0.001	0.002	......	0.001	0.001	0.001	0.001	0.002	......	0.001	0.001	0.001	0.001	0.002
4	......	0.001	0.001	0.001	0.002	0.002	......	0.001	0.001	0.001	0.002	0.002	......	0.001	0.001	0.002	0.002	0.002	0.001	0.001	0.001	0.002	0.002	0.002
5	......	0.001	0.001	0.002	0.002	0.003	......	0.001	0.001	0.002	0.002	0.003	0.001	0.001	0.001	0.002	0.002	0.003	0.001	0.001	0.002	0.002	0.002	0.003
6	......	0.001	0.001	0.002	0.003	0.003	0.001	0.001	0.002	0.002	0.003	0.003	0.001	0.001	0.002	0.002	0.003	0.003	0.001	0.002	0.002	0.003	0.003	0.003
7	......	0.001	0.002	0.002	0.003	0.004	0.001	0.001	0.002	0.002	0.003	0.004	0.001	0.002	0.002	0.003	0.003	0.004	0.001	0.002	0.002	0.003	0.003	0.004
8	......	0.001	0.002	0.002	0.003	0.004	0.001	0.002	0.002	0.003	0.004	0.004	0.001	0.002	0.002	0.003	0.004	0.004	0.001	0.002	0.003	0.003	0.004	0.005
9	......	0.002	0.002	0.003	0.004	0.005	0.001	0.002	0.002	0.003	0.004	0.005	0.001	0.002	0.003	0.003	0.004	0.005	0.001	0.002	0.003	0.004	0.004	0.005
10	......	0.002	0.002	0.003	0.004	0.005	0.001	0.002	0.003	0.003	0.004	0.005	0.001	0.002	0.003	0.004	0.005	0.006	0.001	0.003	0.003	0.004	0.005	0.006
20	0.001	0.003	0.005	0.006	0.009	0.010	0.002	0.004	0.005	0.007	0.009	0.010	0.002	0.005	0.006	0.008	0.009	0.011	0.003	0.005	0.006	0.008	0.010	0.012
30	0.001	0.005	0.007	0.009	0.013	0.015	0.003	0.006	0.008	0.010	0.013	0.016	0.004	0.007	0.009	0.012	0.014	0.017	0.004	0.008	0.009	0.012	0.015	0.017
40	0.002	0.007	0.009	0.013	0.017	0.021	0.003	0.009	0.010	0.014	0.017	0.021	0.005	0.010	0.012	0.015	0.019	0.022	0.006	0.010	0.013	0.016	0.020	0.023
50	0.002	0.008	0.011	0.016	0.022	0.026	0.004	0.011	0.013	0.017	0.022	0.026	0.006	0.012	0.015	0.019	0.024	0.028	0.007	0.013	0.016	0.020	0.024	0.029
60	0.003	0.010	0.014	0.019	0.026	0.031	0.005	0.013	0.016	0.020	0.026	0.031	0.007	0.015	0.018	0.023	0.028	0.034	0.008	0.016	0.019	0.024	0.029	0.035
70	0.003	0.012	0.016	0.022	0.030	0.037	0.006	0.015	0.018	0.024	0.030	0.037	0.009	0.017	0.021	0.027	0.033	0.039	0.010	0.018	0.022	0.028	0.034	0.040
80	0.004	0.014	0.019	0.025	0.035	0.042	0.007	0.017	0.021	0.028	0.034	0.042	0.010	0.020	0.024	0.031	0.038	0.045	0.011	0.021	0.025	0.032	0.039	0.046
90	0.005	0.016	0.021	0.028	0.039	0.047	0.008	0.020	0.024	0.030	0.039	0.047	0.011	0.022	0.027	0.035	0.042	0.050	0.013	0.024	0.028	0.036	0.044	0.056
	0.032-in. Metal Thickness						0.040-in. Metal Thickness						0.051-in. Metal Thickness						0.064-in. Metal Thickness					
3/4	......	......	......	......	......	......	......	......	......	......	......	......	......	......	......	......	......	0.001	......	......	......	......	0.001	0.001
1	......	......	......	......	0.001	0.001	......	......	......	......	0.001	0.001	......	......	......	0.001	0.001	0.001	......	......	......	0.001	0.001	0.001
2	......	0.001	0.001	0.001	0.001	0.001	......	0.001	0.001	0.001	0.001	0.001	0.001	0.001	0.001	0.001	0.001	0.001	0.001	0.001	0.001	0.001	0.001	0.002
3	......	0.001	0.001	0.001	0.002	0.002	0.001	0.001	0.001	0.001	0.002	0.002	0.001	0.001	0.001	0.002	0.002	0.002	0.001	0.001	0.002	0.002	0.002	0.002
4	......	0.001	0.001	0.002	0.002	0.003	0.001	0.001	0.002	0.002	0.002	0.003	0.001	0.002	0.002	0.002	0.003	0.003	0.001	0.002	0.002	0.003	0.003	0.003
5	......	0.002	0.002	0.002	0.003	0.003	0.001	0.002	0.002	0.003	0.003	0.003	0.002	0.002	0.002	0.003	0.003	0.004	0.002	0.002	0.003	0.003	0.004	0.004
6	0.001	0.002	0.002	0.003	0.003	0.004	0.001	0.002	0.002	0.003	0.003	0.004	0.002	0.003	0.003	0.003	0.004	0.005	0.002	0.003	0.003	0.004	0.004	0.005
7	0.001	0.002	0.003	0.003	0.004	0.004	0.002	0.002	0.003	0.003	0.004	0.005	0.002	0.003	0.003	0.004	0.005	0.005	0.003	0.003	0.004	0.004	0.005	0.006
8	0.002	0.003	0.003	0.004	0.004	0.005	0.002	0.003	0.003	0.004	0.005	0.005	0.002	0.003	0.004	0.004	0.005	0.006	0.003	0.004	0.004	0.005	0.006	0.006
9	0.002	0.003	0.003	0.004	0.005	0.006	0.002	0.003	0.003	0.004	0.005	0.006	0.003	0.004	0.004	0.005	0.006	0.007	0.003	0.004	0.005	0.006	0.006	0.007
10	0.002	0.003	0.004	0.005	0.005	0.006	0.002	0.004	0.004	0.005	0.006	0.007	0.003	0.004	0.005	0.006	0.006	0.007	0.004	0.005	0.005	0.006	0.007	0.008
20	0.004	0.006	0.007	0.009	0.011	0.013	0.005	0.007	0.008	0.010	0.012	0.013	0.006	0.008	0.009	0.011	0.013	0.015	0.007	0.010	0.011	0.013	0.014	0.016
30	0.006	0.009	0.011	0.014	0.016	0.019	0.007	0.010	0.012	0.015	0.017	0.020	0.009	0.013	0.014	0.017	0.019	0.022	0.011	0.015	0.016	0.019	0.021	0.024
40	0.008	0.013	0.015	0.018	0.022	0.025	0.009	0.014	0.016	0.020	0.023	0.027	0.012	0.017	0.019	0.022	0.026	0.029	0.015	0.020	0.022	0.025	0.029	0.032
50	0.010	0.016	0.018	0.023	0.027	0.031	0.011	0.017	0.020	0.024	0.029	0.033	0.015	0.021	0.024	0.028	0.032	0.037	0.018	0.024	0.027	0.031	0.036	0.040
60	0.012	0.019	0.022	0.027	0.032	0.038	0.014	0.021	0.024	0.029	0.035	0.040	0.018	0.025	0.028	0.034	0.039	0.044	0.022	0.029	0.032	0.038	0.043	0.048
70	0.013	0.022	0.026	0.032	0.038	0.044	0.016	0.024	0.028	0.034	0.040	0.046	0.021	0.029	0.033	0.039	0.045	0.051	0.026	0.034	0.038	0.044	0.050	0.056
80	0.015	0.025	0.029	0.036	0.043	0.050	0.018	0.028	0.032	0.039	0.046	0.053	0.024	0.034	0.038	0.044	0.052	0.059	0.029	0.039	0.043	0.050	0.057	0.064
90	0.017	0.028	0.033	0.041	0.049	0.057	0.020	0.031	0.036	0.044	0.052	0.060	0.027	0.038	0.042	0.050	0.058	0.066	0.033	0.044	0.049	0.057	0.064	0.072

Courtesy Society for Manufacturing Engineers
Dearborn, MI from Die Design Handbook, 2nd Edition

APPENDIX G

ALLOWANCES FOR BENDS IN SHEET METAL (INCHES)

Radius, in.	Allowance*	\multicolumn{12}{c}{Thickness of Material, in.}
		0.015	0.018	0.020	0.024	0.025	0.030	0.032	0.036	0.040	0.047	0.051	0.060
1/32	D	0.032	0.035	0.038	0.043	0.044	0.052	0.055	0.060	0.065	0.074	0.080	0.091
	E	0.061	0.063	0.065	0.068	0.069	0.070	0.072	0.074	0.077	0.082	0.085	0.091
	F	0.002	−0.001	−0.002	−0.005	−0.006	−0.008	−0.009	−0.012	−0.015	−0.020	−0.022	−0.029
	G	0.00068	0.00070	0.00072	0.00075	0.00076	0.00078	0.00080	0.00083	0.00086	0.00091	0.00094	0.00101
1/16	D	0.045	0.049	0.051	0.056	0.057	0.063	0.066	0.070	0.075	0.084	0.089	0.105
	E	0.110	0.112	0.114	0.117	0.118	0.122	0.123	0.126	0.130	0.135	0.138	0.140
	F	0.015	0.013	0.011	0.008	0.007	0.003	0.002	−0.002	−0.005	−0.010	−0.013	−0.015
	G	0.00122	0.00125	0.00126	0.00130	0.00131	0.00135	0.00137	0.00140	0.00144	0.00150	0.00154	0.00156
3/32	D	0.058	0.062	0.064	0.069	0.071	0.007	0.079	0.084	0.089	0.097	0.102	0.113
	E	0.159	0.161	0.163	0.166	0.167	0.171	0.172	0.176	0.179	0.184	0.187	0.194
	F	0.028	0.026	0.024	0.021	0.021	0.017	0.015	0.012	0.009	0.003	0.000	−0.007
	G	0.00177	0.00179	0.00181	0.00184	0.00185	0.00190	0.00191	0.00195	0.00198	0.00204	0.00208	0.00216
1/8	D	0.072	0.076	0.078	0.083	0.084	0.090	0.093	0.097	0.102	0.111	0.116	0.126
	E	0.208	0.210	0.212	0.215	0.216	0.220	0.222	0.225	0.228	0.233	0.236	0.243
	F	0.042	0.040	0.038	0.035	0.034	0.030	0.028	0.025	0.022	0.017	0.014	0.006
	G	0.00231	0.00234	0.00236	0.00239	0.00240	0.00244	0.00246	0.00250	0.00253	0.00259	0.00263	0.00270
5/32	D	0.085	0.089	0.091	0.096	0.097	0.104	0.106	0.111	0.116	0.124	0.129	0.140
	E	0.257	0.260	0.261	0.264	0.265	0.269	0.270	0.274	0.277	0.282	0.286	0.292
	F	0.055	0.053	0.051	0.048	0.047	0.043	0.042	0.039	0.036	0.030	0.027	0.020
	G	0.00286	0.00288	0.00290	0.00294	0.00294	0.00299	0.00300	0.00304	0.00308	0.00314	0.00317	0.00325
3/16	D	0.099	0.102	0.105	0.110	0.111	0.117	0.119	0.124	0.129	0.138	0.142	0.153
	E	0.306	0.309	0.310	0.313	0.314	0.318	0.320	0.323	0.327	0.331	0.335	0.342
	F	0.069	0.066	0.065	0.062	0.061	0.057	0.055	0.052	0.049	0.044	0.040	0.034
	G	0.00340	0.00343	0.00345	0.00348	0.00349	0.00353	0.00355	0.00358	0.00362	0.00368	0.00372	0.00379
7/32	D	0.112	0.116	0.118	0.123	0.125	0.130	0.133	0.138	0.142	0.151	0.156	0.167
	E	0.355	0.358	0.359	0.362	0.363	0.367	0.369	0.372	0.375	0.380	0.384	0.391
	F	0.082	0.080	0.078	0.075	0.074	0.070	0.069	0.066	0.062	0.057	0.054	0.047
	G	0.00395	0.00398	0.00399	0.00403	0.00404	0.00408	0.00410	0.00413	0.00417	0.00423	0.00426	0.00434

ALLOWANCES FOR BENDS IN SHEET METAL (INCHES)
Continued

Radius, in.	Allowance*	Thickness of Material, in.												
		0.064	0.072	0.075	0.081	0.090	0.102	0.105	0.125	0.134	0.156	0.187	0.250
1/32	D E F G	0.097 0.094 −0.031 0.00104											
1/16	D E F G	0.110 0.143 −0.018 0.00159	0.102 0.149 −0.024 0.00165	0.124 0.151 −0.026 0.00168	0.132 0.155 −0.030 0.00172	0.144 0.161 −0.036 0.00179	0.159 0.170 −0.045 0.00189	0.163 0.172 −0.047 0.00191	0.189 0.186 −0.061 0.00217				
3/32	D E F G	0.118 0.198 −0.010 0.00219	0.128 0.204 −0.016 0.00226	0.131 0.206 −0.019 0.00229	0.142 0.208 −0.021 0.00231	0.157 0.210 −0.023 0.00234	0.173 0.219 −0.031 0.00243	0.177 0.221 −0.033 0.00246	0.203 0.235 −0.047 0.00261	0.214 0.241 −0.054 0.00268	0.243 0.257 −0.069 0.00285	0.283 0.278 −0.091 0.00310	0.365 0.322 −0.135 0.00359
1/8	D E F G	0.131 0.247 0.003 0.00274	0.141 0.253 −0.003 0.00281	0.145 0.255 −0.005 0.00283	0.152 0.260 −0.010 0.00289	0.163 0.267 −0.017 0.00296	0.177 0.277 −0.027 0.00307	0.181 0.279 −0.029 0.00310	0.216 0.284 −0.034 0.00316	0.228 0.290 −0.040 0.00323	0.256 0.306 −0.056 0.00340	0.297 0.327 −0.077 0.00364	0.378 0.372 −0.122 0.00413
5/32	D E F G	0.145 0.296 0.017 0.00328	0.154 0.302 0.010 0.00335	0.158 0.304 0.008 0.00338	0.166 0.309 0.004 0.00343	0.176 0.316 −0.004 0.00351	0.091 0.326 −0.013 0.00362	0.195 0.328 −0.015 0.00364	0.219 0.346 −0.031 0.00382	0.230 0.350 −0.038 0.00389	0.270 0.355 −0.042 0.00394	0.310 0.376 −0.064 0.00429	0.392 0.421 −0.108 0.00468
3/16	D E F G	0.158 0.345 0.030 0.00383	0.168 0.351 0.024 0.00390	0.172 0.353 0.022 0.00392	0.179 0.358 0.017 0.00398	0.190 0.365 0.010 0.00406	0.204 0.375 0.000 0.00416	0.208 0.377 −0.002 0.00419	0.232 0.393 −0.008 0.00436	0.243 0.400 −0.015 0.00444	0.277 0.410 −0.042 0.00463	0.324 0.426 −0.051 0.00473	0.405 0.470 −0.095 0.00522
7/32	D E F G	0.172 0.394 0.044 0.00437	0.181 0.400 0.037 0.00444	0.185 0.402 0.035 0.00447	0.192 0.407 0.030 0.00452	0.203 0.414 0.023 0.00460	0.218 0.424 0.014 0.00471	0.221 0.426 0.013 0.00473	0.246 0.442 −0.004 0.00491	0.257 0.449 −0.011 0.00498	0.283 0.466 −0.029 0.00518	0.329 0.490 −0.053 0.00544	0.419 0.519 −0.081 0.00577

ALLOWANCES FOR BENDS IN SHEET METAL (INCHES)
Continued

Radius, in.	Allowance*	\multicolumn{12}{c}{Thickness of Material, in.}
		0.015	0.018	0.020	0.024	0.025	0.030	0.032	0.036	0.040	0.047	0.051	0.060
1/4	D	0.126	0.129	0.132	0.136	0.138	0.144	0.146	0.151	0.156	0.164	0.169	0.180
	E	0.404	0.407	0.408	0.412	0.412	0.416	0.418	0.421	0.424	0.430	0.433	0.440
	F	0.096	0.093	0.092	0.088	0.088	0.084	0.082	0.079	0.076	0.070	0.067	0.060
	G	0.00449	0.00452	0.00454	0.00457	0.00458	0.00462	0.00464	0.00468	0.00471	0.00477	0.00481	0.00488
9/32	D	0.139	0.143	0.145	0.150	0.151	0.157	0.160	0.164	0.169	0.178	0.183	0.194
	E	0.454	0.456	0.458	0.461	0.461	0.465	0.467	0.470	0.473	0.479	0.482	0.489
	F	0.109	0.107	0.105	0.102	0.101	0.097	0.096	0.092	0.089	0.084	0.081	0.074
	G	0.00504	0.00507	0.00508	0.00512	0.00513	0.00517	0.00519	0.00522	0.00526	0.00532	0.00535	0.00543
5/16	D	0.152	0.156	0.158	0.163	0.164	0.170	0.173	0.178	0.183	0.191	0.196	0.207
	E	0.503	0.505	0.507	0.510	0.511	0.514	0.516	0.519	0.522	0.528	0.531	0.538
	F	0.122	0.120	0.118	0.115	0.114	0.110	0.109	0.106	0.103	0.097	0.094	0.087
	G	0.00558	0.00561	0.00563	0.00566	0.00567	0.00571	0.00573	0.00577	0.00580	0.00586	0.00590	0.00598
11/32	D	0.166	0.169	0.172	0.177	0.178	0.184	0.186	0.191	0.196	0.205	0.209	0.220
	E	0.552	0.554	0.556	0.559	0.560	0.564	0.565	0.568	0.571	0.577	0.580	0.587
	F	0.136	0.133	0.132	0.129	0.128	0.124	0.122	0.119	0.116	0.111	0.107	0.100
	G	0.00613	0.00616	0.00617	0.00621	0.00622	0.00626	0.00628	0.00631	0.00635	0.00641	0.00644	0.00652
3/8	D	0.179	0.183	0.185	0.190	0.191	0.197	0.200	0.205	0.210	0.218	0.223	0.234
	E	0.601	0.603	0.605	0.608	0.609	0.613	0.614	0.617	0.620	0.626	0.629	0.636
	F	0.149	0.147	0.145	0.142	0.141	0.137	0.136	0.133	0.130	0.124	0.121	0.114
	G	0.00667	0.00670	0.00672	0.00675	0.00676	0.00681	0.00682	0.00686	0.00689	0.00695	0.00699	0.00707
7/16	D	0.206	0.210	0.212	0.217	0.218	0.224	0.227	0.232	0.236	0.245	0.250	0.261
	E	0.699	0.701	0.703	0.706	0.707	0.711	0.712	0.716	0.719	0.724	0.727	0.734
	F	0.176	0.174	0.172	0.169	0.168	0.164	0.163	0.160	0.156	0.151	0.148	0.141
	G	0.00777	0.00779	0.00781	0.00784	0.00785	0.00790	0.00791	0.00795	0.00798	0.00804	0.00808	0.00816
1/2	D	0.233	0.236	0.239	0.244	0.245	0.251	0.254	0.258	0.263	0.272	0.276	0.287
	E	0.797	0.800	0.801	0.804	0.805	0.809	0.810	0.814	0.817	0.822	0.826	0.832
	F	0.203	0.200	0.199	0.196	0.195	0.191	0.190	0.186	0.183	0.178	0.174	0.168
	G	0.00886	0.00888	0.00890	0.00894	0.00895	0.00899	0.00900	0.00904	0.00908	0.00914	0.00917	0.00925

Tests conducted and data prepared by H.L. Smith and R.J. Gabler.
* See accompanying text for explanation of types D, E, F, and G allowances.

Courtesy Society for Manufacturing Engineers
Dearborn, MI from *Die Design Handbook*, 2nd Edition

ALLOWANCES FOR BENDS IN SHEET METAL (INCHES)
Continued

Radius, in.	Allowance*	\multicolumn{12}{c}{Thickness of Material, in.}
		0.064	0.072	0.075	0.081	0.090	0.102	0.105	0.125	0.134	0.156	0.187	0.250
1/4	D	0.185	0.195	0.198	0.206	0.217	0.231	0.235	0.259	0.270	0.297	0.350	0.432
	E	0.443	0.449	0.452	0.456	0.463	0.479	0.475	0.491	0.498	0.515	0.524	0.568
	F	0.057	0.051	0.048	0.044	0.037	0.027	0.025	0.009	0.002	−0.015	−0.024	−0.068
	G	0.00492	0.00499	0.00502	0.00507	0.00515	0.00525	0.00528	0.00545	0.00553	0.00572	0.00582	0.00631
9/32	D	0.198	0.208	0.212	0.219	0.230	0.244	0.248	0.272	0.284	0.310	0.364	0.446
	E	0.492	0.498	0.501	0.505	0.512	0.522	0.524	0.540	0.547	0.564	0.573	0.617
	F	0.071	0.064	0.062	0.057	0.050	0.040	0.038	0.022	0.016	−0.002	−0.010	−0.054
	G	0.00546	0.00554	0.00556	0.00561	0.00569	0.00580	0.00582	0.00600	0.00608	0.00627	0.00637	0.00686
5/16	D	0.212	0.222	0.225	0.232	0.243	0.258	0.262	0.286	0.297	0.324	0.377	0.459
	E	0.541	0.548	0.550	0.554	0.562	0.571	0.573	0.589	0.596	0.613	0.622	0.666
	F	0.084	0.078	0.075	0.070	0.063	0.054	0.052	0.036	0.029	0.012	0.003	−0.041
	G	0.00601	0.00608	0.00611	0.00616	0.00624	0.00634	0.00637	0.00654	0.00662	0.00681	0.00691	0.00740
11/32	D	0.225	0.235	0.239	0.246	0.257	0.271	0.275	0.299	0.310	0.337	0.383	0.472
	E	0.590	0.597	0.599	0.604	0.611	0.620	0.622	0.638	0.645	0.662	0.679	0.715
	F	0.097	0.091	0.089	0.084	0.077	0.067	0.065	0.049	0.042	0.025	0.008	−0.029
	G	0.00656	0.00663	0.00665	0.00670	0.00678	0.00689	0.00691	0.00709	0.00717	0.00736	0.00754	0.00795
3/8	D	0.239	0.248	0.252	0.259	0.270	0.285	0.288	0.313	0.324	0.350	0.388	0.486
	E	0.639	0.646	0.648	0.653	0.660	0.669	0.672	0.687	0.694	0.712	0.736	0.764
	F	0.111	0.104	0.102	0.097	0.090	0.081	0.078	0.063	0.056	0.038	0.014	−0.014
	G	0.00710	0.00717	0.00720	0.00725	0.00733	0.00743	0.00746	0.00763	0.00771	0.00790	0.00817	0.00850
7/16	D	0.266	0.275	0.279	0.286	0.297	0.312	0.315	0.340	0.351	0.377	0.415	0.502
	E	0.737	0.744	0.746	0.751	0.758	0.767	0.770	0.785	0.792	0.810	0.834	0.873
	F	0.138	0.131	0.129	0.124	0.117	0.108	0.105	0.090	0.083	0.065	0.041	0.002
	G	0.00819	0.00826	0.00829	0.00834	0.00842	0.00852	0.00855	0.00872	0.00880	0.00899	0.00926	0.00970
1/2	D	0.292	0.302	0.306	0.313	0.324	0.338	0.342	0.366	0.377	0.404	0.442	0.518
	E	0.836	0.842	0.844	0.849	0.856	0.866	0.868	0.884	0.891	0.908	0.932	0.982
	F	0.164	0.158	0.156	0.151	0.144	0.134	0.132	0.116	0.109	0.092	0.068	0.018
	G	0.00928	0.00935	0.00938	0.00943	0.00951	0.00962	0.00964	0.00982	0.00989	0.01008	0.01035	0.01090

Courtesy Society for Manufacturing Engineers
Dearborn, MI from *Die Design Handbook*, 2nd Edition

NCCER CRAFT TRAINING USER UPDATES

The NCCER makes every effort to keep these manuals up-to-date and free of technical errors. We appreciate your help in this process. If you have an idea for improving this manual, or if you find an error, a typographical mistake, or an inaccuracy in the NCCER's Craft Training Manuals, please write us, using this form or a photocopy. Be sure to include the exact module number, page number, a description of the problem, and the correction, if possible. Your input will be brought to the attention of the Technical Review Committee. Thank you for your assistance.

Instructors – If you found that additional materials were necessary in order to teach this module effectively, please let us know so that we may include them in the Equipment/Materials list in the Instructor's Guide.

Write: Curriculum and Revision Department
National Center for Construction Education and Research
P.O. Box 141104
Gainesville, FL 32614-1104
Fax: 352-334-0932

Craft _____ Module Name _____

Module Number _____ Page Number(s) _____

Description of Problem
_____
_____
_____
_____
_____

(Optional) Correction of Problem
_____
_____
_____

(Optional) Your Name and Address
_____
_____
_____

Soldering
Module 04312

NATIONAL
CENTER FOR
CONSTRUCTION
EDUCATION AND
RESEARCH

Task Module 04312

SOLDERING

Objective

Upon completion of this task module, the trainee will be able to identify, use, and skillfully manipulate soldering tools and materials.

INTRODUCTION

Nonferrous metal solders are used for fastening many types of sheet metal parts and for sealing seams. In order to do a professional job of soldering, sheet metal workers must know the kind of material being soldered, the kind of solder and flux best suited to the job, and the proper tools for completing a specific job. The information in this module provides reasons for performing the various steps involved in soldering practices and lists the proper procedures for completing the selected tasks.

Copyright © 1992 National Center for Construction Education and Research, Gainesville, FL All rights reserved. No part of this work may be reproduced in any form or by any means, including photocopying, without written permission of the publisher. Updated: 1998.

USES OF SOLDERING

Soldering is a procedure which fastens metals together with a nonferrous metal of low melting point which adheres to the surface being joined. Soldering has been defined by the American Welding Society (AWS) as "a group of welding processes which produces coalescence of materials by heating them to a suitable temperature and by using a filler metal having a liquidus not exceeding 450° C (840° F) and below the solidus of the base metal." The filler metal is distributed between the closely fitted surfaces by capillary attraction. If the solder melts above temperatures of 840° F the process is called hard soldering or brazing.

Soft soldering is of little value where strength is required and is usually used as a sealing process. Due to the low melting range of soft solders (350° to 800° F), the use of a soldering copper is usually preferred to open flame heat sources.

Hard soldering, sometimes referred to as "silver soldering," is a process between soft soldering and braze welding. The term "silver soldering" comes from the fact that at least 5 percent of silver is one of the alloys of the filler metal. Silver soldering can be used as a sealer (like soft soldering) but is superior due to its high strength and resistance to corrosion.

Because of its strength and resistance to corrosion, silver soldering is very satisfactory for making electrical and refrigeration piping connections. The oxyacetylene flame is a good heat source since temperatures up to 1100° F (590° C) are required. The proper joint design and heat application will produce welds with strengths up to 60,000 psi.

This module will be directed toward the soft soldering process as it applies to sheet metal sealing and fastening practices. Solders generally have lower strength properties than the materials to which they are joined. Thus, structurally loaded joints must be carefully evaluated so that they will be capable of standing up to the applied stresses for the necessary period of time.

Base metal properties have a strong influence on joint design and workers must have a complete understanding of the part or assembly and its intended function in order to select the best joint design, solder, and material. As service or load stresses increase, particular attention should be given to the joint by placing it in a low stress area, by supporting the joint mechanically, and by using a higher strength solder.

Soldering is particularly useful and effective as a means of securing electrical connections, joining sheet metal, and sealing seams against leakage. Soldering can be used to join iron, nickel, lead, tin, copper, zinc, aluminum, many alloys, and, of course, galvanized sheet metal.

SAFETY CONCERNS

Soldering is a safe operation when health and safety practices are followed. Each operation should be carefully studied and necessary safety precautions taken for that particular job.

Possible sources of injury are heat, chemicals, fumes, and electrical hazards. Efficient soldering area ventilation, operator burn protection, and training in the handling of materials will be effective in making the soldering operation safe. Safety glasses should always be worn.

Personal carelessness is one hazard which cannot be covered by rules and regulations, but can be combatted by constant care and vigilance.

Since soldering requires heat, the usual precautions should be taken to prevent burns while handling hot objects. Proper clothing, face protection, and safety glasses or goggles should be worn to ensure personal safety.

Gases and gas-handling equipment are potential hazards and should be used carefully. Equipment must be kept clean and in good working condition. Worn hoses should be replaced and connections must be kept tight and leakproof. Hoses must be kept away from the flame and heated metal. Pliers or pipe wrenches must never be used as connections on regulators.

A torch should never be used on tanks or containers which have contained flammable material until the tank has been thoroughly cleaned and properly purged. Cleaning should be done by high pressure water, hot chemicals, or steam.

After cleaning, the tank may be purged by inserting a hose from a tank of carbon dioxide or nitrogen. If the opening or vent is large enough, cakes of dry ice may also be used. The inert gases, carbon dioxide or nitrogen, should have a concentration mixture of 50 to 80 percent depending upon the flammable material previously in the container.

Do not use carbon monoxide as a purging agent. All tanks and containers should be vented. The operator should never enter tanks or confined spaces unless stringent ventilation and other safety precautions have been observed.

Fumes arise from fluxes and other foreign materials on the surface of the base metal. These residues emit smoke and other fumes which may be annoying, irritating, or toxic. Smoke given off by fluxes such as rosin and petrolatum have been evaluated by the American Conference of Governmental Industrial Hygienists. This organization has established threshold limit values for pyrolysis products of rosin core solder of 0.1 cubic mg/m aliphatic aldehydes, measured as formaldehyde. This standard has not been incorporated by OSHA.

Prolonged inhalation of halides and some of the more recent organic fluxes should be avoided. Aniline and amine type fluxes emit fumes which can cause skin rash.

As previously mentioned, cadmium, lead, zinc metals, and their oxides are toxic when present in the form of fumes or dusts. Adequate ventilation is an absolute necessity for control of fumes and smoke hazards.

Precautions must be taken in the handling and use of acids, alkalis, and other chemicals to avoid getting them on the skin and eyes or equipment. These chemicals can produce burns, cause skin rash, and create other irritations if allowed to come in contact with the eyes or skin and can cause erosion if allowed to get on equipment. Exposed parts must be washed promptly to reduce the effects of the acids and alkalis.

Some chemicals deserve special attention. Zinc chloride can produce severe burns if allowed to remain on the skin for any length of time. The use of carbon tetrachloride, which has been used as a cleaner and degreaser, should be discontinued.

All solders, fluxes, cleaners, and chemicals contain materials which must not be ingested; therefore, operators should be cautioned to wash their hands thoroughly after handling these materials.

SOLDERS

An understanding of the nature of solders and their selection for specific application can be obtained by examining the melting characteristics of soldering metals and alloys. Pure metals transform from solid to liquid state at one temperature, but the melting of alloys is more complicated because they may melt over a range of temperatures. The most effective solder is produced by alloying lead and tin in various percentages. All standard cleaning, fluxing, and soldering techniques can be used with these solders.

A good grade of 50-50 tin-lead solder is generally used for all applications at room temperatures. These tin-lead solders are also used for wiping and sweating solders. Tin-lead solders are classified by a combination number-letter system *(Table 1)*. When the tin content is increased, the flow of the solder and its wetting (tinning) characteristics are increased.

ASTM ALLOY GRADE	TIN % DESIRED	LEAD % NOMINAL	COMPLETELY SOLID SOLIDUS °C	COMPLETELY SOLID SOLIDUS °F	COMPLETELY LIQUID LIQUIDUS °C	COMPLETELY LIQUID LIQUIDUS °F
70A	70	30	183	361	192	378
70B	70	30	183	361	183	361
63A	63	37	183	361	190	374
63B	63	37	183	361	183	361
60A	60	40	183	361	216	421
60B	60	40	183	361	183	361
50A	50	50	183	361	227	441
50B	50	50	183	361	183	361
45A	45	55	183	361	238	460
45B	45	55	183	361	183	361
40A	40	60	185	365	231	448
40B	40	60	183	361	247	477
40C	40	58				
35A	35	65	185	365	243	470
35B	35	65	183	361	255	491
35C	35	63.2				
30A	30	70	185	365	250	482
30B	30	70	183	361	266	511
30C	30	68.4				
25A	25	75	184	364	263	504
25B	25	75	183	361	277	531
25C	25	73.7				
20B	20	80	184	363	270	517
20C	20	79				
15B	15	85	227	440	288	550
10B	10	90	268	514	299	570
5A	5	95	270	518	312	594
5B	5	95				
2A	2	98				

Courtesy: The American Welding Society

Table 1- Classification of Tin-Lead Solders

The classification range of solders is from 2A (2 percent tin and 98 percent lead), to 70A (70 percent tin and 30 percent lead). The 60A and 63A are generally referred to as fine solders and are used whenever temperature requirements are critical. The 70A solder is also a special purpose solder used where high tin content is necessary. All soldering techniques apply to the range of solders referred to.

Solders (*Figure 1*) are commercially available in various sizes and shapes. They come in about a dozen classifications, and in any desired size, weight, or shape by special order. The major groups are:

Pig — available in 50 and 100 pound pigs (22.5 and 45 kg.).

Cakes or ingots — rectangular or circular, 3.5 and 10 lb. (1.5 - 2.5 and 4.5 kg.).

Bars — available in many lengths, cross sections, and weights.

Paste — available as a powdered solder and suitable flux paste mixture.

Foil, sheet, or ribbon — available in various thicknesses and weights.

Segment or drop — triangular bar or wire cut into any length or number of pieces.

Wire, solid — available in spools .010 to .250 inch (.25 to 6.5 mm) diameter.

Wire-flux cored — available in spools .010 to .250 inch (.25 to 6.5 mm) in diameter and cored with rosin, organic, or inorganic fluxes.

Preforms — available in any size and shape to meet special requirements.

FLUXES

Soldering flux has been defined by the AWS as liquid, solid, or gaseous material which, when heated, is capable of promoting or accelerating the wetting of materials by solder.

The purpose of a soldering flux is to remove films and oxides from the base metal and solder, and to prevent reoxidation of the heated surfaces.

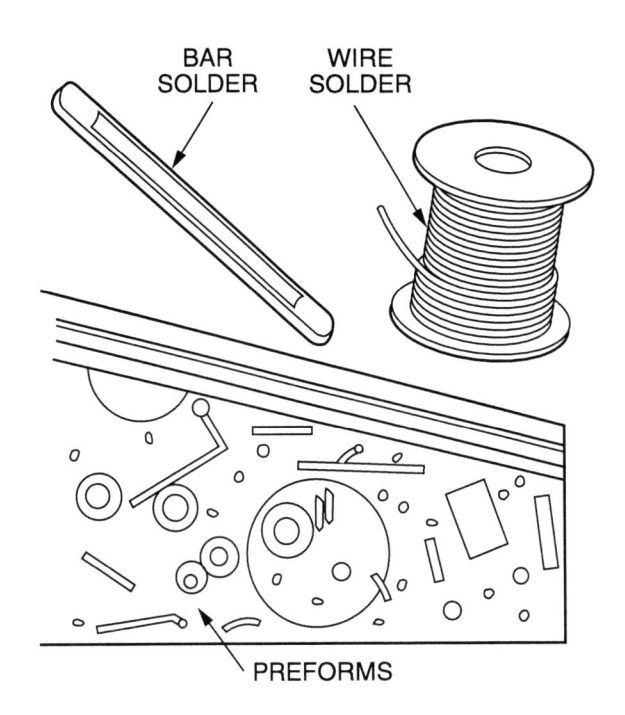

Figure 1 - Types of Solder

Fluxes (*Table 2*) are frequently classified on the basis of their residues and are divided into three main groups: corrosive, intermediate, and noncorrosive. The trainee should always choose the mildest flux that will perform satisfactorily in a specific application.

Corrosive fluxes are more versatile than other types of fluxes and can be applied as solutions, dry salts, or pastes. They work well with all heating methods since they do not char or burn. However, the residue may cause severe corrosion at the joint and are not used to solder closed containers such as thermostats or bellows nor to solder electrical connections.

The main ingredient in most corrosive fluxes is zinc chloride. It is usually prepared by adding zinc to the concentrated hydrochloric acid. Zinc chloride has a melting temperature well above the solidus temperature of most tin-lead solders which, if used alone, may allow unmelted salt particles to become entrapped in the joint. Therefore, zinc chloride should be mixed with other inorganic chlorides to lower the melting temperature of the flux.

SOLDERING — TRAINEE TASK MODULE 04312

TYPE	COMPOSITION	CARRIER	USES	CORROSIVENESS
INORGANIC Acids	Hydrochloric Hydrofluoric Orthophosphoric	Water, Petrolatum Paste	Structural	High
Salts	Zinc Chloride Ammonium Chloride Tin Chloride	Water, Petrolatum Paste, Polyethylene Glycol	Structural	High
ORGANIC Acids	Lactic, Oleic, Stearic Glutamic, Phthalic	Water, Organic Solvents, Petrolatum Paste, Polyethylene Glycol	Structural, Electrical	Moderate
Halogens	Aniline Hydrochloride, Glutamic Hydrochloride, Bromide Derivatives of Palmitic Acid, Hydrazine Hydrochloride (or Hydrobromide)	Same as Organic Acids	Structural, Electrical	Moderate
Amines and Amides	Urea, Ethylene Diamine	Water, Organic Solvents, Petrolatum Paste, Polyethylene Glycol	Structural, Electrical	Noncorrosive Normally
Activated Rosin	Water White Rosin	Isopropyl Alcohol, Organic Solvents, Polyethylene Glycol	Electrical	Noncorrosive Normally
Water White Rosin	Rosin Only	Same as Activated	Electrical	None

Courtesy: The American Welding Society

Table 2 - Flux Selection

SHEET METAL — TRAINEE TASK MODULE 04312

Hydrochloric acid is often known by the commercial name of "muriatic acid," but is usually called "raw acid" in the sheet metal shop. Muriatic acid comes in one strength only (medium); hydrochloric acid can be purchased in any strength.

Other ingredients of corrosive fluxes include ammonium chloride, sodium chloride, potassium chloride, hydrofloric acid, and orthophosphoric acid. Corrosive fluxes are recommended for those metals requiring a rapid and highly active fluxing action.

Intermediate fluxes are weaker than inorganic salt type fluxes. They consist mainly of organic acids such as lactic, citric, benzoic and oxalic and certain other derivatives such as hydrohalides, amines and others. They are useful in quick spot soldering operations and their residue is relatively inert and easily removed with water. Caution should be exercised where undecomposed flux may spread to insulated sleeving or in soldering closed systems where corrosive fumes may be left on critical parts. When fluxes are used on stranded wire, entrapment of the corrosive elements must be avoided.

Noncorrosive Fluxes

These fluxes all have rosin as a common ingredient. Rosin is unique in that it melts at 260° F (127° C) and remains active in the molten state up to 600° F (315° C).

Acetic acid, the active element of rosin, is inert in the solid state; it becomes active when molten, and returns to an inactive state when cooled. Due to the fact that the flux residue is noncorrosive and nonconductive, it is widely used in the electrical and electronics industry. Noncorrosive fluxes are also effective for use when soldering copper, brass, bronze, nickel, and silver connections and joints.

Generally speaking, when applied to mechanically cleaned surfaces, fluxes protect the surface from oxidation during heating, permit easy displacement by the filler metal so that it flows into the joint, floats out remaining oxides, and increases the wetting (tinning) action of the solder by decreasing its surface tension.

SOLDERING TOOLS

A heat source, such as a soldering iron or torch, solder and flux are needed for joining parts by the soft soldering process. The trainee must become familiar with the tools and processes necessary for making strong, effective, structurally loaded joints.

HEAT SOURCES

Soldering irons (*Figure 2*) are used to provide constant heat to joints ensuring that the parts are joined using minimal contact time. This procedure, therefore, safeguards components in close proximity and adjacent areas from being adversely affected by heat absorption.

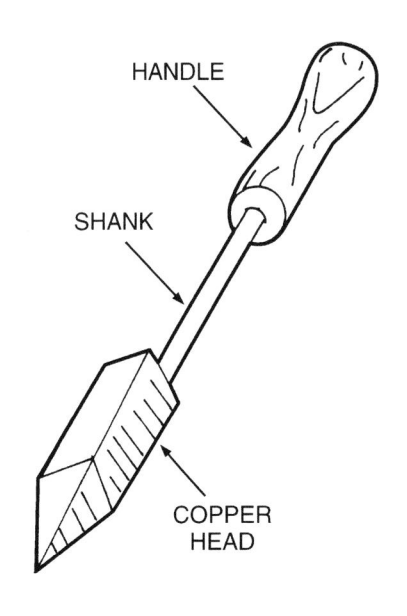

Figure 2 - Soldering Iron

Flame-heated soldering irons are chosen where electric power is not readily available, especially for sheet metal work.

Electrically heated irons are more convenient than gas heated irons especially for use in manual, high-speed, repetitive operations. Industrial soldering irons are available with both plug and screw tips and can be broadly divided into six groups:

1. Instrument irons
2. Medium duty industrial irons
3. Heavy duty industrial irons
4. Temperature irons
5. Transformer type pencil irons
6. Soldering guns

Instrument irons are designed for light duty soldering. They are available in a variety of both copper and iron plated tips to allow for matching the tip to the soldering operation.

Medium duty industrial irons are designed for continuous production operations and can withstand high-speed production use. They are also available with a wide tip and configuration selections.

Heavy duty industrial irons are designed for continuous, fast production use. These irons are available in a number of sizes and wattages to insure heat stability under heavy soldering loads.

Temperature controlled irons are available with sensors in the tips which react to small temperature changes matching the heat requirements of the work.

Transformer type pencil irons are designed for use in light soldering repair work and production operations. They are designed for less than 12 volts (AC) with a rheostat and/or voltage tip to regulate heat output.

Soldering guns are used for light, intermittent soldering of electrical connections. The operator does not have control of the heat output which could result in overheating connections and adjacent areas if the gun is not carefully used.

The properties required for soldering iron tips are:

1. They must have high thermal conductivity.
2. They must be easy to tin.
3. They must have low oxidation properties to insure good heat transfer and to prevent the tip from freezing in the soldering iron.
4. They must be resistant to corrosion.
5. They must be resistant to erosion by the molten solder.

Four basic types of tips that are used are:

1. Copper
2. Iron plated with coated shank
3. Iron plated with stainless steel shank
4. Calorized

Copper tips have high thermal conductivity and tinning properties but have the disadvantage of high oxidation and rapid erosion.

Iron plated tips with a coated shank are made of copper with iron electrodeposit over the entire tip. This tip has an extended life (20 to 50 times that of copper), but it reduces heat conductivity.

Iron plated tips with stainless steel shanks offer the same characteristics of the iron plated tip described above. Additionally, it does not allow the shank to freeze to the iron.

Calorized tips, created by diffusing aluminum into a copper tip, prevent high temperature oxidation and keep the soldering iron shanks from freezing. This type of tip is used primarily on screw tips in iron with internal cartridge type elements.

USE OF SOLDERING IRONS

One of the more important factors in delivering maximum heat to the work is the angle of the soldering iron tip. The flat side of the tip should be applied to the contact areas to ensure maximum heat transfer to the joint connections.

Flux cored solder should not be melted on the soldering iron and carried to the connection because flux effectiveness is reduced and defective connections may result. The solder should be touched to the soldering tip to begin good heat transfer and should then be melted on the work parts to complete the solder joint. The tip can be wiped clean on a wet sponge and the working surface should be kept tinned.

TORCH SOLDERING

Torch soldering is commonly used for plumbing and structural joints and in locations where electricity is not readily available. Torch selection and gas mixture are governed by size, amount of material, and configuration of the assembly to be soldered.

The torch flame will heat large masses of material quickly but is likely to burn or carbonize the flux. One way to prevent this problem is to preheat the assembly before applying the flux and solder. The high temperature of the flame may cause damage to sensitive components or adjacent areas and therefore should be carefully controlled.

DIP SOLDERING

Dip soldering is a useful and cost-effective method of soldering an entire unit. A fixture, made up of any number of joints, can be soldered by simply dipping the prefluxed part in a bath of molten solder. It is probably necessary to use jigs or fixtures to hold the unit and maintain proper joint clearance until the solder solidifies. Preliminary degreasing, cleaning, and fluxing of the unit is required before dip soldering.

SOLDERING PROCESSES

Basic steps in soldering include joint fit-up, precleaning, flux application, heat application, solder application, joint cooling, and joint cleaning of flux residue treatment.

1. Joint fit-up requires that the clearances between the parts being joined should be such that the solder can be drawn into the space between them by capillary action, but not so great that the solder cannot fill the gap. A clearance of .005" (.15mm) is suitable for most work, whereas a clearance of .001" (.025mm) is necessary where precoated metals are used.

2. Precleaning is necessary so that a clean, oxide-free surface is available to insure uniform quality and a soundly soldered joint. All grease, oil, dirt, and oxides must be carefully removed from the base metal.

3. Flux that is applied to the surfaces to be soldered should have the following characteristics.

    a. It should be fluid and effective in removing oxides and other impurities that might be present at soldering temperatures.

    b. It should be a barrier to reoxidation of the base metal.

    c. It should allow displacement of solder.

    d. It should promote tinning (wetting) of the surface.

4. The application of heat is the next step in the process after flux application.

5. Solder application takes place in two steps. The first step requires wetting the surfaces of the base metal and the second step fills the gap between the two surfaces with solder.

When molten solder leaves a continuous permanent film on the base metal, it is said to wet that surface. Wetting is often incorrectly referred to as "tinning." Wetting actually means pre-coating the base metal with solder, whether or not the solder contains tin. This wetting action is partly chemical in nature and is greatly facilitated by the ability of solder to bond to the base metal.

The two steps, tinning and soldering, can be carried out separately or together. Generally, however, it is better done separately because each condition can be more carefully controlled. It is usually better to precoat the base metal prior to soldering for best results.

After the joint has been tinned and soldered, the next step is to cool it to room temperature. The solder should be cooled and solidified as rapidly as possible. Slow cooling may result in embrittlement, and fast cooling from too high a temperature may cause warping and small fractures in the solder.

6. Cooling is done by conducting the heat away to the main mass of the assembly or by spraying the area with water or air.

7. After the soldered joint is completed and cooled, the flux residue should be removed if the degree of corrosiveness requires it. Rosin-base fluxes generally do not require removal unless appearance is important or the joint is to be painted or coated. Corrosive fluxes, such as those having zinc chloride, must be neutralized or removed.

SOLDERING JOINT DESIGN

Solders generally have lower-strength properties than the materials to which they are joined. Thus, structurally loaded joints must be evaluated carefully so that they will be capable of standing up to the applied stresses for the necessary period of time. Electrical conductivity is another important factor to be considered when selecting a suitable joint design or connection.

Base metal properties have a strong influence on joint design. The designer must have a complete understanding of the part or assembly and its intended function in order to select the best joint design, solder, and material. As service or load stresses increase, particular attention should be given to the joint by placing it in a low stress area, by supporting the joint mechanically, and by using a higher-strength solder.

The most desirable and widely used joint is the lap joint and is usually preferred by designers. Butt joints can be made, but have limited value. Many joint design variations are feasible as indicated in *Figure 3* and can be used for many and specialized applications.

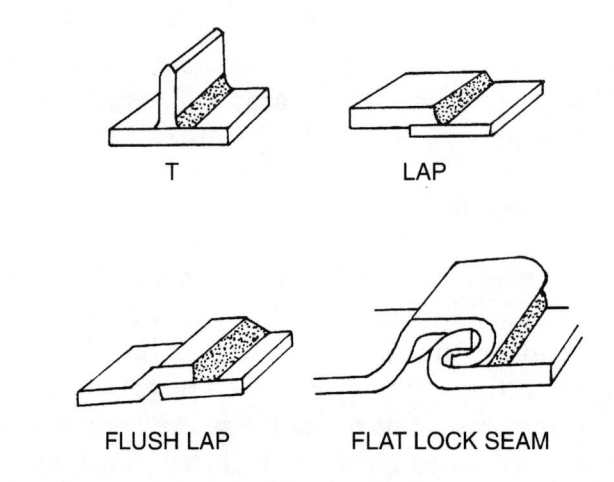

Figure 3 - Joint Design

Joint clearance is a critical factor for optimum performance. If the clearance is too small, inadequate solder flow, voids, and flux entrapment may result. On the other hand, if joint clearances are too large the capillary flow of the solder is impaired. If excessive heat is applied to the joint the solder runs out.

Correct joint clearance should achieve a balance between the competing processes of flux and solder flow, capillary action and solder retention. As previously stated, correct joint clearance should be .003 to .005 of an inch (.1 to .15 mm). Several factors affecting joint design which must be considered for sound joint production are:

1. A molten solder reservoir
2. A capillary feed path
3. Capillary entrance and exit zones
4. Even heating
5. Joint freedom to prevent flux entrapment

SURFACE PREPARATION

Proper precleaning and surface preparation are essential to successful soldering. Frequently encountered organic film, such as oil and grease, must be removed from the base metal because it prevents wetting action by the flux and solder. Frequently used precleaning methods are degreasing, acid cleaning, mechanical cleaning, and etching.

Degreasing is generally accomplished by immersing the parts in a liquid or suspending the parts in vapors of a suitable solvent. The vapor process is recommended because liquid cleaning solvents evaporate from the surface being cleaned and the non-volatile oil that was in the solution will remain on the cleaned object. The vapor cleaning process involves suspending the parts in vapors of a cleaning solvent. Because the parts are colder than the vapor, the vapors condense on the parts and drip off, leaving no residue.

Acid cleaning or pickling is used to remove rust, scale, sulfides, and oxides from the base metal and to provide a chemically clean surface for soldering. Hydrochloric and sulfuric acid are two of the inorganic acids most widely used for this purpose. After pickling, the materials should be thoroughly washed in hot water and dried as quickly as possible.

Various abrasive materials and techniques are used for mechanical cleaning of base metals. All of these are effective and economical but have one definite drawback: abrasive particles may become embedded in the work surface. Abrasive materials such as steel wool, sand, ceramics, emery cloth, and other abrasive grits are not solderable. Even though the surface may appear clean, abrasive particles embedded in the surface result in reduced solderability.

If a brief solderability test indicates abrasive embedment, an etch treatment may be required to remove enough surface material to eliminate the embedded abrasive.

ETCHING

Etching is used to remove a small amount of material from the base metal to repair an abraded surface. Nonplated copper surfaces particularly lend themselves to this technique. Copper etchents such as copper chloride, ferric chloride, and ammonium presulfide are the materials generally used to strip and surface etch printed circuit boards and the like.

Precoating base metal surfaces with more solderable metal or alloy prior to the soldering operation is sometimes desirable and follows the cleaning process. Precoating allows for rapid and uniform soldering and avoidance of strong acid fluxes at the joint. Precoating of aluminum, aluminum bronzes, highly alloyed steels, and cast iron, which have tenacious oxide films, is almost a necessity.

Base metal surfaces may be precoated with solder or tin by the use of a regular or ultrasonic soldering iron, an abrasive wheel, immersion in molten solder or other metal, electro-deposition, or by chemical displacement. Coating thicknesses of .0002" to .0005" (.005 mm to .015 mm) are generally recommended to assure maximum solderability.

SOLDERING SEAMS

Soldering a seam using a lap joint design requires that the surfaces to be soldered must be physically and chemically cleaned. The proper soldering flux can be applied with a brush (*Figure 4*) with care to avoid dropping flux anywhere except on the joint. Apply solder only where it is supposed to stick.

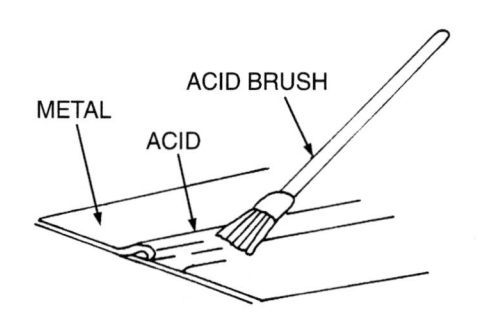

Figure 4 - Applying Flux

The tinned soldering iron must be held in the correct position (*Figure 5*) because it performs two functions: (1) it heats the metal to the melting point of the solder and (2) it melts the solder and carries it along the seam in a liquid state. Since melted solder flows to the hottest point on the metal the soldering iron should be held as indicated. For proper solder transfer it should be remembered that the greatest part of the heat is in the body and base of the point — not the tip. However, special work and tacking of the seam sometimes require using only the tip of the iron for soldering.

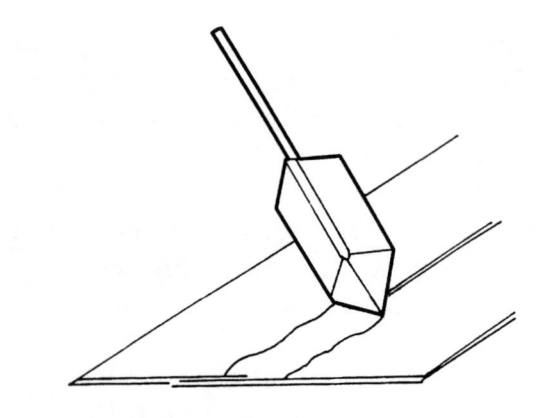

Figure 5 - Iron Position

Lap seams must be tacked before soldering in order to hold the pieces together. Sometimes, however, lap seams and special joints may be held in place by clamps or jigs. Grooved and riveted seams need not be tack soldered as they are held in place by the lock or rivet. One of the problems with the lap joint seam is that the heating system has to transfer heat through at least three thicknesses of base metal and the inner part of the joint may not be hot enough to provide free solder flow. Interlocked joints are sometimes provided with perforations to assist in solder flow observation.

SOLDERING PROBLEMS

Beginning sheet metal workers should practice soldering seams and joints on the materials with which they will be working. The following task sheets are offered so that the trainees can develop a certain amount of expertise in soldering techniques. Many variations of these tasks can be developed once the fundamentals have been mastered.

TASK 1

THE SOLDERING COPPER

Objectives

Upon completion of this task, the trainee will be able to:

1. Describe the factors which necessitate the reshaping of a soldering copper.
2. Clean and shape a soldering copper.
3. Properly tin a soldering copper.

A soldering copper as previously illustrated in *Figure 2* consists of a forged piece of copper connected by an iron rod to a wooden or other heat-resistant handle. The points of soldering coppers are often reshaped by forging or filing to suit a particular job. They must be filed to a smooth finish if they exhibit any of the following conditions:

1. Holes or pits on the surface
2. Scale or corrosion
3. Oxidized surfaces due to overheating
4. Old tinning

Tools and Materials

1. 1 or 1-1/2 pound soldering copper
2. Bastard flat file and coarse flat file
3. Sal-ammoniac block
4. 50/50 bar or wire solder
5. Soldering furnace
6. 14 ounce machinist's or ball peen hammer
7. Vise
8. Anvil
9. Safety glasses
10. Leather or other protective gloves

Procedure

If the soldering copper is so misshapen that filing the point will not form it properly, it must be forged to the desired shape.

1. Heat the iron (soldering copper) to a cherry red.
2. Place the copper in a vise (*Figure 6*) and file the part to be forged with the coarse cut flat file to remove all scale.

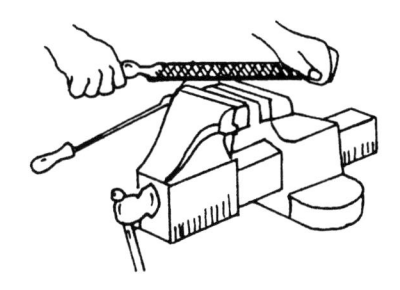

Figure 6 - Filing the Copper

3. Place the shank end of the copper against the anvil (*Figure 7*) and force the misshapen point back into the body of the copper.

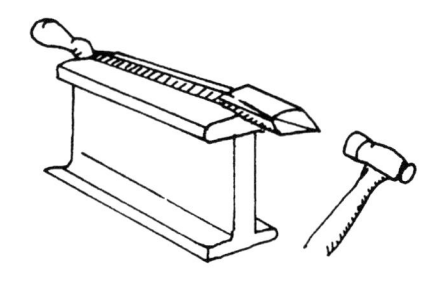

Figure 7 - Forging the Point

4. Reheat the soldering copper and place it on the anvil (*Figure 8*) striking it with heavy blows to reshape the point and body.
5. Repeat the forging operation if necessary.
6. Reheat the body of the copper as if for soldering and clamp it in the vise again. Use the bastard cut file to remove the remaining pits and old tinning.

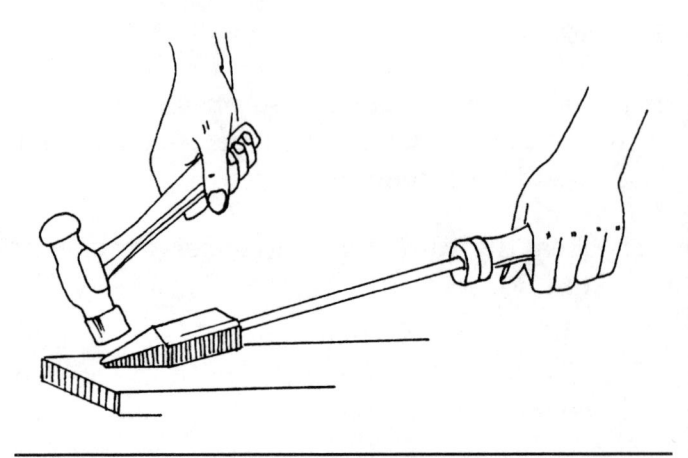

Figure 8 - Reshaping the Body

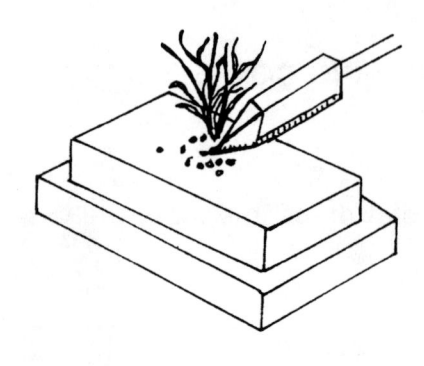

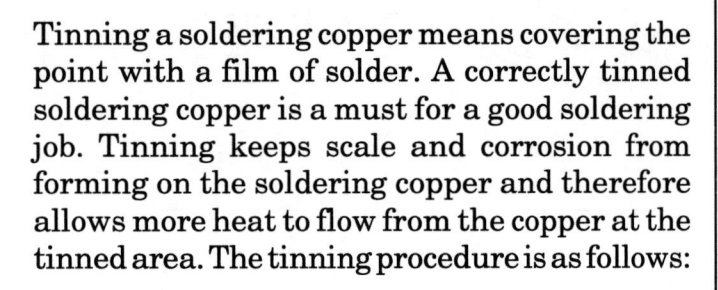

Figure 9 - Tinning a Copper

Tinning a soldering copper means covering the point with a film of solder. A correctly tinned soldering copper is a must for a good soldering job. Tinning keeps scale and corrosion from forming on the soldering copper and therefore allows more heat to flow from the copper at the tinned area. The tinning procedure is as follows:

1. Heat the soldering copper (iron) as for soldering.
2. Place the hot iron in the vise.
3. File the copper with the fine file to remove the rough edges of the corners of the point.
4. After the filing operation is complete, reheat the copper enough to melt the solder.
5. When a small amount of solder has been applied, rub the tip back and forth on the sal-ammoniac block (*Figure 9*) until the copper is tinned. Repeat the process if necessary.

CAUTION:

The soldering copper becomes hot enough to cause white fumes to rise from the sal-ammoniac block. These fumes are toxic and must not be inhaled. Soldering should be done in a well-ventilated area.

The soldering copper should be neither overheated nor underheated. If it is overheated the tin will burn off; if it is underheated, the solder will not adhere to the copper.

SHEET METAL — TRAINEE TASK MODULE 04312

TASK 2

FLAT LAP SEAM

Objectives

Upon completion of this task, the trainee will be able to:

1. Properly tack solder a job to hold pieces in position.
2. Properly solder a lap seam in the flat position (*Figure 10*).

A lap seam must be tacked before soldering in order to hold the pieces in proper position. It must be tacked as often as is necessary to hold the pieces in position, usually at one or one and a half inch intervals.

Tools and Materials

1. Two pieces of 24 gage or lighter galvanized iron, 2" by 6"
2. A properly tinned 1 pound soldering copper
3. Bar or wire 50/50 solder
4. Soldering flux (muriatic acid) swab or brush
5. Soldering furnaces
6. Sal-ammoniac block
7. Transite or other insulating backing sheet material

Procedure

1. Place the job to be soldered in the proper position on the backing sheet.
2. Dip an acid swab or brush in the flux and apply it to the seam area.
3. Heat the soldering copper in the furnace and re-tin if necessary.
4. Pick up some solder with the top of the soldering copper.
5. Hold the copper at one end of the seam until the heat penetrates the metal enough to melt the solder.
6. Use a piece of wood to hold the seam together while tacking into position.
7. Tack at intervals until the stock is securely positioned.
8. Start at one end of the seam and hold the soldering copper with a tapered side flat along the seam, until the solder starts to flow freely into the seam. Melted solder will flow to the hottest point on the metal, thus the soldered copper should be held as indicated.
9. Draw the copper very slowly along the seam and add as much solder as necessary without raising the copper from the job.
10. When the seam is completed, withdraw the copper and wipe the excess flux off the stock with a clean damp cloth.

Note: The soldering copper may be heated as often as is necessary, but the best job is produced without removing the soldering copper from the surface.

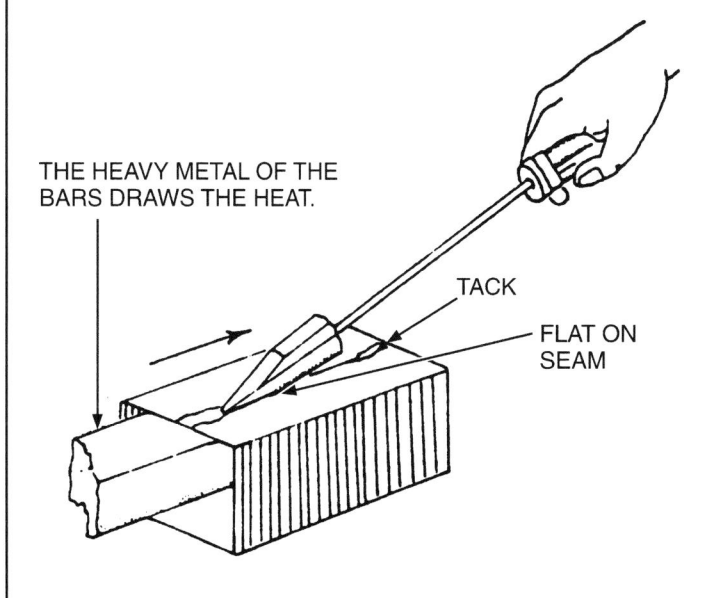

Figure 10 - Soldering a Seam

TASK 3

VERTICAL LAP SEAM

Objectives

Upon completion of this task, the trainee will be able to:

1. Pre-tin a seam.
2. Position solder a vertical lap seam.

Vertical or upright seams are more difficult to solder than flat or horizontal seams because the liquid solder tends to flow away from the top and down toward the lower portion of the stock. These types of seams should also be pre-tinned prior to attempting the soldering operation. Pre-tinning allows sheet metal seams to be sweated during the regular soldering process. Sweating means that the soldering copper must be held in the proper manner, must be kept at the correct temperature, and held in the proper position so that the solder flows completely through the seam (*Figure 11*).

Figure 11 - Lap Seam

Tools and Materials

1. 2 pieces of galvanized sheet metal 24 gage or lighter, 2" by 6"
2. Properly tinned and sized soldering copper
3. Bar or wire 50/50 solder
4. Soldering flux and swab or brush
5. Soldering furnace
6. Sal-ammoniac block
7. Proper holding fixture and material

Procedure

This type of seam requires "pointing up" which is a term used to describe soldering vertical seams. This operation differs from flat soldering since a portion of the soldering practice is done with the tip (point) of the soldering copper.

1. Place the job to be soldered on a flat surface and swab the surfaces to be joined with soldering flux.
2. Properly heat the soldering copper in the furnace and re-tin the surface if necessary.
3. Add some solder to the soldering copper and lay the side flat along the seam until the solder begins to flow freely onto the surface of one piece to be joined.
4. Draw the copper along the edge until the mating surface is completely covered with solder (tinned).
5. Repeat the procedure with the other piece of stock until it is also wet.
6. Place the parts to be joined in a vertical holding device or clamp them on a piece of wood.
7. Place a well-heated soldering iron with the tinned side of the point toward the bottom edge of the seam (*Figure 12*) and keep the handle higher than the iron.
8. Begin the sweating operation by rubbing the soldering iron back and forth across the seam.
9. When the sweating operation is completed, place a reheated copper at the top of the seam with the tip of the iron touching the seam, and the handle elevated above the body of the copper.
10. Add a small amount of solder to the copper and move the copper back and forth across the seam making small ridges (*Figure 13*).
11. Continue until the seam is completed. Cool and clean the seam.

Note: It is virtually impossible to solder a vertical seam correctly with the soldering copper handle lower than the body.

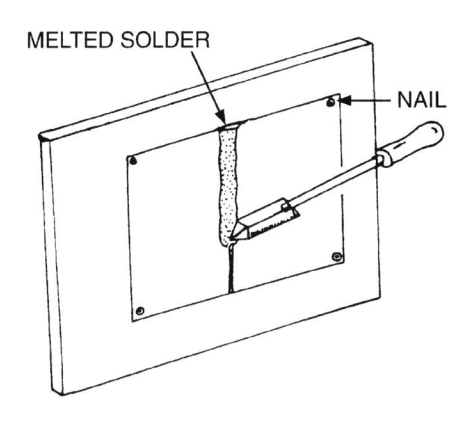

Figure 12 - Vertical Seam

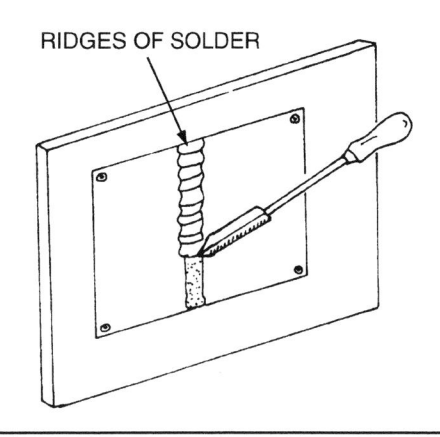

Figure 13 - Ridging

TASK 4

GROOVED SEAM

Objectives

Upon completion of this task, the trainee will be able to:

1. Form and set a grooved lock seam.
2. Properly sweat solder a grooved lock seam.

Tacking is not necessary for holding a grooved lock seam in place because the joint is held together by the lock. It is necessary to correctly apply flux to the mating surfaces to be soldered and to clean the lock area physically and chemically.

Tools and Materials

1. Two pieces of 24 gage or lighter galvanized sheet metal, 2-3/8" by 6"
2. A number 3 size hand groover and anvil
3. A 14 ounce ball peen or setting hammer
4. A properly tinned 1 pound soldering copper
5. Bar or wire solder (50/50)
6. Soldering flux, brush, or swab
7. Soldering furnace
8. Sal-ammoniac block
9. Piece of wood or other suitable backing for the sheet metal seam
10. Hand seamer

Procedure

1. Place the pieces to be formed and soldered on a workbench and physically clean the mating surface.
2. Bend and form the marked edges of the grooved seam areas of the metal.
3. Swab the mating surfaces of the edges with soldering flux.
4. Place the formed edges together and set the seam.
5. Place a properly tinned and heated soldering copper flat upon the flat seam (*Figure 14*) with the flat edge of the copper against the seam and heat the metal until solder will melt along the seam.
6. Move the soldering copper slowly until solder is evident all along the seamed area. Reheat the copper if necessary. Cool and clean the seam.

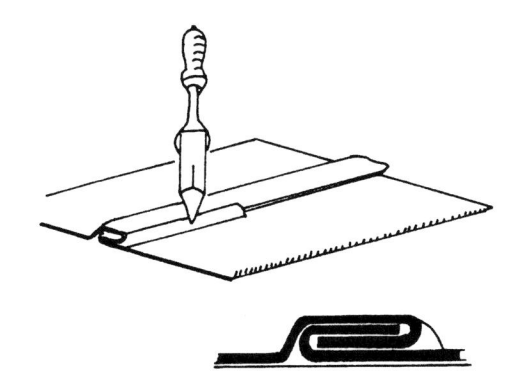

Figure 14 - Soldering a Seam

SOLDERING — TRAINEE TASK MODULE 04312

TASK 5

RIVETED SEAM

Objectives

Upon completion of this task, the trainee will be able to:

1. Form and set a riveted seam.
2. Properly sweat solder a riveted seam.

Rivet seams are often soldered to make them watertight and sweat soldering is probably the most effective method of accomplishing this task.

Tools and Materials

1. 2 pieces of 24 gage galvanized sheet metal, 2-1/2" by 6"
2. A rivet set and four to six rivets (1-1/4" No. tinners)
3. Setting hammer
4. Drill with 1/8" drill bit and a center punch
5. Metal scribe and combination square
6. Properly tinned soldering copper
7. Wire or bar 50/50 solder
8. Soldering flux, brush, or swab
9. Soldering furnace
10. Sal-ammoniac block
11. Suitable backing material and an anvil

Procedure

1. Place the pieces to be fastened and soldered on a workbench and lay out the rivet holes and center punch the marked locations.
2. Drill through both pieces of metal and remove the metal burrs left from the drill.
3. Physically clean the mating edges of the seam.
4. Apply soldering flux, wipe clean, and place the rivets in the proper positions.
5. Set the rivets and form the rivet ends.
6. Heat a soldering copper to the proper temperature and clean it on a sal-ammoniac block and resin if necessary.
7. Place the soldering copper on the seam (*Figure 15*) and allow the metal to heat until the metal will melt the solder.

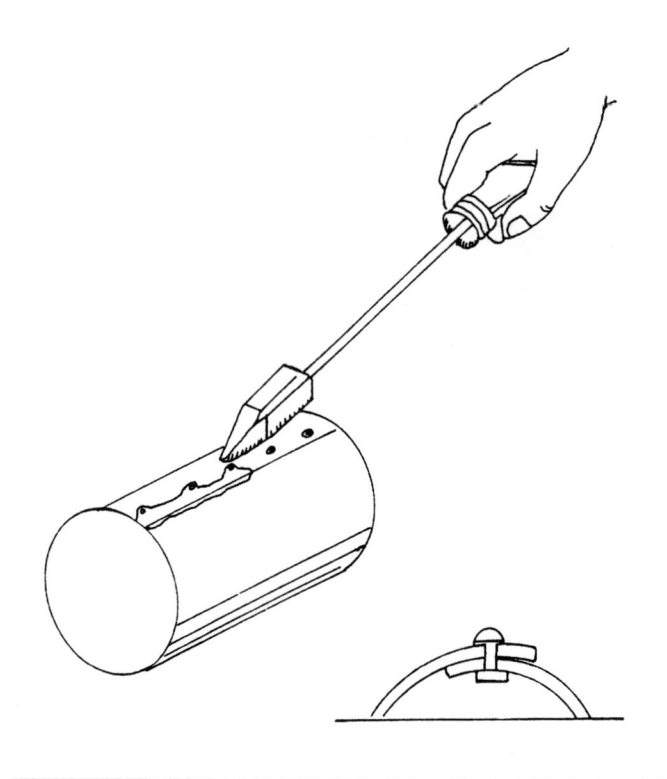

Figure 15 - Riveted Seam Soldering

8. Move the flat edge of the soldering copper slowly along the seam until the solder is drawn into the work area all along the length.
9. Inspect for solder penetration and wipe clean and cool the metal.
10. Restore the work area.

Note: It may be necessary to tin each area of the mating surfaces prior to placing and setting the rivets for proper solder penetration and bonding.

TASK 6

SOLDERING A BOTTOM SEAM

Objectives

Upon completion of this task, the trainee will be able to:

1. Make solder beads.
2. Correctly solder a bottom seam in a square, rectangular, or round container.

Solder beads or shots are sometimes used for soldering seams on containers and therefore must be produced prior to beginning the "container" soldering process.

Tools and Materials

1. Pre-fabricated container, preferably round in shape
2. Wire or bar 50/50 tin lead solder
3. Properly tinned soldering copper
4. Soldering furnace
5. Soldering flux with brush, or swab
6. Sal-ammoniac block

Procedure

1. Properly heat, clean, and tin a soldering copper.
2. Hold the solder against a hot copper and allow the beads to drop onto a clean surface (*Figure 16*).

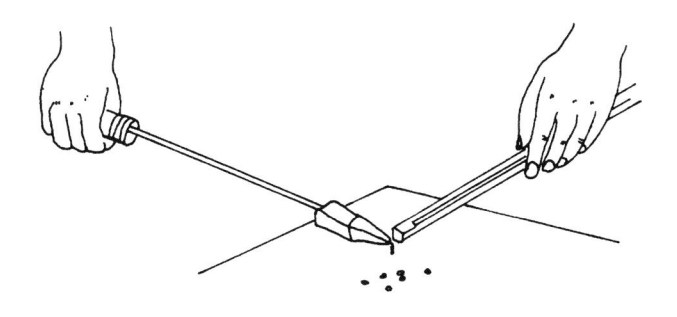

Figure 16 - Making Solder Beads

3. Apply flux to the seam to be soldered and wipe into the seam opening.
4. Reheat, clean, and place the soldering copper against the seam (*Figure 17*).

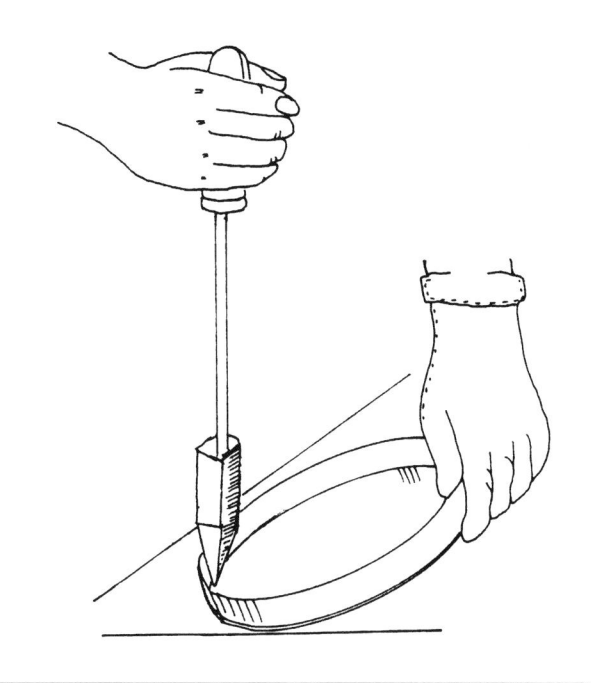

Figure 17 - Bottom Seam Soldering

5. Drop one of the cold beads of solder into the bottom of the container and position it against the seam.
6. Hold the flat side of the copper in one position until the solder bead begins to melt and flow freely into the seam area.
7. Draw the copper slowly along the seam adding more solder beads as necessary.
8. Reheat the soldering copper if necessary.
9. Continue this procedure until the seam is filled and the capillary action has drawn a sufficient quantity of solder into the seam.
10. Cool and clean the work surface.

TASK 7

SOLDERING ALUMINUM

Objective

Upon completion of this task, the trainee will be able to prepare and properly solder a selected aluminum alloy sheet.

Aluminum alloys are generally more difficult to solder than many other metals. The difficulty arises from the fact that aluminum alloys are always covered with a layer of oxide. Many aluminum alloys can, however, be successfully soldered if proper techniques are employed.

Tools and Materials

1. Two pieces of .025" aluminum alloy sheets, 2" by 6".
2. Wire or strip aluminum solder (tin-zinc or tin cadmium).
3. Aluminum soldering flux, brush, or swab.
4. Properly tinned soldering copper.
5. Soldering furnace.
6. File, metal scraper, or wire brush (stainless steel).
7. Proper backing material.
8. Soap and water.

Procedure

1. Clean the mating surfaces completely and remove the oxide with a file, metal scraper, or stainless steel wire brush.
2. Use a corrosive soldering flux to clean the mating surfaces chemically.
3. Tin the surface of the area to be joined with the aluminum solder.
4. Apply flux to the solder and again to the work area.
5. Apply a properly heated soldering copper to the work surfaces and work the aluminum solder well into the surfaces, until both surfaces are tinned.
6. Place the two tinned surfaces together and hold or clamp in place.
7. Work the flat edge of the soldering copper over the surfaces until the area is sweated together.
8. After soldering is complete, clean the joints with the wire brush and wash with soap and water. Remove all flux.

Note: Another soldering procedure which can be used successfully on aluminum alloys is to tin the surfaces with an aluminum solder and then use a regular tin-lead solder to join the tinned surfaces. This procedure is particularly useful when the clearance between parts is excessive and a large amount of solder is required to join the parts.

TASK 8

SOLDERING STAINLESS STEEL

Objectives

Upon completion of this task, the trainee will be able to:

1. Properly prepare stainless surfaces for soldering.
2. Properly solder a selected stainless steel sheet.

Stainless steel is a very difficult metal to solder due to the chromium in the alloy. The chromium not only resists heat and corrosion, but forms an oxide that is very tenacious and difficult to remove.

Tools and Materials

1. Two pieces of 24 gage stainless sheet, 2" by 6"
2. Wire or bar 50/50 tin lead solder
3. Stainless steel flux
4. Hydrochloric acid
5. Fiber brush or swab
6. Clean, damp cloth, soap and water
7. Properly tinned soldering copper
8. Soldering furnace
9. Emery cloth or sandpaper

Procedure

1. Clean the surfaces to be joined of all grease, dirt, and oxide.
2. Roughen the surface with emery cloth or sandpaper. Do not touch the surfaces with your hands after they have been cleaned and roughened.
3. Re-clean the surfaces thoroughly with hydrochloric acid and wipe clean with a damp cloth.
4. Coat the surfaces with a stainless steel flux.
5. Use a properly cleaned, tinned, and heated soldering copper to tin the prepared surfaces.
6. Lay the flat edge of the properly heated soldering copper upon the top surface of the area to be joined and allow the metal to melt the solder. Complete sweat soldering of the seam.
7. Remove all flux residue and wash the work area of the metal with soap and water.

Note: It is mandatory that food containers be soldered with tin and antimony solder (95 percent tin, 5 percent antimony). Solder for food containers cannot contain lead, cadmium, or zinc. Caution should also be exercised so that the stainless steel is not overheated.

REVIEW QUESTIONS

Answer the following questions to review your knowledge of this module and to prepare for the Module Examination.

1. Describe a soldering copper.
2. What is tinning?
3. How are soldering coppers sized?
4. What is the purpose of soldering fluxes? What are the two general classifications?
5. What are the seven steps in soldering procedures?
6. What is sweat soldering?
7. Why must soldering copper heads be reformed?
8. How is a soldering copper reshaped, cleaned, and retinned?
9. What is meant by the term "pointing up"?
10. What is the purpose of a sal-ammoniac block?

SUMMARY

Soldering is a process which joins metals by melting nonferrous metal alloys called solders on the surfaces to be joined. Soft solders, solders that have melting points below 800° F, are most commonly used by the sheet metal worker. Soldered joints are not as strong as welded joints and, therefore, cannot be used where strength is required or where high amounts of vibration exist. Soldering is particularly useful for joining sheet metal seams to insure against leakage. Soldering can be used to join many of the common metal alloys that sheet metal workers are called upon to employ. Safe working habits should be exercised at all times because soldering fluxes produce fumes that are toxic and must not be inhaled.

TRADE TERMS

Capillary action
Corrosive
50/50
Flux
Hard soldering
Liquidus
Solidus
Sort-solder
Sweat soldering
Tacking
Tinning
Wetting

ACKNOWLEDGMENTS

Tables 1 and 2 courtesy of American Welding Society.

NCCER CRAFT TRAINING USER UPDATES

The NCCER makes every effort to keep these manuals up-to-date and free of technical errors. We appreciate your help in this process. If you have an idea for improving this manual, or if you find an error, a typographical mistake, or an inaccuracy in the NCCER's Craft Training Manuals, please write us, using this form or a photocopy. Be sure to include the exact module number, page number, a description of the problem, and the correction, if possible. Your input will be brought to the attention of the Technical Review Committee. Thank you for your assistance.

Instructors – If you found that additional materials were necessary in order to teach this module effectively, please let us know so that we may include them in the Equipment/Materials list in the Instructor's Guide.

Write: Curriculum and Revision Department
National Center for Construction Education and Research
P.O. Box 141104
Gainesville, FL 32614-1104

Fax: 352-334-0932

Craft _____ Module Name _____

Module Number _____ Page Number(s) _____

Description of Problem
_____
_____
_____
_____
_____

(Optional) Correction of Problem
_____
_____
_____

(Optional) Your Name and Address
_____
_____
_____

Blueprints and Specifications
Module 04403

NATIONAL
CENTER FOR
CONSTRUCTION
EDUCATION AND
RESEARCH

Task Module 04403

BLUEPRINTS AND SPECIFICATIONS

The blueprints to be used with this module are provided to trainees with the NCCER Core Curricula Module, *Introduction to Blueprints*.
For replacement blueprints, call Prentice Hall Customer Service at 1-800-922-0579.

Objectives

Upon completion of this module, the trainee will be able to:

1. Demonstrate an ability to interpret blueprints and specifications.

2. Demonstrate an ability to use section, elevation, and detail views or plans for interpreting drawings and blueprints.

3. Demonstrate an ability to use mechanical, electrical, and plumbing drawings to interpret architectural information.

4. Demonstrate an ability to use specifications for information pertaining to specific portions of the construction job.

INTRODUCTION

This module furthers the trainee's knowledge of blueprint interpretation. Building on the information presented in Sheet Metal Level 1, this module introduces techniques for reading blueprints, specifications, and shop drawings. A series of related blueprints is used to illustrate how information is conveyed.

Please note that there are two appendices at the end of this module. *Appendix A* consists of blueprint symbols and abbreviations. *Appendix B* consists of sample specifications. The blueprints to be used with this module are provided to trainees with the NCCER Core Curricula Module, *Introduction to Blueprints*.

Copyright © 1992 National Center for Construction Education and Research, Gainesville, FL All rights reserved. No part of this work may be reproduced in any form or by any means, including photocopying, without written permission of the publisher. Updated: 1998.

READING BLUEPRINTS

The following procedure is suggested as a method of reading a set of blueprints for understanding:

1. Check the list of blueprints in the set. Note the sequence of the various types of plans. Notice that the prints are broken into several categories:

    Architectural
    Site
    Mechanical
    Electrical
    Plumbing

2. Study the site, or plot plan, to observe the location of the building. Also notice that the geographic location of the building may be indicated on the site plan.

3. Check the floor plan for orientation of the building. Observe the location and features of entries, corridors, offsets, and any special features.

4. Study the features that extend for more than one floor, such as plumbing and vents, stairways, heating and cooling ductwork, or piping.

5. Check the floor and wall construction and other details relating to exterior and interior walls.

6. Check the foundation plan for size and types of footings, reinforcing steel, and load-bearing substructures.

7. Study the mechanical plans for the details of heating, cooling, and plumbing.

8. Observe the electrical entrance and distribution panels, and the installation of the lighting or power supplies to special equipment.

9. Check the notes on the various pages and also check the specifications against the construction details. Look for any variations.

10. Thumb through the compilation of sheets until you are familiar with all the plans and structural details.

11. Recognize applicable symbols and their relative locations in the plans. Note any special construction details or variations that will affect your trade.

The Site Plan

The site plan (*S-1 in the set of blueprints*) indicates the location of the building on the land site. A site plan may include topographic features such as contour lines, trees, and shrubs. It may also include some construction features such as walks, driveways, curbs, and gutters. Very often the roof plan, if there is one, is also shown on the site plan. General notes may also be included on the site plan pertaining to grading and shrubbery.

The Floor Plan

The floor plan (*A-1 in the set of blueprints*) is one of the most important of the working drawings because it includes a significant amount of information. The floor plan is the first drawing started by the designer. It shows the length and width of the building and the location of the rooms and other spaces that the building contains. Each floor of the structure has a different floor plan.

A floor plan is a plan view of a horizontal section taken at some distance above the floor, usually midway between the floor and ceiling. The cutting plane of the sectional drawing may be offset to a higher or lower level, so that it cuts through the desired features such as windows and doors. The cut will cross all openings for that floor, or story, give the dimensions of the window and door openings, and indicate which way the doors are to swing.

Elevation Drawings

The elevation view of a structure (*A-2 in the set of blueprints*) shows the exterior features of that structure. Four views are generally used to show the four sides. With very complex buildings, more than four views may be required. Elevation drawings show the exterior style of the building, as well as the placement of doors, windows, chimneys, and decorative trim.

The various views are usually labeled in one of two ways. They may be broken down as Front, Right Side, Left Side, Rear, or they may be designated by compass direction. If the front of the building faces the East, then this becomes the East Elevation. The other elevations are then labeled accordingly: West, South, and North.

Materials used for the exterior finish of a building are also indicated on elevation drawings. Parts of a building hidden from view, foundation walls, and footings are shown by broken lines.

Section Drawings

Section drawings make construction procedures easier by showing how a particular feature looks inside. A feature is drawn as if a cut had been made through the middle of it. Like detail drawings, section drawings are also drawn to a larger scale than that used in plan views.

Sectional views are often given for walls, stairs, cabinets, and other features that require more information than is found on the plan views. Sectional views show how something is put together internally. When the sectional cut is made along the long dimension of a building, it is called a "longitudinal section." When it is made through the short dimension, it is called a "transverse section."

Schedules

Schedules are not drawn but consist of tables describing and specifying the various types and sizes of items used in the construction of a building. Window and door schedules are the most common kinds found in blueprints. Door schedules are usually included on the plan drawings, and window schedules on the elevation drawings. Each item in the schedule is referenced to the appropriate plan.

Additional schedules are also available for mechanical equipment and controls, plumbing fixtures, and any other equipment that needs more complete definition or description.

Detail Drawings

Detail drawings are views of some special features of a building such as windows, doors, or rafter bracings. These drawings are drawn to a larger scale in order to make the details clearer. Often the detail drawings are placed on the same sheet where the feature appears in the plan.

The Plumbing Plans

These plans (*P-1 and P-2 in the set of blueprints*) diagram the layout of water supply, sewage disposal, and fixtures. The plans may be included on the floor plan of regular construction jobs or on a separate plan for a large commercial structure. The plumbing system plan may have a separate plumbing riser diagram that is not often drawn to scale, with additional pages that depict the layout and identification of the piping and fixtures. A plumbing legend is usually on the plan, also.

The Electrical Plan

Normal construction jobs usually contain the electrical plan on the floor plan. Complex commercial blueprints, however, use a tracing of the floor plan, omitting unnecessary details to provide space to show the electrical layout.

The locations for the meter, distribution panel, fixtures, switches, and special items are indicated on the electrical plan along with specifications for load capacities and wire sizes. An electrical legend listing the various symbols pertaining to the plan may also be located on the electrical plan. An electrical distribution riser diagram may sometimes be on the lead-in page to the electrical plan, with a floor plan located on a following page or pages. (*See drawing E-1 in the set of blueprints.*)

The Mechanical Plan

Like the electrical plan, the heating and cooling plan is included on the floor plan for conventional construction (*M1 through M7 in the set of blueprints*). Complex jobs may require the heating and cooling to be laid out on a separate floor plan that details the installation of the conditioned-air system. The air-handling units and affiliated equipment are drawn to scale on the panel that may also include the HVAC legend.

WORKING WITH BLUEPRINTS

When working with any type of drawing found in a set of commercial blueprints, keep the following points in mind:

1. Read the title block. The title block tells you what the drawing is about. It contains critical information about the drawing such as the scale, date of last revision, drawing number, and architect or engineer. If you have to remove a sheet from a set of drawings, be sure to fold the sheet with the title block facing up.

2. Find the north arrow. Always orient yourself to the structure. Knowing where north is enables you more accurately to describe the locations of walls and other parts of the building.

3. Always be aware that blueprints work together as a team. The reason the architect or engineer draws plans, elevations, and sections is that it requires more than one type of view to communicate the whole. Learn how to use more than one drawing, when necessary, to find the information you need.

THE DRAWINGS FOR TASK MODULE 04403

Task Module 04403 uses Drawings S-1, A-1, A-2, A-3, P-1, P-2, E-1, and M-1 through M-7 from the set of blueprints. Your instructor may wish to refer to other drawings in the packet.

To provide you with a demonstration of the information on blueprints, the features of drawings A-1, P-1, and P-2 are discussed in the paragraphs that follow.

DRAWING A-1 — FLOOR PLAN AND DETAILS

Drawing A-1 shows the floor plan for the new classroom addition to the church. The floor plan describes the size and shape of the floor of the building and gives necessary dimensions.

As shown on Drawing A-1, floor plans are generally drawn to scale of 1/8" = 1'0", although there may be times that 1/4" = 1'10" may be necessary for clarity. Either scale permits the required information to be shown in a readable fashion.

Drawing A-1 also contains three schedules, a Door Schedule, a Window Schedule, and a Floor and Finish Schedule. Depending upon the complexity of the project, each of the above schedules may require a separate page or pages.

The designer uses typical conventions to convey information in the schedules. In the door schedule, each door is numbered sequentially. On the drawing, each door is followed by its size, listed as width by height by thickness. Size is followed by material of construction and then type. Information concerning the frame is also listed, followed by any notes necessary for clarification.

SHEET METAL — TRAINEE TASK MODULE 04403

Drawing A-1 also contains two Alternates. Alternates are used when the owner desires bids on the project in several different ways. For example, if there are budgetary considerations, the owner may decide to build the project with two fewer classrooms or four fewer. Thus, Alternate #1 requires bid on the project as drawn but with four fewer classrooms. Alternate #2 requires a bid on the project as drawn with two fewer classrooms. The end result for the owner is three bids: a bid on the full project, the project with two fewer classrooms, and the project with four fewer classrooms.

DRAWING P-1

This drawing, the first of a series of plumbing drawings in this set of plans, has some information in common with the floor plan of the building. Notice that the dimensioning is not as detailed as it was on the architectural drawing, A-1, but that the overall dimensions are the same.

Drawing P-1 also contains three other items of note.

The most obvious is the isometric drawing of the sanitary/vent system for the area of the building shown. Notice how the piping sizes are represented. Compare this isometric to the way the piping is shown on the floor plan.

The drawing also contains a Schedule of Plumbing Systems. This schedule establishes the governing plumbing codes, specifies piping materials, and calls out insulation requirements.

Below the schedules are the Plumbing System Specifications. This section contains information regarding the installation and testing of the systems.

In order to lay out and install the fixtures shown on the drawing, fixture rough-in sheets must be obtained. These can be obtained from the purchasing agent or project manager.

DRAWING P-2

Drawing P-2 shows the plumbing requirements for the water supply system. You should compare this drawing with Drawing A-1 and Drawing P-1 to get a better idea of the requirements for this building.

Request for Information (RFI)

Request for Information, usually abbreviated RFI, is used for clarification. If a discrepancy is noted on the plans, an RFI may be issued to the architect or engineer. There is a hierarchy that is usually followed. For example, should you notice a discrepancy on the plans, you should notify the foreman. The foreman generates the RFI, being as specific as possible and making sure to put the time and date on it. The foreman passes the RFI to the superintendent or project manager who passes it to the general contractor. The general contractor then relays the RFI to the architect or engineer. A sample RFI form is included as *Figure 1*.

**XYZ, Inc
General Contractors
123 Main Street
Bigtown, USA 10001
(111) 444-5555**

PROJECT: ☐

TO: ☐

R.F.I.
Request for Information

XYZ Project #_____
Date: _____
R.F.I. # _____

RE: ☐

Specification Reference: _____

Drawing Reference: _____

SUBJECT:

REQUIRED:

Date Information is Required: _____

XYZ, Inc By: _____

REPLY:

Distribution: Superintendent
Field File

By: _____
Date: _____

Figure 1 - Request for Information

SHEET METAL — TRAINEE TASK MODULE 04403

WORKSHEETS 1-6

Following are lists of questions pertaining to the various drawings included with this module. In general, the only information needed is contained on the identified drawing(s) for each group of questions.

WORKSHEET 1 — SITE PLAN

Refer to Drawing *S-1: Site Plan* to find the answers to the following questions:

DRAWING S-1: SITE PLAN

1. What type of construction is involved?
2. In what city and state is the site located?
3. What is the address?
4. The new construction will be built upon what existing feature?
5. The new building construction ties into what?

WORKSHEET 2 — FLOOR AND DETAILS, ELEVATIONS, AND FOUNDATION PLAN

Refer to Drawings *A-1: Floor and Details*, *A-2: Elevations*, and *A-3: Foundation Plan* to find the answers to the following questions:

DRAWING A-1: FLOOR PLAN AND DETAILS

1. What type of material will be used for door D-4?
2. What type of flooring will be used in the lobby?
3. Which classrooms will be separated by accordion doors?
4. What type of frame material will be used for the window?
5. What type, size, and thickness of glass will be used in the hollow metal doors?
6. What is the scale of the plan for the first floor?
7. What are the dimensions of classroom 135?
8. What is the length of the east hall to the lobby tile?
9. What are the rough-in dimensions of windows W-1?
10. What type of material will be used to face the outside of the building at the north vestibule?
11. What type of material will be used to face the outside of the building at the south vestibule?
12. How are the classroom interior walls soundproofed?

DRAWING A-2: ELEVATIONS

13. What is the roof pitch at the south elevation?
14. What is the roof pitch at the west elevation?

DRAWING A-3: FOUNDATION PLAN

15. How long is the addition's foundation from north to south?
16. How wide is the foundation of the eastern wing of the addition?

BLUEPRINTS AND SPECIFICATIONS — TRAINEE TASK MODULE 04403

WORKSHEET 3 — PLUMBING

Refer to Drawings *P-1: Sanitary Plumbing Plan* and *P-2: Water Plumbing Plan* to find the answers to the following questions:

DRAWING P-1: SANITARY PLUMBING PLAN

1. What is the size of the waste line that extends to the existing sewer?
2. What type of material will be used for the sanitary waste lines?
3. What size pipe connects the floor drains?
4. What size vent will extend to the roof?
5. Where are cleanouts to be located?
6. How many lavatories does the women's room have? The men's room?
7. The drawing which sketches the elevations of the plumbing system is called?

DRAWING P-2: WATER PLUMBING PLAN

8. What faucets are specified for the lavatories?
9. What brands of lavatory faucets are listed as alternatives?
10. What size is the return line to the water heater?
11. Where are the wall hydrants (water spigots)?
12. Do cold or hot water lines extend to the wall hydrants? What size are these lines?
13. What does the abbreviation SA mean?
14. Where is the mop sink located?
15. What does the abbreviation FUT SK indicate? Why?

WORKSHEET 4 — ELECTRICAL

Refer to Drawing *E-1: New Addition Lighting Plan* to find the answers to the following questions:

DRAWING E-1: NEW ADDITION LIGHTING PLAN

1. How many exit lights are there?
2. What is the power source for the exit lights?
3. How many duplex receptacles are in classroom 136? Classroom 128?
4. How many circuits does panel D have?
5. Where is panel D located?
6. What does GFI stand for in bathrooms 130 an 133?
7. What size conductor is used to load the 200 amp WP disconnect for the chiller?
8. How high above the finished floor are the light switches?
9. What type of wire is to be installed for all electrical work?
10. Receptacles in the toilets are provided with what type of protection?
11. How many waterproof electrical outlets are there? Where?
12. What activates the outside lights "A"?
13. How high are receptacles mounted above the floor?
14. All electrical work must be in strict compliance with what?
15. The designation EM represents what type of device?

WORKSHEET 5 — MECHANICAL

Refer to Drawings *M-1: Chilled Water Coil Piping Diagram; M-2: Existing Basement Floor Plan – HVAC Piping; M-3: Chiller Plans; M-4: First Floor Addition – HVAC; M-5: Existing First Floor Plan – HVAC; M-6: Flow Sheet; and M-7: HVAC Specifications*, to find the answers to the following questions:

DRAWING M-1: CHILLED WATER COIL PIPING DIAGRAM

1. What does NTS mean in the hot water coil piping diagram?

2. What does CHWR mean? CHWS?

3. How many air-heating units are there in the new addition?

4. Name the level where all of the air-heating units are located.

5. Are the drain lines above and below the floor the same size?

DRAWING M-2: EXISTING BASEMENT FLOOR PLAN – HVAC PIPING

6. How many restrooms are in the existing church building?

7. What is the size and location of the louver shown on this drawing?

8. In how many locations is hot water routed from the basement to the first floor?

9. In how many locations is chill water routed from the basement to the first floor?

10. How are the coils for the nave AHU serviced?

DRAWING M-3: CHILLER PLANS

11. What scales are used in the drawings of chiller CH-1?

12. What are the dimensions for the underground concrete mounting pad for the fiberglass storage tank?

13. What is placed directly upon the underground concrete mounting pad for the fiberglass tank?

14. For what purpose is #10 rebar installed in the underground concrete pad for the storage tank?

15. What are the requirements for exposed piping?

DRAWING M-4: FIRST FLOOR ADDITION – HVAC

16. How many fire dampers will be installed in the ductwork for the new addition?

17. What is the largest return to be installed? Its CFM?

18. How many exhaust fans will be installed? Where?

19. Are duct work dimensions inside or outside?

20. The AHU section where return air and outside air meet is called?

DRAWING M-5: EXISTING FIRST FLOOR PLAN – HVAC

21. What size are the necks to the grilles in serving room 122?

22. What size are the ductruns to the CFM 300 grilles in classroom 113?

23. What size is the ductrun above the pastor's study 109?

DRAWING M-6: FLOW SHEET

24. All of the new air handling units are equipped with what type of device at the return air connection?

25. What size vent pipe will be installed at the 15,000 gallon storage tank?

DRAWING M-7:
HVAC SPECIFICATIONS
AND
DRAWING M-4:
FIRST FLOOR ADDITIONS – HVAC

26. What type of insulation will be installed for round ductwork?

27. What is the specified fan horsepower for Air Handling Unit No. 1?

28. What is the specified BTU per hour for Air Handling Unit No. 4?

29. What produces the heat for the Cabinet Unit Heaters?

30. What materials are to be used for the metal ductwork?

31. What is the CFM of the supply diffuser in the lobby?

32. What materials are to be used for the metal ductwork?

WORKSHEET 6 — GENERATING AN RFI

Refer to Drawing *A-1: Floor Plan and Details*. Along the south wall, the designer has shown a dimension of 59'-0" from the outside of the face brick at classroom 138 to the outside of the face brick at classroom 136.

Verify this dimension (59'-0") against the dimension shown through classroom 140 to the outside wall of the men's room 130. If there is a discrepancy, issue an RFI using *Figure 1*, requesting clarification.

SPECIFICATIONS

Specifications are written statements that are provided by the architectural and engineering firm to the general contractor and, consequently, to the subcontractors. These define the quality of work to be done and describe the materials to be used. Specifications are very important to the architect and owner to ensure compliance to the standards set for the project by the contractors. Specifications consist of various elements that may differ somewhat for particular construction projects.

Purpose

The elements of a specifications document can be summarized by looking at the contents of *Appendix B*.

Specifications have several important purposes:

1. They clarify information that cannot be shown on the drawings.

2. They identify work standards, type of materials to be used, and the responsibility of various parties to the contract.

3. They provide information on details of construction.

4. They serve as a guide for bidding on the construction job by the contractors.

5. They serve as a standard of quality for materials and workmanship.

6. They serve as a guide for compliance with building codes and zoning ordinances.
7. They serve as the basis of agreement between the owner, architect, and contractors in settling any disputes.

There are two types of information contained in a set of specifications: general conditions and technical aspects of construction. General conditions cover the nontechnical aspects of the contractual arrangements. They cover the following points of information:

1. Contract terms
2. Permits and payment of fees
3. Use and installation of utilities
4. Supervision of construction
5. Other pertinent items

General Conditions

The general conditions section is the area of the construction contract where misunderstandings often occur. Therefore, these conditions are usually much more explicit on large complicated construction projects.

Technical Aspects

The technical aspects of the specifications cover the work to be done by the major divisions and identify the standards for each part. The divisions are usually in the order that the work will be performed; for example, site work is listed before carpentry work.

The technical aspects of the specifications publication include information on materials that are specified by standard numbers and by standard national testing organizations, such as the American Society of Testing Materials (ASTM). The specifications are usually written around some standard format proposed by the American Institute of Architects (AIA).

How Specifications Are Written

Writing accurate and complete specifications for building construction is a serious responsibility for those who design the buildings because the specifications, combined with the working drawings, govern practically all important decisions made during the construction span of every project. Compiling and writing these specifications is not a simple task, even for those who have had considerable experience in preparing such documents. A set of written specifications for a single project usually will contain thousands of products, parts and components, and methods of installing them, all of which must be covered in either the drawings and/or specifications. No one can memorize all of the necessary items required to accurately describe the various areas of construction. One must rely upon reference materials — manufacturer's data, catalogs, checklists, and, best of all, a high-quality master specification.

Specification Format

For convenience in writing, speed in estimating work, and ease in reference, the most suitable organization of the specification is a series of sections dealing successively with the different trades. All the work of each trade should be incorporated into the section devoted to that trade. Those people who use the specifications must be able to find all needed information quickly.

The CSI Format

The Construction Specification Institute (CSI) developed the Uniform Construction Index some years ago that allowed all specifications, product information, and cost data to be arranged into a uniform system. This format is now followed on most large construction projects in North America. All construction is divided into 16 Divisions, and each division has several sections and subsections. The following outline describes the various divisions normally included in a set of specifications for building construction.

Division 1 – General Requirements

This division summarizes the work, alternatives, project meetings, submissions, quality control, temporary facilities and controls, products, and the project closeout. Every responsible person involved with the project should become familiar with this division.

Division 2 – Site Work

This division outlines work involving such items as paving, sidewalks, outside utility lines (electrical, plumbing, gas, telephone, etc.), landscaping, grading, and other items pertaining to the outside of the building.

Division 3 – Concrete

This division covers work involving footings, concrete formwork, expansion and contraction joints, cast-in-place concrete, specially finished concrete, precast concrete, concrete slabs, and the like.

Division 4 – Masonry

This division covers concrete, mortar, stone, masonry accessories, and the like.

Division 5 – Metals

Metal roofs, structural metal framing, metal joists, metal decking, ornamental metal, and expansion control normally fall under this division.

Division 6 – Carpentry

Items falling under this division include rough carpentry, heavy timber construction, trestles, prefabricated structural wood, finish carpentry, wood treatment, architectural woodwork, and the like. Plastic fabrications may also be included in this division of the specifications.

Division 7 — Thermal and Moisture Protection

Waterproofing is the main topic discussed under this division. Other related items such as dampproofing, building insulation, shingles and roofing tiles, preformed roofing and siding, membrane roofing, sheet metal work, wall flashing, roof accessories, and sealants are also included.

Division 8 – Doors and Windows

All types of doors and frames are included under this division: metal, plastic, wood, etc. Windows and framing are also included along with hardware and other window and door accessories.

Division 9 – Finishes

This division includes the types, quality, and workmanship of lath and plaster, gypsum wallboard, tile, terrazzo, acoustical treatment, ceiling suspension systems, wood flooring, floor treatment, special coatings, painting, and wallcovering.

Division 10 – Specialties

Specialty items such as chalkboards and tackboards; compartments and cubicles, louvers and vents that are not connected with the heating, ventilating, and air conditioning system; wall and corner guards; access flooring; specialty modules; pest control; fireplaces; flagpoles; identifying devices; lockers; protective covers; postal specialities; partitions; scales; storage shelving; wardrobe specialties; and the like are covered in this division of the specifications.

Division 11 – Equipment

The equipment included in this division could include central vacuum cleaning systems, bank vaults, darkrooms, food service, vending machines, laundry equipment, and many similar items.

Division 12 – Furnishing

Items such as cabinets and storage, fabrics, furniture, rugs and mats, seating, and other similar furnishing accessories are included under this division.

Division 13 – Special Construction

Air-supported structures, incinerators, and other special items fall under this division.

Division 14 – Conveying Systems

This division covers conveying apparatus such as dumbwaiters, elevators, hoists and cranes, lifts, material-handling systems, turntables, moving stairs and walks, pneumatic tube systems, and powered scaffolding.

Division 15 – Mechanical

This division includes plumbing, heating, ventilating and air conditioning, and related work. Electric heat is sometimes covered under Division 16, especially if individual baseboard heating units are used in each room or area of the building.

Division 16 – Electrical

This division covers all electrical requirements for the building including lighting, power, alarm and communication systems, special electrical systems, and related electrical equipment.

The above sections are further subdivided into many subsections. For example, items covered under Section 16400, Service and Distribution, will usually include the project's service entrance, metering, grounding, service-entrance conductors, and similar details.

Procedure

When reading specifications, proceed as follows:

1. Review the table of contents or index.
2. Become familiar with the information included in the manual.
3. Note the format and organization of the material.
4. Get a general overview of the materials and the section in which specific information may be found.

WORKSHEET 7 — SPECIFICATIONS

Refer to *Appendix B,* Specifications, to answer the following questions:

1. How many divisions are in this set of specifications?
2. Under what section would you expect to find information pertaining to lighting?
3. Where is the statement pertaining to contradictions between the specifications and the drawings?
4. Which shall take precedence?
5. Who is going to furnish the heating and air-conditioning equipment?
6. Who is going to install the heating and air-conditioning equipment?
7. Who is going to install the support for the heating and air-conditioning equipment?
8. Who will direct the setting of the heating and air-conditioning equipment?
9. Who coordinates all operations concerning the remodeling?
10. Who coordinates the distance of the temporary wall from the existing wall?
11. What is to be used to control noise and dust during the remodeling process?

12. How many shop drawings and submittals for electrical and plumbing are to be submitted and to what authority?

13. Does salvaged material become the property of the general contractor? If not, whose property does it become?

14. Who pays for the utility tie-ins?

15. Who is the owner?

16. Who is the architect?

17. Where would you find the definition of the term "contract"?

18. Where would you find the definition of the term "contractor"?

19. Where would you find the statement: "Drawings shall govern when variations from the specifications are found"?

20. Who pays for the extras not reported to the owner or architect?

21. Who becomes the owner of all drawings prepared by the contractor?

22. What happens to shop drawings furnished to and approved by XYZ?

23. If the owner checks and approves the shop drawings and errors are found, who is responsible for the errors?

24. List the types of insurance that must be carried by the contractor.

25. What must be the value of the performance bond furnished by the contractor?

26. Who repairs any damage to the work until the owner accepts the completed work?

27. Can the contractor change superintendents without the owner's consent?

28. Who is responsible for replacing or repairing any work not done to codes and ordinances?

29. Does the owner have the right to disapprove subcontractors used in the work?

30. How can the owner insure that liens levied against the work by the contractor are paid by the contractor?

31. How long must the contractor guarantee materials and workmanship against defects?

32. Can the owner have access to the project at any time for inspection purposes?

33. Is the owner allowed to inspect the reinforcement steel before placement of the concrete?

34. When can the owner inspect the roofing?

35. When must the contractor place a written request with the owner for substitution of specified products or materials of equal quality?

36. What additional information must accompany a request for substitution?

37. When can the contractor submit requests for payment for the work completed to date?

38. What is the amount to be requested at each interval?

SHOP DRAWINGS

There are three types of shop drawings. One type is a detail drawing that a draftsman creates after the engineer designs the structure. These kinds of shop drawings show the size of the member depicted and the finished size. They illustrate the connections used, show the location of all holes and openings, and provide notes specifying how the part is to be made. Assembly instructions are also included. This type drawing is used principally for structural steel members.

A second type of shop drawing (or submittal) pertains to the purchase of special items of equipment for installation in a building. These kinds of shop drawings are usually prepared by the equipment manufacturers. These drawings show overall sizes, details of construction, method for securing the equipment to the structure, and all pertinent data that the architect and contractor need to know for the final placement and installation of the equipment.

A third type of shop drawing that is very similar in development to the structural steel shop drawing is the shop drawing used by sheet metal fabricators and installers. These shop drawings involve sheet metal drafting techniques and evolve from the design drawings. These shop drawings are usually drawn to a scale that is several times larger than the design drawing. Sheet metal shop drawings show the exact layout of the ductwork, the size and type of fittings, the types of connectors and hangers to be used for installation, and notes that will assist in fabrication or installation. This type of shop drawing is shown in *Figure 2*.

The first and second type of shop drawings usually come from the contractor or fabricator and are submitted to the owner or architect for approval and/or revisions or corrections. The design drawing is often put on the same sheet as the shop drawing. Shop drawings are drawn to a large enough scale so that they are clear, but they must not be crowded. They are usually dimensioned to the nearest 1/16th of an inch. One contractor uses the following approach for the development of shop drawings. When the contract is signed by the president of the company, a full set of blueprints is given to the drafting department. Upon receipt of the blueprints, the drafting department, depending upon the work load, immediately begins developing the shop drawings. As the shop drawings are taken from the mechanical prints, the drafting department also researches the plumbing, electrical, HVAC piping, architectural, and structural prints, etc., to see if there will be any conflicts among them.

Cut Lists

Another function of the shop drawing is to assist the subcontractor in identifying the number and size of the fittings and ductrun sections that must be fabricated and subsequently installed on the job.

After the shop drawings are complete, or as they are drawn (depending upon the work load), the drafter makes a cut sheet on each individual fitting and assigns a fitting number to it that matches the numbers on the shop drawing. The straight duct sections are given another number that stays the same until the duct size changes. The cut sheets are given next to the fabrication shop. These cut sheets contain the job number, the quantity required, and the gage of metal from which they are to be fabricated.

Cut lists are a function of the production phase in the fabrication shop and may be either drawn by the drafter *(Figure 3)* or may be generated by a computer *(Figure 4)*. The cut lists identify the fittings and sections by number, type of fitting, amount required, width- and depth, length, the type of flange or connection to be used, the number of parts required for the fitting, the cut size, and the type and gage of metal.

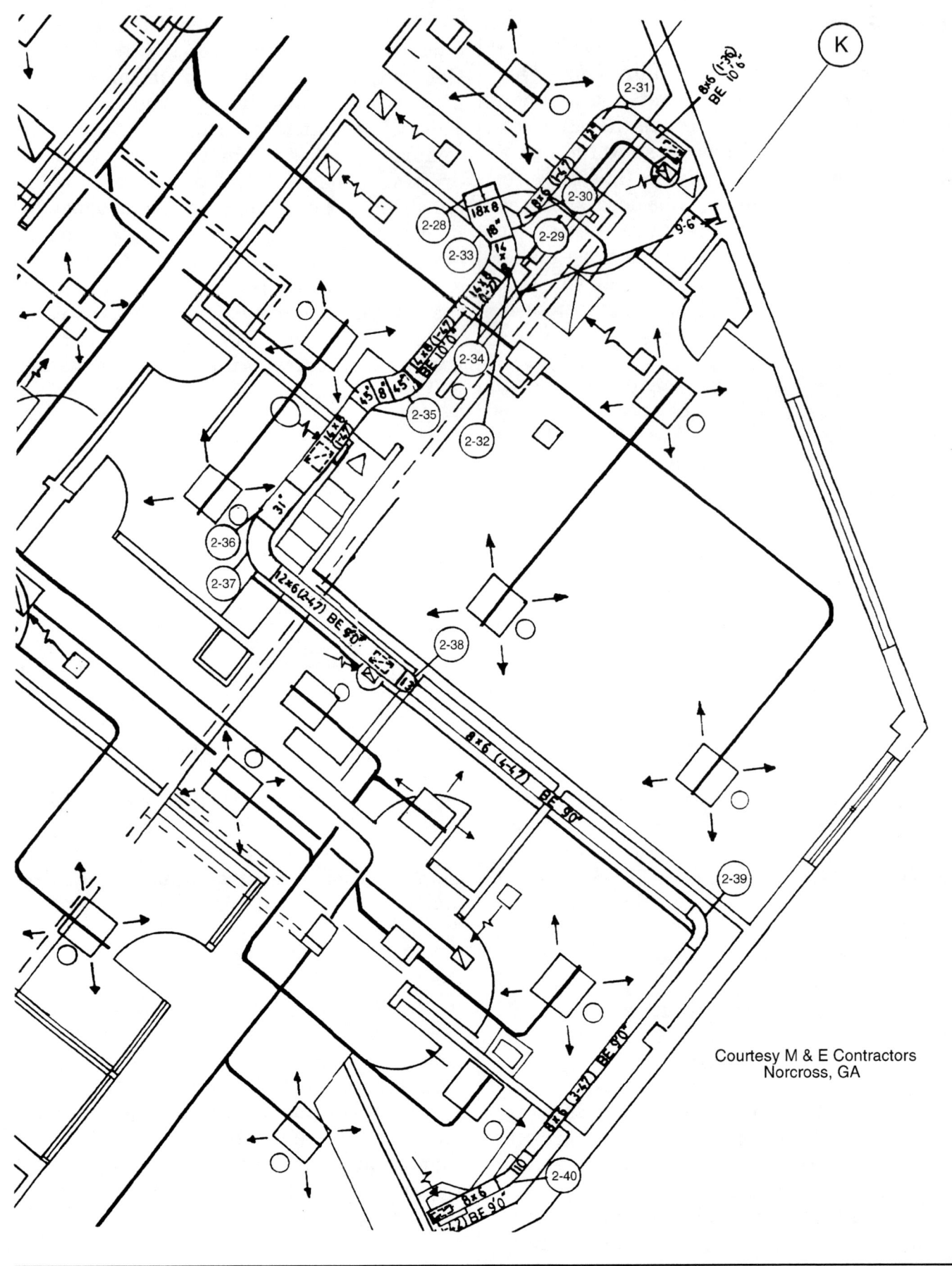

Figure 2 - Shop Drawing

CUT LIST

JOB TYPE _____   DATE RELEASED _____

JOB NO. _____   DATE SCHEDULED _____

LOCATION _____   DATE COMPLETED _____ BY _____

FITTING NO. _____   ASSY NO. _____

QTY. REQ'D _____   NO. OF PIECES _____

PRESSURE CLASS _____   GAUGE _____

SEALER CLASS _____   SEALER TYPE _____

BEADED _____   LONG. SEAM _____

TRANSVERSE JT. _____   REINFORCING _____

LINER _____   LINER TYPE _____

SPECIAL INSTRUCTIONS: _____

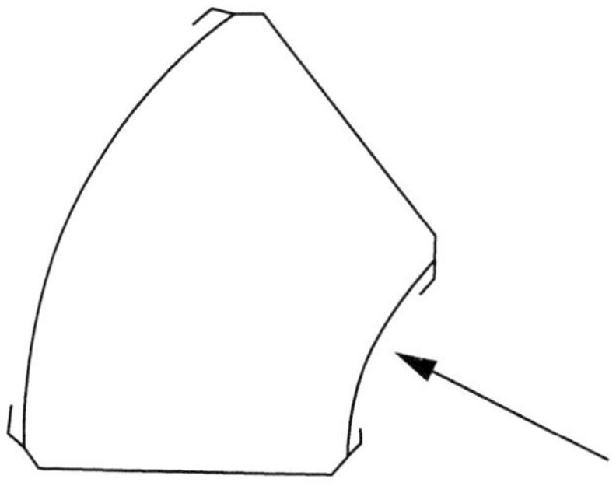

	SHOP			OFFICE	
FAB.	ITEM	QTY.	W x H	S.F.	WT.
TOTAL					

Courtesy M & E Contractors
Norcross, GA

Figure 3 - Cut List

BLUEPRINTS AND SPECIFICATIONS — TRAINEE TASK MODULE 04403

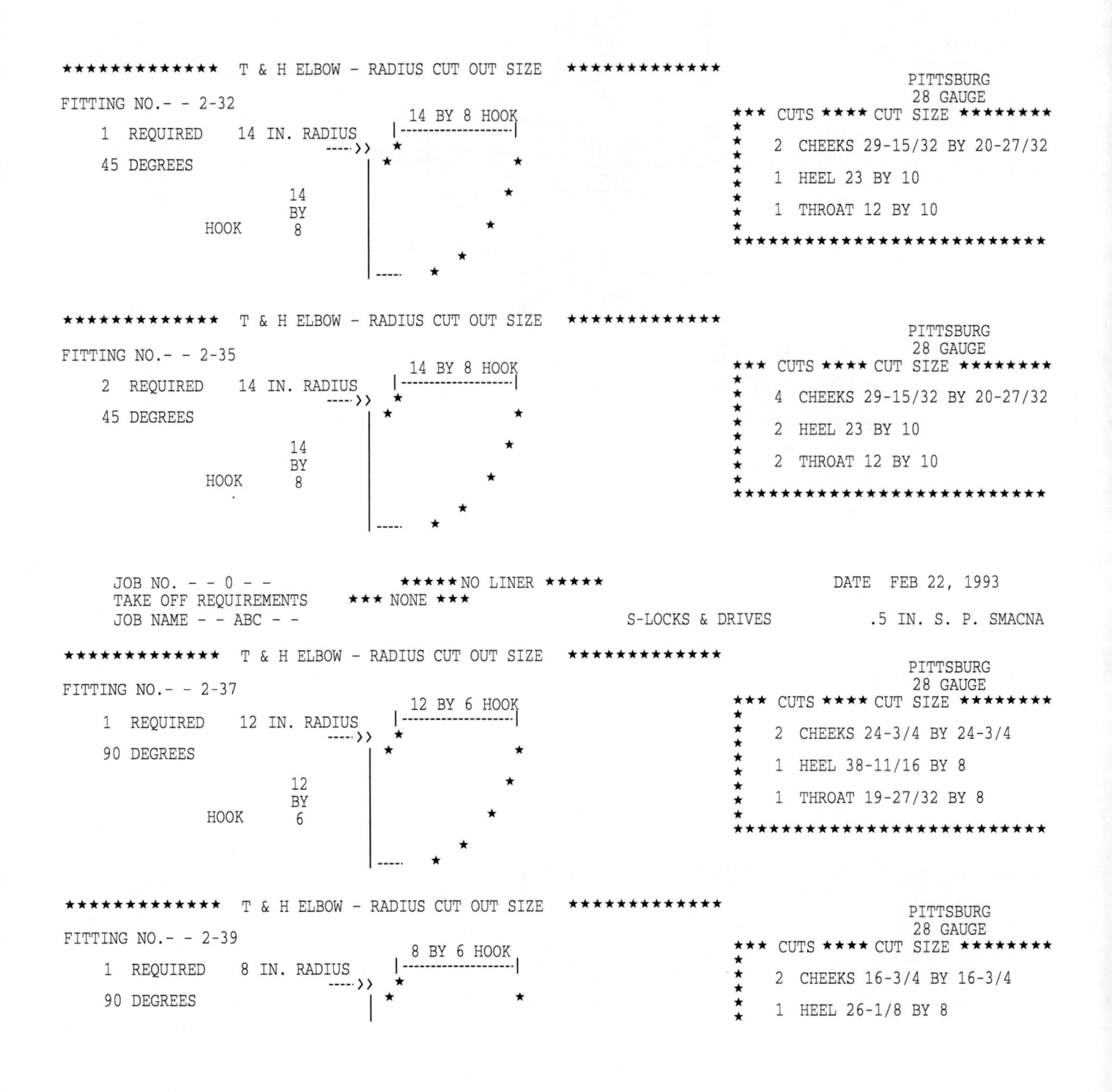

```
************* T & H ELBOW - RADIUS CUT OUT SIZE **************
                                                                            PITTSBURG
FITTING NO.- - 2-32                                                          28 GAUGE
                                    14 BY 8 HOOK              *** CUTS **** CUT SIZE ********
    1  REQUIRED   14 IN. RADIUS   |--------------------|      *
                            ---->>     *              *       *  2 CHEEKS 29-15/32 BY 20-27/32
    45 DEGREES                     *                *         *
                                                              *  1 HEEL 23 BY 10
                          14            *         *           *
                          BY                                  *  1 THROAT 12 BY 10
               HOOK        8              *     *             *
                                                              *******************************
                                             * *
                                   |-----  *


************* T & H ELBOW - RADIUS CUT OUT SIZE **************
                                                                            PITTSBURG
FITTING NO.- - 2-35                                                          28 GAUGE
                                    14 BY 8 HOOK              *** CUTS **** CUT SIZE ********
    2  REQUIRED   14 IN. RADIUS   |--------------------|      *
                            ---->>     *              *       *  4 CHEEKS 29-15/32 BY 20-27/32
    45 DEGREES                     *                *         *
                                                              *  2 HEEL 23 BY 10
                          14            *         *           *
                          BY                                  *  2 THROAT 12 BY 10
               HOOK        8              *     *             *
                                                              *******************************
                                             * *
                                   |-----  *


       JOB NO. - - 0 - -              ***** NO LINER *****               DATE FEB 22, 1993
       TAKE OFF REQUIREMENTS          *** NONE ***
       JOB NAME - - ABC - -                               S-LOCKS & DRIVES    .5 IN. S. P. SMACNA

************* T & H ELBOW - RADIUS CUT OUT SIZE **************
                                                                            PITTSBURG
FITTING NO.- - 2-37                                                          28 GAUGE
                                    12 BY 6 HOOK              *** CUTS **** CUT SIZE ********
    1  REQUIRED   12 IN. RADIUS   |--------------------|      *
                            ---->>     *              *       *  2 CHEEKS 24-3/4 BY 24-3/4
    90 DEGREES                     *                *         *
                                                              *  1 HEEL 38-11/16 BY 8
                          12            *         *           *
                          BY                                  *  1 THROAT 19-27/32 BY 8
               HOOK        6              *     *             *
                                                              *******************************
                                             * *
                                   |-----  *


************* T & H ELBOW - RADIUS CUT OUT SIZE **************
                                                                            PITTSBURG
FITTING NO.- - 2-39                                                          28 GAUGE
                                    8 BY 6 HOOK               *** CUTS **** CUT SIZE ********
    1  REQUIRED   8 IN. RADIUS    |--------------------|      *
                            ---->>     *              *       *  2 CHEEKS 16-3/4 BY 16-3/4
    90 DEGREES                     *              *           *
                                                              *  1 HEEL 26-1/8 BY 8
```

Courtesy M & E Contractors
Norcross, GA

Figure 4 - Computer Cut List

General Procedure

In large shops, the sheet metal drafters are usually sheet metal mechanics who have been trained in the use of drawing instruments and layout procedures. In smaller shops, the owner or journeyman may be required to develop the shop drawings. Freehand sketches from field measurements are often passed on to the drafter to develop a shop drawing. Sometimes, written notes and descriptions are used to work from, and the drafter must translate that information to shop drawings.

A general procedure for producing shop drawings is as follows:

1. Select a scale two to four times larger than the scale used for the design drawing.
2. Arrange the layout to be evenly spaced on the sheet; it may be desirable to center the layout.
3. Use the standard symbols on the drawing.
4. Add notes when and where necessary.
5. Draw in partitions, exterior walls, columns, beams, hanging ceilings, and any other obstructions that appear on the architectural plan.
6. Use the design drawing to calculate all measurements needed to properly locate the ductwork.

When dimensioning:

1. Show the measurements from the finished floor to the bottom of the duct.
2. Show the duct height.
3. Indicate the clearance from the top of the duct to the bottom of the slab, if applicable.
4. If a suspended ceiling is part of the construction, indicate the measurement from the ceiling to the bottom of the slab.
5. Properly locate all access doors, dampers, boots, registers, duct lining, thermostats, and other accessories on the drawing.
6. Allow sufficient clearance all around the ducts so that they can pass through walls easily.
7. Dimension from the centerline of the nearest column to properly locate ducts.
8. Refer periodically to the design drawing to check for interference with other trades.
9. Number all pieces of ductwork on the shop drawing according to the practices in your shop.
10. Make up a tally sheet or cut sheet that indicates the number of the piece, the size, description, quantity, the type and gage of material, and any other pertinent information that will help the fabricator and/or installer.

The following additional factors should be considered when preparing shop drawings:

1. A careful check of the electrical and plumbing mechanical drawings must be made when preparing drawings for ducts.
2. The types of connections used for conventional low- or high-pressure duct or for heavy-gage duct affect the length of the joints and fittings.
3. The thickness and type of acoustical lining must be noted on the shop drawing where it is indicated.
4. Ducts are usually increased to allow for the thickness of acoustical lining, but the plans and specifications should be checked for verification of the designer's intent.
5. Layout dimensions regarding approved HVAC equipment submittal cuts should be available for reference.
6. Gage specifications and types of materials should be checked carefully for boiler breechings, exhaust and fume hoods, and kitchen exhaust components.
7. Watertight duct construction is generally necessary for shower rooms, dishwasher equipment, etc.

8. Horizontal ducts may be pitched downward to drain connections when run through moist environments.

9. Fire dampers are usually shown on the HVAC drawings and generally include a note in reference to the applicable installation and material code.

10. If the location of a fire damper is doubtful, a note should be included that requests the necessary information from the architect or designer.

11. Each fire damper must be accessible through a properly-sized access door for fusible link inspections and maintenance.

12. Additional notes to the attention of the architect or designer must be included if information is necessary to confirm a dimension on the shop drawing in the following cases: when it is not shown on the design or architectural plan, when it is necessary to indicate a specific location that is inadequate for duct clearance, when work must be done by others, and when necessary to identify locations where coordination of the work by other trades is critical.

WORKSHEET 8 — SHOP DRAWINGS

Refer to the Shop Drawing in *Figure 2* and the Core Blueprints to find the answers to the following questions:

1. How are the same ductruns indicated on the shop drawing?

2. How many fittings (highlighted ductrun) are identified as 2-35? What are they?

3. What kind of fitting is designated as 2-36? How long is it (finished size)?

4. What is the distance from the center of the duct section between fittings 2-39 and 2-40?

5. What is the distance from the center of the duct section between fittings 2-39 and 2-40 and the finished wall?

6. What is the width and depth of the straight section of duct between fittings 2-39 and 2-40?

7. How are the straight sections of ductrun designated on the shop drawing?

SUBMITTALS

Submittals are documents that illustrate special pieces of equipment or accessories that are to be furnished and installed by the subcontractor. The submittal document is received from the supplier and is submitted by the subcontractor to the general contractor after the bid by the subcontractor has been accepted and the contract signed.

The submittal sheet *(Figure 5)* illustrates the piece of equipment or accessory that has been defined in the specifications and that must conform to the standards as outlined in the specification manual.

For example, the specifications for an in-line centrifugal duct fan may have been specified as follows:

> Centrifugal in-line duct fans shall be Acme Company, Model VIDB direct drive or Model VIBS belt drive, as shown on the plans and schedules. Fans shall be constructed of heavy-gage steel and electro-coated acrylic enamel finish over phosphate primer. Wheels 12 inches in diameter and larger shall have median foil blades to assure quiet, efficient operation. The motor-drive compartment shall be isolated from the air stream and be externally ventilated. Bearings shall be prelubricated and sealed for minimum maintenance and designed for 200,000 hours of operation.

Internal parts—wheels, shaft, bearings, motor, and drive—shall be accessible for inspection, and repair or replacement without disturbing inlet or outlet ductwork. Fans shall be furnished with a mounted safety disconnect. Single-phase motors shall have integral overload protection. V-belts drives shall be adjustable. Horsepower and noise levels shall not exceed the values shown and oversized motors will not be acceptable. Performance ratings shall be certified for air and sound.

The submittal may be used to describe the specified unit or it may be submitted to the proper authorities for approval of a substitute equivalent piece of equipment. The routing of the submittal begins with the subcontractor, who submits copies of it to the general contractor, who, in turn, submits it to the owner, the architect, and any code enforcement authorities. These people either accept or reject the submittal. If the submittal is accepted by the general contractor, the owner, and the architect, the item may then be installed, as agreed upon, by the subcontractor.

The submittal sheet, as shown, includes the pertinent information that will meet specifications that have been written for the construction project. It will include the size of the unit, the rough opening, the specifications relating to the size of the inlet or outlet, the cfm, the sound ratings, etc. The type of mounting may also be stated along with any accessories that would be applicable, such as electronic speed control, spark-resistant wheels, and explosion-proof motors.

When agreed upon by all, the submittal becomes the genuine specification for the unit or accessory, and it must not be deviated from without approval (by a change order) from all the parties.

Submittal information and shop drawings are usually available from equipment and accessory manufacturers. With this information, the subcontractor has the submittal sheet made up by the drafting department for processing.

AS-BUILTS

"As-built" drawings must be made on alteration or addition jobs, on jobs where modifications must be made to make way for other mechanical trades, or to alter the location of a component. In some cases, particularly for additions or alterations, these drawings may be available from the building or plant engineer. These drawings indicate actual installations of the various mechanical trades and must be used for reference by the drafter when called upon to provide a shop drawing of the modified system or components. As-built drawings usually use dashed lines to indicate ducts, piping, and equipment at close proximity to the work. Separate symbols or notes must be used to distinguish ducts that are to be removed and discarded from those that will be relocated.

The as-built drawings are then placed on the architect's plan (usually in another color such as red) and become part of the permanent files for the building's mechanical system. In addition, notes should be made as to the types of connections and existing duct locations that will be reconnected. Duct openings through existing concrete or masonry walls should also be located, checked, and indicated.

SUBMITTAL SHEET   HV 4-8

IN LINE CENTRIFUGAL DUCT FANS

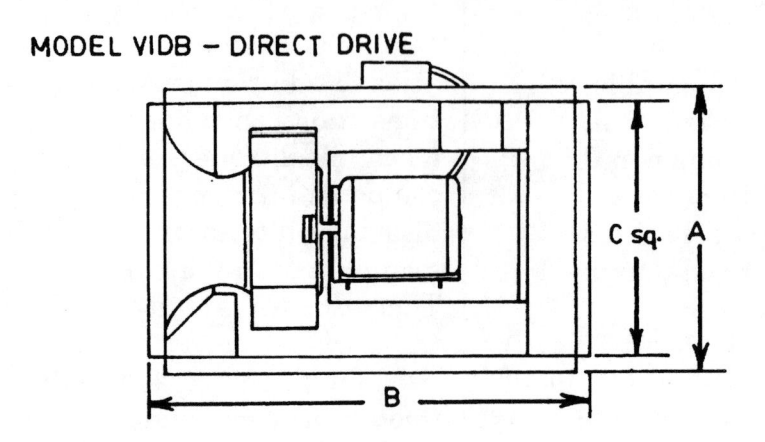

MODEL VIDB — DIRECT DRIVE

UNIT SIZE	A	B	C	INLET OR OUTLET AREA	WHEEL DIA	WT
06	13 7/8"	20"	12"	.979 sq. ft.	10 3/4"	30
08	13 7/8"	20"	12"	.979 sq. ft.	10 3/4"	40
10	13 7/8"	20"	12"	.979 sq. ft.	10 3/4"	40
12	17 7/8"	27 3/8"	16"	1.750 sq. ft.	11 13/16"	75
15	*21 7/8"	31"	20"	2.740 sq. ft.	14 7/8"	90
18	*21 7/8"	33 3/8"	26"	4.650 sq. ft.	17 13/16"	140

* "A"-1" Larger on access door sides

JOB NAME AND LOCATION	SUBMITTED BY

Courtesy Carnes Company

Figure 5 - Submittal Sheet

REVIEW QUESTIONS

Answer the following questions to review your knowledge of this module and to prepare for the Module Examination.

1. Define a schedule.
2. Describe what is meant by the scale of a drawing.
3. Where might one expect to find information pertaining to a specific detail in an architectural plan? In other words, where is the index usually located?
4. In your estimation, is the specification "slanted" in favor of the contractor or the owner?
5. What must a contractor do if it is discovered that he or she has violated a code or ordinance?

SUMMARY

Blueprint reading and specifications for the sheet metal trade are used for the layout, fabrication, and installation of selected ductruns and fittings. Specifications are used when selecting and installing equipment, systems, and construction components. When there is a conflict between the design specifications and the architectural plans, the specification that is most stringent usually applies.

TRADE TERMS

CD
Detail
Elevation
Floor plan
Hose bibb
Location map
MBH
Mechanical print
Riser drawing
Scale
Schedule
Sections
Shop drawing
Site plan

APPENDIX A

Blueprint Symbols

PROPERTY LINE

BOUNDARY LINE (MATCH LINE)

MAIN OBJECT LINE

HIDDEN LINE

CENTER LINE (Used as finished floor line)

DIMENSION AND EXTENSION LINES
2-1/8"

LONG BREAK LINE

SHORT BREAK LINE

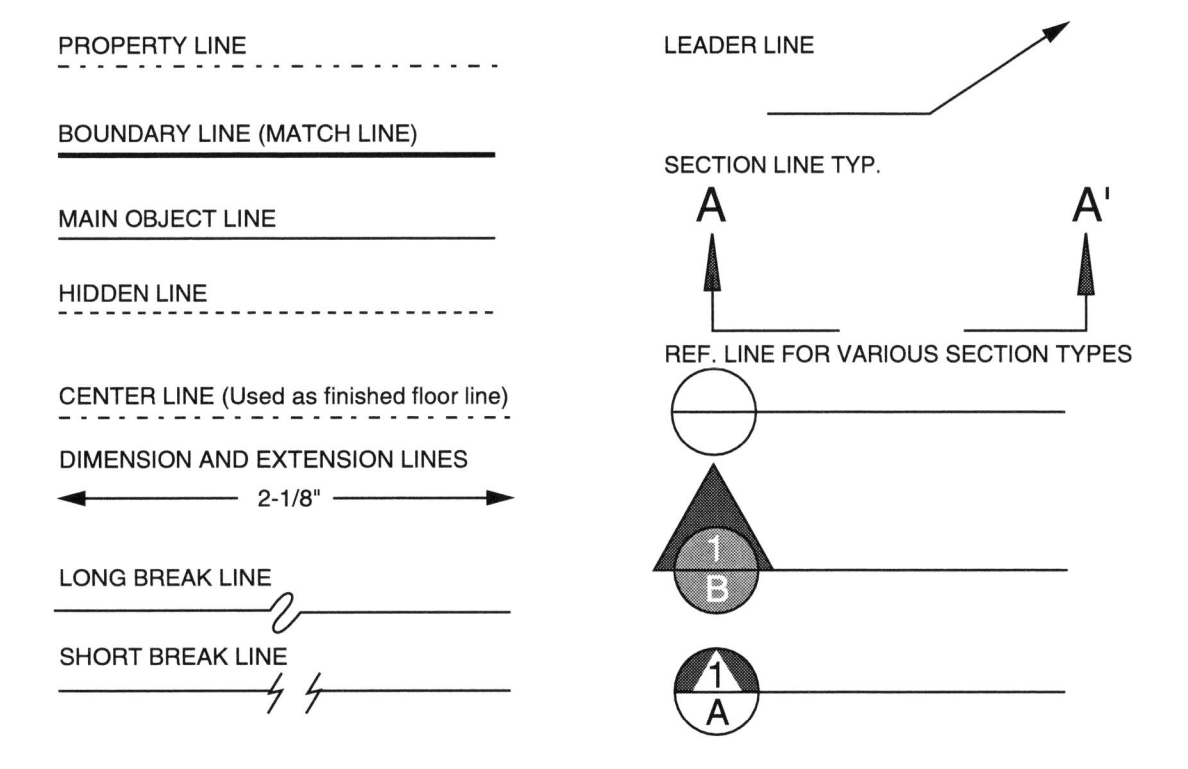

LEADER LINE

SECTION LINE TYP.

A   A'

REF. LINE FOR VARIOUS SECTION TYPES

Figure A-1 - Alphabet of Lines

BLUEPRINTS AND SPECIFICATIONS — TRAINEE TASK MODULE 04403

APPENDIX A
Blueprint Symbols

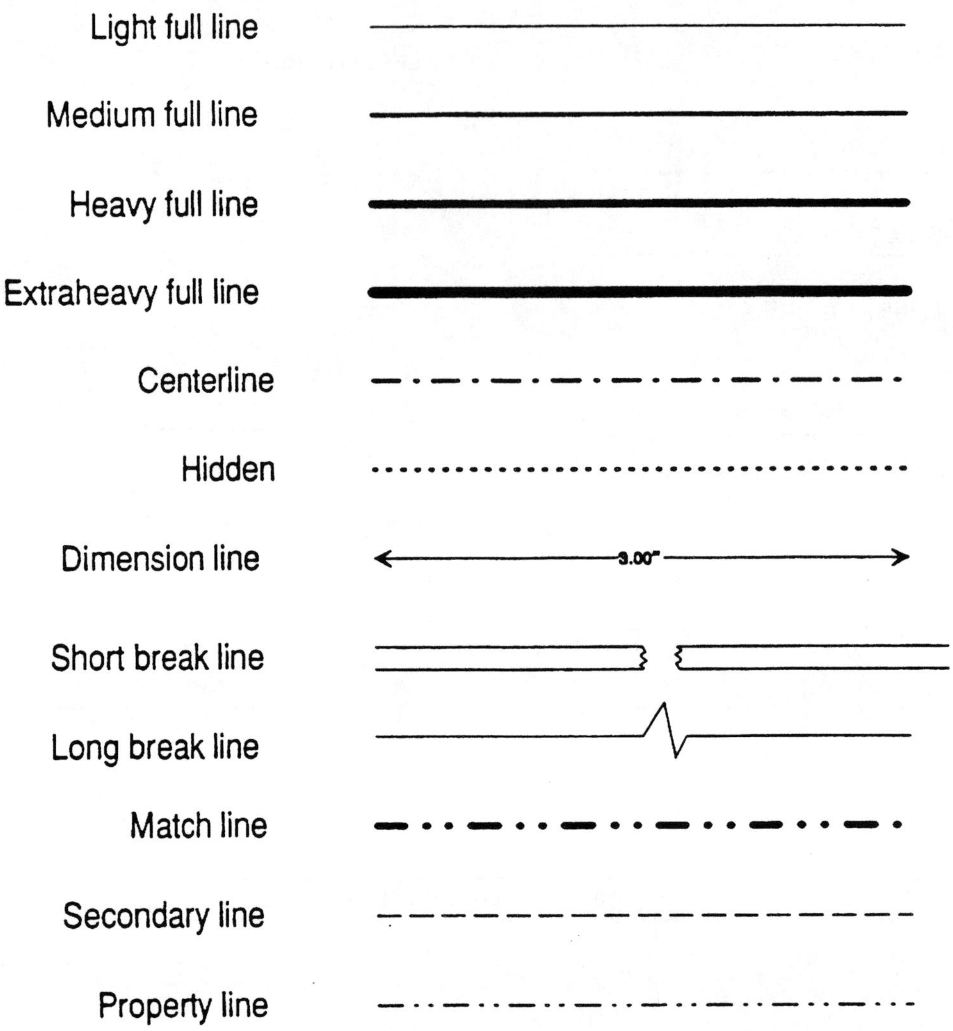

Light full line	———————————
Medium full line	———————————
Heavy full line	———————————
Extraheavy full line	———————————
Centerline	— · — · — · — · —
Hidden	· · · · · · · · · · · ·
Dimension line	←———— 3.00" ————→
Short break line	=⌇= =⌇=
Long break line	———⋀———
Match line	▬ ·· ▬ ·· ▬ ·· ▬
Secondary line	— — — — — — —
Property line	— ·· — ·· — ·· —

Figure A-2 - Typical Drafting Lines

SHEET METAL — TRAINEE TASK MODULE 04403

APPENDIX A

Blueprint Symbols

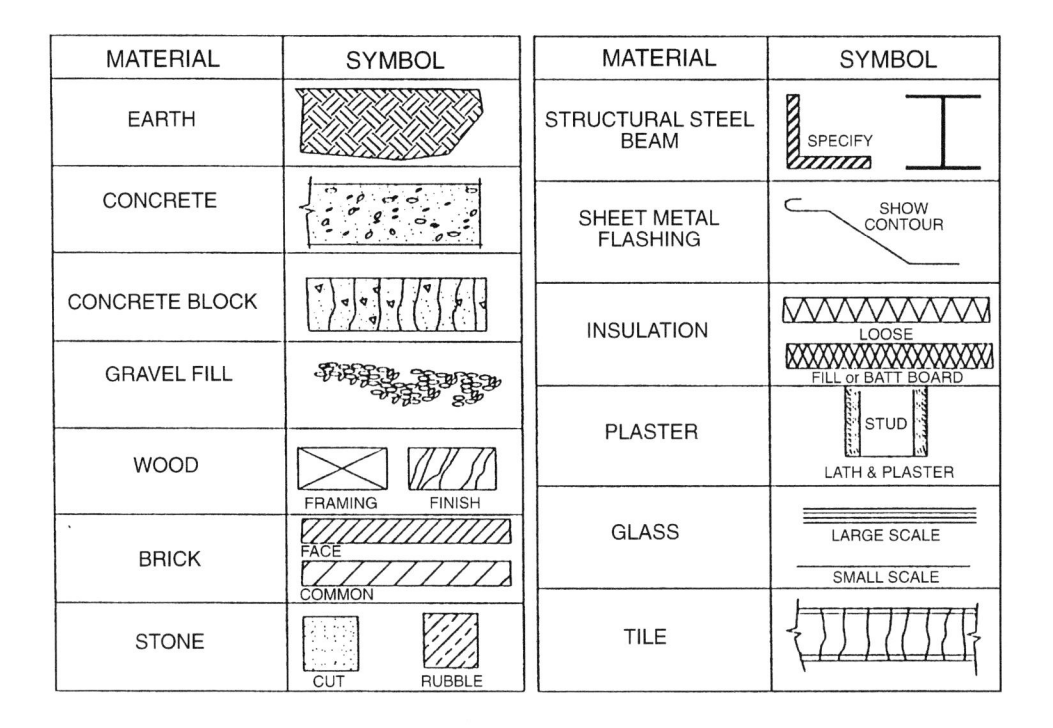

MATERIAL	SYMBOL	MATERIAL	SYMBOL
EARTH		STRUCTURAL STEEL BEAM	SPECIFY
CONCRETE		SHEET METAL FLASHING	SHOW CONTOUR
CONCRETE BLOCK		INSULATION	LOOSE / FILL or BATT BOARD
GRAVEL FILL		PLASTER	STUD / LATH & PLASTER
WOOD	FRAMING / FINISH	GLASS	LARGE SCALE / SMALL SCALE
BRICK	FACE / COMMON	TILE	
STONE	CUT / RUBBLE		

Figure A-3 - Building Material Symbols

DOOR TYPE	SYMBOL	WINDOW TYPE	SYMBOL
SINGLE SWING		AWNING	
SLIDER		FIXED SASH	
BIFOLD		DOUBLE HUNG	
FRENCH		CASEMENT	
ACCORDION		HORIZONTAL SLIDER	

Figure A-4 - Window and Door Symbols

BLUEPRINTS AND SPECIFICATIONS — TRAINEE TASK MODULE 04403

APPENDIX A
Blueprint Symbols

ADD.	addition	N	north
AGGR	aggregate	NO.	number
L	angle	OC	on center
B	bathroom	OPP	opposite
BR	bedroom	O.D.	outside diameter
BM	bench mark	PNL	panel
BRKT	bracket	PSI	pounds per square inch
CLK	caulk	PWR	power
CHFR	chamfer	REINF	reinforce
CND	conduit	RH	right-hand
CU FT	cubic foot, feet	RFA	released for approval
DIM.	dimension	RFC	released for construction
DR	drain	RFD	released for design
DWG	drawing	RFI	released for information
ELEV	elevation	SHTHG	sheathing
ESC	escutcheon	SQ	square
FAB	fabricate	STR	structural
FLGE	flange	SYM	symbol
FLR	floor	THERMO	thermostat
GR	grade	TYP	typical
GYP	gypsum	UNFIN	unfinished
HDW	hardware	VEL	velocity
HTR	heater	WV	wall vent
" or IN.	inch, inches	WHSE	warehouse
I.D.	inside diameter	WH	weep hole
LH	left-hand	WDW	window
MEZZ	mezzanine	WP	working pressure
MO	masonry opening		
MECH	mechanical		

Figure A-5 - Standard Abbreviations Used in Blueprint Drawings

APPENDIX A
Blueprint Symbols

LIGHTING OUTLETS	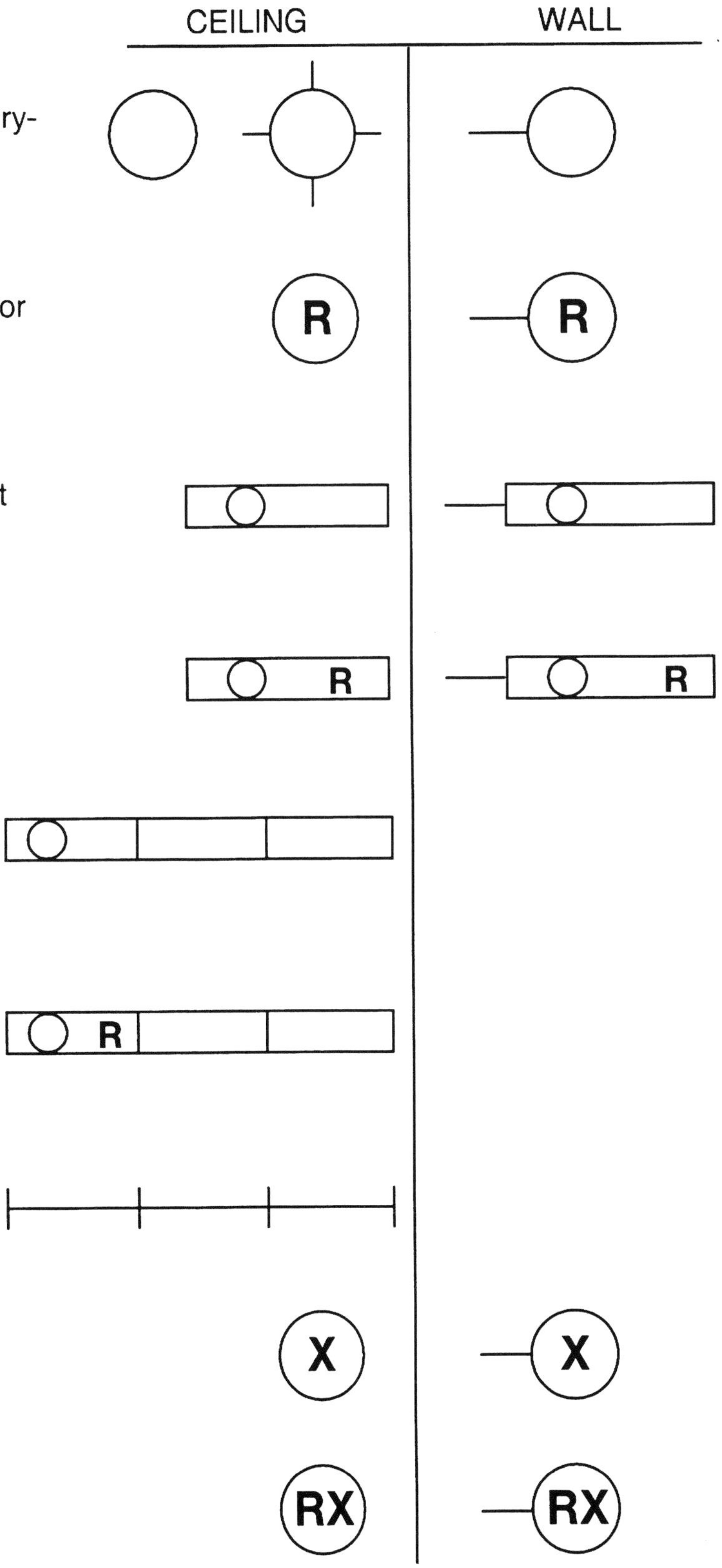 CEILING	WALL
Surface or pendant incandescent, mercury-vapor, or similar lamp fixture	○ ⊕	─○
Recessed incandescent, mercury-vapor or similar lamp fixture	(R)	─(R)
Surface or pendant individual fluorescent fixture	[○]	─[○]
Recessed individual fluorescent fixture	[○ R]	─[○ R]
Surface or pendant continuous-row fluorescent fixture	[○ | |]	─[○ | |]
Recessed continuous-row fluorescent fixture	[○ R | |]	
Bare-lamp fluorescent strip	├───┼───┤	
Surface or pendant exit light	(X)	─(X)
Recessed exit light	(RX)	─(RX)

Figure A-6 - ANSI Electrical Symbols (Page 1 of 8)

APPENDIX A

Blueprint Symbols

	CEILING	WALL
Blanked outlet	B	—B
Fan outlet	F	—F
Drop cord	D	
Juction box	J	—J
Outlet controlled by low-voltage switching when relay is installed in outlet box	L	—L

RECEPTACLE OUTLETS — GROUNDED

Single receptacle outlet	⊖
Duplex receptacle outlet	⊖
Waterproof receptacle outlet	⊖ WP
Triplex receptacle outlet	⊕
Fourplex (Quadruplex) receptacle outlet	⊕
Duplex receptacle outlet, split wired	⊖
Triplex receptacle outlet, split wired	⊕

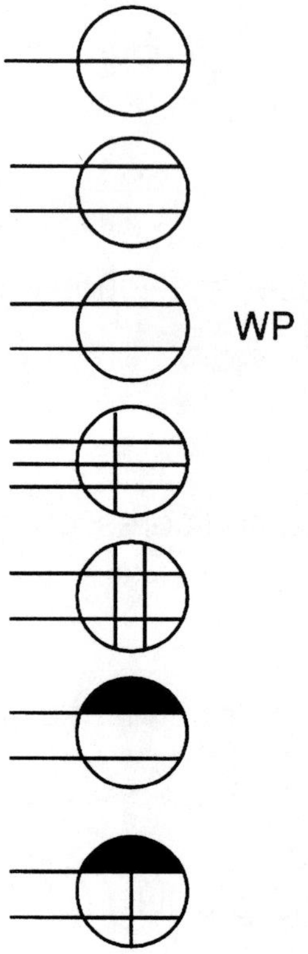

Figure A-6 - ANSI Electrical Symbols (Page 2 of 8)

APPENDIX A

Blueprint Symbols

RECEPTACLE OUTLETS

Floor duplex receptacle outlet

Floor special-purpose outlet

Floor telephone outlet, public

Floor telephone outlet, private

An example of using several floor outlet symbols to identify several gang floor outlets

Underfloor duct and junction box for triple, double, or single duct system, as indicated by the number of parallel lines

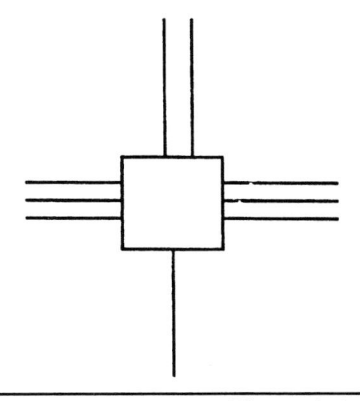

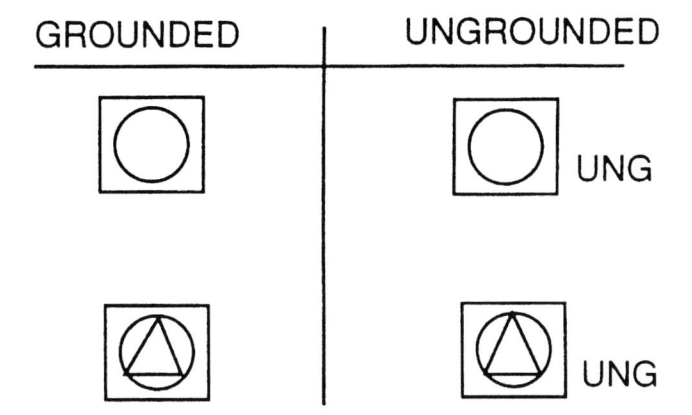

GROUNDED | UNGROUNDED

An example of the use of different symbols to show location of different types of outlets or connections for underfloor duct or cellular floor systems

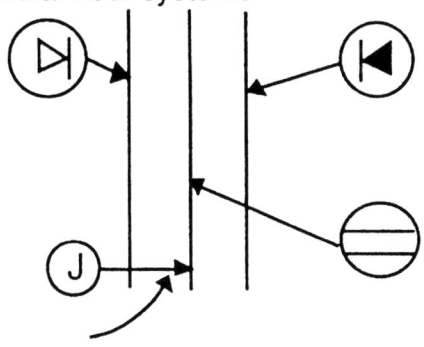

Cellular floor header duct

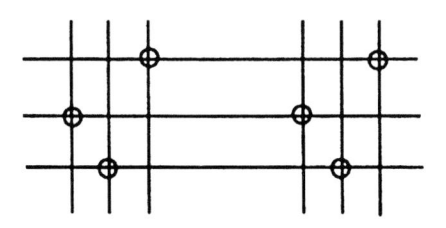

Figure A-6 - ANSI Electrical Symbols (Page 3 of 8)

APPENDIX A

Blueprint Symbols

SWITCH OUTLETS		
Single-pole switch	S	
Double-pole switch	S_2	
Three-way switch	S_3	
Four-way switch	S_4	
Key-operated switch	S_K	
Switch and pilot lamp	S_P	
Switch for low-voltage switching system	S_L	
Master switch for low-voltage switching system	S_LM	
Switch and single receptacle	⊖S	
Switch and double receptacle	⊜S	
Door switch	S_D	
Time switch	S_T	
Circuit breaker switch	S_CB	
Momentary contact switch or pushbutton for other than signalling system	S_MC	
Ceiling pull switch	Ⓢ	

SIGNALING SYSTEM OUTLETS FOR INDUSTRIAL, COMMERCIAL, AND INSTITUTIONAL OCCUPANCIES

Any type of nurse call system device	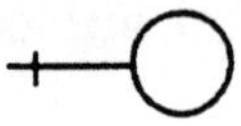 ─○
Nurses' annunciator	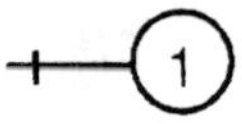 ─①
Call station, single cord, pilot	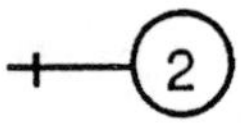 ─②
Call station, double cord, microphone speaker	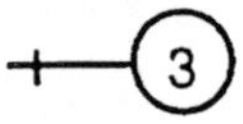 ─③
Corridor dome light, one lamp	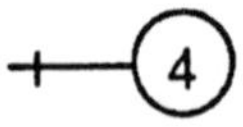 ─④
Transformer	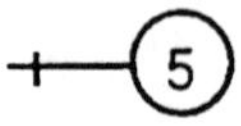 ─⑤
Any other item on same system (use numbers as required)	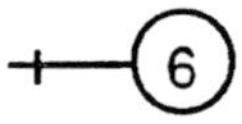 ─⑥
Any type of paging system device	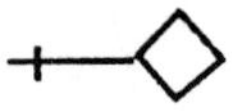 ─◇
Keyboard	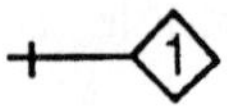 ─◇₁
Flush annunciator	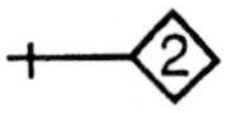 ─◇₂
Two-face annunciator	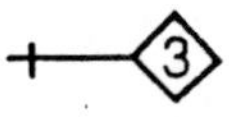 ─◇₃
Any other item on same system (use numbers as required)	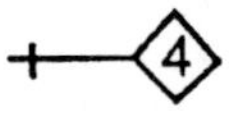 ─◇₄

Figure A-6 - ANSI Electrical Symbols (Page 4 of 8)

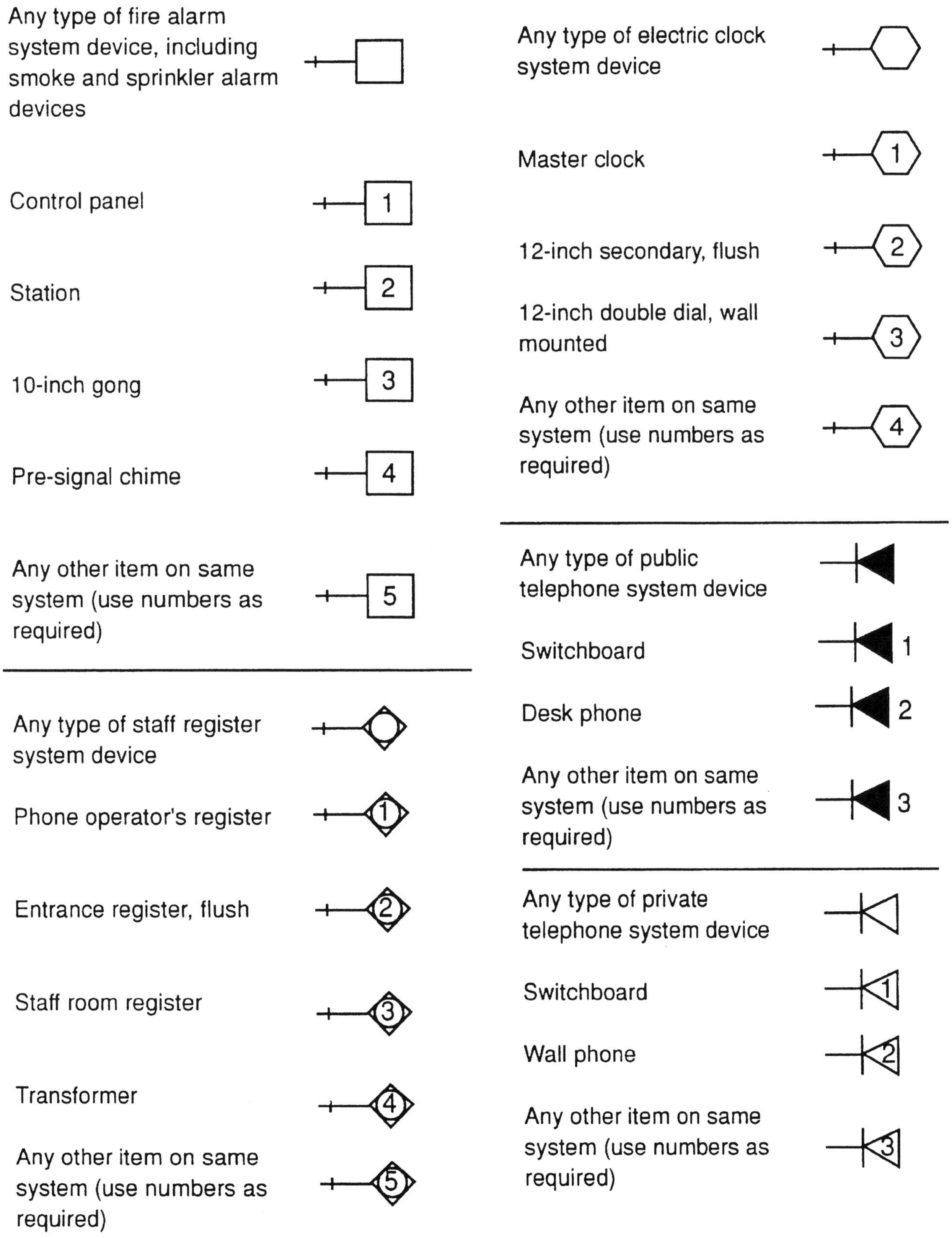

APPENDIX A
Blueprint Symbols

Any type of fire alarm system device, including smoke and sprinkler alarm devices	□	Any type of electric clock system device	⬡
Control panel	1	Master clock	⬡1
Station	2	12-inch secondary, flush	⬡2
10-inch gong	3	12-inch double dial, wall mounted	⬡3
Pre-signal chime	4	Any other item on same system (use numbers as required)	⬡4
Any other item on same system (use numbers as required)	5		
Any type of staff register system device	◇	Any type of public telephone system device	◀
Phone operator's register	◇1	Switchboard	◀1
Entrance register, flush	◇2	Desk phone	◀2
Staff room register	◇3	Any other item on same system (use numbers as required)	◀3
Transformer	◇4	Any type of private telephone system device	◁
Any other item on same system (use numbers as required)	◇5	Switchboard	◁1
		Wall phone	◁2
		Any other item on same system (use numbers as required)	◁3

Figure A-6 - ANSI Electrical Symbols (Page 5 of 8)

APPENDIX A

Blueprint Symbols

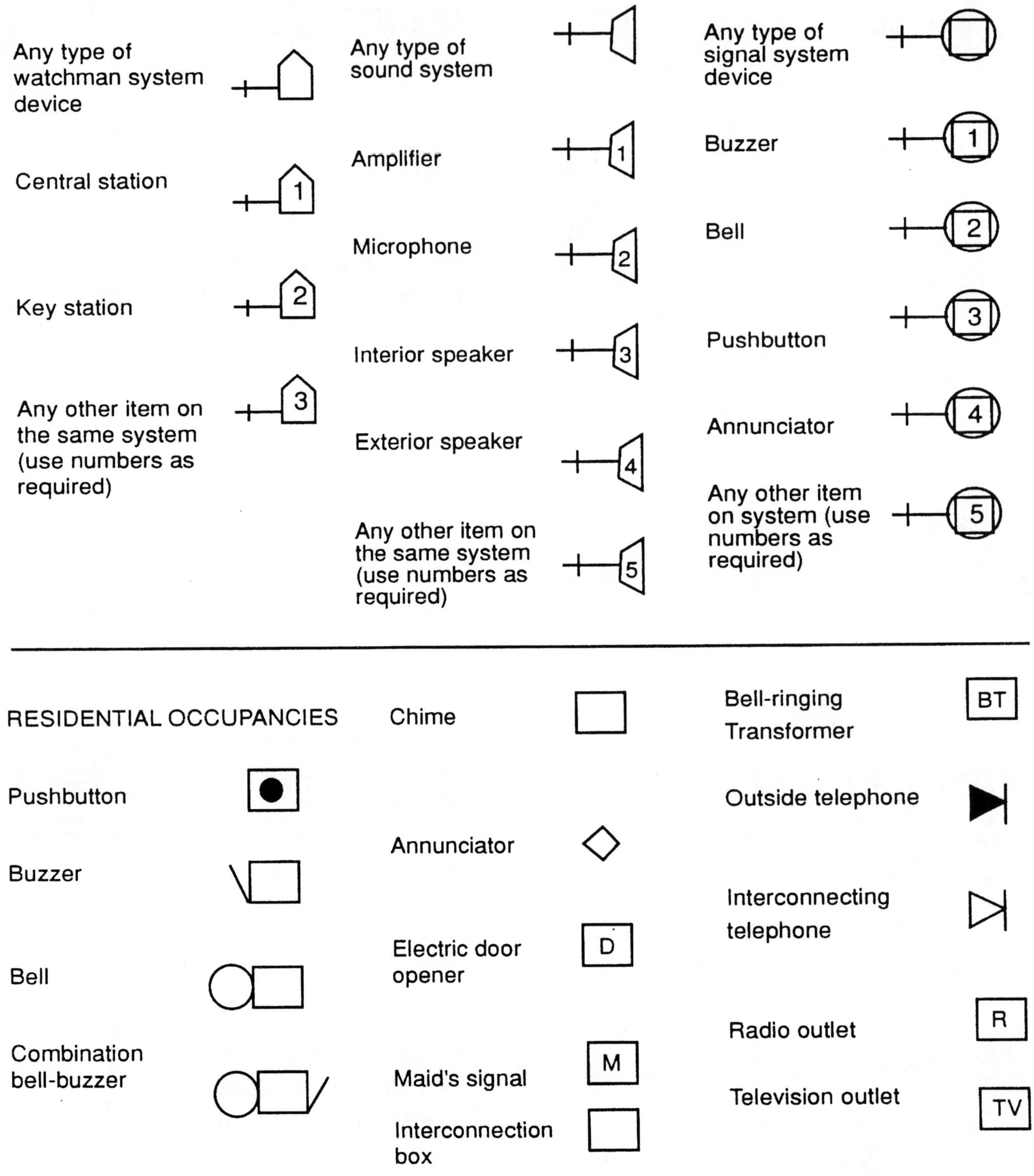

Any type of watchman system device	Any type of sound system	Any type of signal system device
Central station	Amplifier	Buzzer
	Microphone	Bell
Key station	Interior speaker	Pushbutton
Any other item on the same system (use numbers as required)	Exterior speaker	Annunciator
	Any other item on the same system (use numbers as required)	Any other item on system (use numbers as required)

RESIDENTIAL OCCUPANCIES

Pushbutton	Chime	Bell-ringing Transformer — BT
Buzzer	Annunciator	Outside telephone
Bell	Electric door opener — D	Interconnecting telephone
Combination bell-buzzer	Maid's signal — M	Radio outlet — R
	Interconnection box	Television outlet — TV

Figure A-6 - ANSI Electrical Symbols (Page 6 of 8)

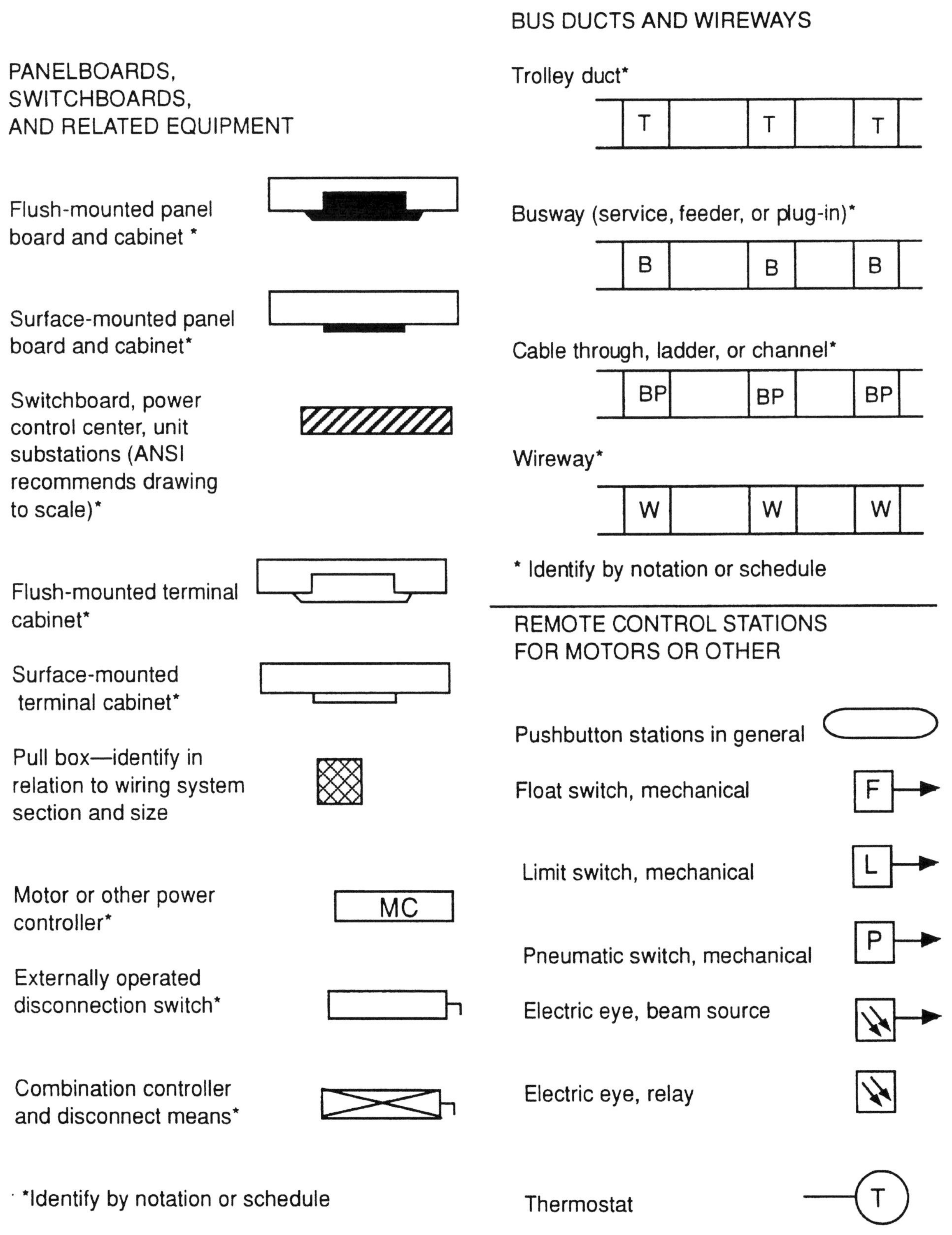

APPENDIX A

Blueprint Symbols

PANELBOARDS, SWITCHBOARDS, AND RELATED EQUIPMENT

Flush-mounted panel board and cabinet *

Surface-mounted panel board and cabinet*

Switchboard, power control center, unit substations (ANSI recommends drawing to scale)*

Flush-mounted terminal cabinet*

Surface-mounted terminal cabinet*

Pull box—identify in relation to wiring system section and size

Motor or other power controller*

Externally operated disconnection switch*

Combination controller and disconnect means*

*Identify by notation or schedule

BUS DUCTS AND WIREWAYS

Trolley duct*

| T | | T | | T |

Busway (service, feeder, or plug-in)*

| B | | B | | B |

Cable through, ladder, or channel*

| BP | | BP | | BP |

Wireway*

| W | | W | | W |

* Identify by notation or schedule

REMOTE CONTROL STATIONS FOR MOTORS OR OTHER

Pushbutton stations in general

Float switch, mechanical — F

Limit switch, mechanical — L

Pneumatic switch, mechanical — P

Electric eye, beam source

Electric eye, relay

Thermostat — T

Figure A-6 - ANSI Electrical Symbols (Page 7 of 8)

APPENDIX A
Blueprint Symbols

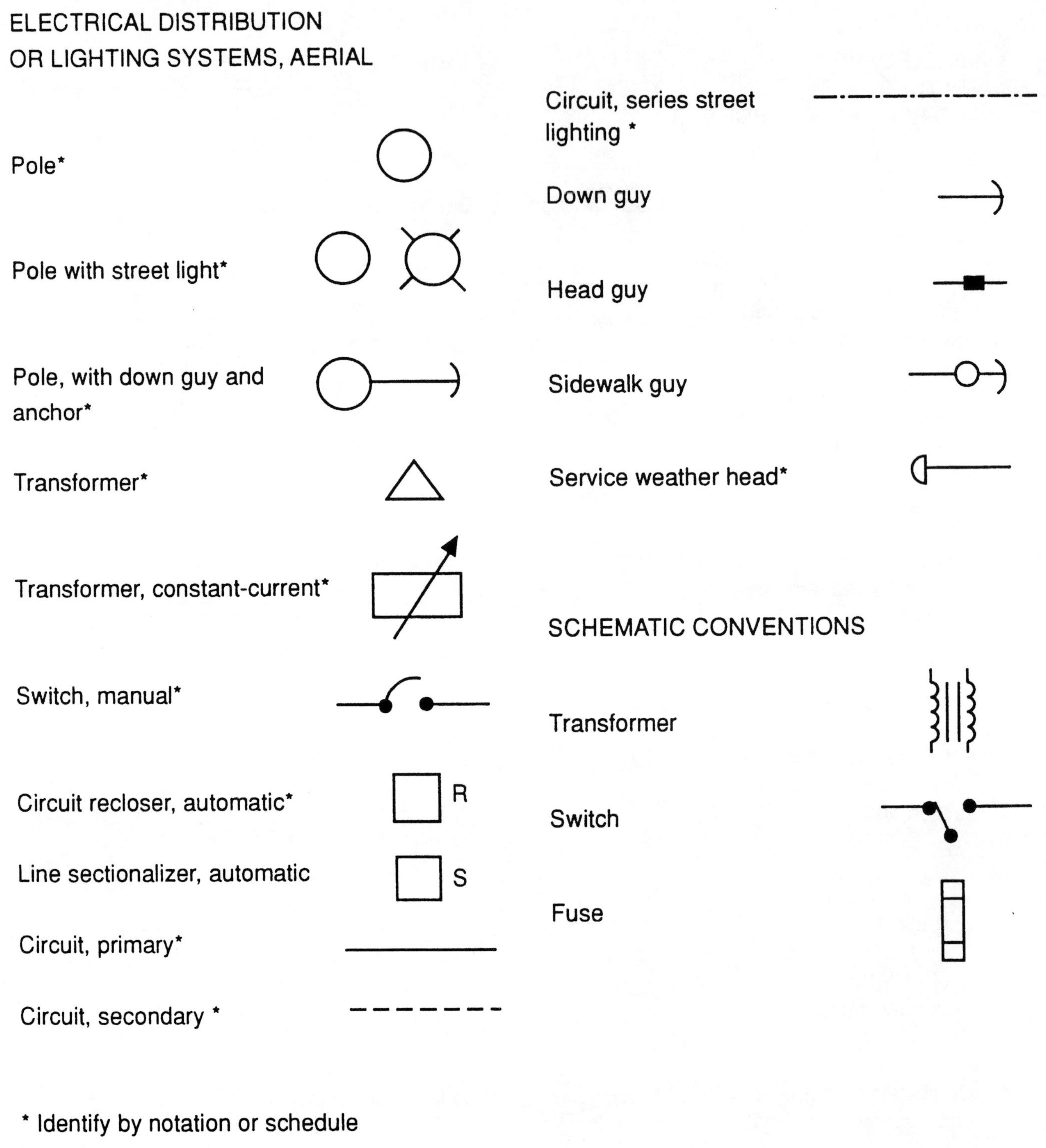

ELECTRICAL DISTRIBUTION
OR LIGHTING SYSTEMS, AERIAL

Pole*	○
Pole with street light*	○ ⊗
Pole, with down guy and anchor*	○—→
Transformer*	△
Transformer, constant-current*	▱ with arrow
Switch, manual*	—•/•—
Circuit recloser, automatic*	□ R
Line sectionalizer, automatic	□ S
Circuit, primary*	———
Circuit, secondary *	— — — —

Circuit, series street lighting *	—·—·—·—
Down guy	—→
Head guy	—■—
Sidewalk guy	—○—)
Service weather head*	⊐—

SCHEMATIC CONVENTIONS

Transformer	(coil symbol)
Switch	—•/•—
Fuse	▯

* Identify by notation or schedule

Figure A-6 - ANSI Electrical Symbols (Page 8 of 8)

APPENDIX A

Blueprint Symbols

Exposed wiring	——— E ———
Wiring concealed in ceiling or wall	———————
Wiring concealed in floor	— — — — — — —
Wiring turned up	———————○
Wiring turned down	———————●
Branch-circuit homerun to panelboard*	———————▸▸ or ** ——————◣◣ 1 2

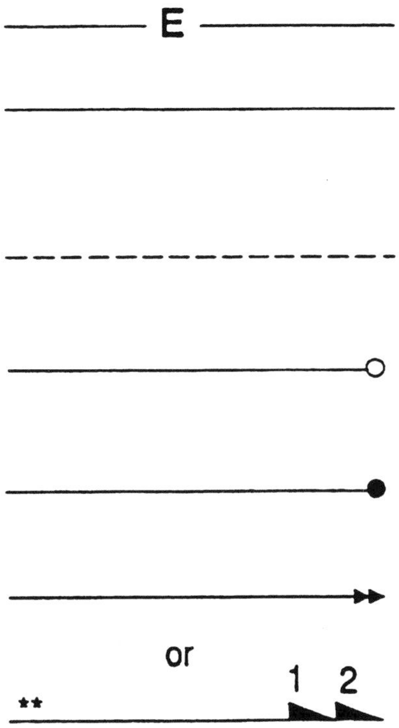

* Number of arrowheads indicate number of circuits. A number at each arrowhead may be used to identify circuit numbers

** Half arrowheads are sometimes used for homeruns to avoid confusing them with drawing callouts

Figure A-7 - Circuit Lines Used on Electrical Drawings

APPENDIX A

Blueprint Symbols

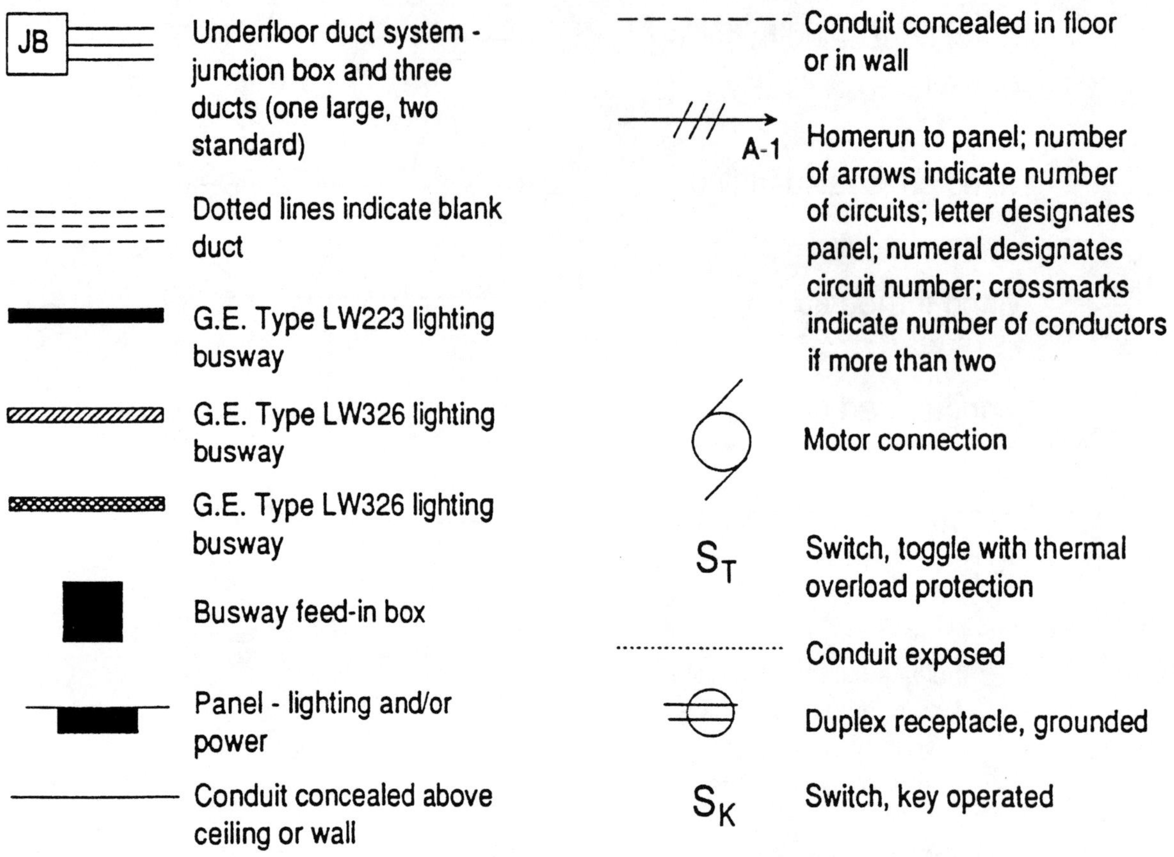

JB	Underfloor duct system - junction box and three ducts (one large, two standard)
======	Dotted lines indicate blank duct
▬▬▬	G.E. Type LW223 lighting busway
▨▨▨	G.E. Type LW326 lighting busway
▦▦▦	G.E. Type LW326 lighting busway
■	Busway feed-in box
▭	Panel - lighting and/or power
———	Conduit concealed above ceiling or wall
– – – –	Conduit concealed in floor or in wall
→/// A-1	Homerun to panel; number of arrows indicate number of circuits; letter designates panel; numeral designates circuit number; crossmarks indicate number of conductors if more than two
◯	Motor connection
S_T	Switch, toggle with thermal overload protection
....	Conduit exposed
⊖	Duplex receptacle, grounded
S_K	Switch, key operated

Figure A-8 - Electrical Symbols Used by One Consulting Engineering Firm

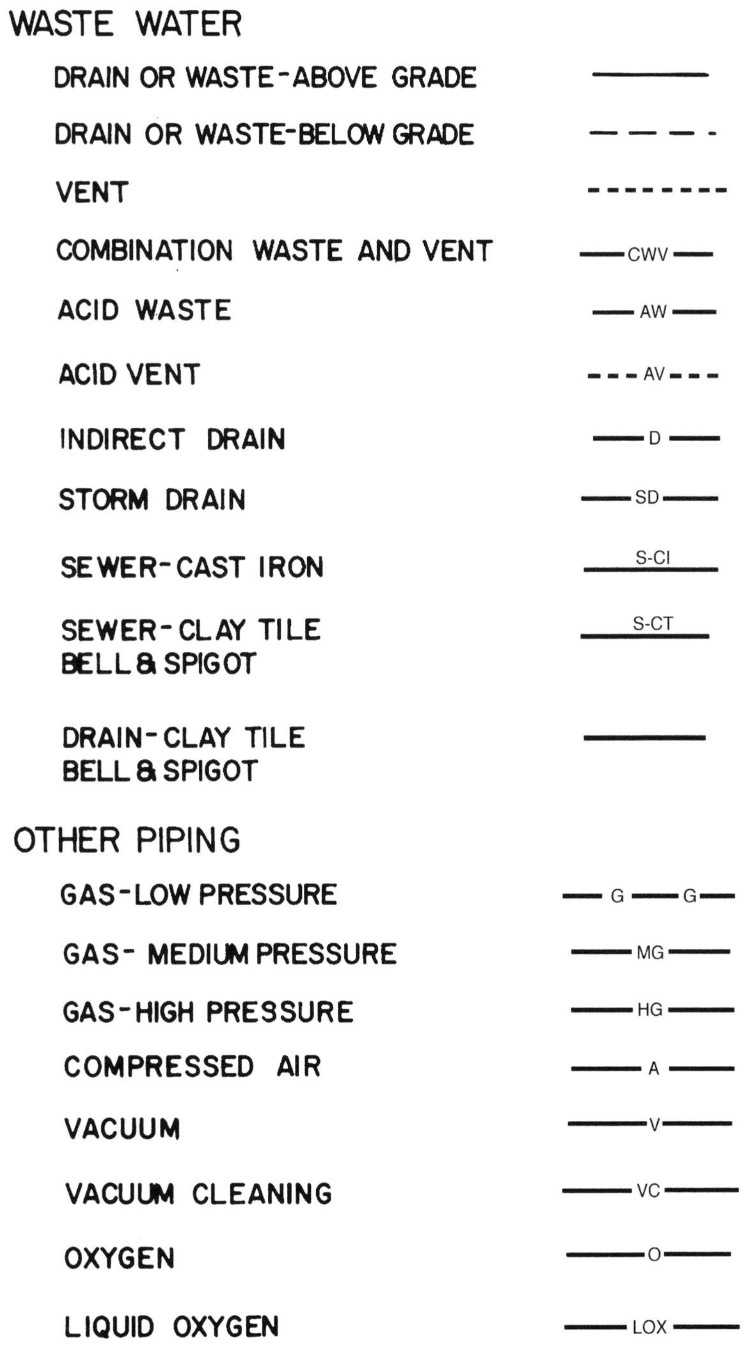

APPENDIX A

Blueprint Symbols

WASTE WATER

DRAIN OR WASTE-ABOVE GRADE	———
DRAIN OR WASTE-BELOW GRADE	— — — -
VENT	- - - - - - -
COMBINATION WASTE AND VENT	—CWV—
ACID WASTE	—AW—
ACID VENT	- - -AV- - -
INDIRECT DRAIN	—D—
STORM DRAIN	—SD—
SEWER-CAST IRON	—S-CI—
SEWER-CLAY TILE BELL & SPIGOT	—S-CT—
DRAIN-CLAY TILE BELL & SPIGOT	———

OTHER PIPING

GAS-LOW PRESSURE	—G—G—
GAS-MEDIUM PRESSURE	—MG—
GAS-HIGH PRESSURE	—HG—
COMPRESSED AIR	—A—
VACUUM	—V—
VACUUM CLEANING	—VC—
OXYGEN	—O—
LIQUID OXYGEN	—LOX—

Figure A-9 - Piping Symbols

APPENDIX A

Blueprint Symbols

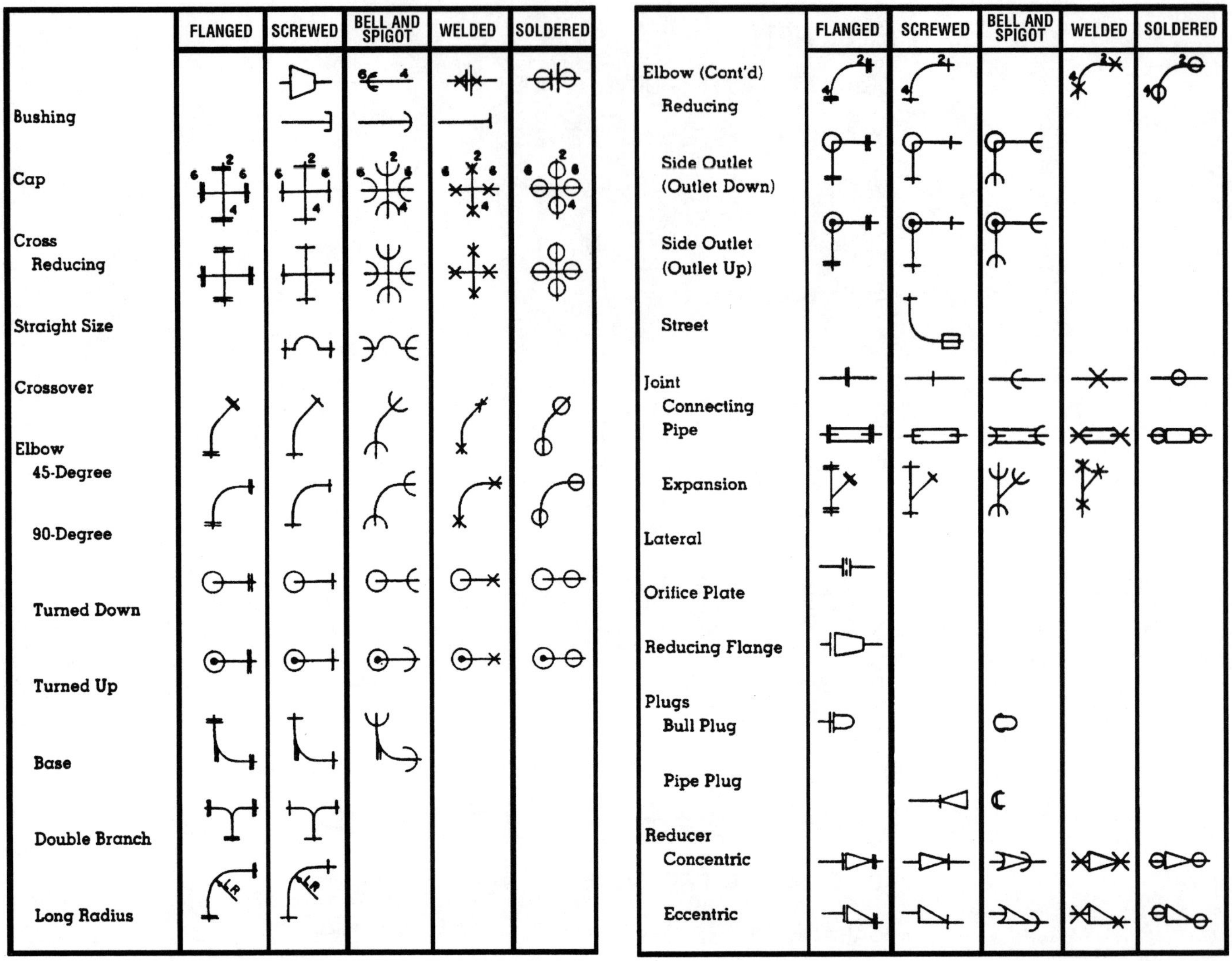

	FLANGED	SCREWED	BELL AND SPIGOT	WELDED	SOLDERED
Bushing					
Cap					
Cross Reducing					
Cross Straight Size					
Crossover					
Elbow 45-Degree					
Elbow 90-Degree					
Elbow Turned Down					
Elbow Turned Up					
Elbow Base					
Elbow Double Branch					
Elbow Long Radius					

	FLANGED	SCREWED	BELL AND SPIGOT	WELDED	SOLDERED
Elbow (Cont'd) Reducing					
Side Outlet (Outlet Down)					
Side Outlet (Outlet Up)					
Street					
Joint Connecting Pipe					
Expansion					
Lateral					
Orifice Plate					
Reducing Flange					
Plugs Bull Plug					
Pipe Plug					
Reducer Concentric					
Eccentric					

Figure A-10 - Fitting Symbols (Page 1 of 3)

SHEET METAL — TRAINEE TASK MODULE 04403

APPENDIX A

Blueprint Symbols

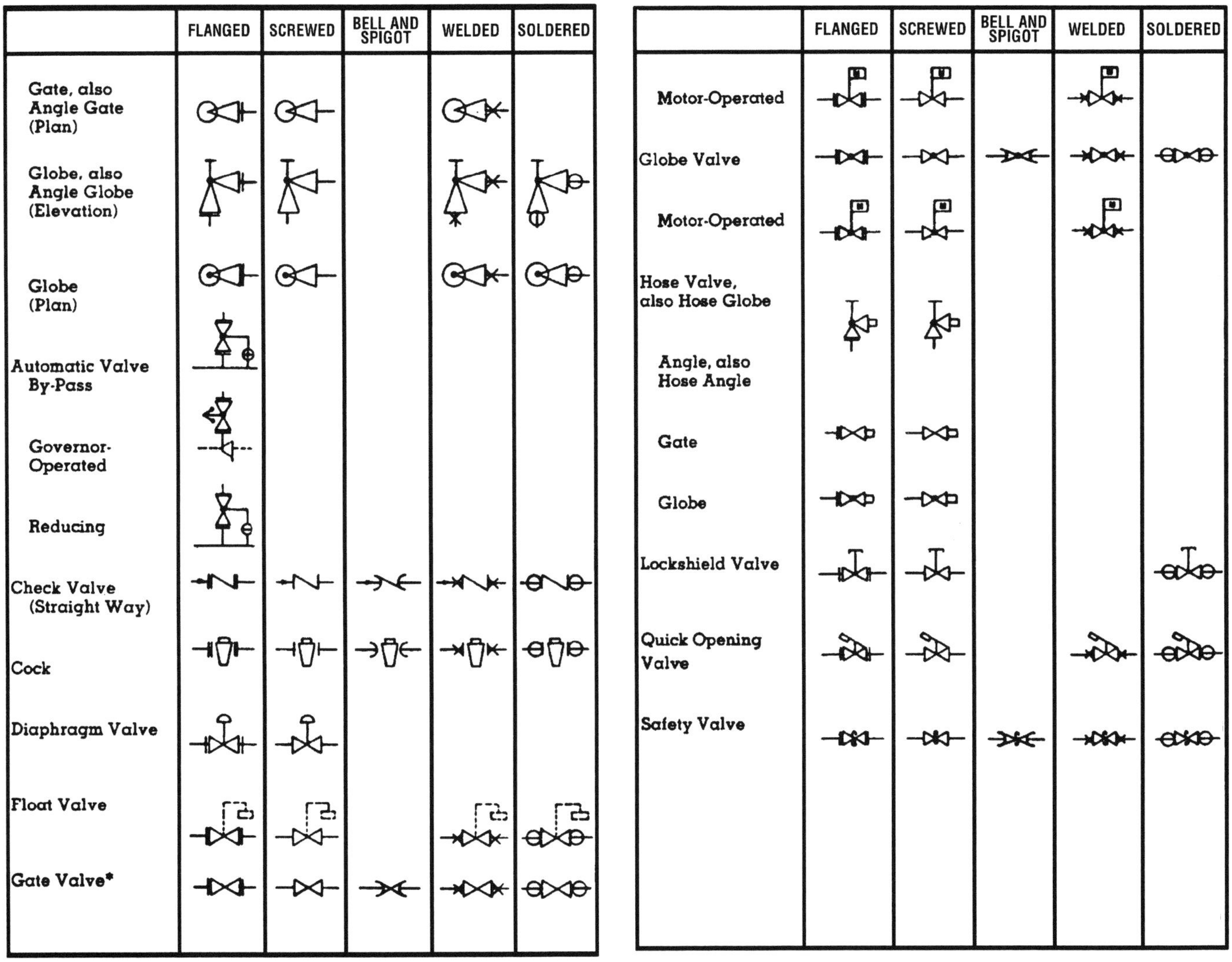

	FLANGED	SCREWED	BELL AND SPIGOT	WELDED	SOLDERED
Gate, also Angle Gate (Plan)	⊖⊲┤	⊖⊲┤		⊖⊲╳	
Globe, also Angle Globe (Elevation)					
Globe (Plan)	⊖⊲┤	⊖⊲┤		⊖⊲╳	⊖⊲⊖
Automatic Valve By-Pass					
Governor-Operated					
Reducing					
Check Valve (Straight Way)	┤∕├	┤∕├	→∕←	╳∕╳	⊖∕⊖
Cock	┤▯├	┤▯├	→▯←	╳▯╳	⊖▯⊖
Diaphragm Valve					
Float Valve					
Gate Valve*	┤⋈├	┤⋈├	→⋈←	╳⋈╳	⊖⋈⊖

	FLANGED	SCREWED	BELL AND SPIGOT	WELDED	SOLDERED
Motor-Operated					
Globe Valve	┤⋈├	┤⋈├	→⋈←	╳⋈╳	⊖⋈⊖
Motor-Operated					
Hose Valve, also Hose Globe					
Angle, also Hose Angle					
Gate	┤⋈├	┤⋈├			
Globe	┤⋈├	┤⋈├			
Lockshield Valve					⊖⋈⊖
Quick Opening Valve					⊖⋈⊖
Safety Valve	┤⋈├	┤⋈├	→⋈←	╳⋈╳	⊖⋈⊖

*Also used for General Stop Valve Symbol when amplified by specification.

Figure A-10 - Fitting Symbols (Page 2 of 3)

APPENDIX A

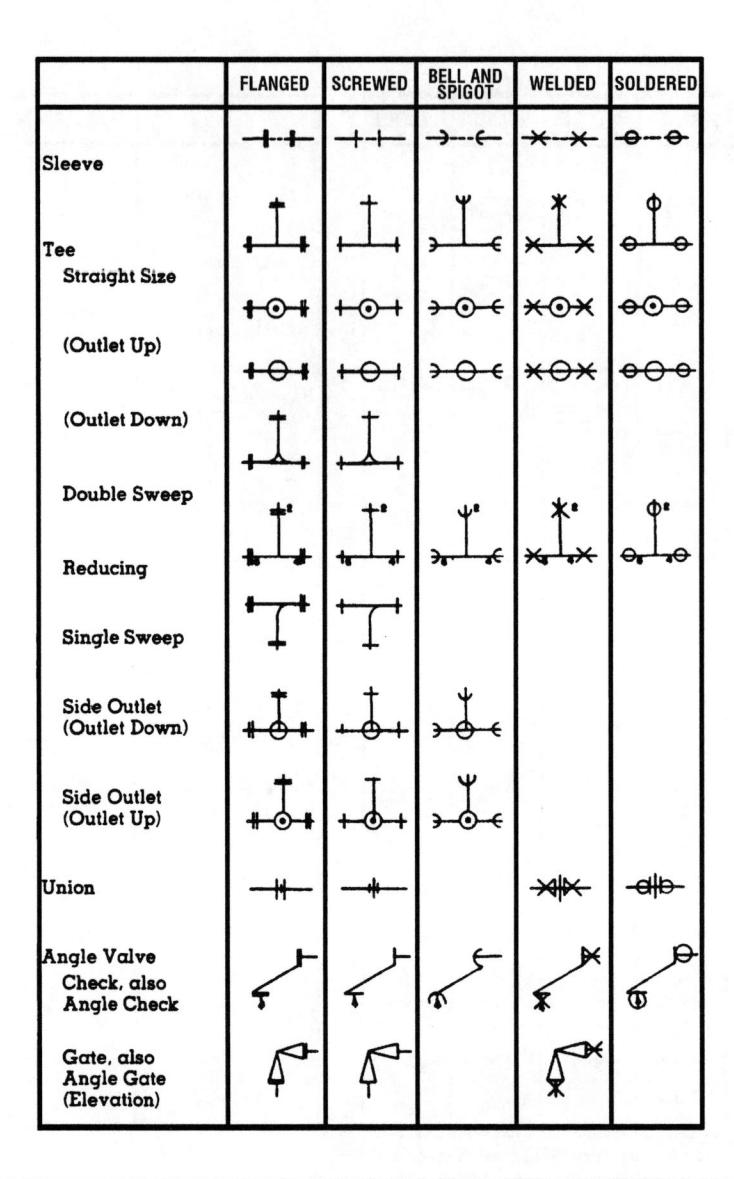

Blueprint Symbols

	FLANGED	SCREWED	BELL AND SPIGOT	WELDED	SOLDERED
Sleeve					
Tee Straight Size					
(Outlet Up)					
(Outlet Down)					
Double Sweep					
Reducing					
Single Sweep					
Side Outlet (Outlet Down)					
Side Outlet (Outlet Up)					
Union					
Angle Valve Check, also Angle Check					
Gate, also Angle Gate (Elevation)					

Figure A-10 - Fitting Symbols (Page 3 of 3)

APPENDIX A

Blueprint Symbols

TYPE OF FITTING		SCREWED OR SOCKET WELD	WELDED	FLANGED
		SINGLE LINE	SINGLE LINE	SINGLE LINE
90° ELBOW	TOP			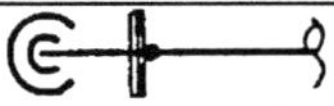
	SIDE	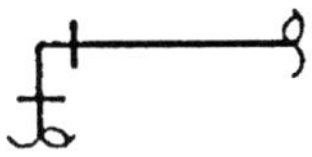	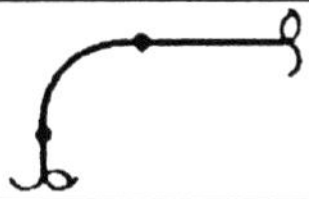	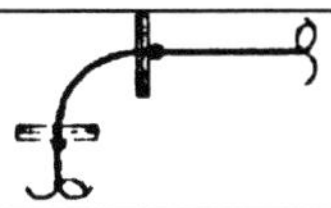
	BOTTOM			

Figure A-11 - Other Piping Symbols

APPENDIX A

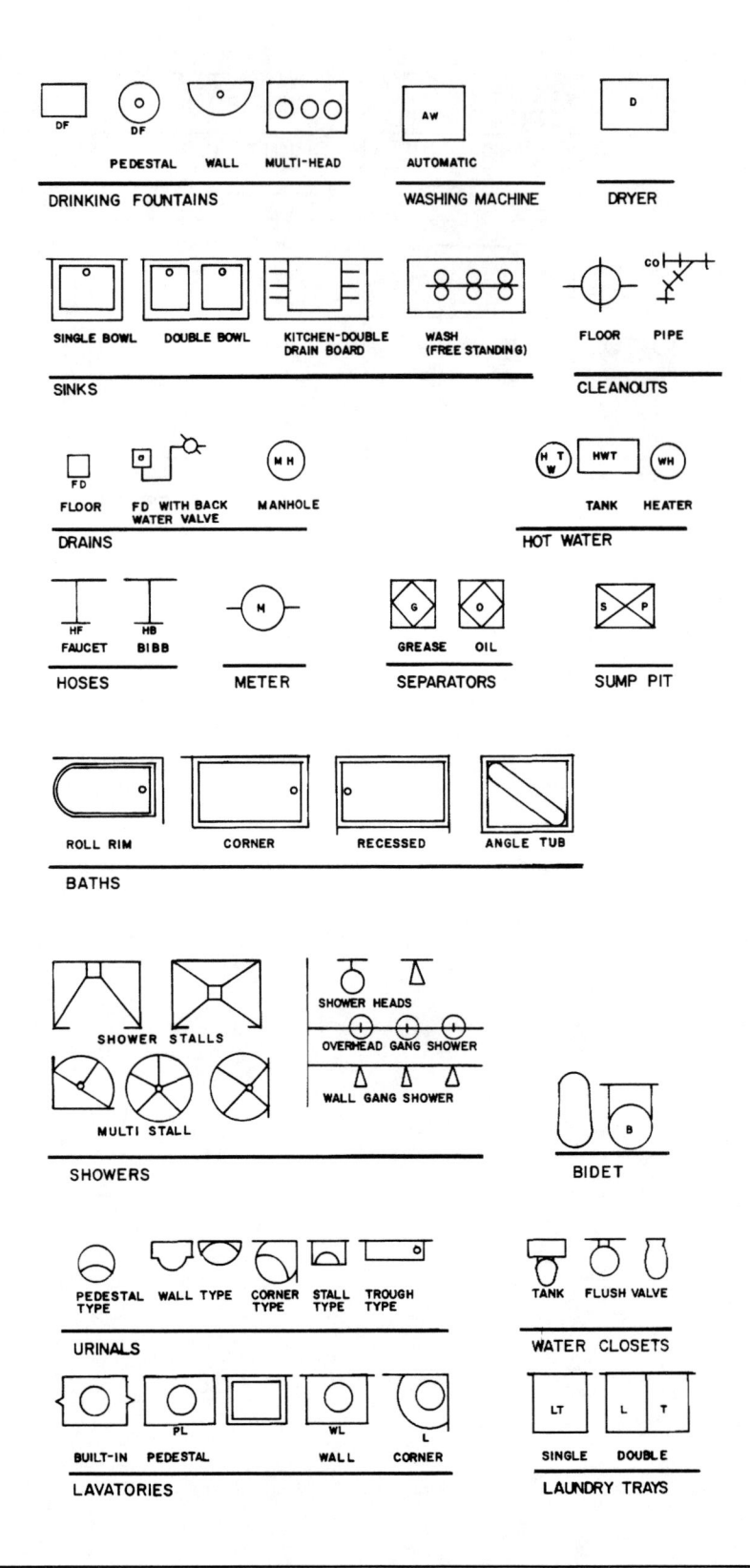

Blueprint Symbols

Figure A-12 - Fixture Symbols

APPENDIX A
Blueprint Symbols

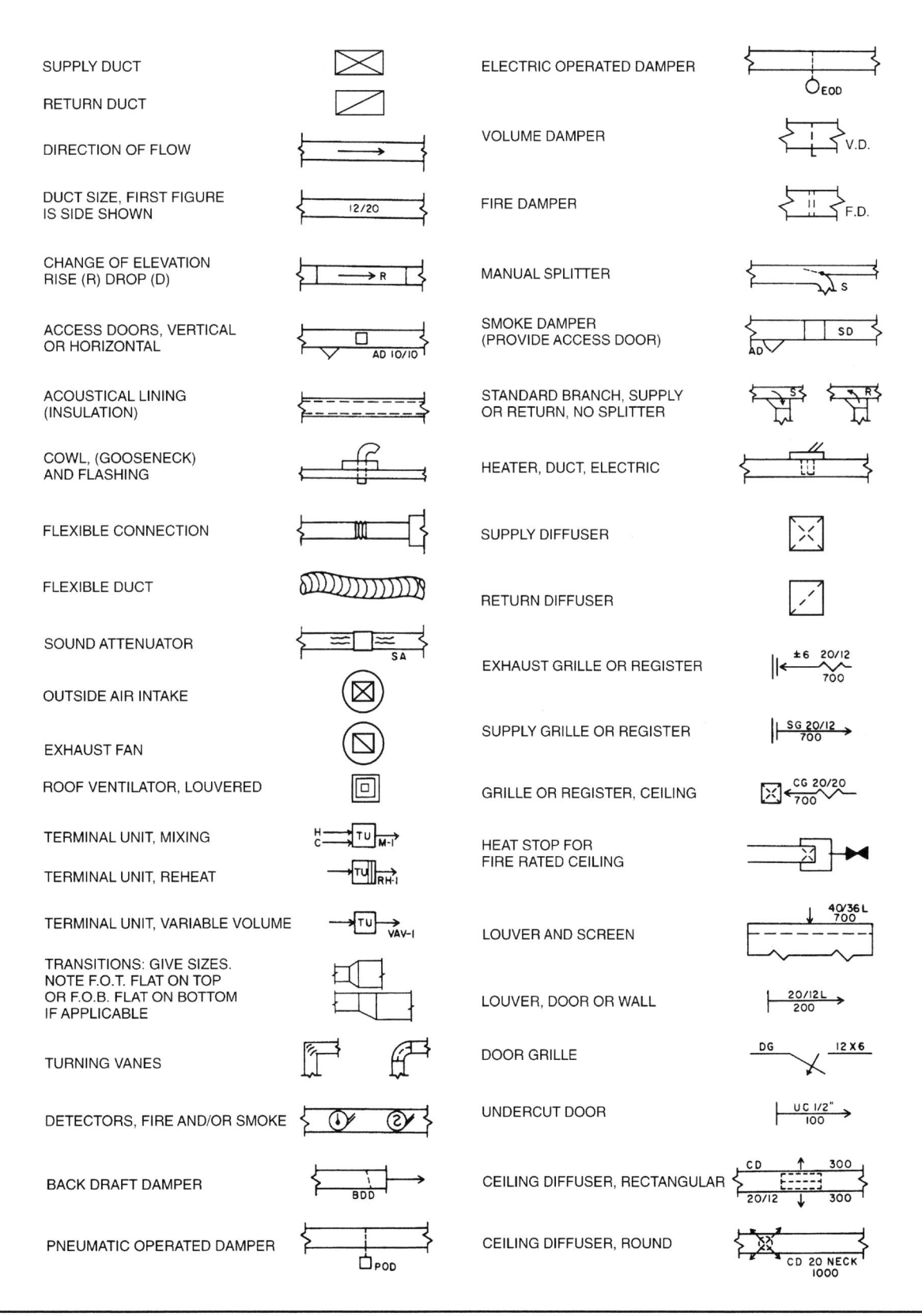

SUPPLY DUCT		ELECTRIC OPERATED DAMPER	
RETURN DUCT		VOLUME DAMPER	
DIRECTION OF FLOW		FIRE DAMPER	
DUCT SIZE, FIRST FIGURE IS SIDE SHOWN		MANUAL SPLITTER	
CHANGE OF ELEVATION RISE (R) DROP (D)		SMOKE DAMPER (PROVIDE ACCESS DOOR)	
ACCESS DOORS, VERTICAL OR HORIZONTAL		STANDARD BRANCH, SUPPLY OR RETURN, NO SPLITTER	
ACOUSTICAL LINING (INSULATION)		HEATER, DUCT, ELECTRIC	
COWL, (GOOSENECK) AND FLASHING		SUPPLY DIFFUSER	
FLEXIBLE CONNECTION		RETURN DIFFUSER	
FLEXIBLE DUCT		EXHAUST GRILLE OR REGISTER	
SOUND ATTENUATOR		SUPPLY GRILLE OR REGISTER	
OUTSIDE AIR INTAKE		GRILLE OR REGISTER, CEILING	
EXHAUST FAN		HEAT STOP FOR FIRE RATED CEILING	
ROOF VENTILATOR, LOUVERED		LOUVER AND SCREEN	
TERMINAL UNIT, MIXING		LOUVER, DOOR OR WALL	
TERMINAL UNIT, REHEAT		DOOR GRILLE	
TERMINAL UNIT, VARIABLE VOLUME		UNDERCUT DOOR	
TRANSITIONS: GIVE SIZES. NOTE F.O.T. FLAT ON TOP OR F.O.B. FLAT ON BOTTOM IF APPLICABLE		CEILING DIFFUSER, RECTANGULAR	
TURNING VANES		CEILING DIFFUSER, ROUND	
DETECTORS, FIRE AND/OR SMOKE			
BACK DRAFT DAMPER			
PNEUMATIC OPERATED DAMPER			

Figure A-13 - HVAC Symbols (Page 1 of 2)

APPENDIX A

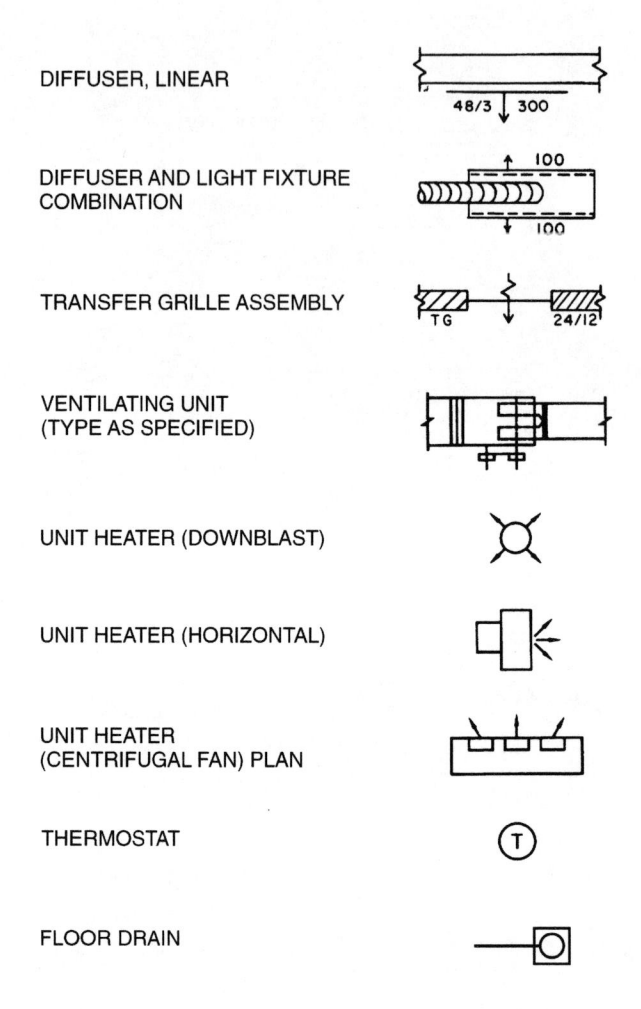

Blueprint Symbols

DIFFUSER, LINEAR	
DIFFUSER AND LIGHT FIXTURE COMBINATION	
TRANSFER GRILLE ASSEMBLY	
VENTILATING UNIT (TYPE AS SPECIFIED)	
UNIT HEATER (DOWNBLAST)	
UNIT HEATER (HORIZONTAL)	
UNIT HEATER (CENTRIFUGAL FAN) PLAN	
THERMOSTAT	
FLOOR DRAIN	

Figure A-13 - HVAC Symbols (Page 2 of 2)

APPENDIX B
Specifications

TABLE of CONTENTS

DIVISION	CATEGORY	PAGE NO.
	Special Conditions	48 - 49
1	General Conditions	50 - 55
14	Plumbing and Sprinkler	56
15	Heating, Ventilating, and Air Conditioning	55 - 59
16	Electrical	60

APPENDIX B

Specifications

XYZ Remodel Project
Bentonville, Arkansas

1. In all instances where contradictions between plans and specifications exist, the plans shall take precedence.

2. The heating and air-conditioning equipment noted in Section 15 of the specifications is not to be a part of the General Contract, but will be furnished and installed by XYZ. The General Contractor will be responsible for installing the support frames and platforms and will work with the XYZ equipment installer in providing crane service and assisting with the setting of the rooftop units as noted on the drawings. XYZ's heating and air-conditioning installer will direct the setting of the rooftop units.

3. SAFETY — All required exits must be kept usable throughout the construction period. Provide lighted enclosed walkways through new construction areas as required by governmental authorities having jurisdiction.

4. COORDINATION OF WORK — All operations concerning the remodel are to be coordinated with the proper XYZ authority in order to minimize disruption of office areas to remain at the east wall of building. These offices are to remain in operation until the open area offices are set for these people to occupy. Then these offices may be demolished, removed, and completion of construction in this area begin.

5. TEMPORARY PARTITION — When the ceiling and floor covering of new addition have been constructed, and prior to removing the existing office walls, install a temporary full height braced 2" x 6" stud wall along the wall of the office area where shown on plan with top of plywood to the roof deck. Distance of temporary wall from existing wall to be coordinated between Owner and Contractor.

6. TEMPORARY INTERIOR ENCLOSURES — The interior remodeling of the building will necessarily require that the work be done in stages and isolated to certain areas. The coordination of the work is to be verified with XYZ Representatives. Areas of the existing work which are undergoing remodeling processes shall be entirely enclosed by the use of temporary partitions and separated from the remainder of the building which is in operation. Partitions shall go from the floor to the ceiling or above the ceiling, as necessary, to control dust and noise.

Method of temporary partitions shall be as approved by XYZ Representative or the Architect.

Special Conditions (Page 1 of 2)

APPENDIX B
Specifications

7. SHOP DRAWINGS — The following shop drawings and submittals are required. Submit five copies of each to designated XYZ Representative.

    A. Folding Acoustical Partitions
    B. Exterior Canopy System
    C. Glass and Glazing in the Storefront
    D. Electrical Submittals
    E. Plumbing Submittals
    F. Millwork, including doors
    G. Hardware Schedule
    H. Ceiling Tile Sample
    I. Overhead Doors and Dock Equipment
    J. Toilet Partitions
    K. Sprinkler Drawings Approved by Mutual Insurance

8. SALVAGED MATERIALS — Drawings and specifications call for the demolition and remodeling of certain portions of the existing building. Salvaged materials shall remain the property of the Owner. If the Owner does not wish to retain these materials, they shall become the property of the Contractor and he shall be responsible for their disposal. These items include but are not limited to the following:

    Unit Heaters
    Doors and Hardware
    Electrical Panels
    Switches, Wiring, and Light Fixtures
    Water Heater
    Plumbing Fixtures and Trim

APPENDIX B

Specifications

1-1 GENERAL — The work to be done hereunder includes the furnishing of all labor, materials, and equipment necessary to complete the construction of an existing building renovation as shown and described in the drawings, specifications, and contract documents.

Before submitting his quotation, the Contractor shall satisfy himself as to the nature and location of the work; the confirmation of the ground; materials, tools, equipment; and other facilities required before and during the work, as well as general and local conditions which can affect the work. The contractor accepts the work site as found, unless otherwise specifically stated in his quotation for the work. No compensation shall be made by the Owner to the Contractors for any Contractors' errors in bids.

The Contractor's quotation shall include the cost of all utility tie-ins, including tap fees for sewage, drainage, water supply, sprinkler system supply, natural gas, electricity, street cuts and replacement, etc., whether or not such work is on Owner's and/or public property in order to insure a complete job. Performance bonds, permits, and/or deposits required are also to be included in the quotation. XYZ will not honor any extras for these items.

1-2 DEFINITIONS — The word "XYZ" shall mean XYZ Properties, Inc., Bentonville, Arkansas, acting through its duly authorized representatives.

The word "OWNER" shall mean XYZ Properties, Inc., Bentonville, Arkansas.

The word "ARCHITECT" shall mean Sam Spearing, Architects and Engineers, who prepared contract documents for the project.

The word "CONTRACTOR" shall mean the person, persons, partnership, company, firm, or corporation entering into the contract for the performance of the work required by it, and the legal representative of said party, or agent appointed to act for said party in the performance of the work.

The word "CONTRACT" shall mean, collectively, all of the covenants, terms, and stipulations contained in the various portions of the contract, to-wit: bid letter, bids, specifications, plans, and shop drawings as well as any addenda, letter of authorization or instruction, and any change orders which may be originated by XYZ.

1-3 CORRELATION AND INTENT OF DOCUMENTS — The contract documents are complementary to the specifications, and what is called for by any one shall be binding as if called for by all. It is the intent of the contractual documents to have a complete operating facility constructed, and with all services that are within the contract connected and in operating condition.

1-4 DRAWINGS AND SPECIFICATIONS — This specification is for general use and may apply to more than one building system such as masonry buildings, pre-engineered metal buildings, etc. Check drawings for items which are included in the work. Drawings shall govern when variations from this specification are found.

Contractor shall promptly call XYZ and the Architect's attention to any apparent contradictions, ambiguities, errors, discrepancies or omissions, in the plans or specifications. No extras shall

APPENDIX B

Specifications

be allowed for any such items which the Contractor fails to report to XYZ and the Architect prior to the award of the contract.

All drawings, prints, specifications, or other documents furnished by XYZ or prepared by the Contractor or his subcontractors specifically for the work shall become the sole property of XYZ and shall be returned to him at completion of the work.

When necessary, furnish shop drawings in sufficient quantity and, after approval by XYZ, these drawings shall be considered a part of the Contract Documents. Checking and approval by XYZ shall not relieve Contractor of any responsibility for errors, omissions, or discrepancies on such shop drawings.

1-5   INSURANCE — The Contractor shall carry insurance as listed below and furnish a certification of insurance before construction is started. The certification must indicate that the insurance will not be cancelled while the work specified therein is in progress, without ten (10) days prior notice to XYZ.

TYPE		LIMITS OF INSURANCE	
Workmen's Compensation		Statutory Amount	
CONTRACTOR'S PUBLIC LIABILITY			
Bodily Injury (including death)		Each Person	$250,000
		Each Accident	$500,000
Property Damage — Each Accident			$100,000
Aggregate			$100,000
CONTRACTOR'S AUTOMOBILE LIABILITY			
Bodily Injury (including death)		Each Person	$250,000
		Each Accident	$500,000
Property Damage			$100,000
CONTRACTOR'S PUBLIC LIABILITY			
Bodily Injury (including death)		Each Person	$250,000
		Each Accident	$500,000
Property Damage — Each Accident			$100,000
Aggregate			$100,000

The contractor shall take out and maintain throughout the course of construction a Builders' All Risks Insurance Policy in the amount of the contract. This policy shall name as insureds the Owner and General Contractor; their subcontractors' loss shall be adjusted with payment to the Owner and General Contractor. Until work is fully completed and accepted by the Owner, Contractor shall promptly repair any damage to the work. The original of said policy shall be delivered to the Owner prior to commencement of work and returned to the Contractor upon completion of work for cancellation and refund of premium, if any.

Division 1 - General Conditions (Page 2 of 6)

APPENDIX B

Specifications

1-6   BOND — The Contractor shall furnish, where required by Owner, an approved performance bond in an amount equal to one hundred percent (100%) of the contract price. Verify with Owner prior to bid. The bond shall contain the following paragraph.

> "And the said surety, for value received, hereby stipulates and agrees that no change, extension of time, alteration or addition to the terms of the contract or to the work to be performed thereunder or the specifications accompanying the same shall in any way affect its obligations on this bond, and it does hereby waive notice of any change, extension of time, alteration or addition to the terms of the contract or to the specifications."

1-7   TAXES — The Contractors shall pay all costs of Social Security payments, unemployment insurance, sales tax, and any other charges imposed by federal, state, and local governments.

1-8   PERMITS AND REGULATIONS — The Contractor shall obtain all permits required for the work, including necessary temporary permits, give all notices, and pay all fees. All equipment, materials, and workmanship shall comply with requirements of federal, state and municipal codes and ordinances, underwriters' rules and specifications. Proposals shall be based on the plans and specifications with any exceptions required by codes and regulations being noted in writing by the Contractor in his proposal so that an equitable adjustment can be made in the contract price. Otherwise, it shall be construed that the Contractor is willing to comply with such codes, ordinances, rules, and regulations without additional cost to the Owner. Any equipment, materials, and workmanship installed contrary to above regulations shall be removed and replaced at the Contractor's expense.

1-9   SUPERINTENDENCE AND EMPLOYEES — The Contractor shall provide competent superintendence satisfactory to the Owner at all times. The superintendent shall not be changed except with consent of the Owner, unless he proves to be unsatisfactory to the Contractor and ceases to be in his employ. The Contractor shall be totally responsible for the employment, supervision, welfare, and compensations of employees, and shall be responsible for any work performed by employees or subcontractors.

1-10   SUBCONTRACTS — The Owner shall have the right to approve or disapprove the subcontractors to be used in the work.

1-11   SEPARATE CONTRACTS — The Owner reserves the right to let other contracts in connection with the work. The Contractor shall give other contractors reasonable opportunity for the storage of their materials and the execution of their work. The Contractor shall properly connect and coordinate work with other contractors. When any other Contractor's work is involved in the proper execution and results of the Contractor's work, he shall inspect and measure the other Contractor's work and report any discrepancy to the Owner.

APPENDIX B

Specifications

1-12 DISCHARGE OF LIENS — If at any time there is evidence that a claim which is chargeable to the Contractor may become a lien against the premises, the Owner may retain out of the contract price an amount sufficient to indemnify it against any lien grown out of such claim, and against all costs and expenses (including attorney's fees) which Owner may incur in connection with the claim of lien or arising out of any action related thereto. If payment of the contract price has been made to the Contractor, he shall reimburse the Owner for all monies, costs, expenses, and disbursements (including attorney's fees) that the Owner may be compelled to pay to discharge any claim or lien against the premises. When requesting the final payment for completion of contract, the Contractor shall submit to the Owner an executed and notarized Contractor's Affidavit stating that all subcontractors and suppliers have been paid in full. Upon Owner's request, Contractor will supply lien waivers from all subcontractors and material suppliers.

1-13 GUARANTEE — The Contractor shall guarantee materials and workmanship against defects for a minimum period of one (1) year from the date of final acceptance. Upon notification from the Owner, the Contractor agrees to promptly repair or replace any defects and all resulting damage to the satisfaction of the Owner and at no cost to the Owner.

1-14 PAYMENTS TO THE CONTRACTOR — At thirty (30) day intervals, the Contractor may submit to the Owner requests for payment for the work completed to date, less a retainage of ten percent (10%) of the amount due, less the amount of payments previously made.

1-15 CREDITS AND EXTRAS — When additions to, or deletions from, the work covered in the contract are required by the Owner, a change order shall be executed by the owner and the Contractor including the costs of the changes involved.

1-16 INSPECTIONS — XYZ and its representatives shall, at all times, have access to the project, and the Contractor shall give XYZ a sufficient advance notice of when the work will be ready for inspection at the following stages of construction:

1. Inspection of soil condition after excavation for footings.
2. Inspection of steel reinforcing before placement of concrete.
3. Inspection after structural steel is in place.
4. Inspection of electrical and plumbing rough-in before floor slab is poured.
5. Inspection of roofing application as roofing contractor begins work.
6. Inspection of electrical and plumbing rough-in before rough-in is covered in walls and ceiling.
7. Final electrical, mechanical, and plumbing inspections.
8. Inspection of driveway base material after it has been set up prior to paving.
9. Final inspection of complete job.

APPENDIX B

Specifications

1-17 CLIMATIC CONDITIONS — When so directed by XYZ, the Contractor shall suspend work that may be subject to damage by climatic conditions.

1-18 TEMPORARY SERVICES — The Contractor shall pay for all fuel, electrical current, and water required for construction purposes. The Contractor shall also provide temporary heat and temporary toilet, if required, as directed by the Owner.

1-19 SUBSTITUTIONS — The Contractor shall base his bid on the cost of the materials and/or products specified. If the Contractor desires to substitute any equal material of another brand or manufacturer, it shall be requested in writing at least five (5) days prior to the bid due date. Requests from subcontractors will not be considered. Samples and/or technical data on the proposed product or material shall accompany these requests.

1-20 MEASUREMENTS, LINES, AND GRADES — The Contractor shall be responsible for the accuracy of all lines and grades of the work. The Contractor shall do all field work necessary to layout and maintain the work. No extra charge or compensation will be allowed due to differences between actual dimensions and the measurements indicated on the drawings; any difference which may be found shall be submitted to the Owner for his consideration before proceeding with the work. The Owner will provide a survey of the property including reference points, property corners, and bench marks.

1-21 OCCUPANCY PRIOR TO FINAL ACCEPTANCE — The Owner reserves the right to take possession and use any completed or partially completed portion of the project, providing it does not interfere with the Contractor's work. Such possession or use of the project shall not be considered as final acceptance of the project, or any portion thereof.

1-22 SAFETY — The Contractor shall provide and continuously maintain adequate safeguards, such as railings, temporary walks, lights, etc., to prevent the occurrence of accidents, injuries, or damage to any person or property. The Contractor shall adhere to the requirements of the Federal Occupational Safety and Health Act a it relates to the work covered in the contract.

1-23 USE OF PREMISES — The Contractor shall occupy, use, and permit others to use the premises only for the purpose of completing the work to be performed under his contract with the Owner. Storage and other uses required by the Contractor shall be in areas designated by the Owner.

1-24 USE OF ADJOINING PREMISES — The Contractor shall confine his operations to the area contained within the property lines as shown on the plot plan. The Contractor may use public streets and alleys as permitted by the jurisdictional authorities. No equipment, forms, materials, scaffold, or persons shall encroach or trespass on any adjoining property, unless prior written consent of the landowner is obtained by the Contractor.

APPENDIX B

Specifications

1-25 PROTECTION OF ADJACENT WORK AND PROPERTY — The Contractor shall protect all adjacent work and property such as structures, fences, trees, hedges, etc., from all damage resulting from the operations. Should it be necessary to remove or trim, etc., an existing tree, hedge, etc., the Contractor shall secure all permits and approvals and pay any and all costs arising therefrom. The Contractor shall check all projects, off-sets, footings, etc., and determine that there are no encroachments of the building or a appurtenances on adjoining property. Where encroachments occur as a result of the work performed under these plans and specifications, the Contractor shall remove such encroachments at his own cost and at no expense to the Owner.

1-26 CLEANING UP — The Contractor shall keep the project clean at all times. No accumulation of waste material or rubbish shall be permitted; and at the completion of the work, the Contractor shall remove all rubbish, tools, and surplus materials, and shall leave the work "broom clean" and ready for use, unless otherwise specified.

1-27 CONSTRUCTION RELATED DOCUMENTS REQUIRED BY XYZ — Prior to the payment by XYZ of the final contract retainage for XYZ built facilities, or the first month's rent for facilities built by developers other than XYZ, the following documents shall have been placed on record with XYZ:

1. Letter from registered consulting engineering firm attesting to the adequacy of the asphalt paving design.

2. Executed copy of roofing guarantee.

3. Completed Maintenance Data Sheet (forms supplied by XYZ).

4. Copies of structural steel columns, beams, bar joists, and steel decking manufacturer's shippers' bills of lading.

5. Copies of soil density tests.

6. Copies of concrete cylinder tests.

7. Copies of test results of asphalt pavement base thickness and density and of asphalt topping conformance with specifications.

8. Final letter of acceptance of fire protection sprinkler system from Mutual Insurance.

9. Copies of manufacturer's five-year warranties on all heating and air-conditioning equipment.

APPENDIX B

Specifications

14-1   GENERAL — Comply with applicable state and local plumbing codes and standards pertaining to materials, products, and installation of potable water and sanitary sewage systems.

14-2   TESTING — Test each plumbing system in accordance with applicable codes and standards, sterilize potable water systems per state and local utility requirements.

Division 14 - Plumbing and Sprinkler

APPENDIX B

Specifications

15-1 **GENERAL** — Comply with applicable mechanical codes and standards pertaining to materials, products, and installation of air handling, metal ductwork, hot water systems, and chilled water systems.

15-2 **DATA** — Submit manufacturer's technical product data, assembly type shop drawings, wiring drawings, and maintenance data for each component of each HVAC system.

15-3 **MATERIALS** — Provide factory fabricated and tested equipment and materials of sizes, rating and characteristics indicated. Referenced equipment and materials indicate style and quality desired. Contact engineer for preliminary approval of any other manufacturer's submittal. Provide proper quantity of materials and equipment as required for complete installation of each HVAC system.

Identify each HVAC system's components with materials and designations as directed.

15-4 **INSTALLATION** — Install each system in accordance with applicable mechanical codes and standards; recognized industry practices, and manufacturer's recommendations.

Test and balance each HVAC system in accordance with applicable mechanical codes and standards; balance air handling system to CFMs shown on drawings. Report findings to engineer.

15-5 **KITCHEN** — Provide and install all supply, return, and ventilation ductwork shown, together with plenums, casings, dampers, turning vanes, grilles, ceiling outlets, heating coils, etc., including the setting of fans, filters, and air units.

Kitchen exhaust duct shall be 16 gauge steel assembled by welding. It shall drain back to the hood, using a slope as required by code. Access doors shall be grease tight construction with hinges and latches: locate where required by code and as required to provide access to fire protection devices in the duct. Make rigid connections to the hood and the fan; transition where required for connection to the fan; mastic at connection to the fan inlet. Coordinate required two hour fire rated drywall enclosure of kitchen exhaust duct provided by others with general contractor.

Spiral conduit and fittings shall be lock forming quality galvanized prime grade steel; both conduits and fittings from the same manufacturer; spiral locks seam; fittings constructed with welded seams.

Kitchen dishwasher exhaust shall be fabricated from new prime grade aluminum or stainless steel per 1985 SMACNA guidelines. Installed water tight with rigid connections with slope back to dishwasher as required by code.

Division 15 - Heating, Ventilating, and Air Conditioning (Page 1 of 3)

APPENDIX B

Specifications

15-6   SHEET STEEL — All other supply, return, and ventilation ductwork, plenums, dampers, etc. shall be new lock forming quality galvanized prime grade steel sheets fabricated, supported, and installed per SMACNA guidelines.

15-7   FLEXIBLE DUCTWORK — Flexible ductwork shall be factory fabricated with vinyl coated spring steel wire helix bonded to a continuous layer of vinyl impregnated and coated fiberglass mesh inner sleeve, a 1-inch thick glass fiber blanket insulation layer, and an outer moisture barrier jacket of Mylar/neoprene or vinyl conductance of 0.23 BTU/hr/sq.ft./OF at 75 degrees Fahrenheit; and shall be UL listed and shall comply with NFPA Standard 90A. All connection points shall be bonded with a mechanical fastener and taped. Maximum length of flexible duct shall be two feet on inlet of all VAV and fan powered boxes and six feet on all grille connections.

15-8   CEILING — Ceiling supply outlets, grilles and registers shall be provided in accordance with the schedule on the drawings by specified manufacturers.

Ceiling mounted devices shall be finished in off-white baked enamel. Sidewall supplies and registers shall be finished in a prime coat or a baked enamel finish and job painted in color required.

15-9   DUCT CONSTRUCTION — Per SMACNA 1985 guidelines, except for special duct construction specified hereinbefore, ductwork shall be constructed in accordance with 1985 SMACNA "HVAC duct construction standards" rated for 2-inch static pressure. This includes all ductwork accessories including but not limited to dampers, vanes and vane runners, hangers, and supports.

15-10   SUPPLY DUCT — Supply duct between air handling units and VAV and fan powered boxes shall be constructed in accordance with 1985 SMACNA "HVAC duct construction standards" reinforced for 4-inch static pressure.

15-11   FIRE WALLS — Where ducts penetrate 2-hour fire walls or floors, fire dampers shall be installed in the construction in a manner directed by the manufacturer of the dampers, with or without attached sleeves as required. Install angles completely framing each opening on both sides and attach to the damper body or sleeve with screws, bolts, or approved fastener. Leave space between the edges of the construction and the face of the sleeve or damper to accommodate expansion and contraction of the metal.

15-12   FITTINGS — All fittings in primary duct shall be radiused per 1985 SMACNA. No vanes, splitters, or dampers are allowed.

15-13   SEAMS AND JOINTS — All ductwork seams and joints shall be sealed according to SMACNA class B requirements. Fabricate ducts to prevent seams of joints being cut for the installation of grilles, registers or outlets.

Division 15 - Heating, Ventilating and Air Conditioning (Page 2 of 3)

APPENDIX B

Specifications

15-14 OPENINGS — Openings through structure required for ductwork will be provided by others unless otherwise shown.

15-15 REINFORCEMENT — Reinforce all ducts to prevent buckling, breathing, vibrations, or unnecessary noises during start-up, shut-down, and continuous operation of air handling system.

15-16 BALANCING DAMPERS — Provide balancing dampers at points of low pressure supply and exhaust where branches are taken from larger ducts. Use splitter dampers only where indicated.

15-17 SPACE REQUIREMENTS — In adherence to ceiling height schedules indicated; consult with other trades, and in conjunction with them, establish necessary space requirements for each trade so as to maintain required clearances. Where no ceiling height is stated, ductwork shall run as high as possible unless noted otherwise. Penetration of ductwork by pipes, conduits, electrical fixtures, or structural members is not acceptable.

15-18 FIRE DAMPERS — Fire damper shall be type A with wall or floor sleeves as required for proper protection of penetration; UL labeled and conforming to UL-555. Dampers shall be 90% free area as a minimum. Mechanical contractor must locate, provide, and install all fire dampers required by code.

15-19 DUCT ACCESS DOORS — Duct access doors shall be Air Balance FSA 100 or equivalent, galvanized steel frame and double wall hinged door with 1-inch insulation, gasketing, and latch. It shall be sized to permit servicing of fusible links in fire dampers and/or sized as noted into plenums for access to coils, filters, etc., where installed in lined ducts and/or plenums.

APPENDIX B

Specifications

16-1   GENERAL — All work shall be in strict compliance with latest edition of the National Electric Code and Applicable State and Local Codes. All work shall be done using 1MC, EMT, PVC, ENT, flexible conduit, surface raceway, cable tray, MC cable, AC cable, NM cable, as appropriate for the specific application.

Material and equipment shall be new, of standard manufacturer's construction, installed in accordance with accepted practice by competent workmen.

16-2   WIRE — Wire shall be #12 AWG minimum unless otherwise noted, with THHN or THW insulation and copper conductor.

16-3   OUTLET BOXES — Outlet boxes shall be 4 inches square, fitted with appropriate device ring or single piece masonry type set flush with finished surface.

16-4   SWITCHES — Switches shall be 15 AMP specification grade equal to P&S 501, 120-277 volts, mounted at 18 inches above floor unless otherwise noted.

16-5   RECEPTACLES — Receptacles shall be 15 AMP self-grounding specification grade equal to 5242, mounted at 18" above floor unless otherwise noted.

Receptacles, switch, telephone, and cover plates shall be smooth ivory plastic equal to sierra "P" series.

Division 16 - Electrical

NCCER CRAFT TRAINING USER UPDATES

The NCCER makes every effort to keep these manuals up-to-date and free of technical errors. We appreciate your help in this process. If you have an idea for improving this manual, or if you find an error, a typographical mistake, or an inaccuracy in the NCCER's Craft Training Manuals, please write us, using this form or a photocopy. Be sure to include the exact module number, page number, a description of the problem, and the correction, if possible. Your input will be brought to the attention of the Technical Review Committee. Thank you for your assistance.

Instructors – If you found that additional materials were necessary in order to teach this module effectively, please let us know so that we may include them in the Equipment/Materials list in the Instructor's Guide.

Write: Curriculum and Revision Department
National Center for Construction Education and Research
P.O. Box 141104
Gainesville, FL 32614-1104
Fax: 352-334-0932

Craft _____ Module Name _____

Module Number _____ Page Number(s) _____

Description of Problem _____

_____

_____

_____

(Optional) Correction of Problem _____

_____

_____

(Optional) Your Name and Address _____

_____

_____

BLUEPRINTS AND SPECIFICATIONS — TRAINEE TASK MODULE 04403

notes

The SMACNA Manuals

Module 04405

NATIONAL
CENTER FOR
CONSTRUCTION
EDUCATION AND
RESEARCH

Task Module 04405

THE SMACNA MANUALS

Objectives

Upon completion of this module, the trainee will be able to:

1. Demonstrate skill in locating standards for selected topics, fittings, or components.

2. Define the difference between standards and codes or ordinances.

3. Demonstrate skill in locating selected information in illustrations and tables.

4. List other pertinent organizations which establish codes and standards.

INTRODUCTION

The SMACNA manuals are technical manuals compiled by skilled personnel in the sheet metal and air conditioning trades. The manuals are written for the Sheet Metal and Air Conditioning Contractors' National Association (SMACNA) and contain technical engineering information pertaining to the design, construction, and field installation of various sheet metal applications. This module will introduce you to the important information and standards found in these manuals.

STANDARDS

The standards found in the **SMACNA** manuals are developed from engineering principles, research, and application data supplied by manufacturers, users, testing laboratories, and others having specialized experience in the sheet metal industry.

For example, the SMACNA manual pertaining to duct standards (which you will use in this module) is entitled *HVAC Duct Construction Standards – Metal and Flexible* (second edition, 1995). This SMACNA manual contains standards, in both English and metric measurements, organized according to the following sections of the book:

1. Introduction to Basic Duct Construction;
2. Fittings and Other Construction;
3. Round, Oval, and Flexible Duct;
4. Hangers and Supports;
5. Exterior Components;
6. Equipment and Casings;
7. Functional Criteria; and
A. Appendices.

Other technical and engineering professional organizations are also involved in defining, or at least assisting in establishing, some of the technical standards contained in the manual.

Particular manuals are revised periodically when experience and evaluation may indicate that a change or updating is necessary. Construction techniques and products that may comply with the standards may not necessarily be acceptable if examination and testing shows that other negative features (which may impair the performance requirements) are found to exist.

Local authorities tend to use SMACNA standards in developing their own codes or building ordinances, but remember that SMACNA standards by themselves do not carry any force of law. There is a difference between national construction association standards and lawful building requirements enforced by national, state, or local building codes.

Standards are more like agreed policies that contractors use to govern their work, because they desire consistent quality of construction from job to job. Codes or ordinances often incorporate such standards and give them the force of law, although lawmakers are free to adopt different standards instead. Standards are made by those associated with the construction industry, while codes are adopted by those in government. In other words, standards are *voluntary*, but codes are *mandatory*.

Professionalism

Regardless of how well material and equipment have been designed and manufactured, poor installation can easily ruin the best system. A good installation requires more than technical or mechanical skills; it requires personal integrity to do the best job possible. It demands a professional approach.

Of course the installation of the equipment depends on the type of product and system involved, but there are some factors which are common to almost any situation. The common factor here is "standards." Some standards are related to the design and performance of the product, its application, or its safety considerations. Others are directed at various phases of installation. In general, you will find many of the most important sheet metal industry and trade standards contained in the SMACNA manuals.

Compliance with local codes is an important phase of providing a good installation. Codes and ordinances are specific and mandatory rules you must comply with, but standards serve as guidelines to improve the performance and reliability of any given installed system. If you maintain pride in your workmanship, you will always want to follow these standards in order to make your installations the best they can be.

The following is a detailed discussion of the topics covered in *HVAC Duct Construction Standards – Metal and Flexible*.

1. BASIC DUCT CONSTRUCTION

Unlike earlier editions of SMACNA manuals, the current *HVAC Duct Construction Standards* manual does not divide rectangular duct construction simply into low- or high-pressure classifications. In fact, SMACNA no longer uses any such words as "low," "medium," or "high" to describe air **pressures** that ducts are designed to handle. Now the various duct systems are categorized by tables according to their specific w.g., or water gage, and by equivalent Pascal (Pa) pressures. These classes are 1/2, 1, 2, 3, 4, 6, and 10 w.g. positive or negative pressure and 125, 250, 500, 750, 1000, 1500, and 2500 Pa positive or negative pressure. These tables define, by pressure, the minimum gage and connector code for all rectangular straight duct and fittings. The class designation system is described on pages 1.3 through 1.7, with a graphic explanation shown in the manual's Figure 1-1.

Tables 1-1 and 1-15 show the standards for pressure class. The notes under the tables explain what the letters "A," "STD," and "STV" mean. The letter A, for example, indicates that other details or standards are *available* for such duct types in those particular pressure or **velocity** classes, and they are, in general, shown in other parts of this manual.

Other information in the first section of the manual include standards pertaining to sealing ducts, reinforcements, transverse joints, tie rods, seams, and other assembly and attachment specifications. Through the use of figures, tables, and word descriptions, the manual gives you the information you need for properly fabricating, assembling, and installing various types of rectangular ductruns.

2. FITTINGS & OTHER CONSTRUCTION

The second section of this SMACNA manual contains standards for fittings and other sheet metal constructions. Graphic illustrations are included on pages 2.2 through 2.30 in relation to these construction or assembly standards for duct fittings, connections, access doors, dampers, hoods, liners, and other ductrun components.

Included in this section are construction details for: elbows, vanes, duct branches, offsets and transitions, diffuser plenums, dampers, exhaust hoods, acoustical liners, flexible liners, and many other components you will likely be fabricating for any given duct system.

In this section you will find details pertaining to construction and placement of various duct-run fittings, internal components such as vanes and dampers, branch duct connections, reinforcements, hoods, and duct liners. Illustrations showing supply and return duct configurations, hood and vapor exhaust systems, and other basic assemblies are shown. Appropriate cross-references to the text and/or other parts of the manual are always noted in the drawings.

Sometimes individual standards or illustrations of standards will refer you to other standards provided by other associations, testing laboratories, or governmental agencies. An example is found in this section at Figure 2-22, Duct Liner Interruption. Here you are directed to the National Fire Protection Association (**NFPA**) Standard 90A, which in this case requires that any duct liner must be interrupted wherever a fire damper is installed in a duct. Fire damper operation must never be impaired by anything else you install in a ductrun.

3. ROUND, OVAL, AND FLEXIBLE DUCT

An entire section has been designed to specify and illustrate SMACNA standards pertaining to non-rectangular ducts. These standards address such matters as: round duct schedules and specifications; round duct longitudinal seams and transverse joints; elbows, tees, and other fittings; oval duct fittings; flexible duct specifications, accessories, and supports; underslab duct construction standards; and anchorage of ducts to be encased in concrete.

The specifications for these types of ducts are given in similar fashion to the standards specified for rectangular ductruns. That is, depending upon different pressure classes of the duct, various size and metal gage specifications are listed, as well as types and specifications for their seams and joints. Seams, in the example of round ducts, might be longitudinal or spiral; they may be grooved, lapped, riveted, or welded; and they will vary in required size and gage depending upon the type of duct metal, duct diameter, and pressure (measured in w.g. units) for which the ductrun is designed.

As always, these standards are published as design references, so that non-rectangular systems can be engineered safely and correctly. Round duct standards are shown in tables, figures, and text on pages 3.2 through 3.12. Flat oval and flexible duct standards are contained on pages 3.13 through 3.22. Underslab and encased duct standards start on page 3.23 and conclude this manual section.

See the Sheet Metal Level 1 Module, *Fasteners, Hangers and Supports* for more information pertaining to flexible duct.

4. HANGERS AND SUPPORTS

The fourth section in this SMACNA manual relates to procedures for hanging and supporting various duct systems. Standard types of fasteners and hangers, hanger spacings, trapeze hangers, and riser supports are covered.

Tables show the minimum size and spacing standards for duct hangers that apply to various duct sizes, which are stated in terms of half-perimeter duct measurements (to given maximums). These spacings are allowed to change, depending upon the type of hanger used.

For example, with rectangular duct where the maximum half-perimeter (P/2) equals no more than 72" (total perimeter equals no more than 144"), SMACNA standards call for a pair of 18-gage metal strap hangers, 1" wide, to be spaced every 10 feet. However, you must use an 8-foot spacing if your hangers are no heavier than 20-gage by 1"-wide; or you must use a 4- or 5-foot spacing if your hangers are no heavier than 22-gage by 1". These hanger sizes and spacings are shown in Table 4-1, and they pertain to metal straps (one on each side of the duct). Also shown in Table 4-1 are sizes and spacings for metal rod or wire hangers.

Table 4-2 lists the hanger size and spacing standards for round duct; Table 4-3 specifies allowable loads for trapeze hangers; and Figure 4-5 gives you a proper trapeze load diagram, together with mathematical formulas for computing the trapeze bending stress, deflection, and shear stress according to total duct load.

Such things as deflection formulas, hanger stress, and metal fatigue considerations are of much greater importance to the architect or design engineer than they are to the sheet metal mechanic. But you do need to be aware of the figures and illustrations in a SMACNA manual, showing you correct assembly and installation procedures for the various hangers and supports you'll be working with.

This section of the manual contains several such figures, showing you proper installations of various types of duct hangers and supports and how they are attached to ducts, ceilings, walls, and floors. In addition, Figure 4-10 illustrates correct suspension of HVAC equipment, such as fans or blowers, which are installed this way for improved sound and vibration control.

But SMACNA also recommends that any duct hanging system be at the discretion of the installation contractor—with approval of the mechanical engineer—because of the many variables associated with conditions and materials involved at each installation site. So, again, it is extremely important for you to ask before you are tempted to use a method that is not standard, or one that is not specified in the plans.

5. EXTERIOR COMPONENTS

The fifth section of the *HVAC Duct Construction Standards* manual contains information pertaining to sheet metal components that remain on building exteriors. These components include louvers, rooftop ducts, flashings, exhaust vents, and covers for intake or exhaust ventilation.

Standard formulas for calculating such things as **free area** and the percent of free area are given on page 5.4. Free area represents the minimum area in a louver through which air can pass. This is an important consideration because (for insulation and other energy purposes) you don't want to have to install bigger louvers and make bigger holes in walls or roofs than the HVAC system requires. But it is even more important (for an efficient system) that every louver be correctly sized.

A reference is also given on this page to the AMCA Standard 500, which is a technical publication of the Air Movement and Control Association. The **AMCA** is similar in function to SMACNA and other construction associations in that it publishes standards, manuals, and other publications for consistency of quality and uniformity of products and procedures within its own particular phase of the industry. "Standard 500" contains extensive information on free area, water penetration, cfm ratings, and static pressure loss.

Installation procedures for louvers and screens are illustrated in Figure 5-1 (of this SMACNA manual section) by means of several detail drawings.

This section also contains guidelines for rooftop units and intake and exhaust system installations and support construction. For example, a recommendation is made that all duct penetrations of roofs utilize curbs. Metal flashing should also extend at a minimum of 4" below the top of each curb.

Detailed diagrams in this section also depict cover constructions for intake or exhaust vents, both in regular and large size configurations. The rectangular **gooseneck**, illustrated in Figure 5-5, is a type of roof vent that curves downward and therefore does not require a cover (other than a screen) to protect its opening from the open sky.

6. EQUIPMENT AND CASINGS

Informational standards in regard to heating, air conditioning, and ventilating equipment and **casings** (such as **plenums**) are included in this section. Additional graphic illustrations are included for curbs, eliminators and drain pans, pipe penetrations of casings, and casing access doors.

Casing and plenum construction standards are listed on pages 6.2 and 6.3. They include such specifications as w.g. and Pa pressure classifications for fan casings, water seals, drains, and types of metal recommended for drain pans and other components.

Two pages (6.19 and 6.20) are set aside for textual information in regard to equipment casing. Included here are guidelines for casing wall construction, anchorage, access doors, joint sealing, drainage, penetrations, and low pressure casing protection. General arrangements of casing configurations are mentioned and it is recommended that they should be built in a rectangular box shape.

SMACNA also indicates for casings that tapered sides and roofs should be avoided because of the difficulty in developing adequate strength and air tightness at joints. Even if theory suggests that tapered casings conserve energy and facilitate uniform air distribution, they are still not practical because the tapers required for expansion or contraction are rarely given enough accommodating space in most equipment rooms.

Also mentioned is the standard that bracing, curb, roof and sidewall connections, access doors, and so on, must be carefully constructed to carry their share of the casing load.

Throughout the manual SMACNA is careful to note that, regardless of how well all these HVAC construction standards are followed, there is no guarantee that equipment start-up and shut-down will not produce rumbles or other noise. If a perfectly quiet system is required, additional noise suppressing equipment or soundproofing materials will need to be installed.

7. FUNCTIONAL CRITERIA

This section of the manual generally contains information about testing and analysis of various aspects of duct construction and installation. It explains how SMACNA itself has tested in various situations to arrive at its standards. And it also provides engineers and civil authorities with information needed to conduct their own tests of assemblies not previously covered.

Therefore this section is of more use to the HVAC designer or inspector than it is to the sheet metal mechanic. However, if you are ever called upon to assemble the various components needed for a test, you may need to refer to the illustrations shown here. These show you proper assemblies for such things as duct testing (Figure 7-2) and deflection and leakage measurements (Figure 7-3), while the text explains procedures for testing joint performance, noise levels, vibration, and other factors of ductrun design.

APPENDICES

In this final section of the manual, you will find many useful charts and graphs giving you mathematical or statistical information. You may need to refer to such information, for example, whenever you perform calculations in the shop or on the job.

Charts listed on these pages give you complete technical information on such things as: thickness measurements for various metals, metal properties, rectangular and round duct areas and weights, mathematical and measuring conversion charts, pressure and gage tables, pressure comparisons and reinforcement requirements for different duct metal thicknesses, models of typical HVAC systems and equipment arrangements, diagrams of typical belt guards and isolation devices, leak shielding radiation protection installation procedures, and so on.

OTHER ASSOCIATIONS AND MANUALS

In addition to SMACNA, as mentioned earlier, there are quite a few other construction-related associations that publish standards and information that pertain to their own aspects of the industry. Some of them that you may encounter through your work in the sheet metal trade are as follows:

ASHRAE	American Society of Heating, Refrigeration and Air Conditioning Engineers
ACCA	Air Conditioning Contractors of America
TIMA	Thermal Insulation Manufacturers Association
AMCA	Air Movement and Control Association
ADC	Air Diffusion Council
ADI	Air Distribution Institute
ARI	Air-Conditioning and Refrigeration Institute
FMA	Fabricators and Manufacturers Association, International
ASTM	American Society for Testing and Materials
NFPA	National Fire Protection Association
ANSI	American National Standards Institute
ASME	American Society of Mechanical Engineers
AWS	American Welding Society
FM	Factory Mutual Engineering Research Corporation
UL	Underwriters' Laboratories, Inc.
ACGIH	American Conference of Governmental Industrial Hygienists
BOCA	Building Officials and Code Administrators, International
MCAA	Mechanical Contractors Association of America
NEBB	National Environmental Balancing Bureau

Other SMACNA Publications

SMACNA itself has published at least 25 different manuals or other publications relating to most aspects of the sheet metal industry. As of 1998, these manuals are:

- *Accepted Industry Practice for Industrial Duct Construction*
- *Architectural Sheet Metal*
- *Building Systems Analysis and Retrofit Manual*
- *Ducted Electric Heat Guide for Air Handling Systems*
- *Energy Systems Analysis and Management*
- *Energy Recovery Equipment and Systems*
- *Fibrous Glass Duct Construction Standards*
- *Fire, Smoke, and Radiation Damper Guide for HVAC Systems*
- *Guidelines for Roof-Mounted Outdoor Air Conditioner Installations*
- *Guide for Steel Stack Construction*
- *HVAC Air Duct Leakage Test Manual*
- *HVAC Duct Construction Standards – Metal & Flexible [The manual discussed in this module]*
- *HVAC – Duct Design*
- *HVAC Duct Systems Inspection Guide*
- *HVAC Systems Commissioning Manual*
- *HVAC Systems – Applications*
- *HVAC Systems – Testing, Adjusting and Balancing*
- *Indoor Air Quality – A System Approach*
- *Indoor Air Quality Manual*
- *Indoor Air Quality Guidelines for Occupied Buildings Under Construction*
- *Installation Standards for Residential Heating and Air Conditioning Systems*
- *Kitchen Equipment Fabrications Guidelines*
- *Manager's Guide for Welding*
- *Rectangular Industrial Duct Construction Standards*

THE SMACNA MANUALS — TRAINEE TASK MODULE 04405

- *Residential Comfort System Installation Standards Manual*
- *Retrofit of Building Energy Systems and Processes*
- *Round Industrial Duct Construction Standards*
- *Seismic Restraint Manual: Guidelines for Mechanical Systems*
- *Standard Practice in Sheet Metal Work*
- *Testing, Balancing and Adjusting of Environmental Systems*
- *Thermoplastic Duct (PVC) Construction Manual*
- *Thermoset FRP Duct Construction Manual*

To order manuals or a current catalog of publications, SMACNA can be contacted at:

Sheet Metal & Air Conditioning Contractors' National Association, Inc.
4201 Layafette Center Drive
Chantilly, VA 20151-1209
Phone: 703-803-2989

Fire and Smoke Protection

One of the more critical standards in the Fire Damper and Heat Shop Guide pertains to the function and use of **fire and smoke dampers**. Reference is made in regard to the organizations and standards of those organizations which must be adhered to when planning fire and smoke protection for various structures.

Some of the critical concepts of fire and smoke protection involve early warning, suppression, evacuation, safe refuge zones, monitoring and information systems. Designers also realize that modern HVAC systems are expected to supply fresh air for life support, pressurization of corridors and exit routes to control smoke spreading, exhaust the various products of combustion, and shutdown of some systems or portions of systems upon demand.

This information, according to the text, should be in the hands of designers, and it becomes their responsibility to show all required dampers on the drawings. They must coordinate all requirements pertaining to barrier locations, occupancy assignments, protection planning, and rating and identification of compartments and structural components. Also they should not rely solely upon written designations in the specifications, but they must use recognized symbols to relate this information in the building plans.

You'll need to be aware of such fire protection systems when you encounter them in your installation work in the field. You should also be aware of such publications as those listed in this module, and know where to look for more information whenever you need it during the course of your work in the sheet metal trade.

REVIEW QUESTIONS

Answer the following questions to review your knowledge of this module and to prepare for the Module Examination.

1. List several professional organizations that assist in developing codes and standards.
2. What does the acronym "SMACNA" stand for?
3. What is the difference between a standard and a code or ordinance?
4. Where could you find information on correct hanger sizes and spacings?
5. Why should you be aware of fire and smoke dampers?
6. What does "w.g." stand for?
7. Where would you look to find installation standards for flexible duct?
8. Where can you find guidelines for offset and transition fabrications?
9. Where do you find information on plenums?
10. Where can you find more complete information pertaining to louvers and free area?

SUMMARY

The SMACNA *HVAC Duct Construction Standards* manual is one of many technical publications developed for use by system designers, construction contractors, and sheet metal mechanics. It contributes to your professional development by providing a handy reference to sheet metal construction guidelines and standards adopted for the industry. If you are to develop pride in your workmanship, you'll need to let these standards guide you in your work. Whereas codes are mandatory rules that must be complied with, standards serve as agreed industry guidelines to assure consistent quality for all constructed systems. Knowing where to obtain such information and following these guidelines will help you improve your standard of performance and maintain consistent quality in your workmanship.

TRADE TERMS

AMCA
Casings
Fire damper
FPM
Free area
Gooseneck
NFPA
Plenums
Pressure
SMACNA
Smoke damper
Velocity
W.G.

NCCER CRAFT TRAINING USER UPDATES

The NCCER makes every effort to keep these manuals up-to-date and free of technical errors. We appreciate your help in this process. If you have an idea for improving this manual, or if you find an error, a typographical mistake, or an inaccuracy in the NCCER's Craft Training Manuals, please write us, using this form or a photocopy. Be sure to include the exact module number, page number, a description of the problem, and the correction, if possible. Your input will be brought to the attention of the Technical Review Committee. Thank you for your assistance.

Instructors – If you found that additional materials were necessary in order to teach this module effectively, please let us know so that we may include them in the Equipment/Materials list in the Instructor's Guide.

Write: Curriculum and Revision Department
National Center for Construction Education and Research
P.O. Box 141104
Gainesville, FL 32614-1104
Fax: 352-334-0932

Craft _____ Module Name _____

Module Number _____ Page Number(s) _____

Description of Problem _____

_____

_____

_____

_____

(Optional) Correction of Problem _____

_____

_____

(Optional) Your Name and Address _____

_____

_____

notes

Sheet Metal Duct Fabrication Standards

Module 04406

Sheet Metal Trainee Task Module 04406

NATIONAL
CENTER FOR
CONSTRUCTION
EDUCATION AND
RESEARCH

SHEET METAL DUCT FABRICATION STANDARDS

Objectives

Upon completion of this module, the trainee will be able to:

1. Understand the terminology associated with sheet metal duct fabrication.
2. Understand the effect of operating pressure on the construction of a duct system and identify the various duct pressure classes.
3. Determine the minimum metal gage requirements for a selected ductrun by using reference charts and tables.
4. Determine the sealing requirements for a selected ductrun by using reference charts and tables.
5. Determine the minimum connector and reinforcing requirements for a selected ductrun by using reference charts and tables.
6. Describe the purpose of tie rods and determine when tie rods are optional or mandatory by using reference charts and tables.
7. Identify the different types of acceptable longitudinal seams, including applications and any limitations.

Prerequisites

Successful completion of the following Task Modules is required before beginning study of this Task Module: Sheet Metal Level 1; Sheet Metal Level 2, Modules 04106, 04303, 04304, 04312, and 04403.

Required Trainee Material

1. Trainee Task Module
2. Appropriate Personal Protective Equipment
3. Pencils and eraser
4. Paper and notebook

Copyright © 1992 National Center for Construction Education and Research, Gainesville, FL All rights reserved. No part of this work may be reproduced in any form or by any means, including photocopying, without written permission of the publisher. Updated: 1998.

TABLE OF CONTENTS

Section	Topic	Page
1.0.0	Introduction	4
1.1.0	Operating Pressure	4
1.2.0	Leakage	5
1.3.0	Seal Class	6
2.0.0	Duct Fabrication	8
2.1.0	Selecting Duct Gage, Connectors, And Reinforcement	8
2.2.0	Duct Tables	8
2.3.0	Gage	8
2.4.0	Gage — Intermediate Reinforcing	11
2.5.0	Intermediate Reinforcing	11
2.6.0	Connector and Intermediate Reinforcing	13
2.7.0	Connector Joint	14
3.0.0	Duct Construction	16
3.1.0	Connector With Tie Rod	16
3.2.0	Intermediate Reinforcement With Tie Rod	18
3.3.0	Longitudinal Seams	19
	Summary	21
	Review/Practice Questions	22
	Answers to Review/Practice Questions	24
	Appendix A	25
	Appendix B	37
	Appendix C	42
	Appendix D	43

Trade Terms Introduced In This Module

Constant volume system: A system in which the volume of air supplied to all conditioned spaces remains constant and the temperature of each conditioned space is controlled by the temperature of the supply air.

Diffuser: Device used to disperse air from a ductrun at low pressure in various directions and planes within a conditioned space.

Equal friction: A method of duct sizing wherein the selected duct friction loss value is used throughout the design of a low-pressure duct system.

in. w.g.: Duct operating air pressure expressed in inches of water gauge.

Pa: Duct operating air pressure expressed in Pascals (Newtons per square meter).

Pressure class: Any one of seven standard operating air pressures used to determine the fabrication of duct systems.

Reinforcement: Used at transverse connector joints or at intermediate points on certain sizes and pressure classes of ductrun sections to provide strength and reduce deflection of the duct sheet metal. In some cases, it enables the use of lighter gage sheet metal.

Seal class: Any one of three types of sealing methods used to control duct leakage on certain pressure classes of ductruns.

Static regain: A method of duct sizing wherein the duct velocities are systematically reduced, allowing a portion of the velocity pressure to convert to static pressure, offsetting the duct friction losses.

Tie rod: Used with transverse joints and with intermediate reinforcement for certain sizes and pressure classes of ductrun sections to provide strength and reduce deflection of the sheet metal. In some cases, it enables the use of lighter gage reinforcement members.

Total pressure: A method of duct sizing which allows the designer to determine all friction and dynamic losses in each section of a duct system as well as the total system loss.

Transverse connector: Various types of joints used to connect sections of rectangular ductruns.

Variable air volume (VAV): A device used to reduce air volume (and pressure) in a ductrun.

Variable volume system: A system in which the temperature of each conditioned space is controlled by the temperature and/or volume of air supplied to that space.

Velocity reduction: A method of duct sizing in which arbitrary reductions are made in air velocity after each duct or outlet.

1.0.0 INTRODUCTION

The duct system is an assembly that conveys air between the fan supply equipment and the room diffusers. The system can be used to supply, remove, recycle, filter, or condition air in the room space. The system may operate with both positive and negative pressures exerted on the ductruns. Generally speaking, duct strength, deflection, and leakage are more functions of pressure than of velocity. In conventional systems, noise, vibration, and friction loss are more related to velocity than to pressure.

Sheet metal mechanics are not expected to design the system or size the duct. Their primary function is to select joint, seam, reinforcement, sealing, and support options that provide the proper duct strength and leakage rate for the pressure and seal classes or criteria given on the engineering drawings or job specifications. The sheet metal mechanic must also adhere to local construction codes and recognized industry standards and practices such as those given in the SMACNA manual, *HVAC Duct Construction Standards – Metal and Flexible*.

To develop the drawings and contract specifications, a designer will have evaluated all of the factors that affect the building, and then will have sized and selected the equipment along with the location and capacity of the **diffusers**. To do this, the designer uses a heat loss/heat gain analysis. The factors considered are usually divided into internal and external factors. Internal factors include the lights, people, equipment, and building heat loss/heat gain parameters. External factors include the outside air temperature range, relative humidity range, and position of the sun. To calculate duct size, the designer may use any one of a number of available sizing methods. These methods include **equal friction**, **static regain**, **velocity reduction**, and **total pressure**.

The part of the design that includes the capacity of the equipment, the duct pressure and seal class, or the location and capacity of the diffusers, is not subject to change without the formal approval of the designer. The duct size and location on the small scale drawing are normally schematic and are not exact. An experienced draftsperson (sketcher) may have to refer to the architectural, structural, mechanical drawings, and the reflected ceiling along with the equipment cuts to finalize the duct sizes and location to clear the structure and lights. Many times, ¼ inch (or larger) scale shop drawings are required to show the final location and length of each piece so that the system will fit precisely. The detailer who picks off the job for fabrication also needs to understand local construction codes, the minimum SMACNA construction standards, shop standards, and the job specifications to develop the shop tickets.

1.1.0 OPERATING PRESSURE

The duct size of the straight duct and fittings and the operating pressure of the system must be known to determine the sheet metal gage (thickness), connectors, seams, reinforcement, and seal class that are required for duct fabrication. The operating pressure, which is provided, is measured as inches of water gauge (**in. w.g.**). The unit in. w.g. is a measurement of duct pressure in pounds per square foot (lb./ft.^{2}). A cubic foot (ft.^{3}) of water in a standard 1' × 1' × 1' vessel weighs 62.4 pounds at sea level. The unit weight of the vessel would be stated as 62.4 pounds per square foot (lb./ft.^{2}) for its 1 foot (12 inch) height. The weight is proportionate to its height. Therefore, duct pressure measured in in. w.g. relates to lb./ft.^{2} pressure. A measurement of 1 in. w.g. is equal to 5.2 lb./ft.^{2} (62.4 ÷ 12) duct pressure or, in the metric system, 250 Pascals (**Pa**).

The SMACNA *HVAC Duct Construction Standards* manual provides fabrication standards for most commercial rectangular duct systems operating from 0.5 in. w.g. (125 Pa) to 10 in. w.g. (2,500 Pa) positive or negative pressure. *Table 1* lists the **pressure classes** normally used in commercial work.

DUCT PRESSURE CLASS		OPERATING PRESSURE
Pa	Inches of water gauge	Pounds per square foot
125	0.5	Up to 2.6
250	1	2.6 to 5.2
500	2	5.2 to 10.4
750	3	10.4 to 15.6
1,000	4	15.6 to 20.8
1,500	6	20.8 to 31.2
2,500	10	31.2 to 52.0

Table 1. Static Pressure Classes (Positive Or Negative)

1.2.0 LEAKAGE

Duct leakage specifications have new criteria for determining expected leakage. Previously, a specified percentage was designated as the maximum allowable leakage. Unfortunately, the former specified percentages were sometimes impossible to attain. By today's standards, duct leakage is expected and is directly related to the following:

1. Operating pressure
2. Square footage of duct system
3. Duct construction and sealing

The designer is responsible for selecting the pressure class and **seal class**. The SMACNA standards manual provides sealing guidelines when the engineering drawings or job specifications do not specify the pressure class and seal class. The pressure class refers to seven standard categories of 0.5 in. w.g. (125 Pa), 1 in. w.g. (250 Pa), 2 in. w.g. (500 Pa),

3 in. w.g. (750 Pa), 4 in. w.g. (1,000 Pa), 6 in. w.g. (1,500 Pa), and 10 in. w.g. (2,500 Pa) positive or negative. Refer to *Table 1* and *Figure 1*.

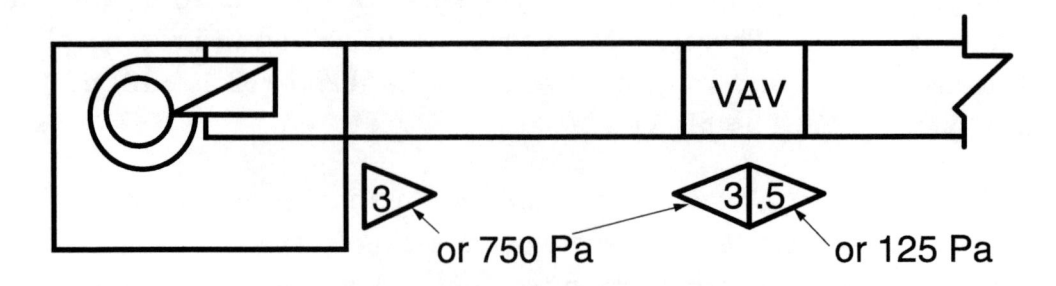

Figure 1. Duct Pressure Class Designation

If the seal class and the pressure class are not selected by the designer, these general guidelines can be used. For **constant volume systems**, use 1 in. w.g. (250 Pa) pressure class with no seal. For **variable volume systems**, use 2 in. w.g. (500 Pa) pressure class with a Class C seal. See *Table 2* for all seal class requirements.

Class C	Connector joint sealed for 2 in. w.g. pressure class and also for .5 in. w.g. or 1 in. w.g. pressure classes when specified.
Class B	Both connector joints and longitudinal seams for 3 in. w.g. pressure class.
Class A	All connector joints, longitudinal seams, and duct wall penetrations for 4 in. w.g. pressure class and up.

Table 2. Pressure Seal Requirements

When sealing is required, adhesives, gaskets, tape systems, or a combination thereof may be used to seal the ductwork. SMACNA does not specify any particular product or method.

1.3.0 SEAL CLASS

Duct sealing requirements are categorized by pressure class (*Table 2*). Sealing .5 in. w.g. (125 Pa) or 1 in. w.g. (250 Pa) pressure class is recommended but not required unless specified or unless it is upstream of a **variable air volume (VAV)** box. In this case, seal Class C is required.

If no sealing is done, it is estimated that a commercial ductrun will leak at the rates shown in *Table 3* per 100 ft.^{2} of duct surface. If desired, additional information may be found in the *SMACNA HVAC Air Duct Leakage Test Manual*.

Duct Pressure in. w.g. (or Pa)	Leakage Rate CFM/100 Ft.²
0.1 (25 Pa)	11
0.2 (50 Pa)	17
0.5 (125 Pa)	31
1.0 (250 Pa)	48

Table 3. Unsealed Duct Leakage Rate

Figure 2 presents leakage values for all pressures and seal classes for rectangular duct.

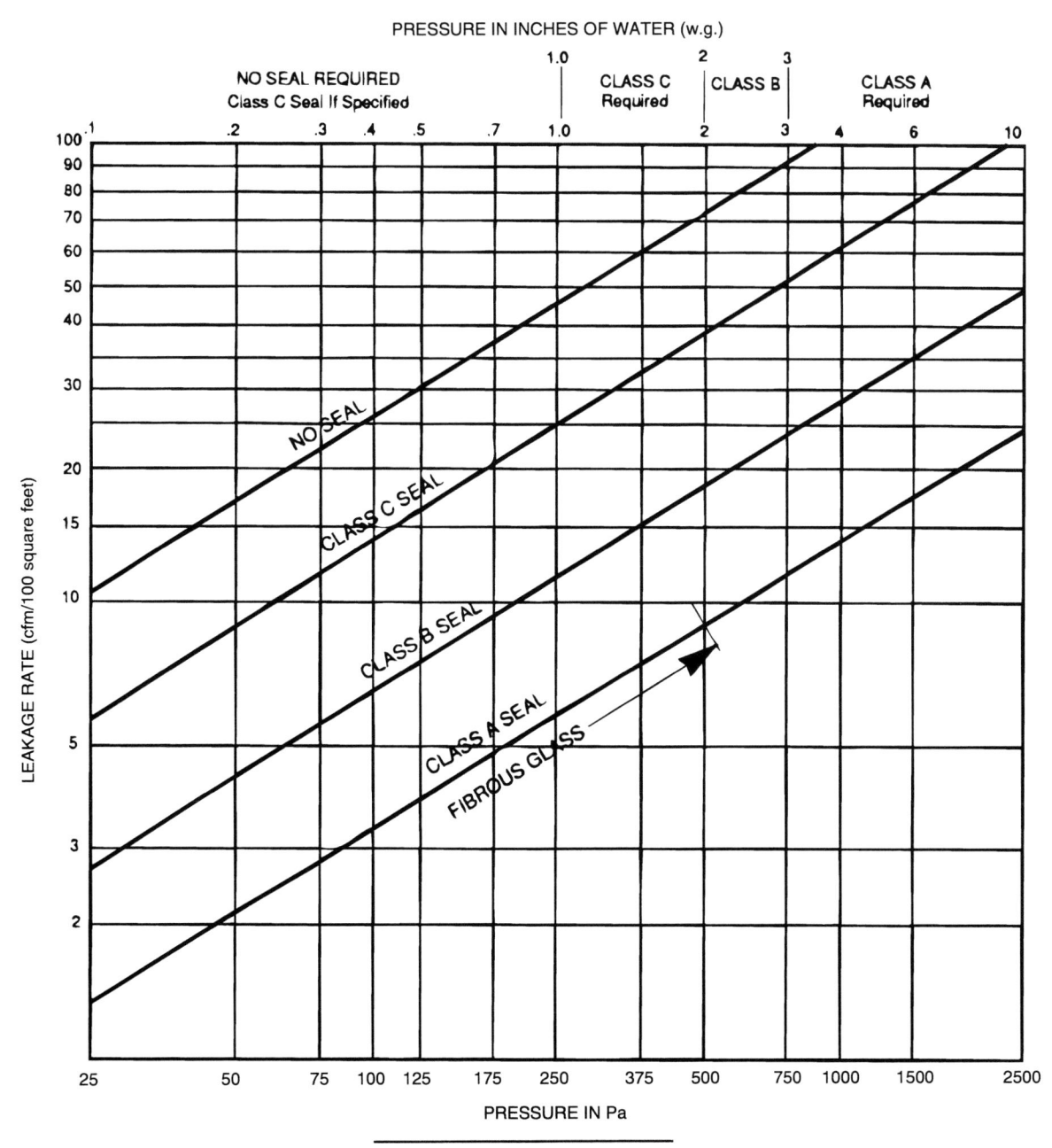

Figure 2. Leakage Values

SHEET METAL DUCT FABRICATION STANDARDS — TRAINEE MODULE 04406

2.0.0 DUCT FABRICATION

2.1.0 SELECTING DUCT GAGE, CONNECTORS, AND REINFORCEMENT

As with duct seal class, the water gage or Pa pressure classifications are used to select the duct gage, connector, and **reinforcement** that will minimize the duct wall panel deflection caused by internal or external pressure. As previously stated, these pressures, even at a pressure level of 2 in. w.g. (500 Pa), are substantial at over 10 lb./ft.² The SMACNA standard is designed to limit the deflection of the duct panel to ¾ inch for widths over 24 inches, and the maximum deflection of the connector or reinforcing member to ¼ inch.

2.2.0 DUCT TABLES

SMACNA has a Rectangular Duct Reinforcement Table for each of the seven standard pressure classifications in both in. w.g. and Pa. The tables have two purposes:

1. To determine the minimum gage required in relation to duct span and length.
2. To determine the rigidity class as defined by a generic alphabet letter code for the connector and reinforcement.

Table 4 is a simplified modification of the information presented in the SMACNA 3 in. w.g. table. This table is used in the same manner as the original SMACNA table, except that reinforcement spacing requirements are only shown for distances of only 5, 4, 3, 2.5, and 2 feet.

2.3.0 GAGE

Using *Table 4* to select the minimum gage for the example in *Figure 3* is straightforward. By using the largest transverse dimension of the duct and the reinforcing spacing, the fabricator can determine the correct duct gage. The example in *Figure 3* has a 48 × 28 inch ductrun with a reducer to 48 × 10 inch duct and a 90° elbow for a 3 in. w.g. system.

The ductrun example is divided into five sections consisting of various duct lengths and an elbow. On the vertical scale in the first column of *Table 4*, the various spans of duct (width or depth) are shown. The horizontal scale shows reinforcement spacing for 5-foot to 2-foot intervals. Beneath the spacing interval are the rigidity class and minimum gage for corresponding duct spans in column one. By referring to the 43 to 48 line, the fabricator can select the minimum gage for each duct section.

Duct Sect. 1 — At 5 feet, the minimum gage is 18.

Duct Sect. 2 — At 4 feet, the minimum gage is 20.

3" W.G. STATIC POS. OR NEG. PRESSURE

DUCT DIMENSION (INCHES)	\multicolumn{5}{c}{REQUIRED REINFORCEMENT SPACING (FEET)}
	5	4	3	2.5	2
	\multicolumn{5}{c}{MINIMUM RIGIDITY CLASS WITH MAXIMUM GAGE DUCT}
10	A-24	←	Same		→
11 & 12	A-24	←	Same		→
13 & 14	A-24	←	Same		→
15 & 16	A-24	←	Same		→
17 & 18	A-24	←	Same		→
19 & 20	A-24	←	Same		→
21 & 22	B-24	←	Same		→
23 & 24	B-24	←	Same		→
25 & 26	C-24	←	Same		→
27 & 28	C-22	C-24	←	Same	→
29 & 30	C-22	C-24	←	Same	→
31 to 36	E-20	D-24	←	Same	→
37 to 42	E-20	E-22	E-24	← Same →	
43 to 48	G-18	F-20	E-22	E-24	← Same →
49 to 54	H-18 F + rod	H-18 F + rod	G-22 F + rod	E-24	← Same →
55 to 60	H-16 F + rod	H-18 F + rod	G-20 F + rod	G-24 F + rod	← Same →
61 to 72		I-16 F + rod	H-20 F + rod	H-22 F + rod	H-24 F + rod
73 to 84			J-18 F + rod	J-20 F + rod	I-22 F + rod
85 to 96			L-16 G + rod	K-18 G + rod	J-20 G + rod
97 & UP				H-18t	H-18t

Rect Duct

Table 4. Standards For Duct Construction

SHEET METAL DUCT FABRICATION STANDARDS — TRAINEE MODULE 04406

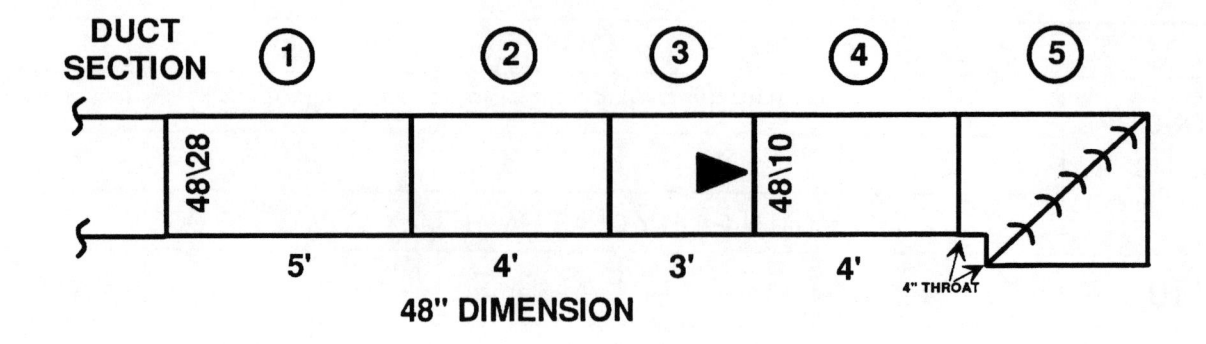

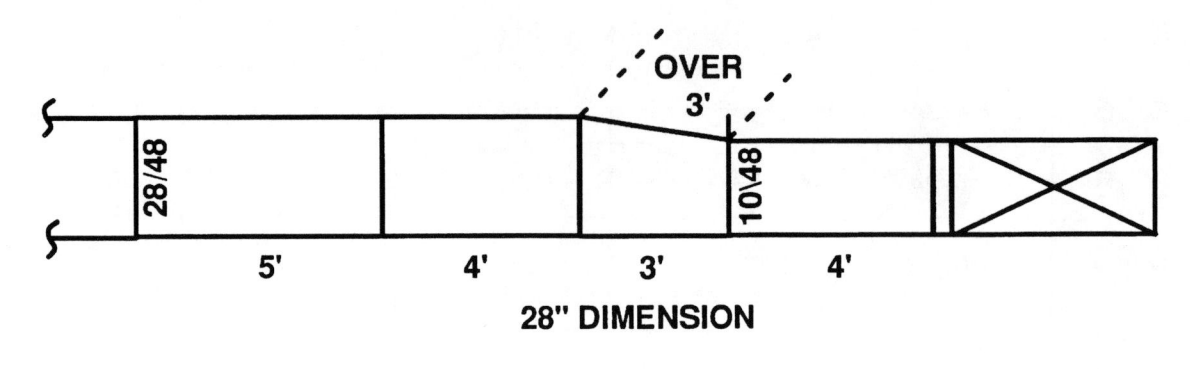

Figure 3. Ductrun With Reducer

Duct Sect. 3 — The reducer has a finished length of 3 feet, but a closer look shows that the sloping panel is longer than 3 feet. Therefore, a 4-foot spacing with 20-gage duct is needed, or the fitting needs to be reduced until the sloping panel is 3 feet or less. If reduced, a 22-gage duct could be used.

Duct Sect. 4 — The width dimension is still 48 inches; therefore, with 4-foot spacing, the reducer duct would be 20 gage.

Duct Sect. 5 — The elbow width (*Figure 4*) is still 48 inches. The elbow length is 52 inches, which is the same as the heel length; therefore, the elbow duct gage is 18.

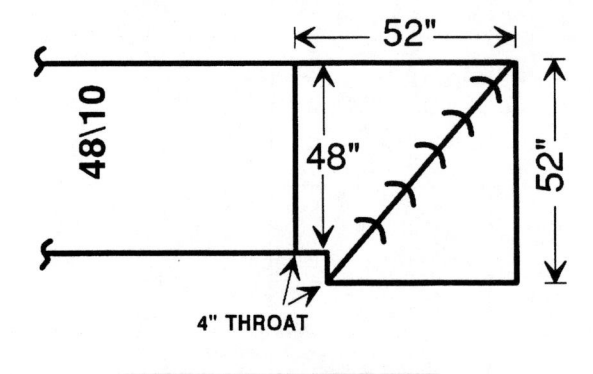

Figure 4. Ductrun Elbow

SHEET METAL — TRAINEE TASK MODULE 04406

2.4.0 GAGE — INTERMEDIATE REINFORCING

In the first example, the connector spacing was used to determine the unsupported panel and, therefore, to determine the gage. Intermediate reinforcement can be used to reduce the panel distance and, therefore, the gage required (*Figure 5*).

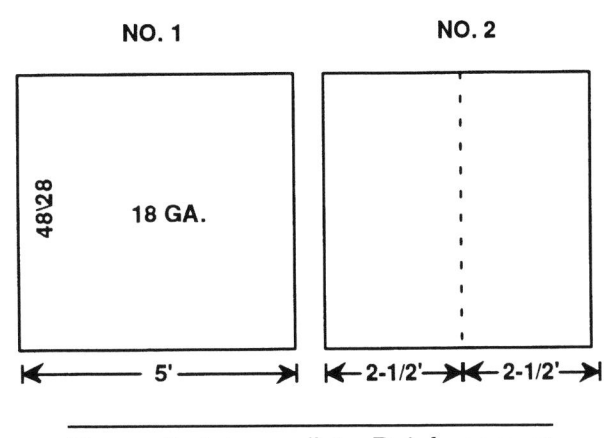

Figure 5. Intermediate Reinforcement

The largest dimension is still 48 inches, and so with 5-foot spacing, 18 gage is needed. By installing an appropriate reinforcement in the middle of this duct, the span is reduced to 2.5 feet. However, this does *not* mean that 24 gage can be used, because the 28-inch side of the duct still has 5 feet between reinforcements. The 28-inch dimension with 5-foot reinforcement requires a minimum of 22 gage. Therefore, if the 24 gage were used, the 28-inch side would have to be reinforced.

Even though selecting the gage by using the space between reinforcements is relatively straightforward, introducing intermediate reinforcing or fittings requires a careful look at both dimensions.

2.5.0 INTERMEDIATE REINFORCING

An alternative to using a heavier gage and connector on 5-foot reinforcement spacing is to install intermediate reinforcement on the width or both the width and depth of the duct. This reinforcement can be a standard structural angle or various bent sections, such as zee or cee, hat, or flat channel (*Figure 6*).

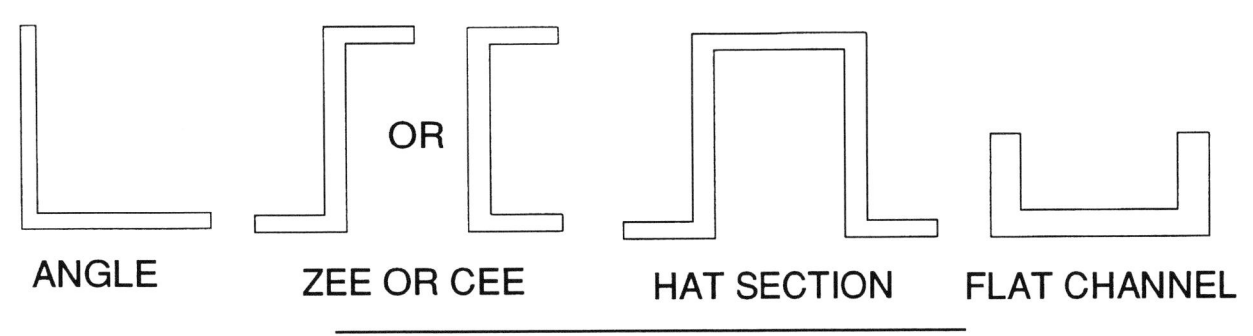

Figure 6. Types Of Intermediate Reinforcements

SHEET METAL DUCT FABRICATION STANDARDS — TRAINEE MODULE 04406

A single piece of intermediate reinforcement can be used for duct up to 3 in. w.g. pressure. The reinforcement is attached using any of the following methods: tack weld, spot weld, bolt, screw, or rivet within 2 inches from each duct corner and at maximum intervals of 12 inches. For systems over 3 in. w.g. pressure, the reinforcement ends must be secured with a ¼-inch **tie rod** or at least a 1 × 1 × 12 gage angle even if the side dimension does not require intermediate reinforcing. Acceptable methods for intermediate reinforcement are shown in *Figure 7*.

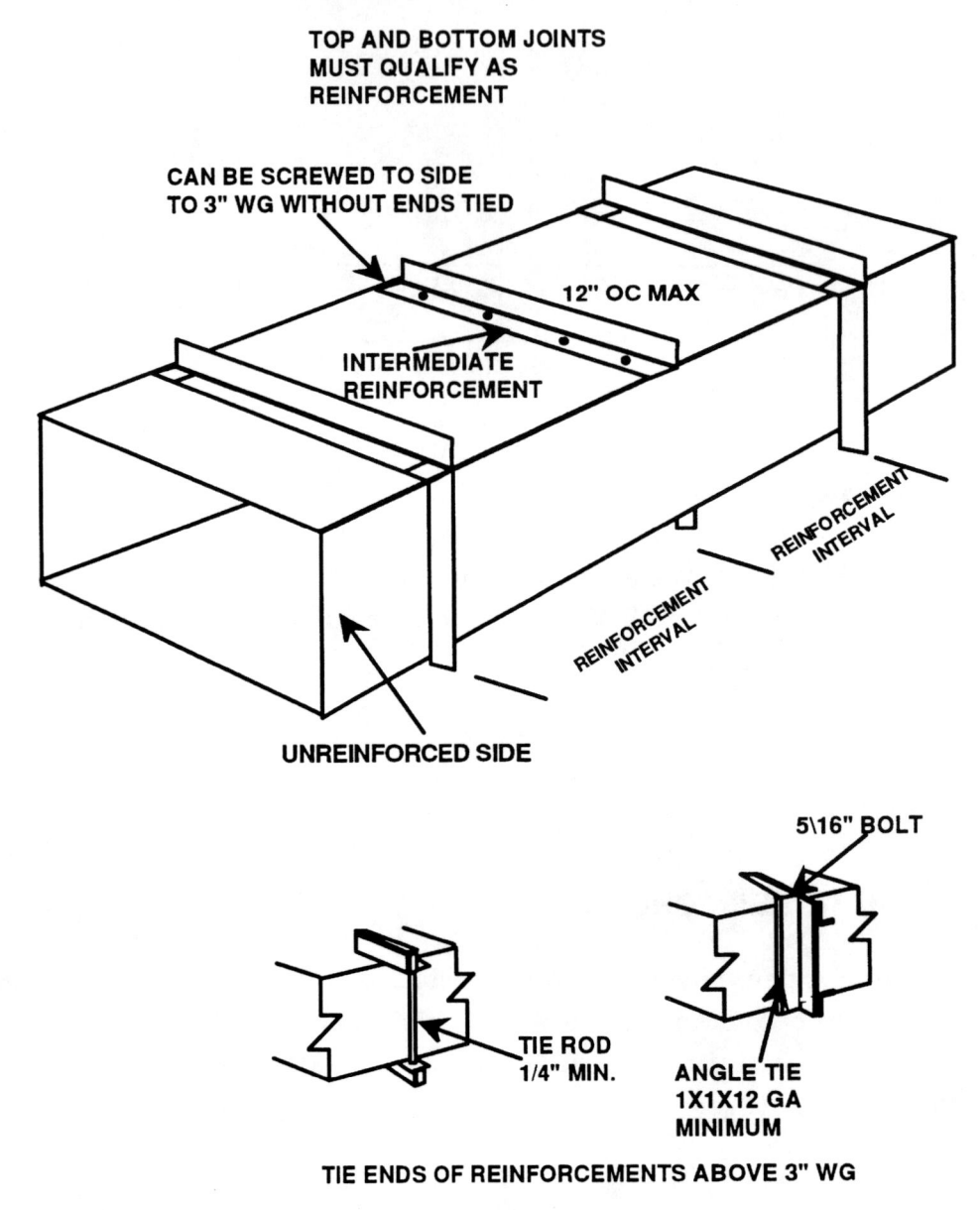

Figure 7. Duct Reinforcement On One Or Both Dimensions

2.6.0 CONNECTOR AND INTERMEDIATE REINFORCING

Any confusion using the tables comes in evaluating the reinforcement spacing for connectors. The intermediate reinforcement spacing is not evaluated in the same way that gage is evaluated. The reinforcement spacing is half the distance on both sides of the connector or reinforcement (see *Figure 8*). The SMACNA Rectangular Duct Reinforcement Tables give distance values for 10, 8, 5, 4, 2.5, and 2 feet.

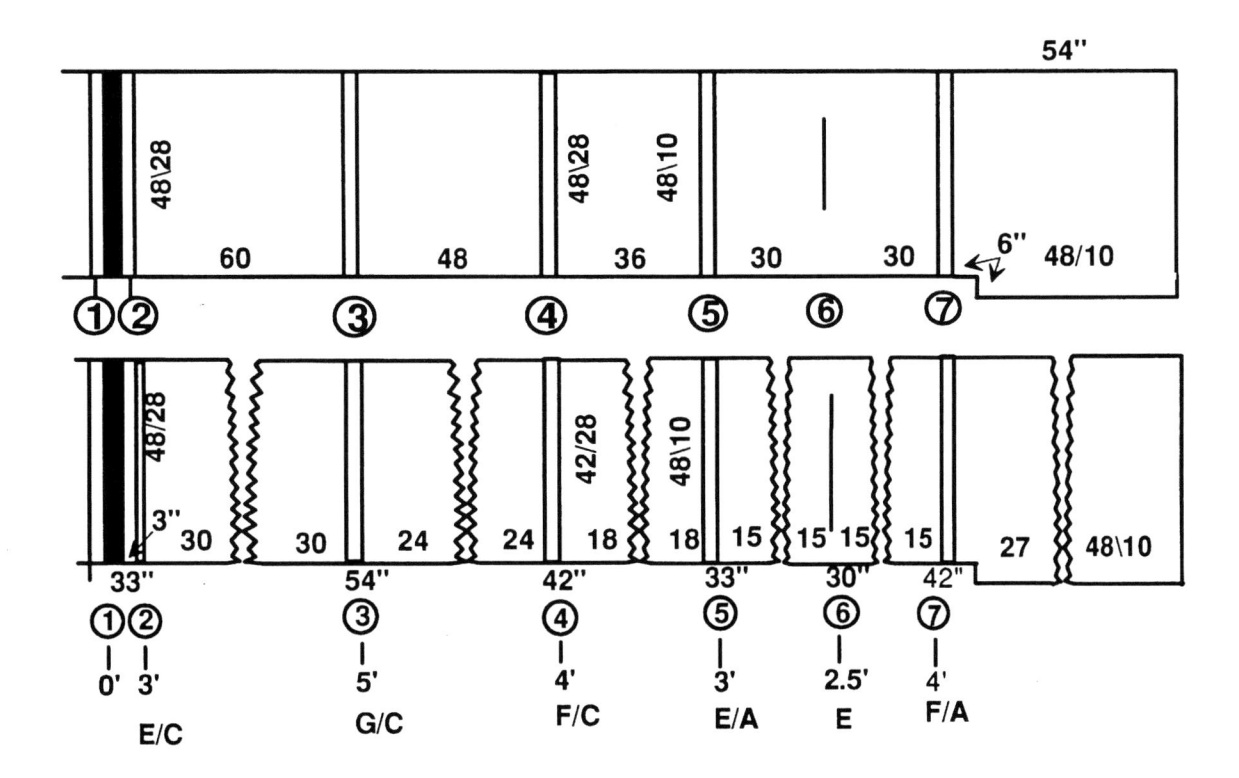

Refer to *Table 4* (page 9).

1. A flex connector attached is such a minimum amount that using the minimum gage in the applicable wg table will suffice.
2. One-half flex plus one-half 5' duct is 3" + 30" = 33". The 33" is more than 2.5', but less than 3'. Therefore, 3' spacing values are used. 48" - E, 28" - C.
3. One-half 5' duct plus one-half 4' duct is 30" = 24" = 54". The 54" is more than 4' but less than 5'. Therefore, 5' spacing values are used. 48" - G, 28" - C.
4. One-half 4' duct plus one-half reducer is 24" + 18" = 42". The 42" is more than 3' but less than 4'. Therefore, 4' spacing is used. 48" - F, 28" - C.
5. One-half reducer plus one-half distance to intermediate reinforcement is 18" + 15" = 33". The 33" is more than 2.5' but less than 3'. Therefore, 3' spacing values are used. 48" - E, 10" - A.
6. One-half distance to intermediate reinforcement plus one-half to elbow is 15" + 15" = 30". The 30" is equal to 2.5'. Therefore, the 2.5' spacing values are used. 48" - E, 10" @ 5', 24 ga - No intermediate reinforcement needed.
7. Elbow: One-half intermediate brace straight plus one-half heel is 15" + 27" = 42". Therefore, 4' spacing values are used. 48" - F, 10" - A.

Figure 8. Connector Reinforcement Spacing

SHEET METAL DUCT FABRICATION STANDARDS — TRAINEE MODULE 04406

2.7.0 CONNECTOR JOINT

There are two general methods to reinforce and connect duct joints:

1. The standard **transverse connectors**, *Figure 9*.
2. The proprietary gasket-mated flange connector, *Figure 10*.

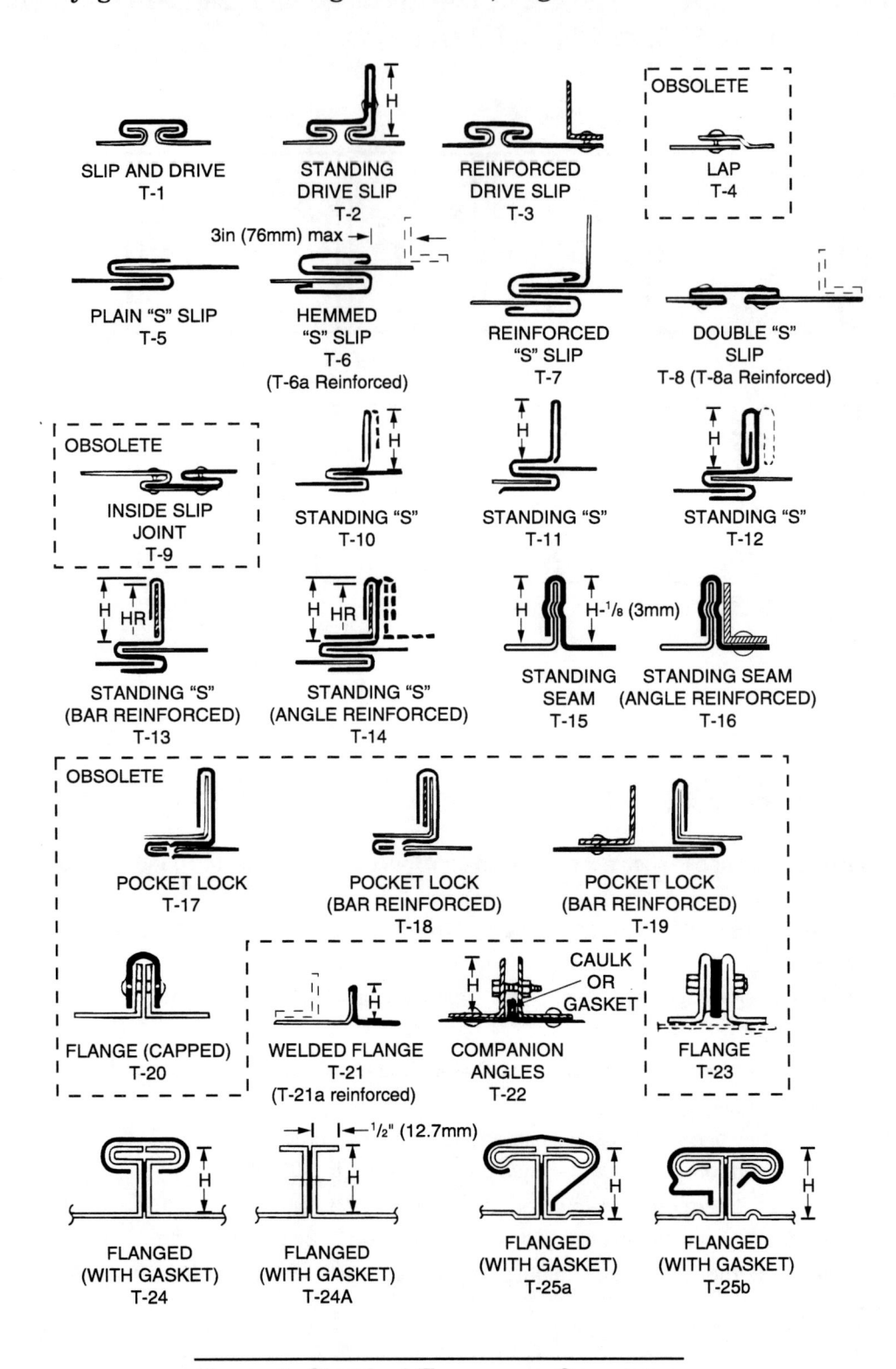

Figure 9. Standard Transverse Connectors

Courtesy of Ductmate Industries, Inc.

Courtesy of Ductmate Industries, Inc.

A

B

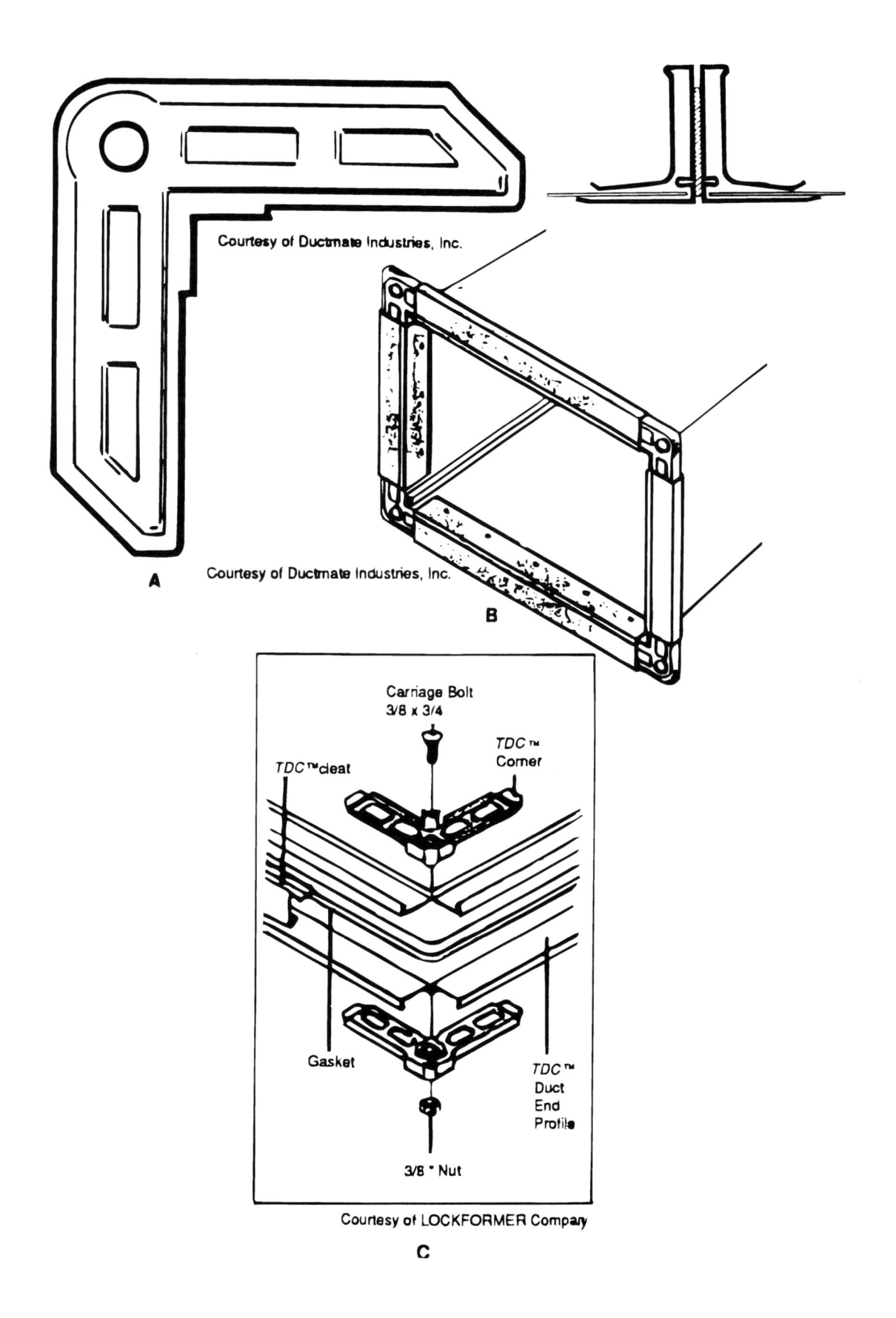

Carriage Bolt
3/8 x 3/4

TDC™ cleat

TDC™ Corner

Gasket

TDC™ Duct End Profile

3/8" Nut

Courtesy of LOCKFORMER Company

C

Figure 10. Proprietary Connector

SHEET METAL DUCT FABRICATION STANDARDS — TRAINEE MODULE 04406

The standard connectors are presented in the SMACNA standards manual and include the slip and drive (or slide and drive). These connectors can be reinforced by an additional bar or angle to bring them up to proper rigidity. Although there are reinforced drive joints available, the contractor may consider the second method, proprietary gasket-mated flange connectors, when a duct size goes beyond the limits of a normal flat drive or when a duct requires a Class C seal. Proprietary gasket-mated flange connectors are available as a preformed connector. Ductmate-type connectors are available in 20-foot lengths, are cut to the desired length, and then, by adding corners, are made into frames that are added to the raw edge of the duct. This reinforcement can be a standard structural angle or various bent sections, such as zee/cee, hat, or flat channel (refer back to *Figure 6*).

3.0.0 DUCT CONSTRUCTION

The general requirements and standards for duct construction have been discussed and may now be interpreted and applied. There are wide variations in shops and equipment. *Table 5* in *Appendix A* uses a generic letter code to define the minimum connector and reinforcing requirements. There are several ways to meet the reinforcing code. Some shops may have the machinery to roll form-mated TDC or TDF flange connectors (SMACNA types T-24 through T-25b). Other shops may adopt preformed connectors such as Ductmate while some may still use slip or double slip joints with angle reinforcing.

This text makes no attempt to deal with all available options except to recognize that they do exist. The industry standards, as well as the job specifications, need to be understood in the context of a particular shop's standards. The shop's equipment should be compared to industry standards to develop shop standards.

The "sketcher" who develops the shop drawings may also be the "detailer" who "picks off" the job. This person will also be the one who implements the various requirements.

3.1.0 CONNECTOR WITH TIE ROD

A tie rod, as stated in the SMACNA Rectangular Duct Reinforcement Tables, can be used as an option with a lesser-rated reinforcement code to equal a stiffer connector. In some cases, it is the only acceptable way to reinforce the duct. The table defines whether the tie rod is optional or mandatory.

As an option for a 3 in. w.g. pressure duct with 54-inch dimensions and 5-foot reinforcement spacing, *Table 4* shows the following figure:

H-18

F + rod

The letter *H* defines the reinforcement grade class with 18-gage duct. The *F + rod* gives the option of using a lesser grade class of reinforcement (F) with a tie rod equal to the H. A ¼-inch rod is used for lengths of up to 36 inches, and a ⅜-inch rod is used for 37-inch lengths and over.

For duct lengths 97 inches and over, *Table 4* shows only:

H-18t

The mandatory solution is to use a grade class *H* reinforcement with a tie rod. *Figures 11* and *12* show several tie rod attachment methods.

Specific requirements for installing connectors, tie rods, and intermediate bracing are discussed in the *Duct Construction* section of this module.

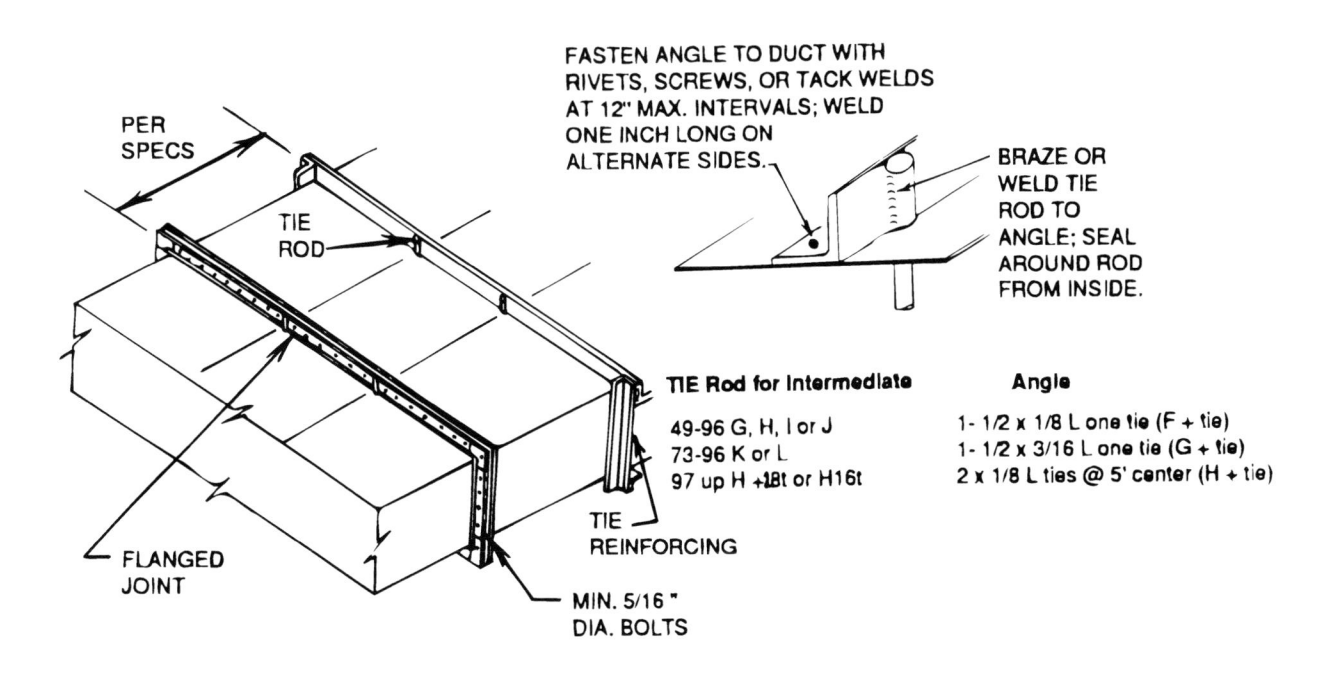

Figure 11. Connector And Intermediate Reinforcement With Tie Rod

SHEET METAL DUCT FABRICATION STANDARDS — TRAINEE MODULE 04406

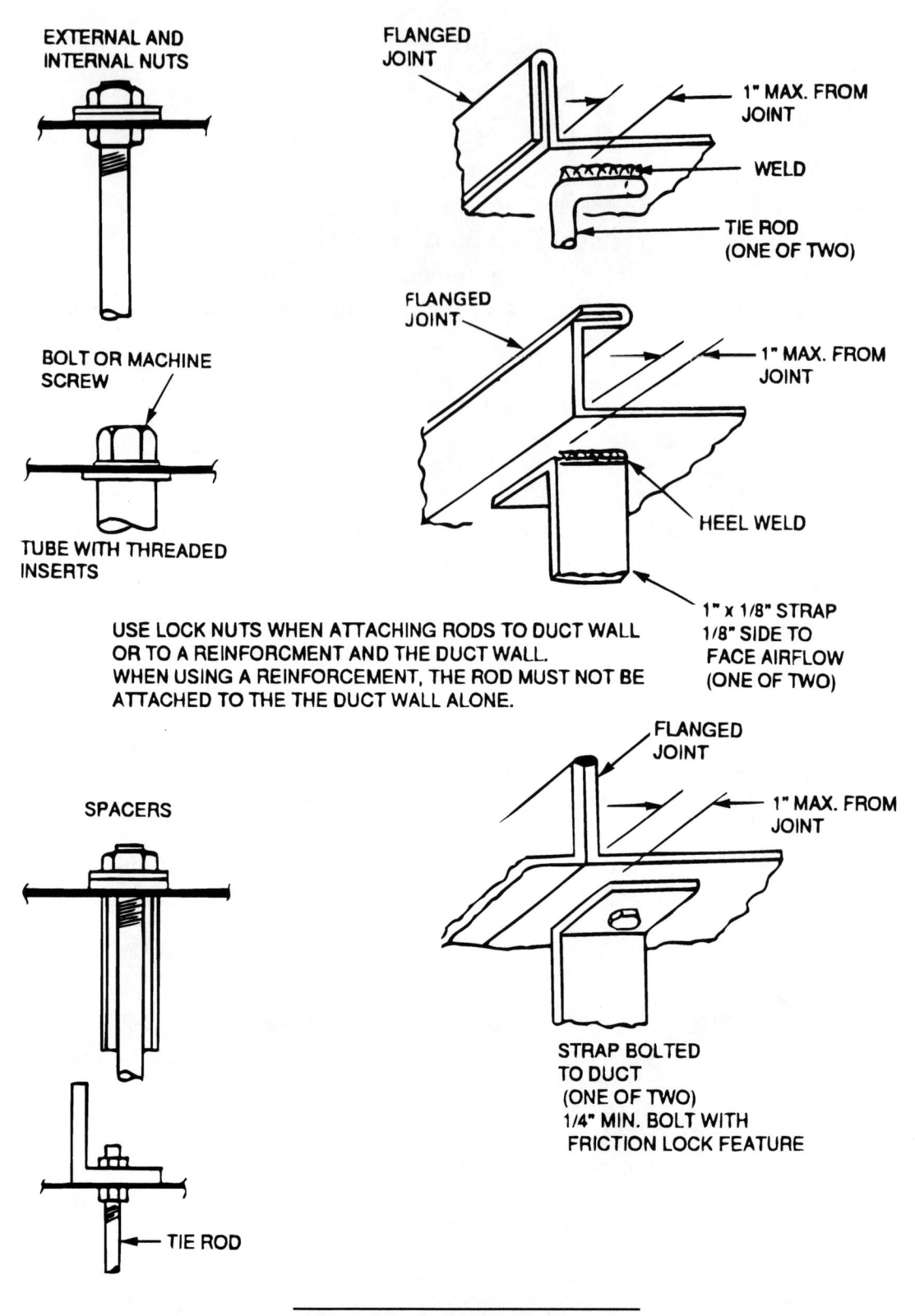

Figure 12. Tie Rod Attachments

3.2.0 INTERMEDIATE REINFORCEMENT WITH TIE ROD

The intermediate reinforcing, like the connector, can use a lighter member with a tie rod. Refer back to *Figure 11*.

SHEET METAL — TRAINEE TASK MODULE 04406

3.3.0 LONGITUDINAL SEAMS

Longitudinal seams are constructed to withstand one and one-half times the designed operating pressure of the system without duct failure or metal deformation. *Figure 13* shows the different types of acceptable longitudinal seams and recommended locations. The two most common longitudinal seams are the Pittsburgh and the button lock snap lock.

The Pittsburgh seam pocket depth varies with the roll form equipment to a maximum pocket depth of ⅝ inch. The larger pocket is for heavier duct. Pittsburgh seams can be used for all pressure classes.

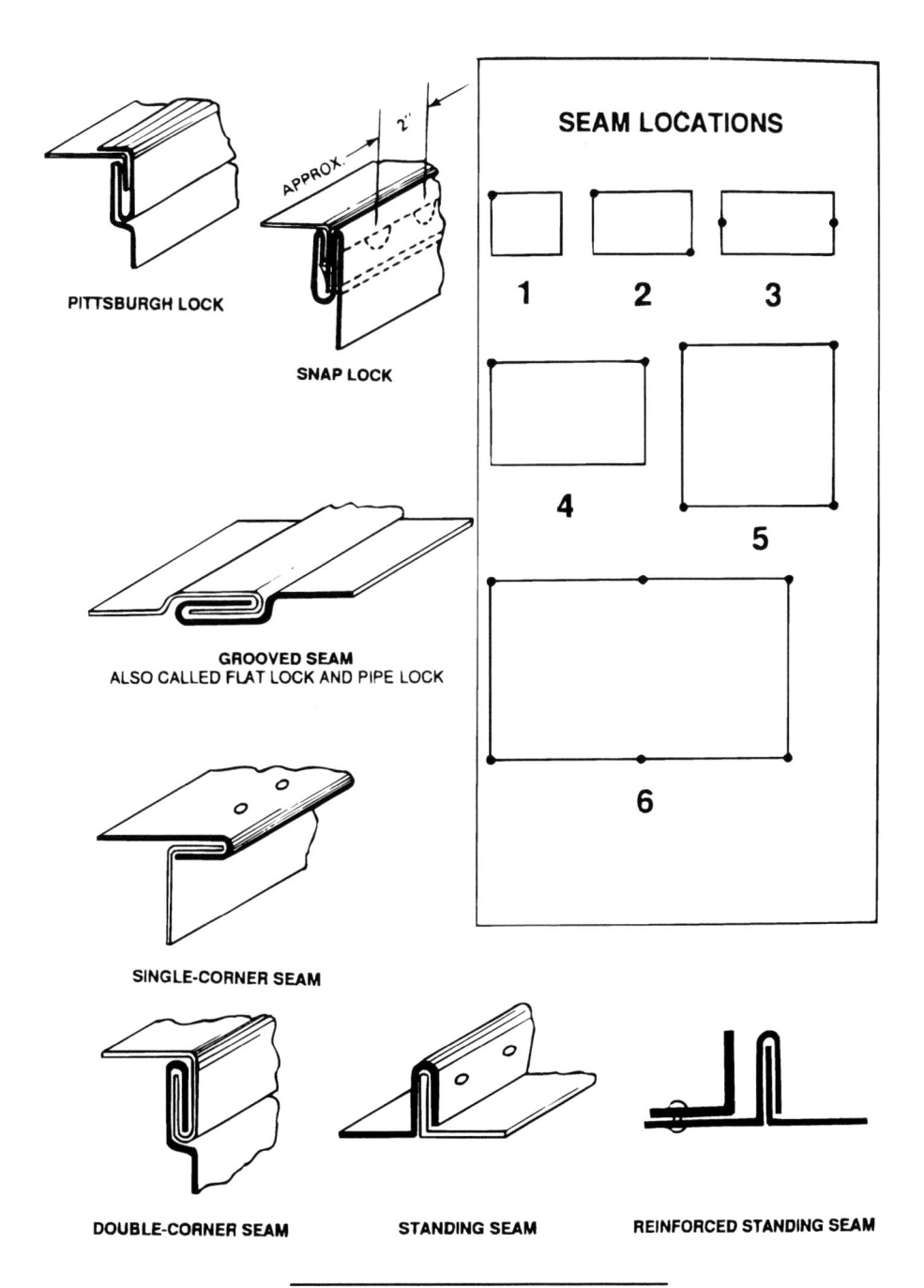

Figure 13. Longitudinal Seams

SHEET METAL DUCT FABRICATION STANDARDS — TRAINEE MODULE 04406

Snap lock seams have the following limitations:

- Snap lock seams can be used only for pressure classes up to 4 in. w.g. maximum.
- Snap lock seams are not recommended for aluminum or other soft metal duct.
- Duct that is over 48 inches in dimension with 3 in. w.g. pressure and all duct with 4 in. w.g. pressure must have screws added at the ends.

The other longitudinal seams are the grooved seam (also known as *pipe lock* or *flat lock*), standing seam, single-corner seam, and double-corner seam. Of these, the standing seam is most commonly used to splice duct panels. Normally a 1-inch seam is used for ducts with widths of up to 42 inches. A 1.5-inch seam is used for larger ducts. The seam is fastened together at the ends and at 8-inch intervals.

Cross-breaking or beading (*Figure 14*) must be used if the duct is greater than 18 inches and the panel is more than 10 square feet, and all of the following are true:

- The duct is uninsulated.
- The duct pressure is less than 3 in. w.g.
- The duct is less than 18 gage.

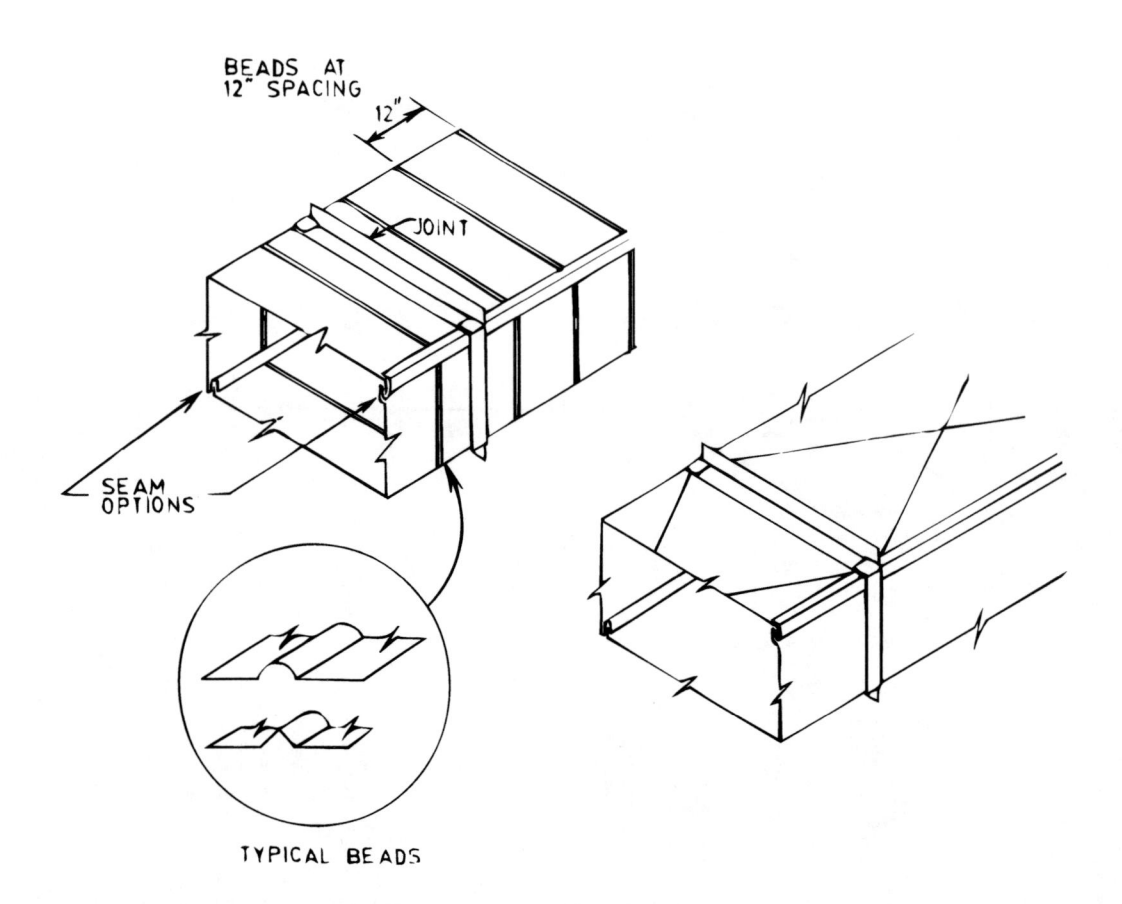

Figure 14. Cross-Breaking And Beading

SUMMARY

The operating pressure of the HVAC system is used to determine the sheet metal gage of the duct. The duct gage, connectors, and reinforcements are selected to minimize deflection caused by internal pressure. Ducts are sufficiently sealed so that the HVAC system operates efficiently. Intermediate reinforcement is used to reduce unsupported panel distances so that lighter gage duct material can be used. Lighter gage connectors with tie rods are used to provide the same rigidity as a heavier gage connector. Longitudinal seams are constructed to withstand $1\frac{1}{2}$ times the designed operating pressure of the system without duct failure or metal deformation.

References

For advanced study of topics covered in this task module, the following books are suggested:

HVAC Air Duct Leakage Test Manual, First Edition, Sheet Metal and Air Conditioning Contractors National Association, Inc., Chantilly, VA.

HVAC Duct Construction Standards – Metal and Flexible, Second Edition, Sheet Metal and Air Conditioning Contractors National Association, Inc., Chantilly, VA.

HVAC Systems – Duct Design, Third Edition, Sheet Metal and Air Conditioning Contractors National Association, Inc., Chantilly, VA.

ACKNOWLEDGMENTS
Figure 1 courtesy of Hydro-Test Products, Inc.
Figure 2 courtesy of LeRoi Division, Dresser Industries, Inc. and ITT Pneumotive, Inc.
Figures 3 - 5 courtesy of General Pump and Equipment Company, Inc.

REVIEW / PRACTICE QUESTIONS

1. Duct strength, deflection, and leakage are primarily functions of _____.
   a. joint connections and reinforcement
   b. velocity
   c. air pressure
   d. None of the above.

2. There are _____ duct pressure classes normally used in commercial work.
   a. five
   b. seven
   c. three
   d. eight

3. There are _____ duct seal classes normally used in commercial work.
   a. five
   b. seven
   c. three
   d. eight

4. Rectangular duct gage is determined directly from the _____.
   a. engineering drawings
   b. SMACNA Rectangular Duct Reinforcement Tables
   c. job specifications
   d. None of the above.

5. In some applications, intermediate duct reinforcement allows the use of heavier gage metal.
   a. True
   b. False

6. There are _____ general methods used to reinforce and connect duct joints.
   a. ten
   b. seven
   c. five
   d. two

7. In some applications, tie rods allow the use of lighter gage duct reinforcement members.
   a. True
   b. False

8. Longitudinal seams are constructed to withstand _____ the designed operating pressure of the system.
    a. one and one-half times
    b. twice
    c. three times
    d. None of the above.

9. The two most common longitudinal seams are the Pittsburgh and the flat lock.
    a. True
    b. False

10. Cross-breaking or beading must be used on duct panels that are uninsulated, less than 18 gage, subject to less than 3 in. w.g., greater than 18 inches long, and more than _____ square feet in area.
    a. ten
    b. twelve
    c. fifteen
    d. twenty

ANSWERS TO REVIEW / PRACTICE QUESTIONS

Answers	Section Reference
1. c	1.0.0
2. b	1.1.0
3. c	1.2.0
4. b	2.2.0
5. b	2.5.0
6. d	2.7.0
7. a	3.2.0
8. a	3.3.0
9. b	3.3.0
10. a	3.3.0

APPENDIX A

DEVELOPING SHOP STANDARDS

After reviewing how to use the pressure, span, and length to determine the seal, gage, and connector/reinforcement of individual pieces, the challenge remains to establish a set of shop fabrication rules for complete duct systems. Before we equate the generic reinforcement code to a real connector, we need to look more closely at the diversity in whole ductruns.

Figure 15A presents how the three primary connector spacing choices: 5', 4', and 3' with the 2' 6" determined using various fitting or straight duct lengths with the standard straight duct choices.

Fitting or Straight Duct

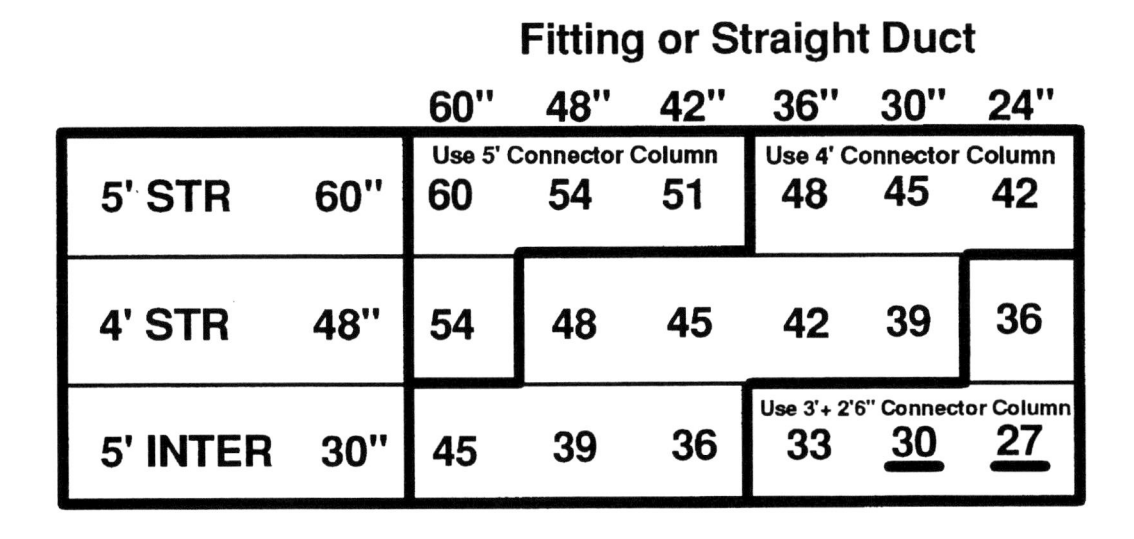

		60"	48"	42"	36"	30"	24"
5' STR	60"	60	54	51	48	45	42
4' STR	48"	54	48	45	42	39	36
5' INTER	30"	45	39	36	33	30	27

(60"/48"/42" use 5' Connector Column; 36"/30"/24" use 4' Connector Column on 5' STR row; Use 3' + 2'6" Connector Column for 5' INTER row at 36"/30"/24")

Figure 15A. Reinforcement Spacing With Combinations Of Straight Duct Or Fittings

The ductrun in *Figure 15B* shows how two pieces of straight duct (48/18 - 5 ft.) have three connector joints with 4', 5', and 3' reinforcement codes or how two pieces of straight duct (42/12) with three connector joints need the 2' 6", 4', and 3' connector codes. If your shop chooses to apply the rules exactly, each of these straight ducts is unique and cannot be exchanged. Most shops would probably like to standardize the straight duct so they would be interchangeable. To do this we need to adopt two simple rules:

1. To avoid confusion or even duplicate connectors when we have three joints with two pieces of straight duct, we will evaluate only one end of each piece. We suggest End 1, the end toward the air handler.

2. We will assume the straight piece to be our standard length of 4', 5', or 5' intermediate, and this piece is joined to another straight duct of the same length.

SHEET METAL DUCT FABRICATION STANDARDS — TRAINEE MODULE 04406

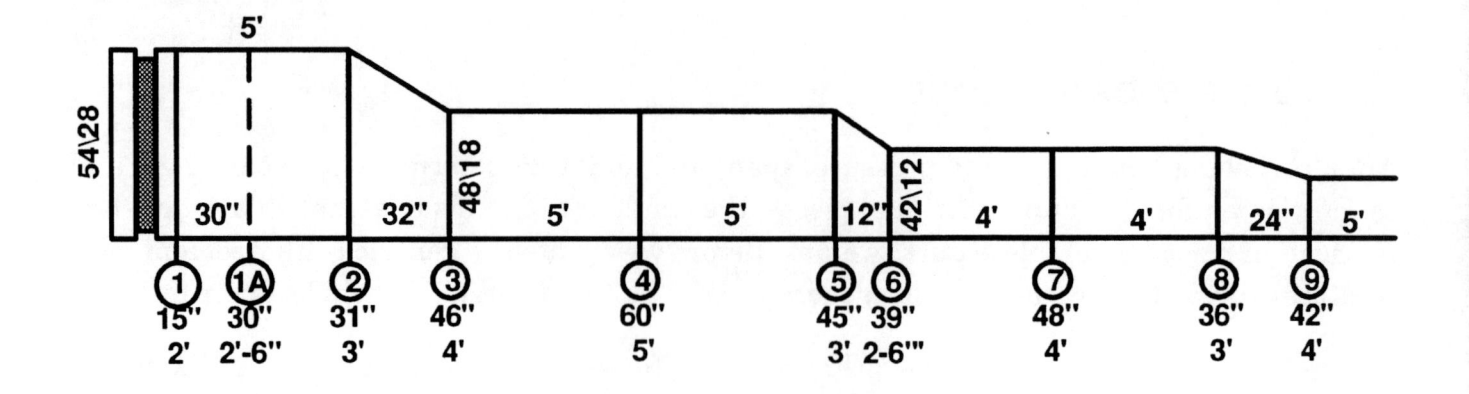

Figure 15B. Sample Ductrun

To standardize the fittings, we adapt the same End 1 rule and also assume the fitting is connected to whichever of the standard straight ducts we are using: 4', 5', or 5' intermediate. See *Figure 15C*.

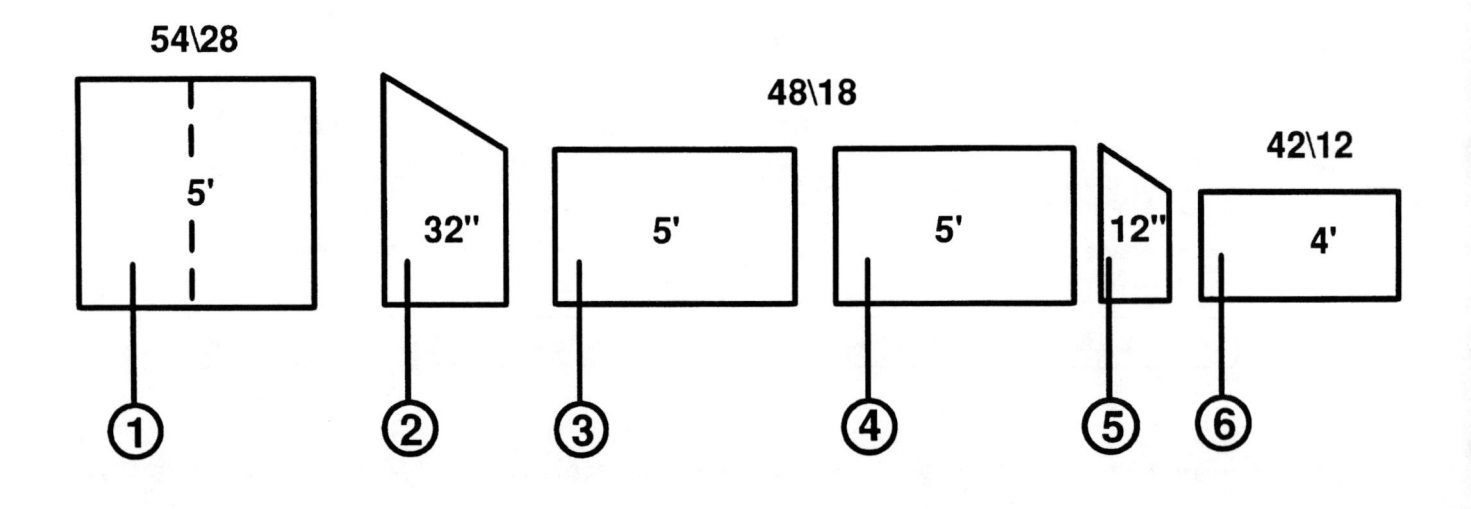

Figure 15C. Breakdown Of Sample Ductrun

With these rules, we have constructed simple look-up tables (*Table 5*) for the gage and connectors. The first determination needed to convert this generic table to a shop standard is whether you are a 4' or 5' shop. Most light commercial shops work with 4×8 or 4×10 sheets and sometimes 4' coil. The heavier commercial shops that also do industrial work usually use 5' coil. The tables emphasize 5' straight and 5' intermediate straight, but also make a 4' shop look-up easy.

SHEET METAL — TRAINEE TASK MODULE 04406

HOW TO USE THE TABLES

The left half of the chart gives you the 5' reinforcement connector that will allow you to use the same connector for any straight duct or fitting up to 5' length. There is an optional connector in the 4' gage column that can be used for 4' shops or for 36" length fittings used with 5' straight duct. As you can see, there is a reinforcement code reduction for only a few of the widths between the 5' and 4' column.

To determine the connector and gage of the duct without intermediate reinforcement, we would use the same connector code for all straight duct and fittings. The gage is chosen from the 5', 4', or 3' columns.

The right half of the chart is the optional 5' intermediate chart. It begins as an option when there is a 2-gage reduction from 20 gage or when 18 gage is required. The weight reduction between 20 and 24 gage helps offset some of the cost of the intermediate reinforcement. Some of the light commercial shops may find it difficult to roll form the 18 gage, so the lighter gage may not only be more convenient but also necessary. When you use this side of the table, both the connector and intermediate reinforcement use the same code except when noted otherwise in the INTER column.

Notice that a 5' intermediate straight (30") with a 42" maximum length fitting can use the 3' reinforcement value. The gage options to the 4" w.g. table are 2' 6" used for straight duct with 3' and 42" for fittings. The 6" and 10" w.g. tables gage columns are 2', 2' 6" for straight duct, and 3'. The 3' connector column becomes the 2' 6" or 2' value when 3' or 2' 6" gage columns are not used. The last column of the right half is the reinforcement code for 2' 6" when it is less than 3' value. Don't forget the smaller duct dimension is looked up in addition to the wide dimension.

This look-up table with the optional intermediate straight duct length allows you to determine the generic code and the minimum gage for various pressure/spans. The table also allows you to use a lighter reinforcement with a tie rod in place of a heavier reinforcement. For example, (Ft) H allows a F connector with a tie rod as an option to an H connector. There are cases where the tie rod with the connector is mandatory and those are noted by Ht. The last step in developing a shop standard is to determine how your shop will meet the generic code and if your shop would rather use the heavier gage than the minimum.

The General Notes area summarizes a number of construction details. The limitations of snap lock, pocket lock, and standard connectors should guide your shop standards. The table shows where the flat "S" or flat drive can be used. Your shop may choose to change from the standard connector when the flat drive can no longer be used. Sometimes the seal class might encourage your shop to consider a mated flange connector instead of field sealing the duct.

SHEET METAL DUCT FABRICATION STANDARDS — TRAINEE MODULE 04406

+ or − 1/2" w.g. SIZE	ALL STR & FTG to 5' MAX				SEAMS – Pittsburgh or Snaplock CONNECTOR – Standard connector Class C seal recommended minimum, but required only when specified						
	CONN. GAGE YOUR SHOP	CONN.	GAGE								
		(TIE) 5'	5'	4'	3'
18		SLIP	26			5' INTER STR & 42" MAX FTG				
20		DRIVE	26			CONN. GAGE YOUR SHOP	CONN	GAGE			INTER CODE
26		A	26				(TIE) 3'	2/6'	3'	42"	
30		B	26								
36		C	26								
42		D	26	C*							
48		D	26								
54		D	26								
60		E	24	26							
72		F	22	24							
84		(Ft) H	22	G*24							
96		(Ft) H	20	24							
97 UP		(Ft) H	18								

* ALT CONN FOR 4' STR & 4' FTG OR 36" MAX FTG WITH 5' STR

©1992 Michael Bergen All Rights Reserved

Table 5A. Duct Connector Selection

+ or − 1" w.g. SIZE	ALL STR & FTG to 5' MAX						GENERAL NOTES
	CONN. GAGE YOUR SHOP	CONN. (TIE) 5'	GAGE 5'	4'	3'	**SEAMS** – Pittsburgh or Snaplock **CONNECTOR** – Standard connector **INTERMEDIATE REINFORCING** – Need only to be screwed to duct 2" from ends, 12" oc Class C seal recommended minimum, but required only when specified
10		SLIP	26			
20		DRIVE	26			
26		A	26			

						5' INTER STR & 42" MAX FTG				
30		B	26			CONN. GAGE YOUR SHOP	CONN. (TIE) 3'	GAGE 2/6'	3'	42"	INTER CODE
36		C	26								
42		D	24	26		W					
48		E	24	D*26							
54		E	22	24							
60		F	22	24							
72		(Ft) H	18	G*22	24	72	(Ft) G	24	24	22	
84		(Ft) I	18	H*20	20	84	(Ft) H	20	20	20	
96		(Ft) J	16	I*18	20	96	(Ft) I	20	20	18	
97 UP						97 UP	Ht	18	NO	NO	

* ALT CONN FOR 4' STR & 4' FTG OR 36" MAX FTG WITH 5' STR

©1992 Michael Bergen All Rights Reserved

Table 5B. Duct Connector Selection

SHEET METAL DUCT FABRICATION STANDARDS — TRAINEE MODULE 04406

+ or − 2" w.g. SIZE	ALL STR & FTG to 5' MAX					GENERAL NOTES					
	CONN. GAGE YOUR SHOP	CONN.	GAGE			**SEAMS** – Pittsburgh or Snaplock **CONNECTOR** – Standard connector **INTERMEDIATE REINFORCING** – Need only to be screwed to duct 2" from ends, 12" oc Class C seal minimum required					
		(TIE) 5'	5'	4'	3'					
10		SLIP	26							
20		DRIVE	26							
22		A	26			5' INTER STR & 42" MAX FTG					
26		B	26			CONN. GAGE YOUR SHOP	CONN.	GAGE			INTER CODE
30		C	24	26			(TIE) 3'	2/6'	3'	42'	
36		D	22	24							
42		E	22	24							
48		F	20	E*22	24	48	E	24	24	22	
54		(Ft) G	18	F*20	24	54	F	24	24	20	
60		(Ft) H	18	G*20	22	60	(Ft) G	24	22	20	
72		(Ft) I	16	H*18	20	72	(Ft) H	22	22	18	
84		(Ft) J	NO	18	20	84	(Ft) I	20	20	18	
96		(Gt) K	NO	16	18	96	(Gt) K	20	18	16	J
						96 UP	Ht	18	18	NO	

* ALT CONN FOR 4' STR & 4' FTG OR 36" MAX FTG WITH 5' STR

©1992 Michael Bergen All Rights Reserved

Table 5C. Duct Connector Selection

+ or − 3" w.g. SIZE	ALL STR & FTG to 5' MAX					GENERAL NOTES				
	CONN. GAGE YOUR SHOP	CONN. (TIE) 5'	GAGE				**SEAMS** – Pittsburgh or Snaplock – (Screw ends of duct over 48")
			5'	4'	3'		**CONNECTOR** – Standard connector not recommended over 36". No slip allowed. Use double slip with angle reinforced over 36".
18		DRIVE	24				**INTERMEDIATE REINFORCING** – Check gage required when depth is above 26"; screw reinforcement 2" from end, 12" oc.
20		A	24				Class B seal minimum required
24		B	24			5' INTER STR & 42" MAX FTG TO 72" WIDE				
26		C	24			CONN. GAGE YOUR SHOP	CONN. (TIE) 3'	GAGE		INTER CODE
30		C	22	24				2/6'	3'	42"
36		E	20	D*24		36	D	24	24	24
42		E	20	22	24	42	E	24	24	22
48		(Ft) G	18	F*20	22	48	E	24	22	20
54		(Ft) H	18	18	22	54	(Ft) G	24	22	18	E
60		(Ft) H	16	18	20	60	(Ft) G	24	20	18
72		(Ft) I	NO	16	20	72	(Ft) H	22	20	16
						84	(Ft) J	20	18	NO
						96	(Gt) L	18	16	NO	K
						96 UP	Ht	18	NO	NO

* ALT CONN FOR 4' STR & 4' FTG OR 36" MAX FTG WITH 5' STR

©1992 Michael Bergen All Rights Reserved

Table 5D. Duct Connector Selection

+ only 4" w.g. SIZE	ALL STR & FTG to 5' MAX					GENERAL NOTES					
	CONN. GAGE YOUR SHOP	CONN. (TIE) 5'	GAGE				**SEAMS** – Pittsburgh or Snaplock – (Screw ends of duct) **CONNECTOR** – Standard connector not recommended over 30". No pocket lock, no slip allowed. Use double slip with angle reinforced over 30". **INTERMEDIATE REINFORCING** – Both W & D or tie ends 1x1x12 ga. min. or 1/4" rod Class A seal required
			5'	4'	3'					
16		DRIVE	24							
18		A	24							
22		B	24			5' INTER STR & 42" MAX FTG TO 60" WIDE					
26		C	22	24		CONN. GAGE YOUR SHOP		CONN. (TIE) 3'	GAGE			INTER CODE
30		D	22	24					2/6'	3'	42"	
36		E	20	22	24	36		D	24	24	22	
42		F	18	20	24	42		E	24	22	20	
48		(Ft) G	18	18	22	48		F	22	22	18	
54		(Ft) H	16	18	20	54		(Ft) G	22	20	18	
60		(Ft) I	16	16	20	60		(Ft) H	22	20	16	
						72		(Ft) I	20	18	NO	
						84		(Gt) K	18	16	NO	J
						96		(Gt) L	18	NO	NO	
						96 UP		Ht	18	NO	NO	

©1992 Michael Bergen All Rights Reserved

Table 5E. Duct Connector Selection

SHEET METAL — TRAINEE TASK MODULE 04406

+ only 6" w.g. SIZE	ALL STR & FTG to 5' MAX			
	CONN. GAGE YOUR SHOP	CONN. (TIE) 5'	GAGE		
			5'	4'	3'
12		DRIVE	24		
16		A	24		
20		B	22	24	
22		C	22	24	
24		C	22	22	24
28		D	20	22	24
30		D	18	22	24
36		F	18	E*20	22
42		(Ft) G	16	18	20

*ALT CONN FOR 4' STR & 4' FTG OR 36" MAX FTG WITH 5' STR

GENERAL NOTES

SEAMS – Pittsburgh, No Snaplock

CONNECTOR – Standard connector not recommended. Use double slip with angle reinforcement.

INTERMEDIATE REINFORCING – Both W & D. Notice spacing limits above 72".

Class A seal required

5' INTER STR & 42" MAX FTG TO 42" WIDE					
CONN. GAGE YOUR SHOP	CONN. (TIE) 3'	GAGE			INTER CODE
		2'	2/6'	3'	
28	C		24	24	
30	D		24	24	
36	E		22	20	E
42	F		22	20	
48	(Ft) H		22	18	G
54	(Ft) H		20	18	
60	(Ft) H		20	18	
72	(Ft) J		18	16	
84	(Gt) L		16	NO	
96	(Gt) L	18	NO	NO	
96 UP	Ht	18	NO	NO	

©1992 Michael Bergen All Rights Reserved

Table 5F. Duct Connector Selection

+ only 10" w.g. SIZE	ALL STR & FTG to 5' MAX				GENERAL NOTES
	CONN. GAGE YOUR SHOP	CONN. (TIE) 5'	GAGE 5'	GAGE 4' / 3'	**SEAMS** – Pittsburgh, No Snaplock

SIZE	CONN. GAGE YOUR SHOP	CONN. (TIE) 5'	5'	4'	3'
8		A	24		
12		A	22	24	
14		A	20	22	24
16		B	20	22	24
18		C	20	B*22	24
20		C	18	20	24
22		C	18	20	24
24		D	18	20	24
26		D	18	20	22
28		E	18	D*20	22
30		E	16	18	22
36		F	16	18	20
42		(Ft) H	NO	16	18

GENERAL NOTES

SEAMS – Pittsburgh, No Snaplock

CONNECTOR – Standard connector not recommended. No slip or drive allowed. Use double slip with angle reinforcement.

INTERMEDIATE REINFORCING – Both W & D. Note – Over 72" same construction

Class A seal required

5' INTER STR & 42" MAX FTG TO 42" WIDE

CONN. GAGE YOUR SHOP	CONN. (TIE) 3'	GAGE 2'	2/6'	3'	INTER CODE
20	B		24	24	
22	C		24	24	
24	C		24	24	
26	D		24	22	C
28	D		24	22	
30	D		24	22	
36	F		22	20	E
42	(Ft) G		20	18	
48	(Ft) H		18	18	
54	(Ft) I		18	16	H
60	(Ft) J		18	16	I
72	(Gt) K		16	NO	
72 UP	Ht	16	NO	NO	

©1992 Michael Bergen All Rights Reserved

* ALT CONN FOR 4' STR & 4' FTG OR 36" MAX FTG WITH 5' STR

Table 5G. Duct Connector Selection

STANDARD CONNECTORS

The typical method used to join duct sections up to 4 in. w.g. pressure has been *slip and drive* or *slide and drive*. Before proprietary gasket-mated flange connectors such as Ductmate came into use, the pocket lock (otherwise known as *government lock* or *Baker slip*) was used extensively. Now that rolled flanges such as TDC or TDF have been introduced, there are even more alternatives to duct construction.

The SMACNA manual specifies test and performance criteria so that these other materials or methods can be tested and used. Consult manufacturer information and tables to apply these products to the table.

Table 6 and *Figure 16* present some of the common "standard connector" options that are presented in the SMACNA manual. This will help to illustrate how the generic reinforcement code can be equated to actual connectors.

The flat drive (T-1) provides a class A reinforcement for certain sizes as defined the SMACNA manual. The limits are listed in *Table 6*.

GENERIC CODE	STANDARD CONNECTORS (All Dimensions in Inches)
A	Flat "S" and drive – conforms to A where allowed to 2" wg pressure (T-1 & T-5) T-5 - PLAIN "S" SLIP T-1 - SLIP AND DRIVE
A, B, C B C	Hemmed "S" with 1 x 1 x 18 ga angle – A, B or C to 2" wg pressure (T-7) Standing Drive (T-2) 1 - 1/8 x 26 ga 1 - 1/8 x 22 ga T-7 REINFORCED "S" SLIP T-2 STANDING DRIVE SLIP
C D	Standing "S" 1 x 26 ga 1 x 24 ga – (T-10 & T-11) T-10 STANDING "S" T-11 STANDING "S" (Alt.)
F G	Standing "S" reinforced with bar (T-13) 1-1/2 x 24 ga + 1-1/2 x 1/8 bar 1-1/2 x 22 ga + 1-1/2 x 1/8 bar T-13 STANDING "S" (Bar Reinforced)
H I J	Standing "S" reinforced with angle (T-14) 1-1/2 x 20 ga + 1-1/2 x 3/16 2 x 20 ga + 2 x 1/8 2 x 20 ga + 2 x 3/16 T-14 STANDING "S" (Angle Reinforced)
	Limit Length 3" wg – 36" 4" wg – 30" Not recommended above 4" wg If above 3" wg and 4" wg limits (see above) or 6" wg and 10" wg, use inside slip or double slip with angle reinforcement. The letter "T" is a prefix assigned by SMACNA to identify transverse connectors.
	INTERMEDIATE REINFORCEMENT
C D E F G H I J K L	Angle (inches) 1 x 18 ga 1-1/4 x 18 ga 1-1/2 x 16 ga 1-1/2 x 1/8 ----------- 1 (Ft) 1-1/2 x 1/8 with tie rods = G - J 1-1/2 x 3/16 ---------- 2 (Gt) 1-1/2 x 3/16 with tie rods = K - L 2 x 1/8 ---------------- 3 (Ht) 2 x 1/8 with tie rods = Ht 2 x 3/16 2-1/2 x 1/18 2-1/2 x 3/16 2-1/2 x 1/4

Table 6. Summary Of Connectors And Intermediate Reinforcements

Sheet metal screws at 6" max. intervals

← 1" MIN. → ← 1" MIN. →

24 GA for ducts up to 30"
22 GA for ducts over 30"

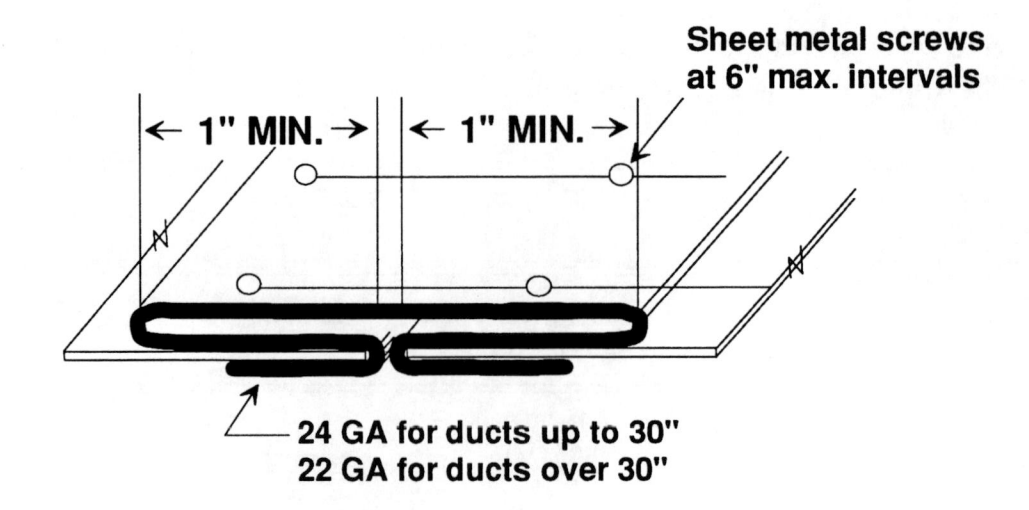

DOUBLE SLIP JOINT

Above 3" and 4" WG limits, use double slip joint with angle reinforcement.

Figure 16. Standard "S" Connector

The flat slip "S" (T-5) or the reinforced flat "S" (T-6) are allowed up to 2 in. w.g. pressure. The SMACNA manual allows the flat "S" to be used on the duct sizes and gages that do not need to be reinforced. A hemmed "S" with a $1 \times 1 \times 18$ gage angle driven into the slip (T-7) and screwed at both ends can be substituted for A, B, or C connectors up to 2 in. w.g. pressure.

The standing "S" drive (T-2), as well as the rest of the standing "S" family (T10-14), is primarily used for 2 in. w.g. pressure and is not to be used for pressures above 4 in. w.g. From 2 in. w.g. to 3 in. w.g., connectors are limited to 36" dimensions, and from 3 in. w.g. to 4 in. w.g., they are limited to 30" dimensions. Securing the bar or angle used to reinforce the standing "S" is recommended even though the SMACNA manual does not specify this procedure. Secure both the bar or angle to the connector and the connector to the duct 2" from each side and then 12" center to center. This will keep the connector from slipping or rolling when the duct is pressurized or when a weight is applied to the sheet next to the joint.

The double "S" (T-8) or inside slip (T-9) is used above 2 in. w.g. pressure or beyond the limits of the standing "S." This joint with separate reinforcement is considered to be the best standard method to join duct.

APPENDIX B

ROUND DUCT

Longitudinal seams and joint specifications for round ducts are presented in *Tables 7A, 7B, 7C,* and *7D* and *Figures 17* and *18.*

Maximum Diameter (Inches)	+2 in. w.g. Spiral	+2 in. w.g. Long.	+4 in. w.g. Spiral	+4 in. w.g. Long.	+10 in. w.g. Spiral	+10 in. w.g. Long.
6	28	28	28	28	28	28
8	28	28	28	28	28	26
10	28	26	28	26	28	26
12	28	26	28	26	26	24
14	28	26	26	24	26	24
16	26	24	24	24	24	22
18	26	24	24	24	24	22
19 to 26	26	24	24	22	24	22
27 to 36	24	22	22	20	22	20
37 to 50	22	20	20	20	20	20
51 to 60	20	18	18	18	18	18
61 to 84	18	16	18	16	18	16

Table 7A. Round Duct Gage Seam Standards

Maximum Diameter (Millimeters)	+500 Pa Spiral	+500 Pa Long.	+1,000 Pa Spiral	+1,000 Pa Long.	+2,500 Pa Spiral	+2,500 Pa Long.
150	0.48	0.48	0.48	0.48	0.48	0.48
200	0.48	0.48	0.48	0.48	0.48	0.55
250	0.48	0.55	0.48	0.55	0.48	0.55
300	0.48	0.55	048	0.55	0.55	0.70
360	0.48	0.55	0.55	0.70	0.55	0.70
400	0.55	0.70	0.55	0.70	0.70	0.85
460	0.55	0.70	0.70	0.70	0.70	0.85
660	0.55	0.70	0.70	0.85	0.70	0.85
910	0.70	0.85	0.85	1.00	0.85	1.00
1,270	0.85	1.00	1.00	1.00	1.00	1.00
1,520	1.00	1.31	1.31	1.31	1.31	1.31
2,130	1.31	1.61	1.31	1.61	1.31	1.61

Table 7B. Round Duct Gage Seam Standards

SHEET METAL DUCT FABRICATION STANDARDS — TRAINEE MODULE 04406

Maximum Diameter (Inches)	-2 in. w.g. Spiral	-2 in. w.g. Long.	-4 in. w.g. Spiral	-4 in. w.g. Long.	-10 in. w.g. Spiral	-10 in. w.g. Long.
6	28	28	28	28	26	26
7	28	28	28	28	26	26
8	28	28	28	28	26	26
9	28	28	28	26	26	24
10	28	28	26	26	26	22
11	28	26	26	24	26	22
12	28	26	26	24	24	22
13	28	26	26	24	24	20
14	28	24	24	22	24	20
15	28	24	24	22	22	20
16	26	24	24	22	22	18
17	26	24	24	20	22	18
18	24	22	24	20	22	18
19	24	22	24	20	22	18
20	24	22	22	20	22	18
21	24	20	22	18	22	18
22	24	20	22	18	22	16
23	24	20	22	18.	20	16
24	22	20	22	18	20	16
25 to 26	22	20	20	18	20	18 A4
27 to 29	22	18	20	16	18	16 A4
30	22	18	20	16	18	16 B4
31 to 33	20	18	20	16	18	16 B4
34	20	18	20	20 A6	18	16 B4
35 to 36	20	16	20	20 A6	18	16 B4
37 to 42	20	16	18	18 B6	18 F12	- -
43 to 48	20	18 A6	18	18 B5	18 F6	- -
49 to 60	18	18 B4	18 F6	16 B4	18 F6	- -
61 to 72	16	- -	18 F6	- -	16 F4	- -

An alphabet letter in the table means that reinforcement angles or their equivalent must be used at the foot interval following the letter. The angle sizes are as follows:
A = 1" x 1" x 1/8"; B = 1-1/4" x 1-1/4: x 3/16"; C = 1-1/2 x 1-1/2: x 3/16"; D = 1-1/2" x 1-1/2" x 1/4";
E = 2" x 2" x 3/16"; F = 2" x 2" x 1/4".
If companion flange joints are used as reinforcements, those for 25" to 36" diameter shall be
1-1/2" x 1-1/2" x 3/16"; for 37" to 48" diameter 2" x 2" x 3/16"; for 40" to 60" diameter 2-1/2" x 2-1/2" x 3/16";
for 61" to 72" diameter 3" x 3" x 1/4".

Table 7C. Round Duct Gage Seam Standards

Maximum Diameter (Millimeters)	-500 Pa Spiral	-500 Pa Long.	-1,000 Pa Spiral	-1,000 Pa Long.	-2,500 Pa Spiral	-2,500 Pa Long.
150	0.48	0.48	0.48	0.48	0.55	0.55
180	0.48	0.48	0.48	0.48	0.55	0.55
200	0.48	0.48	0.48	0.48	0.55	0.55
230	0.48	0.48	0.48	0.55	0.55	0.70
250	0.48	0.48	0.55	0.55	0.55	0.85
280	0.48	0.55	0.55	0.70	0.55	0.85
300	0.48	0.55	0.55	0.70	0.70	0.85
330	0.48	0.55	0.55	0.70	0.70	1.00
360	0.48	0.70	0.70	0.85	0.70	1.00
380	0.48	0.70	0.70	0.85	0.85	1.00
400	0.55	0.70	0.70	0.85	0.85	1.31
430	0.55	0.70	0.70	1.00	0.85	1.31
460	0.70	0.85	0.70	1.00	0.85	1.31
480	0.70	0.85	0.70	1.00	0.85	1.31
500	0.70	0.85	0.85	1.00	0.85	1.31
530	0.70	1.00	0.85	1.31	0.85	1.31
560	0.70	1.00	0.85	1.31	0.85	1.61
580	0.70	1.00	0.85	1.31	1.00	1.61
600	0.85	1.00	0.85	1.31	1.00	1.61
660	0.85	1.00	1.00	1.31	1.00	1.31 A1.2
740	0.85	1.31	1.00	1.6	1.31	1.61 A1.2
760	0.85	1.31	1.00	1.6	1.31	1.61 B1.2
840	1.00	1.31	1.00	1.6	1.31	1.61 B1.2
860	1.00	1.31	1.00	1.00 A1.8	1.31	1.61 B1.2
910	1.00	1.61	1.00	1.00 A1.8	1.31	1.61 B1.2
1,070	1.00	1.61	1.31	1.31 B1.8	1.31 F3.6	- -
1,220	1.00	1.31 A1.8	1.31	1.31 B1.8	1.31 F1.8	- -
1,520	1.31	1.31 B1.2	1.31 F1.8	- -	1.31 F1.2	- -
1,830	1.61	- -	1.31 F1.8	- -	1.61 F1.2	- -

An alphabet letter in the table means that reinforcement angles or their equivalent must be used at the foot interval following the letter. The angle sizes are as follows:
A = 25 x 25 x 3.2 mm; B = 32 x 32 x 4.8 mm; C = 38 x 38 x 4.8 mm; D = 38 x 38 x 4.8 mm; E = 51 x 51 x 4.8 mm; F = 51 x 51 x 6.4 mm.
If companion flange joints are used as reinforcements, those for 630 to 910 mm diameter shall be 38 x 38 x 6.4 mm; for 940 to 1,220 mm diameter 51 x 51 x 4.8 mm; for 1,240 to 1,520 mm diameter 64 x 64 x 4.8 mm; for 1,550 to 1,830 mm diameter 76 x 76 x 6.4 mm.

Table 7D. Round Duct Gage Seam Standards

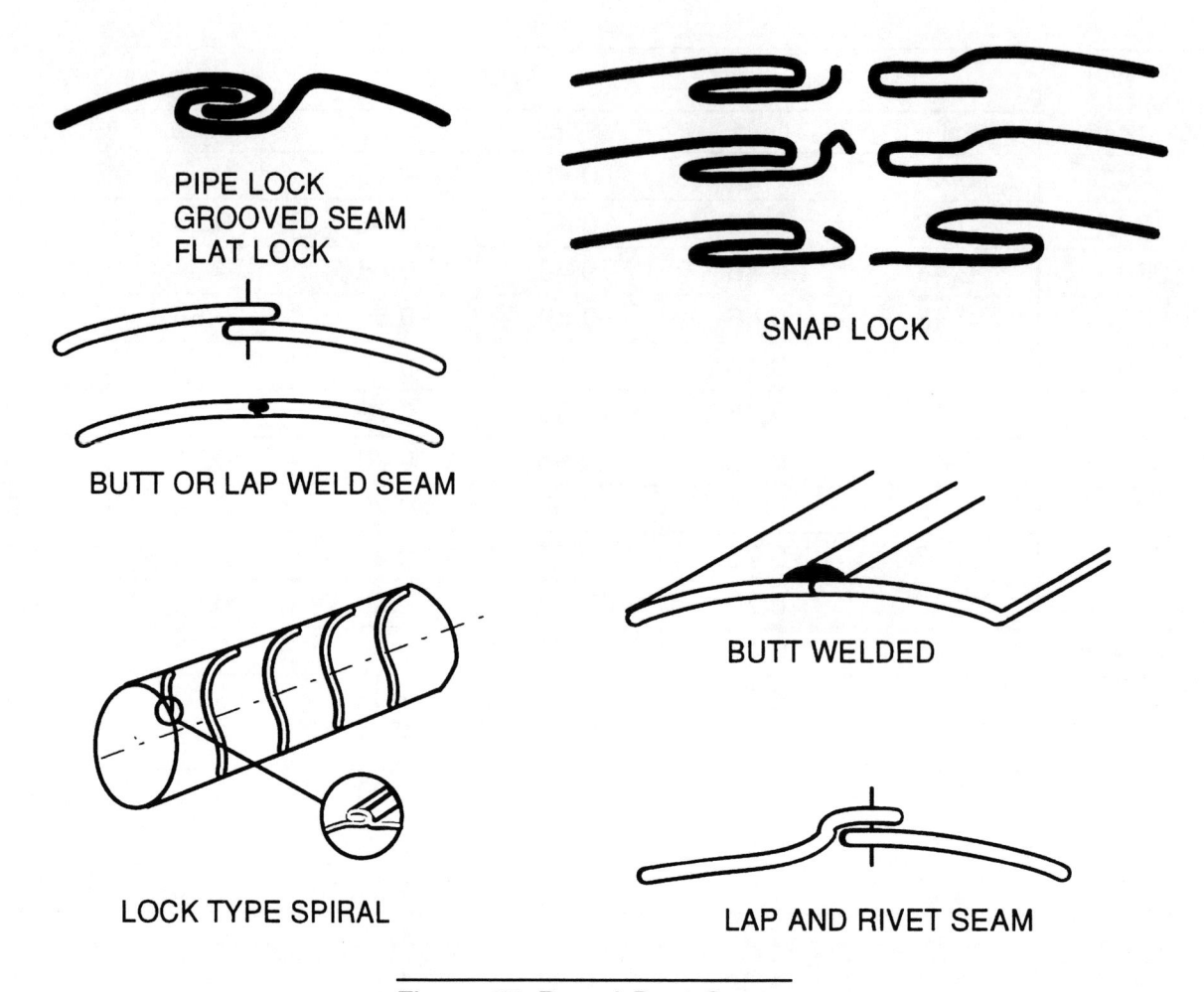

Figure 17. Round Duct Seams

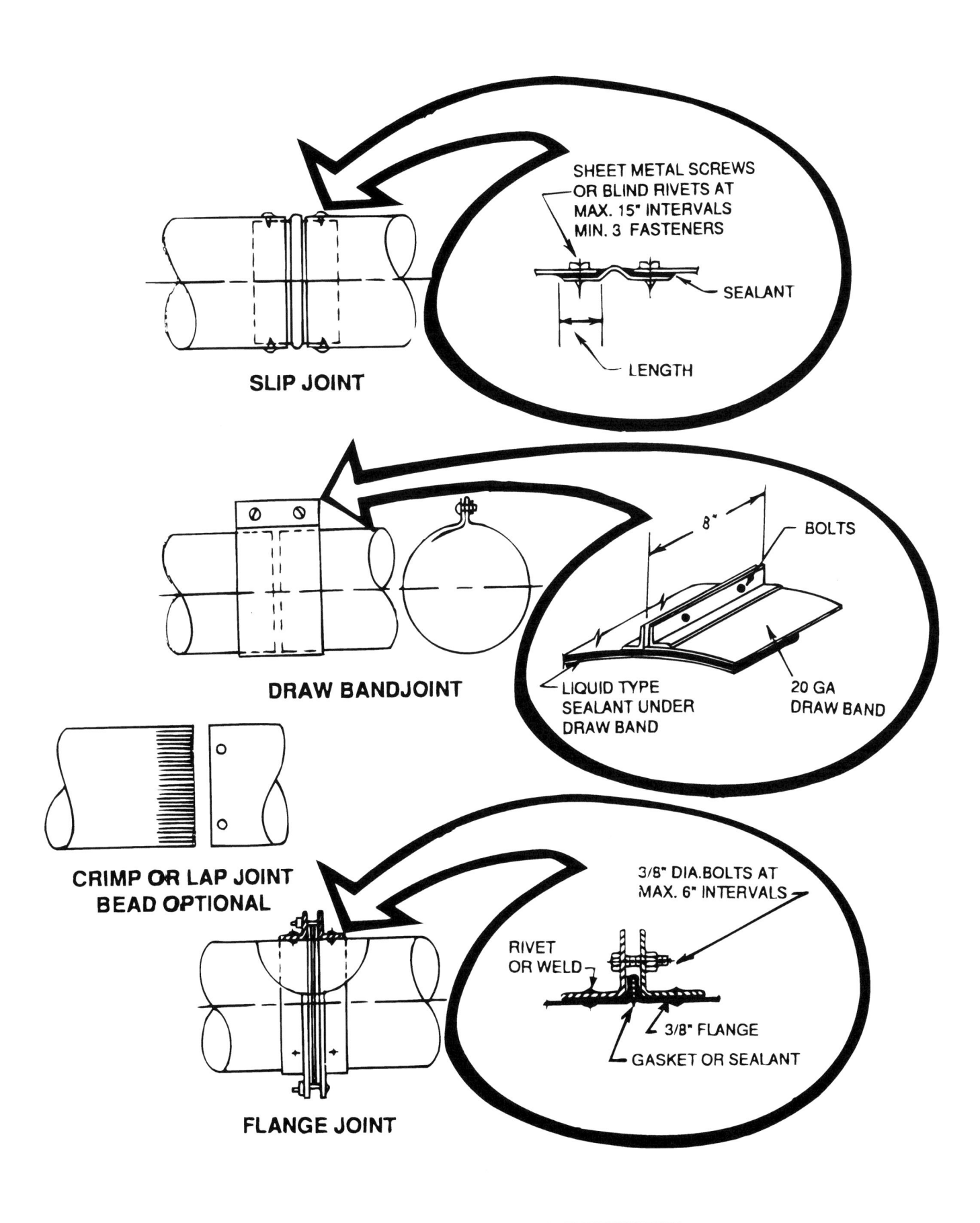

Figure 18. Round Duct Transverse Joints

SHEET METAL DUCT FABRICATION STANDARDS — TRAINEE MODULE 04406

APPENDIX C

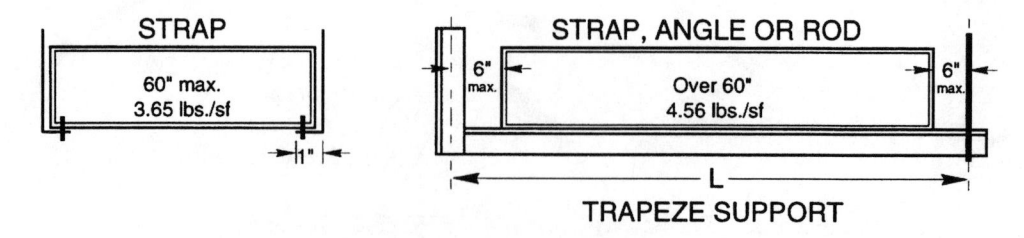

STRAP — 60" max. 3.65 lbs./sf — 1"

STRAP, ANGLE OR ROD — 6" max. / Over 60" 4.56 lbs./sf / 6" max. — L

TRAPEZE SUPPORT

Max. Semi W&D	SF/LF	Pair at Spacing Max. Sq. Ft. Duct				Pair of Rod			
		10'	8'	5'	4'	10'	8'	5'	4'
30"	5 SF	1" x 22 GA 50	40	1" x 22 GA 25	20				
60"	10 SF	1 x 20 GA 100	80	1 x 22 GA 50	40	1/4	1/4	1/4	1/4
72"	12 SF	1 x 18 120	1 x 20 96	1 x 22 60	48	3/8	1/4	1/4	1/4
96"	16 SF	1 x 16 160	1 x 18 128	1 x 20 80	1 x 22 64	3/8	1/4	1/4	1/4
120"	20 SF	1 x 16 200	— 160	1 x 18 100	1 x 20 80	1/2	3/8	3/8	1/4

ALLOWABLE LOADS/SQ. FT. OF DUCT FOR TRAPEZE ANGLES

	3' (lbs./sf)	4' (lbs./sf)	5' (lbs./sf)	6' (lbs./sf)
1 x 1 x 1/8	130/36	80/22		
1-1/2 x 1-1/2 x 1/8	340/93	290/80		
1-1/2 x 1-1/2 x 3/16		450/123	350/96	
1-1/2 x 1-1/2 x 1/4 or 2 x 2 x 1/8			490/135	320/70

	6' (lbs./sf)	7' (lbs./sf)	8' (lbs./sf)	9' (lbs./sf)
2 x 2 x 3/16	620/136	380/84		
2 x 2 x 1/4	900/198	660/145	320/71	
2-1/2 x 2-1/2 x 3/16		940/206	600/132	
2-1/2 x 2-1/2 x 1/4			1060/233	610/134

Figure 19. Hanger Straps

APPENDIX D

FITTING AND DESIGN STANDARDS

The duct sizing rules assume that the fitting geometry will not exceed certain criteria. These maximum angles have been established to minimize turbulence. Where the velocity is the same or less than the entering velocity, use the 20° diverging/30° converging angle rule (*Figures 20, 21A,* and *21B*).

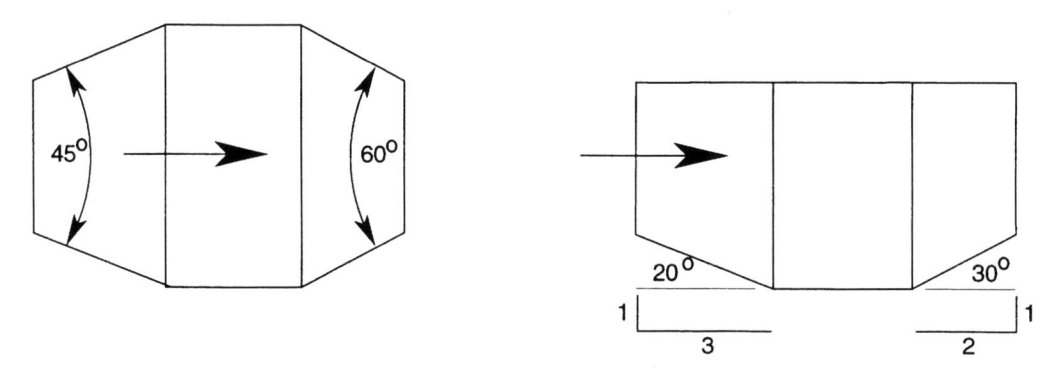

Normal duct size changes are limited to 30° converging and 20° diverging angles, but the center line taper can be 45° total.

Figure 20. Transitions

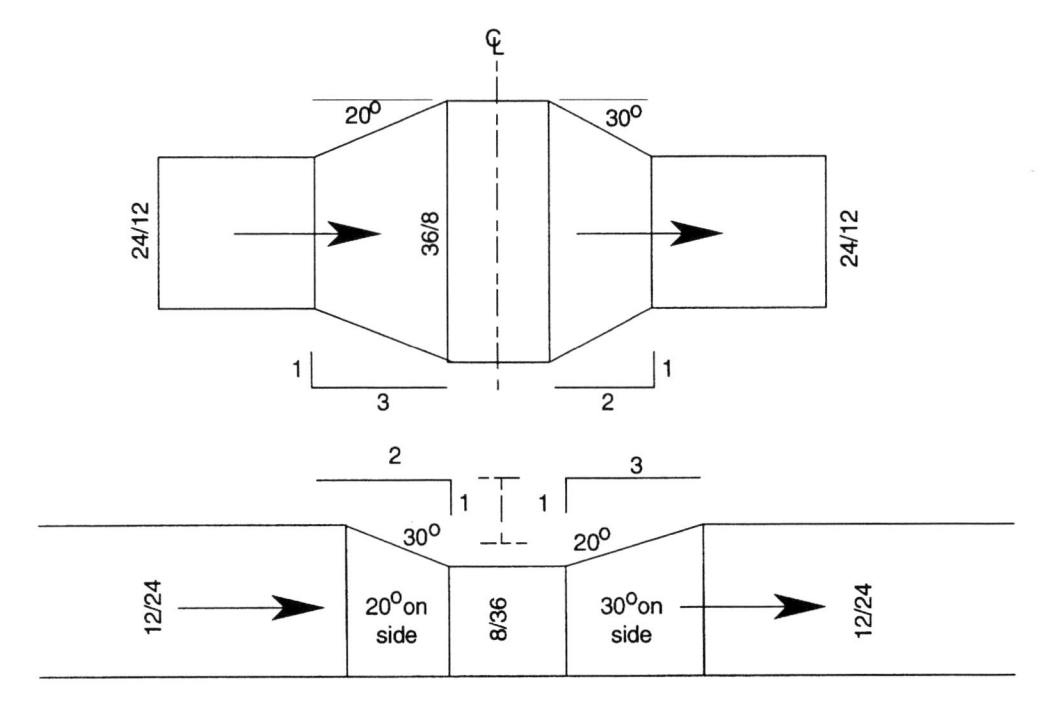

Under-beam transitions clear obstacles and then return to the same size.
To maintain the same velocity through the size change, use the same square inch area.
 24" x 12" = 288 sq. in.
8" will clear; therefore, 288/8 = 36" wide.

Figure 21A. Underbeam Transitions

SHEET METAL DUCT FABRICATION STANDARDS — TRAINEE MODULE 04406

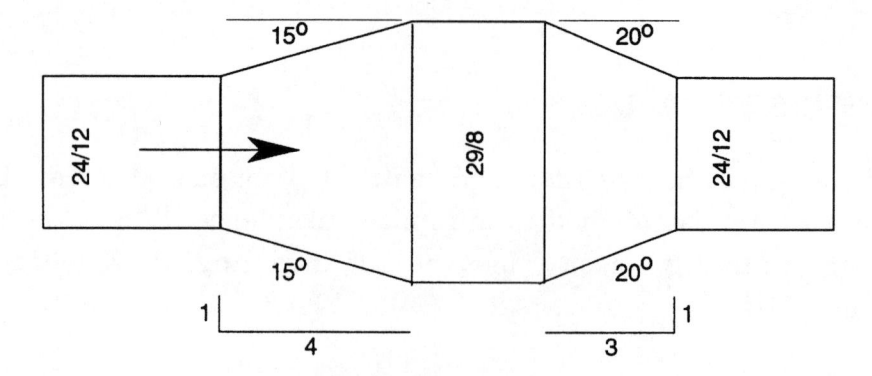

SMACNA standards allow up to a 20% reduction in area with obstacles, so the area could be as small as 288" x .8" = 230 sq. in. or 29" x 8", but maximum angles are 15°. Reduce the angles to 15° and 20°.

Figure 21B. Underbeam Transitions

There are two additional applications that do not follow the general 20°/30° rule.

Heating or Cooling Coil Transitions – The velocity at these coils is generally low, and, therefore, we can use 30°/45° (*Figure 22*).

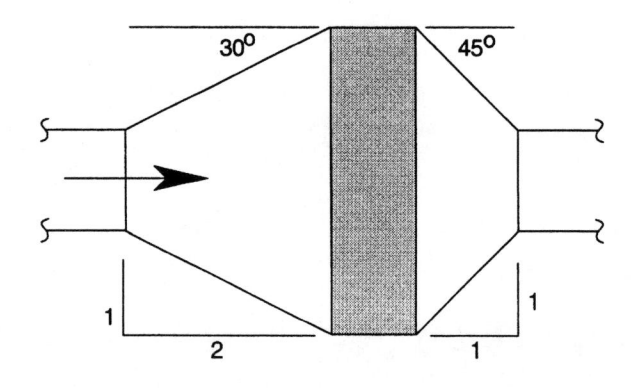

Figure 22. Heating Cooling Coil Transitions

Fan Outlet – The opposite situation is found at the discharge of the fan. The blast area after the fan is not uniform, and attention needs to be paid to the inlet and discharge to ensure the full effect of the fan. (*Figure 23*).

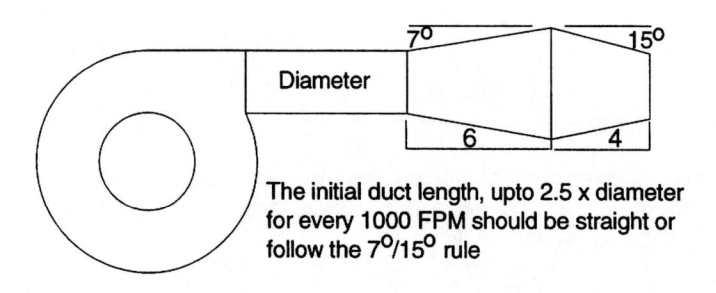

The initial duct length, upto 2.5 x diameter for every 1000 FPM should be straight or follow the 7°/15° rule

Figure 23. Fan Discharge

44   SHEET METAL — TRAINEE TASK MODULE 04406

Offsets

There are four typical layouts for offsets that have the maximum angles allowed *(Figure 24)*.

Straight offset is limited to 15° because of the depth reduction experienced.

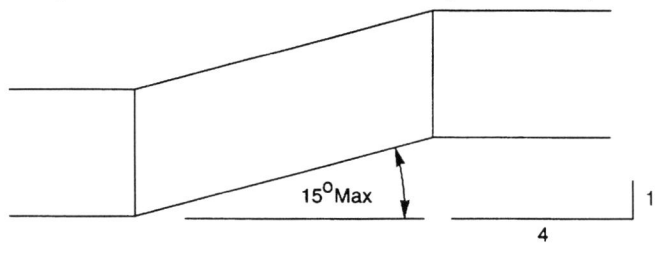

15° Max
4
1

Heel extension set will compensate for most of the reduction seen in straight set.

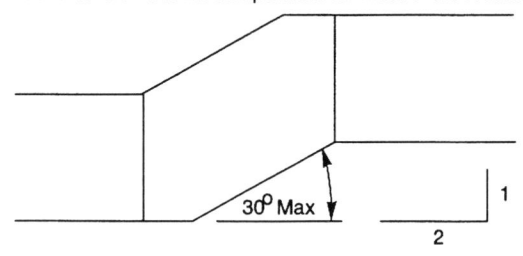

30° Max
2
1

The mitered set will compensate for the depth reduction.

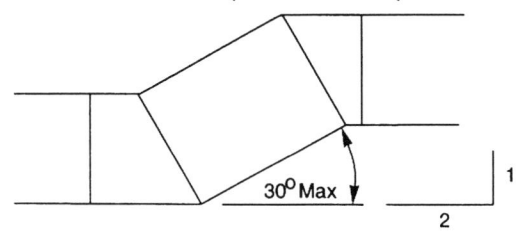

30° Max
2
1

Ogee or radius set is used above 30° to 45°.

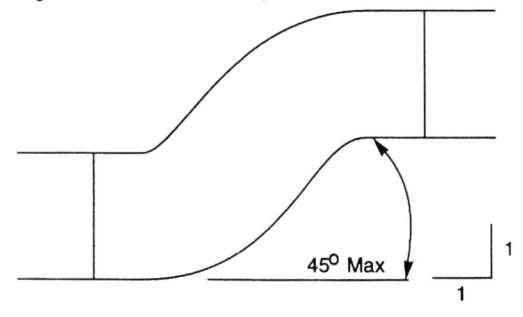

45° Max
1
1

RULES FOR COMMON ANGLES

Figure 24. Typical Offsets

SHEET METAL DUCT FABRICATION STANDARDS — TRAINEE MODULE 04406

Elbows

Radius elbows with a throat radius equal to the width of the duct is the standard. The advantage of the radius elbow is that it can be designed to change size and/or elevation. The angle change can be between 0° and 90°. Square elbows with turning vanes are a reasonable substitute for radius elbows when there is no change to duct size or elevation. Recent industry information suggests that a single-blade vane is more efficient than a double-blade vane.

	Radius	Spacing	Ga	Max. Length
Single	2	1-1/2	24	36
	4-1/2	3-1/4	22	36
Double	2	2-1/2	26	60
	4-1/2	3-1/4	24	72

Over 1,000 fpm, weld every 6th vane or center tie rod.

Square elbows must have the same width in as out, or special provisions must be made. Standard turning vanes are made to turn air at only 45°. Any other angle will produce turbulence. See *Figure 25*.

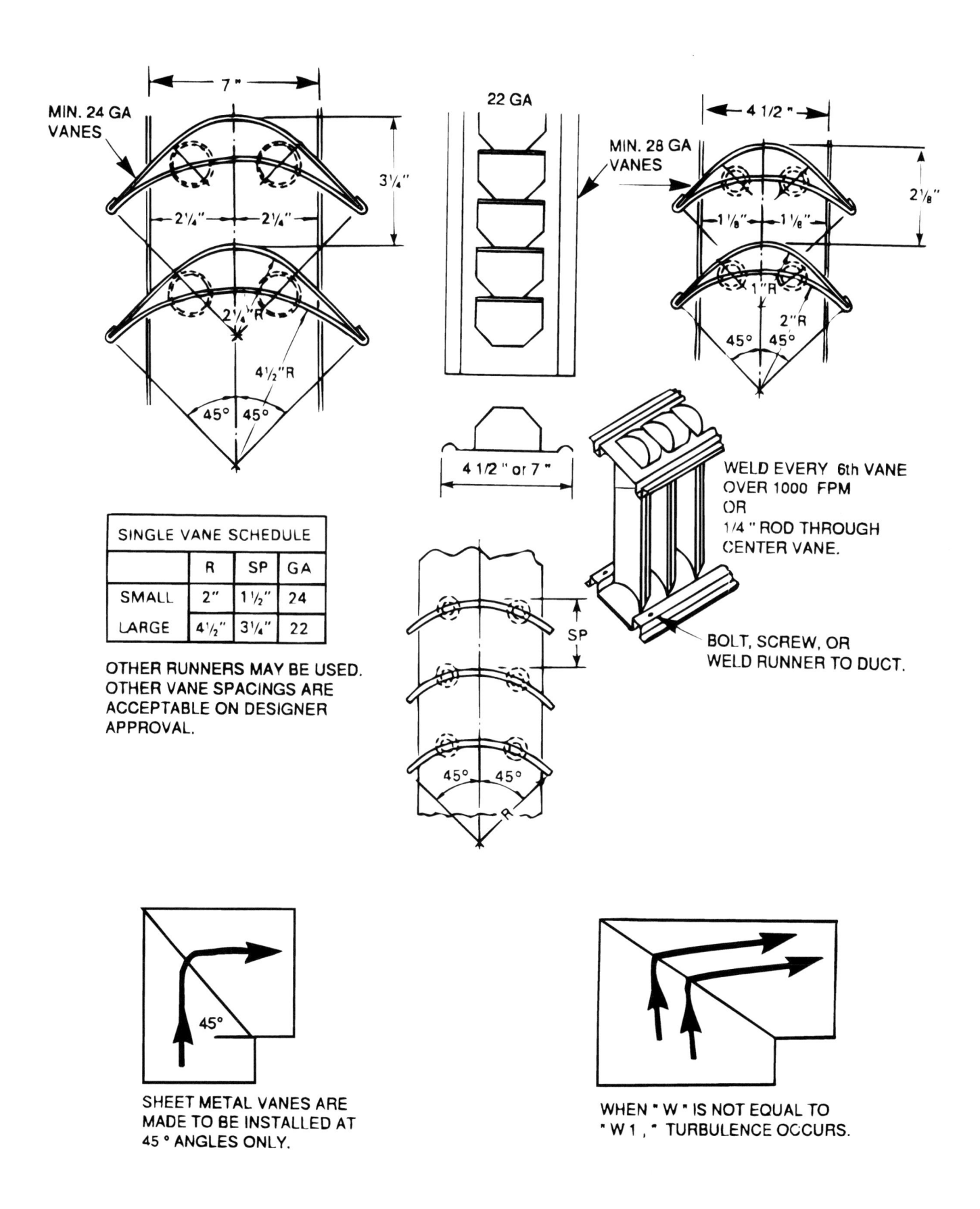

Figure 25. Vanes

NCCER CRAFT TRAINING USER UPDATES

The NCCER makes every effort to keep these manuals up-to-date and free of technical errors. We appreciate your help in this process. If you have an idea for improving this manual, or if you find an error, a typographical mistake, or an inaccuracy in the NCCER's Craft Training Manuals, please write us, using this form or a photocopy. Be sure to include the exact module number, page number, a description of the problem, and the correction, if possible. Your input will be brought to the attention of the Technical Review Committee. Thank you for your assistance.

Instructors – If you found that additional materials were necessary in order to teach this module effectively, please let us know so that we may include them in the Equipment/Materials list in the Instructor's Guide.

Write: Curriculum and Revision Department
National Center for Construction Education and Research
P.O. Box 141104
Gainesville, FL 32614-1104
Fax: 352-334-0932

Craft _____ Module Name _____

Module Number _____ Page Number(s) _____

Description of Problem
_____
_____
_____
_____

(Optional) Correction of Problem
_____
_____
_____

(Optional) Your Name and Address
_____
_____

Insulation
Module 04409

NATIONAL
CENTER FOR
CONSTRUCTION
EDUCATION AND
RESEARCH

Task Module 04409

INSULATION

Objectives

Upon completion of this module, the trainee will be able to:

1. Describe the principles of thermal and acoustic insulation as they apply to the sheet metal industry.

2. Describe the types of insulation commonly used in the sheet metal trade.

3. Demonstrate a degree of competency in the installation of selected types of duct insulation.

INTRODUCTION

"Thermal" insulation is any material preventing or retarding heat transfer from one source to another. The sheet metal mechanic must also be knowledgeable about sound insulation or "acoustical" insulation which separates the noise-sensitive areas of a structure or air-conditioning system from the noisy areas. This module will introduce you to the basic principles and practices of insulation techniques.

Insulation should be designed to reduce heat loss, reduce noise problems, and provide vapor barriers. The insulation selected should be able to support itself and should not shrink or settle. It must not deteriorate in the presence of moisture, and it must not emit any unpleasant odor. The insulation should also be vermin-proof and fire-resistant. The type of insulation to be used depends, to some extent, upon the method of application, the availability of material, and the economics of installation.

Insulation and adhesives have material safety data sheets (MSDS) that describe their proper use and the hazards of handling them. The trainee is responsible for reading and following the MSDS and the manufacturer's recommendations for the use and application procedures.

Copyright © 1992 National Center for Construction Education and Research, Gainesville, FL. All rights reserved. No part of this work may be reproduced in any form or by any means, including photocopying, without written permission of the publisher. Updated: 1998.

PRINCIPLES OF THERMAL INSULATION

Thermal insulations are those materials or combinations of materials which retard the flow of heat energy by conduction, convection, or radiation.

Insulation materials may be fibrous, particulate, film or sheet, block, or formed. They may be composed of materials without joints or seams, which may be open- or closed-cell; or they may be composites, which may be chemically or mechanically applied or supported.

By retarding the transfer of heat, thermal insulations are said to do one or more of the following:

1. Conserve energy by reducing heat loss or gain through ducts and structures.
2. Control surface temperatures of equipment and structures for personal comfort and protection.
3. Facilitate temperature control of a piece of equipment or a structure.
4. Prevent vapor condensation at surfaces having a temperature below the dewpoint of the surrounding environment.
5. Reduce temperature fluctuations within an enclosure.

Some thermal insulations may *also* have one or more of the following features:

1. Add structural strength to a wall, ceiling, or other surface.
2. Provide support for a surface finish.
3. Impede water vapor transfer.
4. Reduce damage to equipment or structures from exposure to fire and/or freezing conditions.
5. Reduce noise and vibration.

Thermal insulation is commonly used to control heat transfer in temperature ranges from absolute zero through 3000° F and higher.

PRINCIPLES OF ACOUSTIC INSULATION

Some thermal insulations are also effectively used as **sound attenuating** acoustical materials. Their acoustical efficiency depends on the physical structure of the material. Materials with open, porous surfaces have sound absorption capabilities. Those of high density and resilient characteristics can act as vibration insulators. Either alone or in combination with other materials, they may provide an effective barrier to sound transfer.

Thermal insulations used for sound conditioning include flexible and semi-rigid materials, and rigid insulation which is used for such purposes as lining equipment platforms for sound attenuation. Materials used for sound absorption are normally installed on interior surfaces or are used as interior surfacing materials.

Interior duct liner (*Figure 1*) is a common example of flexible insulation. An example of semi-rigid insulating material is fiberglass **duct board**. Yet another type of insulation used for sound control is composed of formed-in-place fibrous material, and an example of this is **acoustical spray-on** insulation.

Some of the problems encountered in acoustic installations are actually due to lack of adequate space. This lack may produce too much equipment in too little space or an unrealistic expectation of better performance from too-small equipment, thus operating the equipment beyond its design capabilities.

Figure 1- Interior Duct Liner

Ductborne Noise

Ductborne noise is objectionable sound generated by the air handling equipment and transmitted to habitable parts of the building. The fan or blower is the primary source of noise in any ventilation system. A small part of the horsepower supplied to the fan is radiated out as sound power. The higher the power supplied to the blower, the greater its sound or acoustic power. The fan should be selected to operate at the point of maximum efficiency, which will also prove to be the optimum point acoustically.

For stable fan operation, it is important not to select a fan that is too large for the application. Most manufacturers express the noise of their fans in **sound power level**. Once the characteristics of the fan or blower have been established, the next step is to examine the duct systems served by each fan in order to evaluate the silencing required. Unlined ducts provide a small amount of sound reduction, but suitable lining materials can greatly increase the silencing effect.

When laying out the system, it is important to avoid as much as possible obstructions in the duct, particularly if the velocities are high. If any obstructions are absolutely necessary, those obstructions should have an airfoil section. Duct components that are likely to cause turbulence, such as **dampers**, should not be placed close to bends or any other member that would create turbulence. A minimum separation of six diameters is recommended as an allowance factor.

It is recommended that the use of dampers for balancing the system should be kept to a minimum. If, however, dampers are necessary, they should be situated as far away as possible from the habitable rooms or diffusers. It is generally better to install two sets of 20%-closed dampers rather than one set of 40%-closed, because the sound generated by the two sets will usually be less than the noise from one highly restricted damper.

Vibration Noise

All rotating and reciprocating machines transmit vibrations and low frequency noise to the structure to which they are rigidly fixed. Anti-vibration mountings, therefore, are usually necessary between machine and structure, if vibrations and noise are to be avoided. These mountings may consist of springs, rubber, or resilient materials.

With air flowing through the ductwork, additional noise may be generated where the air flow meets obstructions, sharp bends, sudden enlargements, or contractions. Even straight duct lengths give rise to velocity-generated noise under certain conditions. Sound attenuators, like any other duct member, may also generate noise at the higher air velocities. So, improperly designed installations can sometimes be noisier with sound attenuators than without them.

Terminal outlets and diffusers are not the only paths for noise to enter conditioned space. A duct carrying large volumes of air at high velocities can be subject to drumming, causing noise to radiate into the conditioned space. This is generally known as **duct breakout noise**. Even in low-velocity systems, it is possible for the noise generated by the fan to escape the ductwork and cause problems in any area through which it passes.

One common situation arises when the fan noise breaks out of the duct into an area such as a plant room and gets back into the duct, just past the silencer, thereby short-circuiting or **flanking** the silencer. A heavy-density, impervious false ceiling may help to keep the breakout noise from reaching a critical room.

Sound power can get into ducts just as easily as it can come out. For example, if two rooms are served by a common duct, a problem can arise if sound from one room passes into the ductwork and out into the adjoining room. Thus, suitable methods for providing attenuation within the duct between two rooms is generally necessary.

INSULATION — TRAINEE TASK MODULE 04409

Materials

There are two kinds of acoustic materials that cannot be substituted for one another. They are insulating materials and absorbent materials.

"Insulating materials" restrict the transmission of sound through themselves. One example is a brick wall. A less effective example is the metal wall of a duct. Each of these materials tend to be airtight and rather heavy. A useful rule of thumb for checking insulation is to check first whether it is airtight, and then to check the weight per square foot (superficial density) at the lightest point.

The densest materials, such as lead, are particularly effective at diverting sounds. Remember, insulating materials restrict the passage of sound—they do not make it disappear. The sound is simply reflected back in roughly the same way as a mirror reflects light, and this causes a build-up of sound on the source side.

"Absorbent materials" reflect either no sound at all or only a small portion of it. Mineral wool is a typical absorber. When sound falls on mineral wool, it does not return. Sound directed at mineral wool (and similar materials) tends to get "lost" in the interstices of the material, but not very much is reflected. A high proportion of the sound passes through to the other side, like it would through an open window. Therefore, absorbent materials cannot be considered the same as insulating materials and cannot be used as such.

Material Selection

When unlined ducts and elbows prove too noisy, ducts may be lined with porous sound-absorbing material, or a prefabricated **attenuator** (silencer) may be placed in the system. When selecting absorption material, several important matters must be considered. These include: type of material, material thickness, and surface of the material.

The sound-absorbing capacity of a material is rated by an absorption coefficient, which is the percentage of sound absorbed when a sound wave strikes the material. Absorption of low-frequency sound increases as the thickness of the absorption material lining the duct increases. Low-frequency absorption may require lining material from 2 to 12 inches thick. Increased absorption of low-frequency sound may be obtained by using perforated facing on the material and by incorporating an air space between the metal duct and the lining material.

The location of the sound-absorbing material in the duct system is important. One of the most effective and economical locations for absorbing material is in a fan suction or discharge plenum.

TYPES OF THERMAL INSULATION

Both thermal and acoustical insulations come in a wide variety of different types. The basic materials used for thermal insulations normally consist of the following materials or composites:

1. Mineral, fibrous, or cellular materials, such as glass, rock or slag wool, calcium silicate, bonded perlite, vermiculite, and ceramic products.

2. Organic fibrous materials such as cotton, animal hair, wood, cane, or synthetic fibers, and organic cellular materials, such as cork, foam rubber, polystyrene, and polyurethane.

3. Metallic or metallized organic reflective membranes.

The physical structure of insulation may be cellular, granular, or fibrous, providing gas-filled voids within the solid material that retard heat transfer. Reflective insulation consists of spaced, smooth-surfaced sheets made of metal or having metallized surfaces.

Loose-fill insulation consists of powders, granules, or nodules, which are usually poured or blown into walls or other enclosed spaces. Insulating cement is a loose material which, when mixed with water, may be troweled or blown wet on a surface and dried in place to serve as insulation.

Flexible and Semi-Rigid

Flexible and semi-rigid materials are insulation materials with varying degrees of compressibility and flexibility. They usually come in blanket, batt, or felt form, and are available in sheets and rolls. Coverings and facings may be fastened to one or both sides and serve as reinforcing vapor barriers, reflective surfaces, or surface finishes. These coverings include combinations of laminated foil, glass, cloth, plastics, paper, wire mesh, or metal lath. Thickness and shapes of insulation may be of any conveniently handled dimensions.

Blanket

Flexible **blanket** fiberglass duct insulation (*Figure 2*) is a lightweight, resilient blanket-type thermal (and acoustical) insulation made of long, fine, flame-attenuated glass fibers bonded with a thermosetting resin. This type of flexible blanket insulation is readily available in 1-1/2", 2", 2-1/2", and 3" thicknesses. It is supplied in roll form and with either of two factory-applied vapor-barrier facings. Roll width is usually 48" and the lengths can vary from 50 feet for the 3" thickness to 100 feet for the 1-1/2" thickness.

This type of insulation is recommended as a thermal insulation for the exterior of rectangular and round sheet metal ducts in heating and cooling systems. It may be used for the exterior of plenums or other surfaces where temperatures must be controlled. Care must be exercised to minimize compression when installing the material. It can be cut with an ordinary knife and can be attached to duct surfaces with adhesive or mechanical fasteners.

Figure 2 - Flexible Blanket Fiberglass Duct Insulation

Rigid

Rigid insulation materials are available in rectangular dimensions called block, board, or sheet. When manufactured, they are usually preformed to standard lengths and other dimensions. Insulation for pipes and curved surfaces is supplied in half sections, with radii of curvature available to suit all standard sizes of pipe.

Reflective

Reflective material is available in sheets and rolls of single- or multi-layer construction, and in preformed shapes with integral air spaces.

Formed-In-Place

Formed-in-place insulation materials are available as liquid or expandable pellets, which may be poured or sprayed in place to form rigid or semi-rigid foam insulation. Fibrous materials mixed with binders may also be sprayed in place.

INSULATION — TRAINEE TASK MODULE 04409

TYPES OF ACOUSTIC INSULATION

Insulations used for sound absorption are normally installed on interior surfaces or used as interior surfacing materials. The rigid insulations are fabricated into tiles or blocks, edge-treated to facilitate adhesive or mechanical application, and prefinished during manufacture. Some sections have a natural porous surface, whereas others require mechanical perforations to facilitate the entry of sound waves.

Some sound absorption materials employ a diaphragm or decorative film surfacing attached only to the edges of the units, allowing the sound to reach the fibrous backing by diaphragm action.

Accessory materials used for thermal and sound insulation include adhesive and mechanical fasteners, interior and exterior finishes, vapor barrier and weather coatings, jackets, sealants, membranes, and flashing compounds.

Flexible Duct Liner

Flexible fiberglass duct liner (as shown earlier in *Figure 1*) is an interior insulation designed for use in rectangular sheet metal ducts. Flexible duct liner is available in blanket form and packaged rolls. Standard sizes and packaging include thicknesses of 1/2", 1", 1-1/2", and 2"; widths of 36", 48", and 60"; and roll lengths of 50 feet for the 1-1/2" and 2" thicknesses, and 100 feet for the thinner material.

This particular duct liner can be used in either heating or cooling ducts operating at velocities up to 5000 **fpm** (feet per minute), and where thermal properties are required for temperature control and prevention of condensation. It is considered to be fire resistant, meeting NFPA Standard 90A. The National Fire Protection Association publishes various fire safety standards that pertain to many construction trades, and are often incorporated in building codes that govern your work. See the Sheet Metal Level 2 Module, *The SMACNA Manuals*.

Flexible fiberglass duct liner is also said to be effective in absorbing low-frequency sound from mechanical equipment, air rush noise, and room-to-room cross talk. It can be applied by regular shop equipment and methods. (Installation is discussed later in this module.)

Rigid Plenum Liner Board

Rigid fiberglass plenum liner board (*Figure 3*) is made from long, flame-attenuated glass fibers bonded with a thermosetting resin. The air stream surface is covered with a smooth, black-coated mat. This insulation is available in board form, in thicknesses of 1" and 1-1/2". The standard size is 48" by 96" or 48" by 120". Other board sizes can also be specially ordered.

Rigid fiberglass liner is specifically designed as a liner for plenums. It offers acoustical and thermal performance in systems operating at velocities up to 5000 fpm and at temperatures up to 250° F. It is also fire resistant, meeting NFPA 90A standards, and can be cut with regular shop tools.

Figure 3 - Rigid Plenum Liner Board

INSTALLATION

Both flexible and rigid liner materials are available for rectangular ducts, but flexible lining is more commonly used. The liner manufacturer's recommendations should be followed regarding installation details. While flexible liner can be formed to shape on a brake along with the metal, rigid duct liner would be damaged under such circumstances.

Therefore, when rigid duct liner is specified, the duct is formed first and the liner is installed afterward. Duct liner should not be used in exhaust ducts, or with air streams removing solids or corrosive gases.

Once the type of insulation is specified, duct liners are applied with adhesives and/or such mechanical fasteners as mechanically-secured fasteners, weld-secured fasteners, or adhesive-secured fasteners. All three types of mechanical fasteners are available in various lengths to accommodate the thickness of the specified duct liner, and some are corrosion resistant.

Typical liner specifications require mechanical fasteners at intervals along the leading edge and at intervals both ways in the remainder of the duct. Special protection is required for the leading edge of the liner in high-velocity systems to prevent the air stream from delaminating the liner or peeling it off the metal.

In some cases, mechanical fastener pins are applied prior to insulation on the duct (welded pin or adhesive type). In other cases the pin has a preattached cap and these are pressed through the insulation and attached to the duct in a single operation (mechanical and some welded types). See the various mechanical fasteners illustrated in *Figures 4* through *8*.

Non-Mechanical Fasteners

Each manufacturer provides instructions for spraying, roller coating, or brushing adhesive on the duct before the insulation is applied directly to the duct. Adhesives used with duct liner are devised to meet performance conditions pertaining to NFPA Standard 90A.

Most of the types of adhesives employ solvents with low boiling points in order to develop fast drying and early bond strength capabilities. The solvent vapors are toxic and flammable; therefore, precautions must be observed to limit accumulation of these fumes. Caution should be observed when lining any enclosure at the job site (such as plenums) while using solvent-base adhesives. Be sure to read all adhesive container labels and observe all safety precautions.

Adhesives having a water base instead of solvent are also available. While they are non-flammable and do not emit toxic vapors, these adhesives may not develop fast tack and early bond strength as quickly as the solvent-base adhesives.

Mechanical Fasteners

In addition to insulation adhesives or tapes, larger ducts or higher velocity ducts require attachment reinforcement in the form of mechanical fasteners.

Mechanically-secured fasteners generally perform the required mechanical attachment to the sheet metal duct. These fasteners are shown in *Figures 4* and *5*. The impact-applied, hardened steel fasteners (which bite into the sheet metal) can be applied to insulation with thicknesses greater than 1/2" (see *Figure 4*). On the other hand, staples (*Figure 5*), sheet metal screws, or pop rivets should not be used in systems above 2" w.g. or with duct liner insulation thicker than 1/2".

Impact-applied pins (*Figure 4*) are installed with a special type of hammer. The pins are available in various lengths to accommodate the specified thicknesses of the material (see *Table 1*). The liner is held in place by a self-locking washer on the pin. The teeth at the point of the pin bite into the metal but do not puncture it. However, you need to back up the duct with a heavy steel plate whenever you set these pins.

Weld-secured fasteners, such as the welded pins shown in *Figures 6* and *7*, are applied by a special welding unit. Installation is done with either resistance welding or capacitance discharge welding techniques.

Adhesive-secured fasteners usually have a large base for use with an adhesive. (See *Figure 8*. Note that adhesive secures the base to the duct at the bottom of the figure.) When adhesives are used in conjunction with welded pins, a sufficient time must be allowed to achieve adequate bond strength. Then the duct liner is forced over the pin and a spring clip or washer is attached to the pin for holding back the liner.

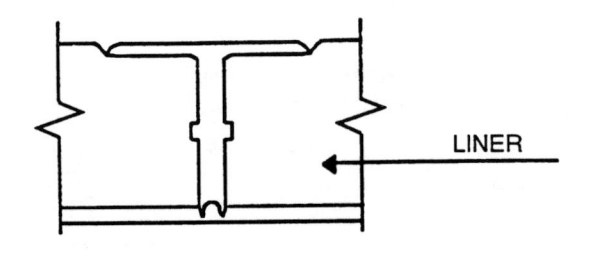

Figure 4 - Hardened Steel Fastener

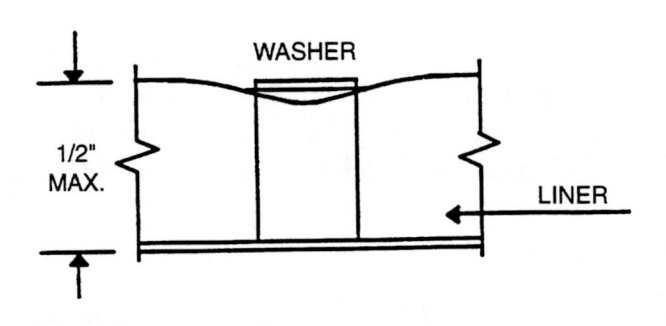

Figure 5 - Staple Fastener

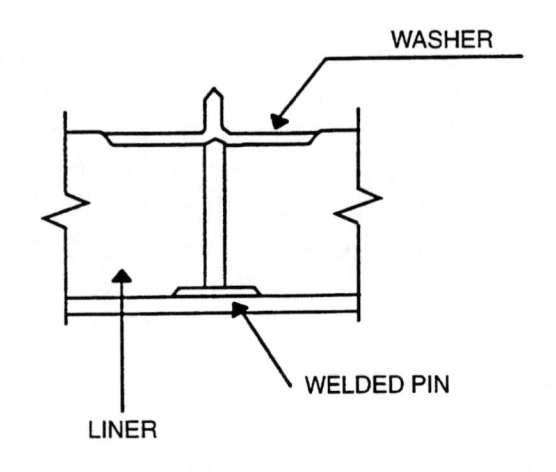

Figure 6 - Welded Fastener

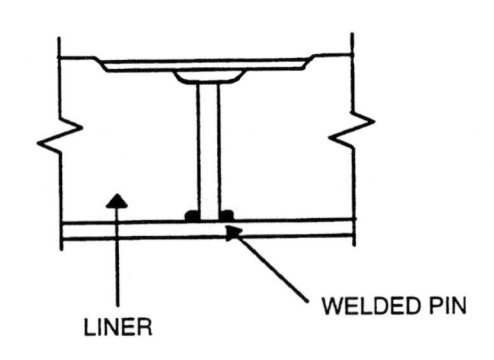

Figure 7 - Welded Fastener

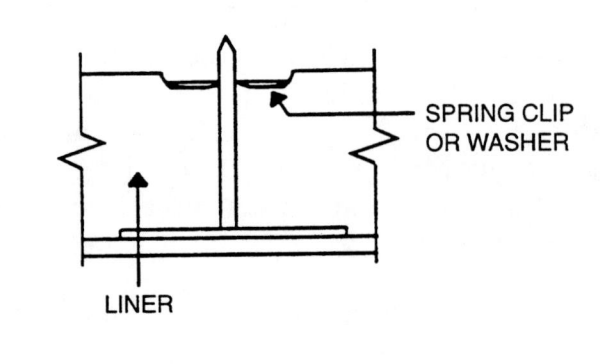

Figure 8 - Adhesive Fastener

SHEET METAL — TRAINEE TASK MODULE 04409

LINER SIZE	PIN SIZE
1/2" x 2"	3/8" or 1/2"
1/2" x 3"	1/2"
1" x 1-1/2"	3/4" - 7/8" - 1"
1" x 3"	1"
2"	1-1/2"

Table 1

Standards

Installation standards for either flexible or rigid duct liner may be found in the manufacturer's application or fabrication manuals, or in the applicable SMACNA manuals (see the Sheet Metal Level 2 Module, *The SMACNA Manuals*).

Generally speaking, however, the following rules apply for both flexible and rigid duct liner installations:

1. All areas of the duct designated to receive duct liner must be completely covered with liner.

2. Transverse joints must be neatly butted with no interruptions or gaps.

3. Liner surface designed to be exposed must face the air stream.

4. Duct liner must be affixed to the sheet metal duct with 100 percent coverage of adhesive. ALL EXPOSED LEADING EDGES and all transverse joints must also be coated with adhesive.

5. The liner must be additionally secured in place with mechanical fasteners.

Flexible duct liner installation standards include the following recommendations for duct application with velocities to 1500 fpm:

1. The liner must meet the Life Safety Standards as established by NFPA Standard 90A.

2. The duct liner must be applied with 100 percent coverage of approved fire-resistant adhesive. On ducts over 20" wide or deep, the liner must be additionally secured with mechanical fasteners on maximum centers of 15". Fasteners must start within 2" of the leading edge of each section and within 3" of the leading edge of all cross-joints within the duct section (see *Figure 9*).

3. All exposed edges and the leading edge of all cross-joints of the liner must be heavily coated with an approved fire-resistant adhesive.

4. The duct liner must be cut to assure snugly closing corner joints. The black surface of the liner (if applicable) must face the air stream. Transverse joints must be neatly butted, and any damaged areas must be heavily coated with an approved fire-resistant adhesive.

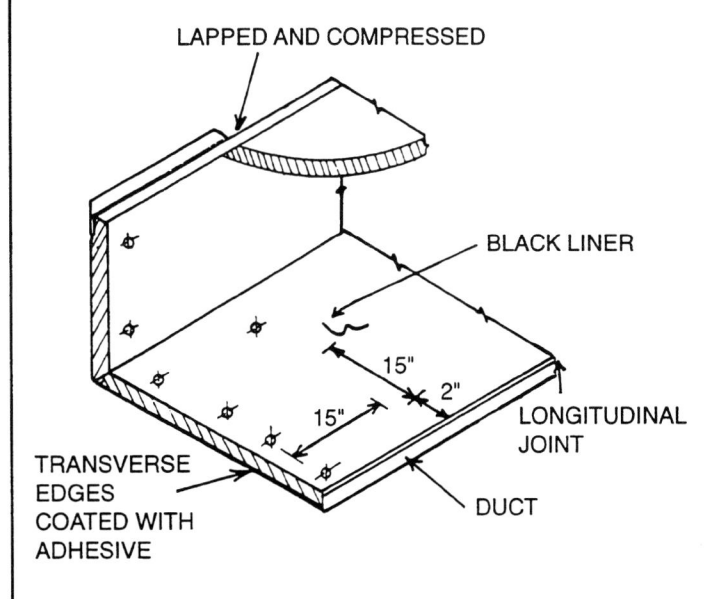

Figure 9 - Flexible Duct Liner Installation

INSULATION — TRAINEE TASK MODULE 04409

For velocities from 1500 to 4000 fpm:

1. The duct liner must be applied with 100 percent coverage of approved fire-resistant adhesive.

2. On horizontal runs, tops of duct over 12" wide and/or sizes over 16" in height must additionally be secured with mechanical fasteners on a maximum of 15" centers.

3. On vertical runs, mechanical fasteners must be spaced on a maximum of 15" centers on all width dimensions over 12". Fasteners must start within 2" of the leading edge of each section, and within 3" of the leading edge of all cross-joints within the duct section.

4. Mechanical fasteners must be flush with the liner surface. All exposed edges and the leading edge of all cross-joints of the liner must be heavily coated with approved fire-resistant adhesive.

5. The duct liner must be cut to assure snugly closing corner joints. The black surface of the liner must face the air stream. Transverse joints must be neatly butted, and any damaged areas must be heavily coated with approved fire-resistant adhesive.

For velocities from 4000 to 5000 fpm:

1. The duct liner must be installed as indicated in the recommendations for 1500 to 4000 fpm applications, plus metal nosings must be placed on all leading edges of the liner. (See Detail in *Figure 10*.) It is further recommended that metal nosings be placed on leading edges of first pieces of duct liner after a flexible connector (*Figure 10*).

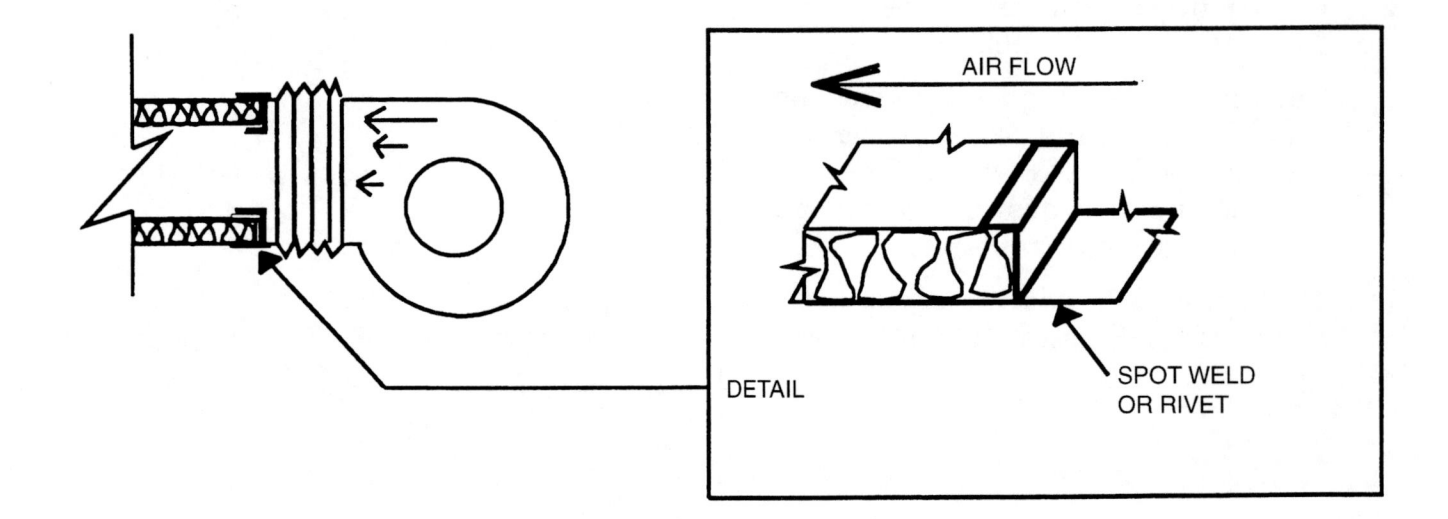

Figure 10 - Metal Nosing

SHEET METAL — TRAINEE TASK MODULE 04409

Plenum liner installation standards include the following recommendations:

1. The plenum liner must be applied to all interior surfaces with a 100 percent coverage of approved fire-resistant adhesive.

2. The insulation must be additionally secured with welded studs or mechanical fasteners on 12" centers.

3. The insulation must be tightly butted and all exposed edges of the liner must be sealed with adhesive.

    CAUTION: When pressure-sensitive tapes are used, make sure all surfaces of the duct liner to be covered are wiped clean and are free from dust and grease. Rub well to insure a satisfactory air seal.

4. The black surface of the liner must face the air stream, and all damaged areas of the insulation must be heavily coated with an approved fire-resistant adhesive.

Standards for applying faced duct insulation include the following recommendations:

1. All ducts must be insulated (where applicable) with flexible fiberglass blanket. Insulation must be furnished with a factory-applied foil-scrim foil facing consisting of aluminum foil reinforced with fiberglass yarn mesh and laminated to 30 pounds, chemically treated, UL rated.

2. Faced duct insulation must be applied over clean, dry sheet metal surfaces that have been sealed airtight.

3. Insulation must be cut slightly longer to allow maximum thickness on all areas and to avoid excessive compression.

4. All joints must be overlapped at least 2" and stapled in place.

5. Stapled seams must be sealed with a minimum 3" wide pressure-sensitive tape designed for use with duct insulation. All breaks in the vapor barrier must also be sealed with approved pressure-sensitive tape.

6. The underside of duct work 24" or greater in width must have the insulation additionally secured with mechanical fasteners and speed clips spaced approximately 18" on center. The protruding ends of the fasteners must be cut off flush after the speed clips are installed, and then sealed with approved pressure-sensitive tape.

7. In place of the above method of sealing, all joints, breaks or punctures in the vapor barrier facing may be sealed with two coats of vapor barrier mastic reinforced with one layer of 4" wide open-weave glass fabric. In geographic locations where high humidity is prevalent and the problem of moisture condensation is a common concern, *proper sealing of all joints and breaks in the vapor barrier is a must.*

Rigid duct liner installation recommendations for velocities up to 2000 fpm are:

1. All rigid duct liner must be cut so as to assure tight, overlapped corner joints (see *Figure 11*).

2. The top pieces must be supported by the side pieces.

3. Where the duct width or height exceeds 20" for horizontal runs, the liner must be additionally secured with fasteners starting within 3" of the upstream transverse edges of the liner, and be spaced at a maximum of 15" on center and 15" from longitudinal joints. On vertical runs, the fasteners must be used when either dimension (width or height) exceeds 12".

Additional recommendations for rigid liner installations where velocities range from 2000 to 4000 fpm are:

1. When the width exceeds 12" or the height exceeds 16" on horizontal runs, the liner must be additionally secured with mechanical fasteners starting within 3" of the upstream transverse edges of the liner, and spaced at a maximum of 15" on center and 15" from longitudinal joints. Mechanical fasteners must be used when either dimension exceeds 12".

For velocities from 4000 to 6000 fpm, the rules listed in number 1 above (for 2000 to 4000 fpm) must apply except that mechanical fasteners must be spaced at a maximum of 12" on center, and metal nosings (*Figure 10*) must be installed to secure the liner at all upstream transverse edges. The nosings should be attached by rivets or welds.

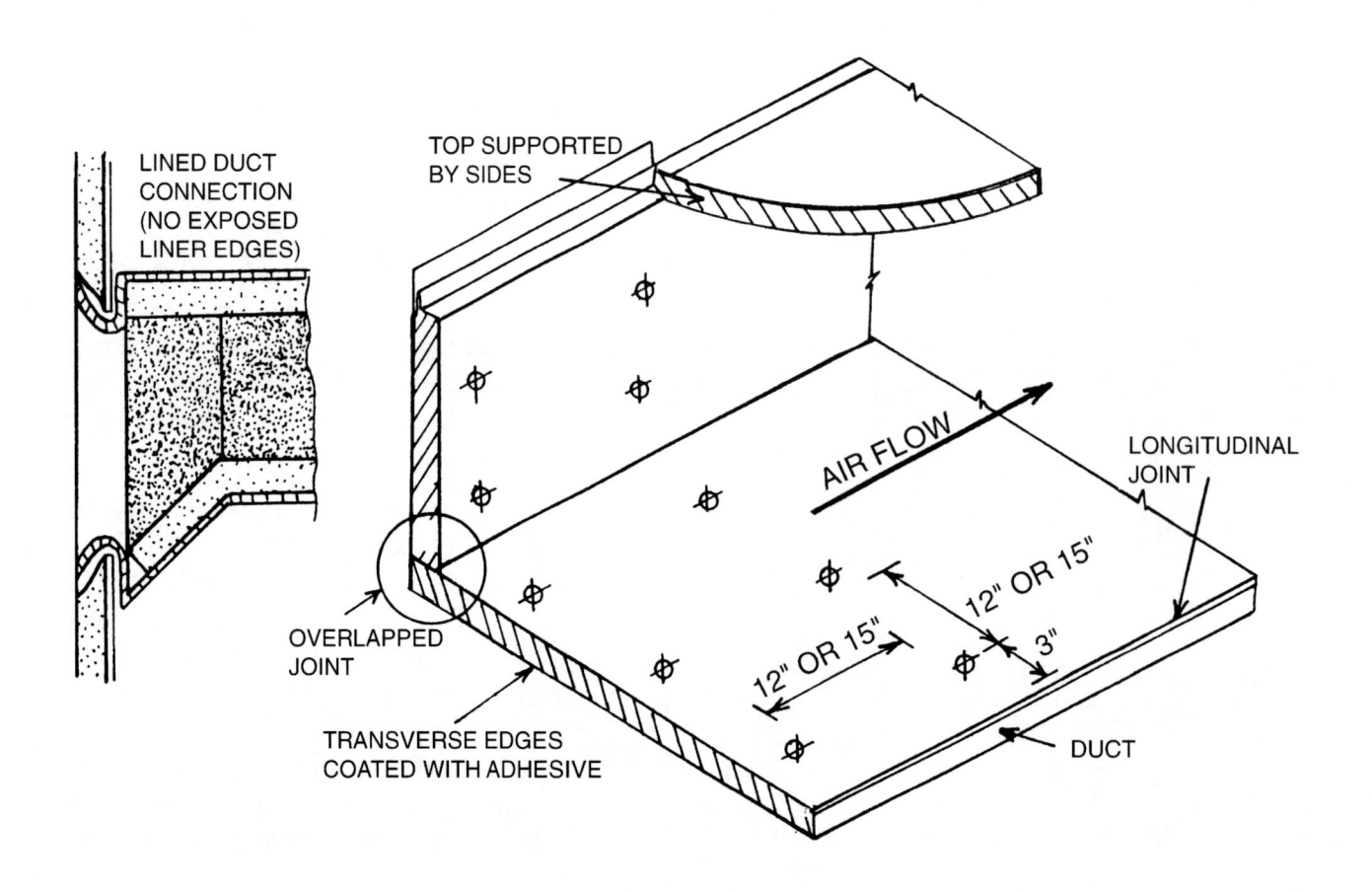

Figure 11 - Installation of Rigid Duct Liner

Fiberglass Duct Board

Fiberglass duct board (*Figure 12*) is used to fabricate rectangular air handling ducts. The standard thickness is 1" or 1-1/2", and the other dimensions are either 48" by 96" or 48" by 120". It can be used for any size duct up to 96" span. It is made from glass fibers, bonded with a thermosetting resin.

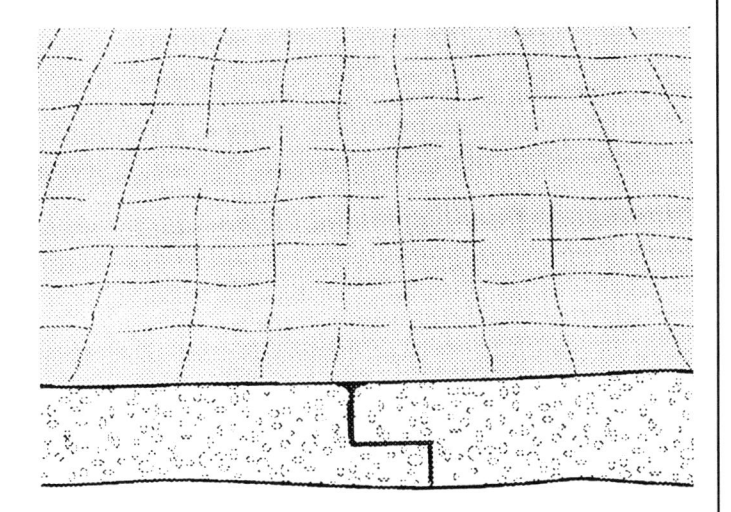

Figure 12 - Fiberglass Duct Board

Rigid Round Fiberglass Duct

Rigid round high-pressure preformed fiberglass duct (*Figure 13*) is a high-pressure, high-velocity duct designed for a maximum air velocity of 4000 fpm, a positive pressure maximum of 8 inches **w.g. (water gage)**, and a maximum negative pressure of 2 inches w.g. (See Module 04405, *The SMACNA Manuals,* for information on water gage measurements.)

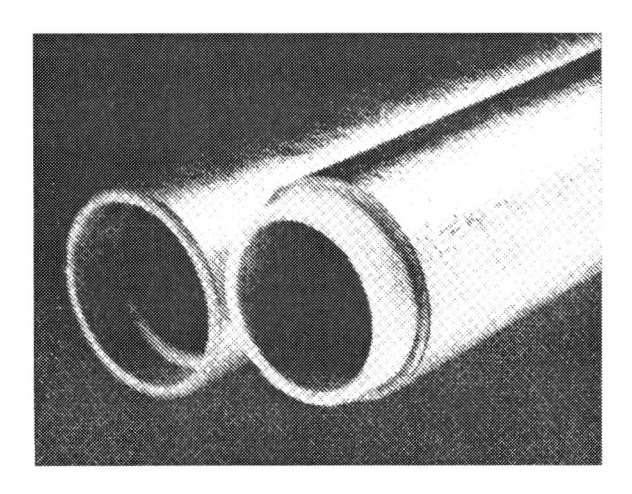

Figure 13 - Rigid Round Fiberglass Duct

The preformed duct is made from long, fine, flame-blown glass fibers and is designed to provide acoustical absorption in addition to thermal insulation and vapor barrier characteristics. The cylindrical sections are covered with reinforced foil jacketing.

It also features an integral slip-joint, which allows for tight connections between sections. The duct wall is 1" thick and comes in 6-foot lengths. It is available in standard round duct sizes from 4" through 10" in 1-inch increments, and from 12" through 30" in 2-inch increments.

Thermal activated tape, a special cutting tool for making slip-joint ends on shortened pieces, and a knife are all you need to assemble this duct work. The cylindrical, one-piece construction also provides good structural strength.

INSULATION — TRAINEE TASK MODULE 04409

Insulated Flexible Round Fiberglass Duct

Insulated flexible round fiberglass duct is designed for both heating and cooling applications in low-pressure air conditioning systems. It consists of three major components: a highly flexible, vinyl-coated, spring steel helix bonded to a black polyethylene; a thick insulating fiberglass blanket; and an outer vapor barrier jacket of metallized laminate reinforced with fiberglass scrim (durable plain woven fabric). This scrim is visible in *Figure 14*.

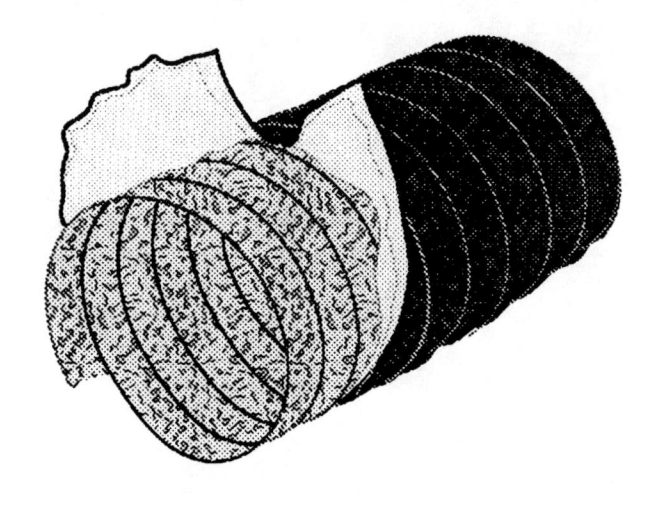

Figure 14 - Insulated Flexible Round Fiberglass Duct

These types of ducts are designed to provide air duct sound absorption, thermal insulation, and vapor barrier qualities. Available forms include tubular styles from 4" through 10" in 1-inch increments, and 10" through 16" in 2-inch increments. Standard lengths are 25 feet, which can be field cut to a minimum length for final connection from a duct or pipe to an air terminal.

You should note, however, that flexible duct is *not* recommended for use on the return air side of an HVAC system.

Insulated flexible fiberglass ducts are used as run-outs from low-pressure ducts or mixing boxes, induction units, diffusers, or other low-velocity terminal units in commercial and industrial heating and cooling systems. These types of ducts can operate at velocities up to 5000 fpm, and static pressures of 2" w.g. for low-pressure joint method and 6" w.g. for high-pressure joint method.

Because of their adaptability, flexible fiberglass ducts are also used to replace fabricated elbows and fittings in confined and obstructed areas. When field cut, the ducts require no metal end fittings. The spring steel helix inner core provides a built-in end finish that permits cutting to exact length and joining to other duct sections, metal collars, plenums, fittings, or straight to a grille.

This attachment is accomplished by putting the inner core on the collar or fitting and using a specialized flexible panduit strap and tensioning tool to secure it. (*See Figure 15*.) The protruding insulation is folded back and then taped down over the panduit strap after the strap has been tightened. The duct should be installed fully extended, using the minimum length required to make the connection. Crimping or compressing the duct will increase friction loss (*Figure 16*). The duct should be supported with a minimum of sag between the supports (*Figure 17*).

Flexible Insulated Metal Duct

Flexible insulated metal duct (*Figure 18*) is a flexible aluminum duct that can be used in high- or low-pressure systems. It can be used for bends or straight runs. The flexible metal duct has the fiberglass insulation encased in a vinyl vapor barrier for low-pressure and aluminized mylar for high-pressure applications.

Insulated flexible metal duct can be used for bends and straight runs on residential and mobile home heating and air conditioning supplies, commercial building air-handling systems, and other industrial and construction uses. Because of its flexibility and light weight, it can be installed above suspended ceilings and in other areas of limited clearance and access. Insulated flexible metal duct is available in regular duct sizes. Again, flexible duct is recommended for use only with supply air.

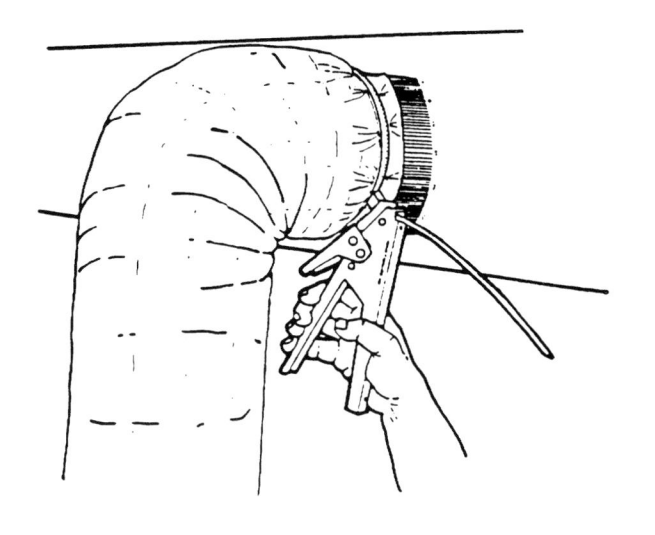

Figure 15 - Panduit Strap with Tensioning Tool

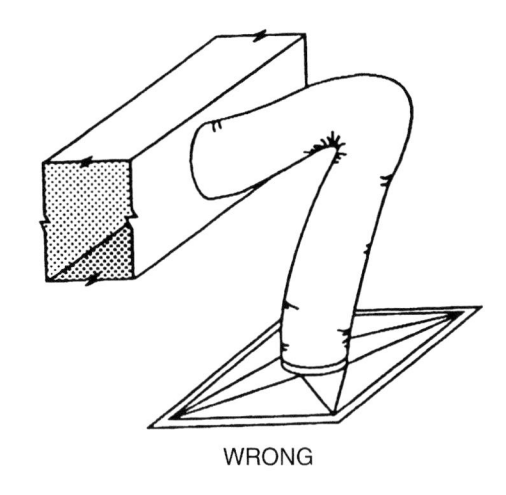

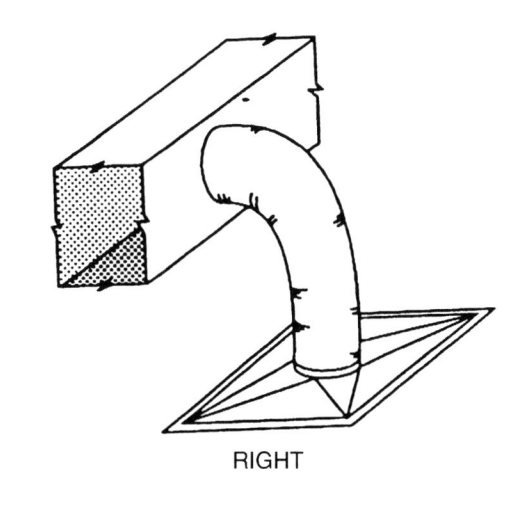

Figure 16 - Installing Flexible Duct

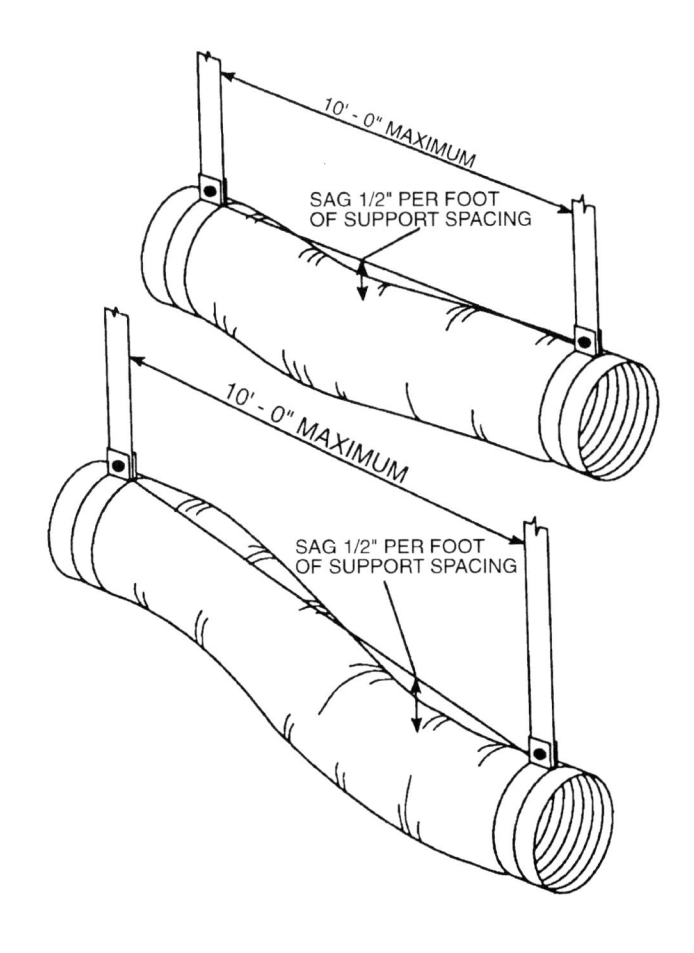

Figure 17 - Supporting Flexible Duct

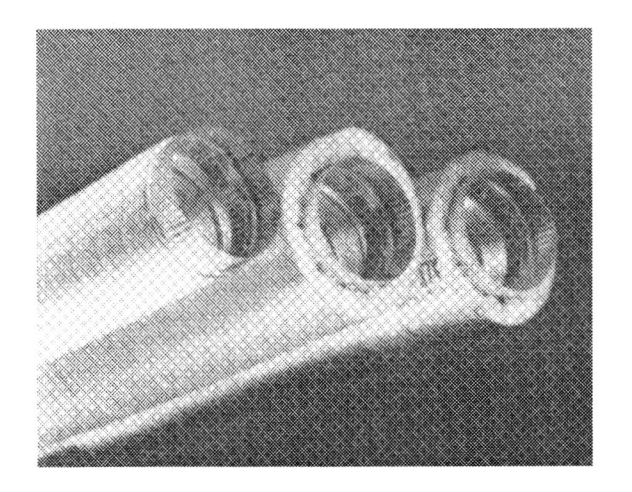

Figure 18 - Flexible Insulated Metal Duct

INSULATION — TRAINEE TASK MODULE 04409

15

REVIEW QUESTIONS

Answer the following questions to review your knowledge of this module and to prepare for the Module Examination.

1. Explain the difference between sound attenuation and thermal insulation.
2. What are the more common forms of sheet metal insulation?
3. Define "vapor barrier" and tell why such a thing is necessary.
4. Describe the approved method of installation for flexible duct liner.
5. List several accepted standards for applying rigid duct liner.
6. What tools and materials are needed to join sections of rigid, round fiberglass duct?
7. Why do you suppose nosings need to be welded or riveted instead of screw attached?
8. How is a ductrun like a telephone connection?
9. How is insulated flexible round fiber-glass duct attached to a round metal fitting?
10. Why should flexible duct never be used for return air?

SUMMARY

The introduction of forced-air systems established the need for insulation to conserve heat and to prevent condensation on ductruns in cooling systems. Insulations with vapor barriers have been developed which provide thermal insulation when applied to the exterior of sheet metal duct systems.

Duct lining provides sound absorption and also provides thermal insulation while using the duct as an air and vapor barrier. The basic material in duct liner is glass processed from the molten state into fibrous form. Insulating materials are available in various dimensions of thickness, width, and length. As with any other component of a heating or cooling system, proper installation of insulating materials is of the utmost importance for proper and efficient operation of the total system.

TRADE TERMS

Acoustical spray-on
Adhesive-secured fasteners
Attenuator
Blanket
Dampers
Duct board
Duct breakout noise
Facing
Flanking
Fpm
Impact-applied pins
Mechanically-secured fasteners
Metal nosings
Sound attenuating
Sound power level
Thermal
W.G.
Weld-secured fasteners

ACKNOWLEDGMENTS

Figures 1, 2, 3, 12, 13 & 18: Johns Manville Corp.
Figure 15: Malco Products, Inc.

NCCER CRAFT TRAINING USER UPDATES

The NCCER makes every effort to keep these manuals up-to-date and free of technical errors. We appreciate your help in this process. If you have an idea for improving this manual, or if you find an error, a typographical mistake, or an inaccuracy in the NCCER's Craft Training Manuals, please write us, using this form or a photocopy. Be sure to include the exact module number, page number, a description of the problem, and the correction, if possible. Your input will be brought to the attention of the Technical Review Committee. Thank you for your assistance.

Instructors – If you found that additional materials were necessary in order to teach this module effectively, please let us know so that we may include them in the Equipment/Materials list in the Instructor's Guide.

Write: Curriculum and Revision Department
National Center for Construction Education and Research
P.O. Box 141104
Gainesville, FL 32614-1104

Fax: 352-334-0932

Craft _____ Module Name _____

Module Number _____ Page Number(s) _____

Description of Problem
_____
_____
_____
_____

(Optional) Correction of Problem
_____
_____
_____

(Optional) Your Name and Address
_____
_____
_____

Gutters and Downspouts

Module 04502

NATIONAL
CENTER FOR
CONSTRUCTION
EDUCATION AND
RESEARCH

Task Module 04502

GUTTERS AND DOWNSPOUTS

Objectives

Upon completion of this task module, the trainee will be able to:

1. Demonstrate skill in understanding the principles of roof design and drainage systems.

2. Demonstrate skill in calculating downspout and gutter sizes.

3. Identify, lay out, and fabricate selected drainage components.

INTRODUCTION

Although most contemporary drainage and gutter system members are prefabricated, a knowledge of the principles involved in layout, development, and fabrication of these parts is still useful. Drainage systems are designed to carry water away quickly and to avoid pockets in which moisture can collect. The criterion for drainage systems is that they should shed water directly and speedily to gutters and downspouts which carry it away with maximum efficiency. Sheet metal components must be fabricated to meet the established criterion.

DESIGN PRINCIPLES

One of the most essential parts of a building is the roof because it protects the interior of the building from the elements of the weather. Once an architect determines the type of roof intended for use, equal attention must be given to the design of the roof drainage system. When designing roof drainage systems, factors to considered are the area to be drained, the size of the gutters, downspouts, and outlets, and the slope of the roof; the type of building; and, of course, the appearance of the system. The design capacity for a roof drainage system depends on the quantity of water to be handled, which in turn depends upon the roof area, slope, and the intensity of rainfall.

Rain-water gutters and leaders are needed to catch the rain water falling on roofs or other catchment areas above the ground and to conduct that rain water to some point of discharge. It is usually forbidden to discharge such drainage into the sanitary sewer. Therefore, storm sewers are sometimes provided for this purpose.

Rain-water leaders can be placed either inside or outside a building. When they are placed inside, they are sometimes called conductors. When they are placed outside, they may be called leaders. Inside locations are favored due to convenience, safety, appearance, and freedom from freezing. The lower cost, however, usually mandates that rain-water leaders are placed on the outside of structures.

The building storm drain usually connects to the roof drain(s) and conveys the rainwater to the building storm sewer. The building storm sewer, in turn, conveys the rainwater to the storm sewer which will convey it to other points for disposal.

DOWNSPOUT SIZING

When considering roof area for downspout sizing, it must be kept in mind that rain does not fall vertically and that maximum conditions exist only when rain falls perpendicular to a surface. The roof area increases as its pitch increases, therefore, it is not advisable to use the plan area of a pitched roof when calculating the capacity of a drainage system. Thus, the use of the true area of a pitched roof often leads to oversizing of gutters, downspouts, and drains.

Conventional roof-drainage sizing information contained in a number of plumbing codes is based upon the "maximum projected roof area, in square feet," that can be handled with each pipe size in a given range of sizes as shown in *Table 1*. For example, to calculate the size and number of roof drains required for a 200 × 300 flat roof (60,000 square feet), with a rainfall intensity of 11 inches per hour, consult *Table 1*. Notice that a roof drain size of 4 inches will drain 4,600 square feet or roof area per drain or leader. Thus, 60,000 square feet divided by

Rainfall in Inches	Size of Drain or Leader in Inches					
	2	3	4	5	6	8
1	2,880	8,800	18,400	34,600	54,000	116,000
2	1,440	4,400	9,200	17,300	27,000	58,000
3	960	2,930	6,130	11,530	17,995	38,660
4	720	2,200	4,600	8,650	13,500	29,000
5	575	1,760	3,680	6,920	10,800	23,200
6	480	1,470	3,070	5,765	9,000	19,315
7	410	1,260	2,630	4,945	7,715	16,570
8	360	1,100	2,300	4,325	6,750	14,500
9	320	980	2,045	3,845	6,000	12,890
10	290	880	1,840	3,460	5,400	11,600
11	260	800	1,675	3,145	4,910	10,545
12	240	730	1,530	2,880	4,500	9,660

Table 1 - Sizing Roof Drains

4,600 equals 13 roof drains. However, it has been found through controlled studies of roof drainage systems that a minimum of one roof drain for each 10,000 square feet of projected roof area is practical for both sloped and flat roofs. Consequently, 60,000 divided by 10,000 equals 6 drains or leaders as the recommended number to drain a roof of this size. Again, consulting *Table 1* it can be found that a 6 inch size drain for each of the 6 drain locations would be needed to meet the requirements. Each 6 inch drain should be able to drain 13,500 square feet of roof under a rainfall intensity of 4 inches per hour. A five inch drain would be inadequate because it can drain only 8,650 square feet of roof under a 4 inch per hour rainfall intensity.

The data indicated in *Table 1* are based upon a maximum rate of rainfall of 4 inches per hour. Therefore, the figures for projected roof areas must be adjusted proportionately for the correct rate of rain fall for a specific geographic area. Each of the figures in the table must be multiplied by 4 and then divided by the correct rate of rainfall. For example, if a 3-inch rainfall rate as calculated from the rainfall map (*Figure 1*) is to be followed, the figures in *Table 1* would be multiplied by 4 and then divided by 3 to produce a different set of values. Consequently, each rate of rainfall will require a completely different set of table figures.

The rainfall map can be used to find the rate of rainfall in inches per hour or local codes may have specific stipulations pertaining to sizing of roof drainage systems per local rainfall intensities.

The vertical leaders or drains and the horizontal storm drainage piping or gutters must be sized according to the total maximum projected roof area they are expected to drain in relation to the maximum rate of rainfall in inches per hour.

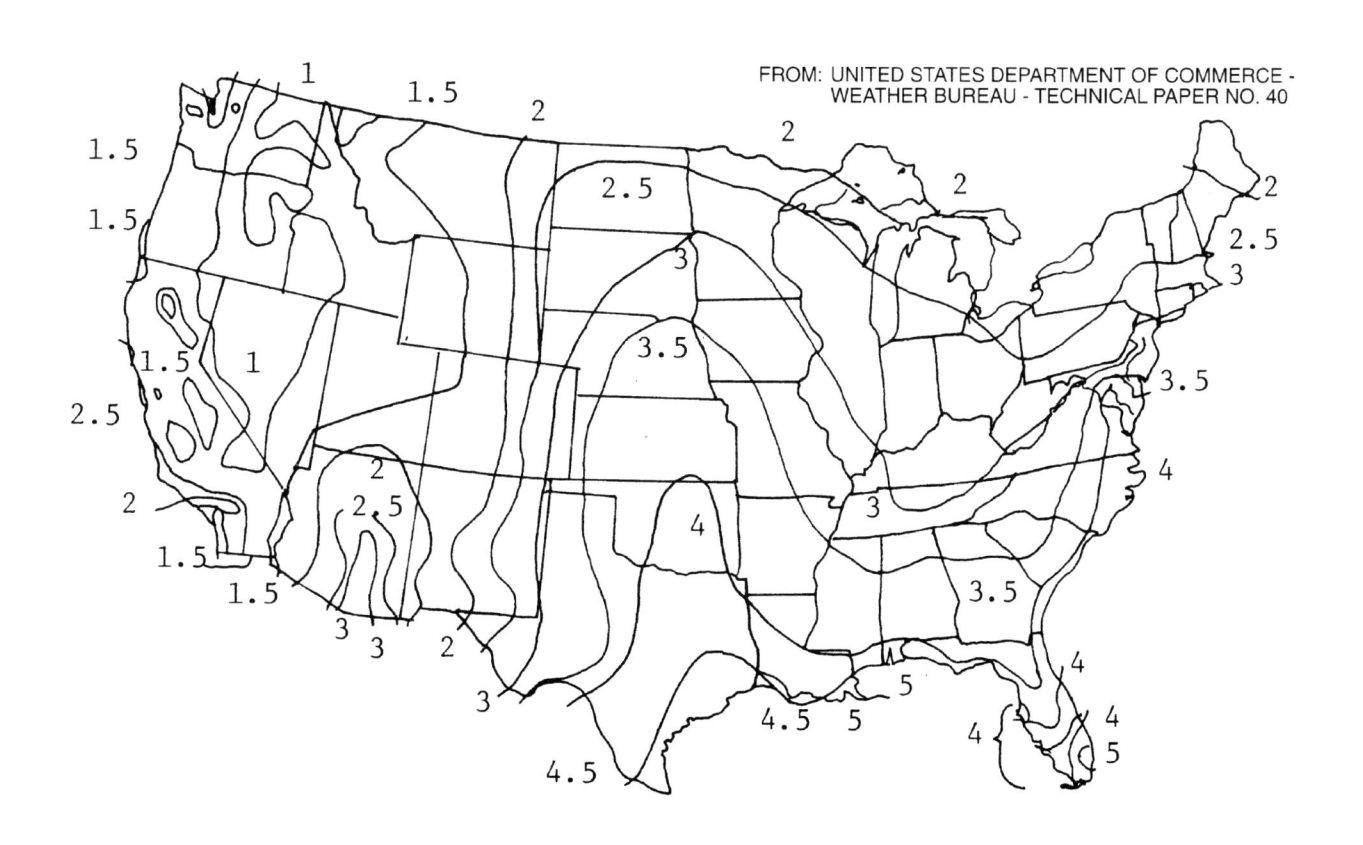

Figure 1 - Rainfall Map

GUTTERS AND DOWNSPOUTS — TRAINEE TASK MODULE 04502

GUTTER SIZING

When considering factors which influence the size of gutters, it must be remembered that the gutter can never be any more effective than the downspout designed to drain it. It must be wide enough so that water from a steeply pitched roof will not spill over the front edge. It also depends upon the area to be drained and the rainfall intensity per hour over the length of gutter in feet and the ratio of depth to width of gutter.

Sizing Drains and Gutters

The size of a structure's rainwater piping or any of its horizontal branches should be sized in accordance with the rainfall intensity and the horizontal or maximum projected roof area.

Using *Table 2* as a reference, for example, one could calculate the size of the rainwater piping needed to drain a roof area of 6,000 square feet, located in Florida (rainfall intensity of 5", according to *Figure 1*), with a pipe slope of 1/4 inch.

Step 1. Select the roof area (6,000 square feet), and the rainfall intensity (5 inches) from that part of the table relating to a pipe slope of 1/4".

Step 2. Find the projected roof area in the column under 5 inches of rainfall (6040).

Step 3. Find the size of the piping relating to the area under the size of pipe in inches column at the left side of the table. Read 6 inches.

Round, square or rectangular rain-water piping may be used. Each of the configurations is considered to be equivalent in diameter when they would enclose a scribed circle equal to the diameter of the leader.

Sizing of the semi-circular roof gutters should be based on the maximum roof area to be drained. These calculations can be made using information obtained from *Table 3*.

For example, to drain a roof in Southern Illinois with a rainfall intensity of 3 inches (*Figure 1*), first select the table pertaining to the pitch or slope of the gutter and proceed as in the problem presented above.

Step 1. Select the table section pertaining to the gutter slope, 1/4 inch, for instance, and the rainfall intensity (3 inches).

Step 2. Find the projected roof area to be drained, 2,000 square feet.

Step 3. Find the rainfall intensity (3 inches).

Step 4. Select the gutter size from the left-hand column in relation to the next larger roof area. Find that 1668 under the rainfall intensity would indicate that a 5 inch gutter diameter should be used. With a projected roof area of 2,000 square feet to be drained, the 5 inch gutter would be inadequate, therefore, a gutter size of 6 inches must be used to adequately drain the 2,000 square feet of roof area (6 inch drain equals 2560 square feet).

Some practical rules pertaining to sizing and placement of rain-water gutters and leaders are:

1. Each leader should be the same size as its outlet for its full length.

2. Runoff computations should probably be based on double the rainfall intensity; calculate runoff conductors at 8 inches per hour if the rainfall intensity for the area is 4 inches per hour.

3. Maximum spacing of leaders should never exceed 75 feet. One square inch of leader should be allowed for each 150 square feet of projected roof area.

4. No leader should be less than 3 inches in diameter (circular).

5. The gutter size depends on the spacing and number of outlets; the slope of the roof; and the gutter spacing.

Size of Pipe in Inches 1/8" Slope	Maximum Rainfall in Inches per Hour				
	2"	3"	4"	5"	6"
3"	1,644	1,096	822	657	548
4"	3,760	2,506	1,880	1,504	1,253
5"	6,680	4,453	3,340	2,672	2,227
6"	10,700	7,133	5,350	4,280	3,566
8"	23,000	15,330	11,500	9,200	7,600
10"	41,400	27,600	20,700	16,580	13,800
11"	66,600	44,400	33,300	26,650	22,200
15"	109,000	72,800	59,500	47,600	39,650

Size of Pipe in Inches 1/4" Slope	Maximum Rainfall in Inches per Hour				
	2"	3"	4"	5"	6"
3"	2,320	1,546	1,160	928	773
4"	5,300	3,533	2,650	2,120	1,766
5"	9,440	6,293	4,720	3,776	3,146
<u>6"</u>	15,100	10,066	7,550	<u>6,040</u>	5,033
8"	32,600	21,733	16,300	13,040	10,866
10"	58,400	38,950	29,200	23,350	19,450
12"	94,000	62,600	47,000	37,600	31,350
15"	168,000	112,000	84,000	67,250	56,000

Size of Pipe in Inches 1/2" Slope	Maximum Rainfall in Inches per Hour				
	2"	3"	4"	5"	6"
3"	3,288	2,295	1,644	1,310	1,096
4"	7,520	5,010	3,760	3,010	2,500
5"	13,360	8,900	6,680	5,320	4,450
6"	21,400	13,700	10,700	8,580	7,140
8"	46,000	30,650	23,000	18,400	15,320
10"	82,800	55,200	41,400	33,150	27,600
12"	133,200	88,800	66,600	53,200	44,400
15"	238,000	158,800	119,000	95,300	79,250

Table 2 - Size of Horizontal Rainwater Piping

Diameter of Gutter 1/16" Slope	Maximum Rainfall in Inches per Hour				
	2"	3"	4"	5"	6"
3"	340	226	170	136	113
4"	720	480	360	288	240
5"	1,250	834	625	500	416
6"	1,920	1,280	960	768	640
7"	2,760	1,840	1,380	1,100	918
8"	3,980	2,655	1,990	1,590	1,325
10"	7,200	4,800	3,600	2,880	2,400

Diameter of Gutter 1/8" Slope	Maximum Rainfall in Inches per Hour				
	2"	3"	4"	5"	6"
3"	480	320	240	192	160
4"	1,020	681	510	408	340
5"	1,760	1,172	880	704	587
6"	2,720	1,815	1,360	1,085	905
7"	3,900	2,600	1,950	1,560	1,300
8"	5,600	3,740	2,800	2,240	1,870
10"	10,200	6,800	5,100	4,080	3,400

Diameter of Gutter 1/4" Slope	Maximum Rainfall in Inches per Hour				
	2"	<u>3"</u>	4"	5"	6"
3"	680	454	340	272	226
4"	1,440	960	720	576	480
5"	2,500	1,668	1,250	1,000	834
6"	3,840	<u>2,560</u>	1,920	1,536	1,280
7"	5,520	3,680	2,760	2,205	1,840
8"	7,960	5,310	3,980	3,180	2,655
10"	14,400	9,600	7,200	5,750	4,800

Diameter of Gutter 1/2" Slope	Maximum Rainfall in Inches per Hour				
	2"	3"	4"	5"	6"
3"	960	640	480	384	320
4"	2,040	1,360	1,020	816	680
5"	3,540	2,360	1,770	1,415	1,180
6"	5,540	3,695	2,770	2,220	1,850
7"	7,800	5,200	3,900	3,120	2,600
8"	11,200	7,460	5,600	4,480	3,730
10"	20,000	13,330	10,000	8,000	6,660

Table 3 - Size of Gutters

6. Minimum gutter depth should equal one-half of the gutter width, but should not exceed three-quarters (75 percent) of the width. Thus gutter is referred to by its width only.

7. A gutter smaller than 4 inches should be avoided.

8. Half-round gutters are most economical in material.

9. If the leader spacing is 50 feet or less, the gutter should be the same size as the leader, but never less than 4 inches.

10. If leader spacing is more than 50 feet, add 1 inch to the leader diameter for every 20 feet of additional spacing on peaked roofs.

11. Add 1 inch to the leader size for every 30 feet of additional gutter length on flat roofs.

12. For residential application, 3 inch or 4 inch round or 2 inch by 4 inch rectangular leaders will usually suffice.

13. Five inch half-round gutter size will meet most residential needs.

14. Gutters should have a pitch (slope) of not less than 1 inch in 16 feet.

15. Scuppers should be provided for all roofs enclosed with a parapet wall.

16. All outlets should be provided with a screen or strainer.

Roof span is another factor that is considered when sizing roof drainage systems. The following recommendations are offered:

1. For roof spans up to 50 feet, 6 inch gutters should be used, with 4 inch leaders placed every 40 feet.

2. For roof spans 50 to 70 feet, 7 inch gutters should be used, with 5 inch leaders placed every 40 feet.

3. For roof spans 70 to 100 feet, 8 inch gutters should be used, with 5 inch leaders placed every 40 feet.

Gutters having shapes other than round or rectangular can be sized by calculating the rectangular or semicircle area that most closely corresponds to the irregular cross section. Half-round gutter size need not be calculated if the downspout size has been determined. The size of half-round gutter is directly related to the downspout size and is usually equal to or one inch larger than the calculated downspout size.

Gutters serve a special purpose in building design. Standard gutter sizes and shapes are available as stocked items but sheet metal workers may be called upon to design and build-in special gutter application. When designing gutters a few factors must be considered. The material should be:

1. Corrosion resistant

2. It should be easy to solder or seal

3. Expansion joints must be provided

4. The highest point on the front of the gutter must be a minimum of 1 inch lower than the back edge of the gutter.

Gutters may be hung level or pitched toward the downspout unless appearance is a consideration and the building lines must be straight, then level gutters are preferred.

TASK 1

CONDUCTOR ELBOW

Objectives

Upon completion of this task, the trainee will be able to:

1. Lay out and develop the pattern for a 60° two-piece conductor elbow.
2. Fabricate the selected plain round conductor elbow.
3. Form and set a soldered lap seam and a soldered butt seam at the intersection.

Tools and Materials

1. One piece of 24 gage galvanized sheet metal of the appropriate size according to *Figure 2*.
2. Soldering equipment and supplies.
3. Layout and development tools.
4. Slip roll forming machine.
5. Tin snips.
6. Measuring instruments (combination square, flexible steel rule, circumference rule, steel square).

Procedure

1. For a side profile (elevation view) of a 60° two-pieced conductor elbow, scribe a curved throat and heel to a 60° angle. Bisect the heel curve and scribe a straight line from the center of the radius point "A" through the division point G on the heel curve.
2. Draw a squaring line from the base FR (FR = 4) through the division point on the heel curve, point G.
3. Scribe a squaring line from point F upward to the division line on the throat curve and mark point E.
4. Establish distances AG and BE.
5. Below the profile view, describe a circle (4" diameter) and scribe a line through the circle (plan view) and divide the lower half of the circle into a number of equal parts as indicated.
6. From each of these points, scribe perpendicular lines intersecting the miter line EG.
7. Scribe horizontal lines at right angles to the vertical arm of the elbow.
8. Draw the **stretchout** line and upon this line, step off the number of spaces from the circle (plan view).
9. From these points scribe squaring lines upward to be intersected by like numbered horizontal lines scribed from the miter line 1-7.
10. Trace a line through these numbered points establishing the pattern for the vertical arm of the elbow. Distances 4-4 are equal to the seam line in the vertical arm of the elbow.
11. The stretchout of both pieces are of equal length. Therefore, the pattern for the upper arm of the elbow is generally obtained from a matching piece of stock. The total size of the stock for the stretchout of both patterns would be equal to the length of the stretchout (**LS** = Circumference of the circle plus seam allowances) times the width of the stretchout (**WS** = Distance RG + AG).
12. Cut out and form the pattern.
13. Solder the lap seam and butt solder the miter.
14. Restore the work area.

Questions

1. How is the miter line established?
2. How is the width of the stretchout established?

SHEET METAL — TRAINEE TASK MODULE 04502

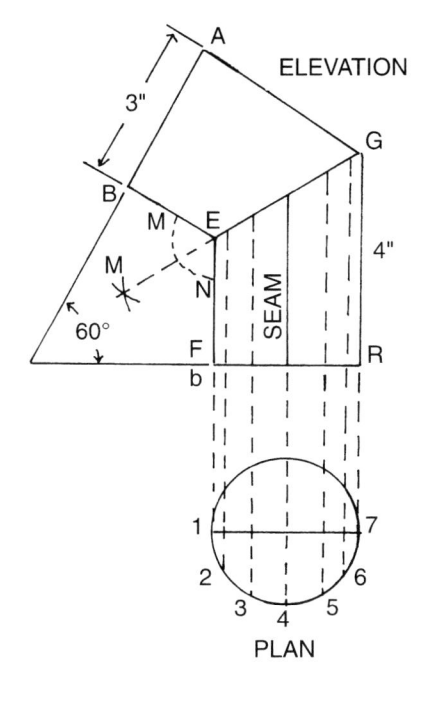

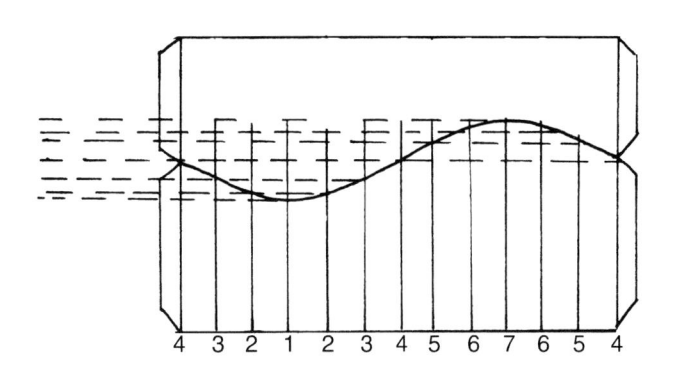

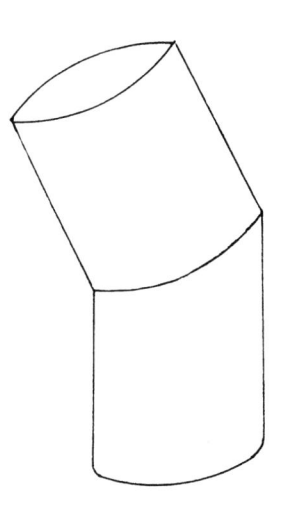

Figure 2 - Conductor Elbow

GUTTERS AND DOWNSPOUTS — TRAINEE TASK MODULE 04502

TASK 2

RECTANGULAR CONDUCTOR SHOE

Objectives

Upon completion of this task the trainee will be able to:

1. Lay out and develop a pattern for the rectangular-shaped 72° conductor shoe.
2. Shape and form the selected fitting.
3. Form and solder a lap seam.

Tools and Materials

1. One piece of 24 gage galvanized sheet metal of the size indicated in the working drawing *Figure 3*.
2. Soldering equipment and supplies.
3. Layout and development tools.
4. Tin snips.
5. Measuring instruments.
6. Box and pan brake.

Procedure

1. Lay out and scribe the lines on the profile or elevation view as indicated.
2. Scribe the stretchout x-x at right angles to the vertical arm of the elbow.
3. Mark off the spaces x-1, 1-2, 2-3, 3-4, 4-x from the plan view on the stretchout.
4. Scribe horizontal lines from points 2-3, 1-x-4 in the profile view to the lines just established.
5. Connect the points located by the intersecting, producing the desired pattern on the stretchout.
6. Make seam allowances.
7. Mark the bend lines on the stretchout.
8. Cut and bend the two parts of the pattern.
9. Sweat solder the lap seam. Solder the butt joint (lap seam) at the miter.
10. Restore the work area.

Questions

1. What establishes the miter line?
2. Where are the lap seams located in relation to each other on the finished fitting?

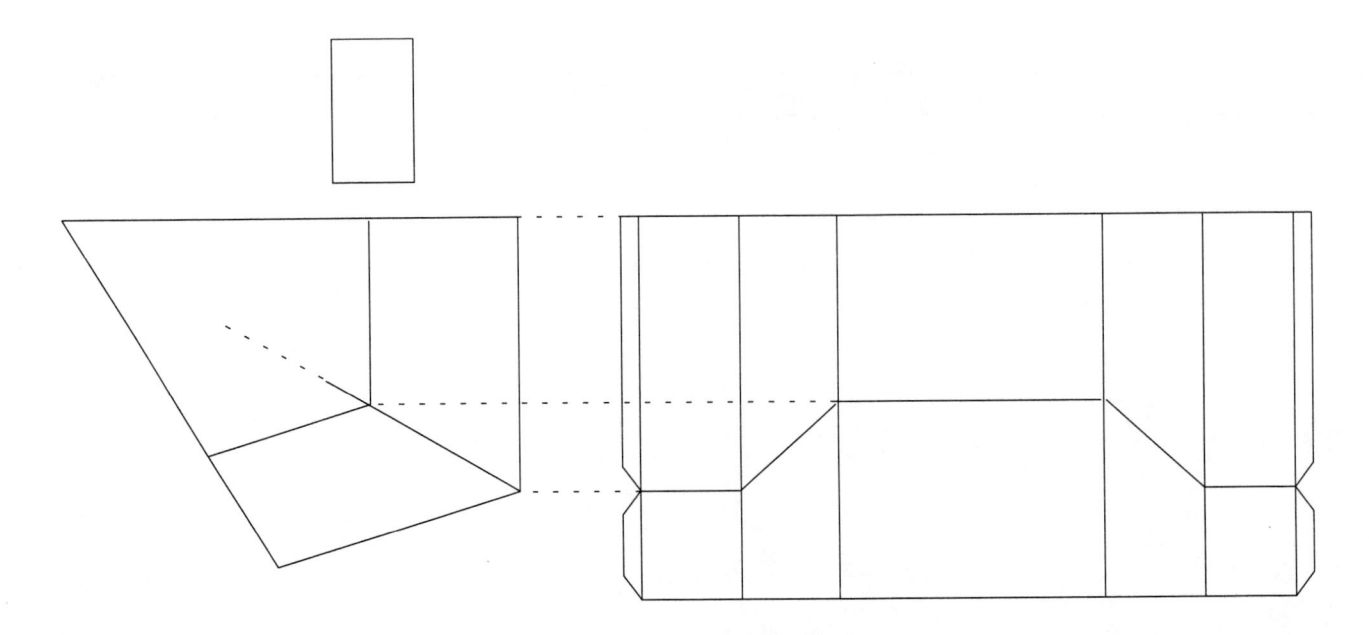

Figure 3 - Conductor Shoe

TASK 3

RECTANGULAR OUTLET TUBE

Objectives

Upon completion of this task, the trainee will be able to:

1. Lay out and develop a pattern for a rectangular outlet tube.
2. Shape and form the selected fitting.
3. Form and solder a grooved lock seam.

Tools and Materials

1. One piece of 26 gage galvanized sheet metal of the size indicated in the working drawing, *Figure 4*.
2. One No. 3 hand groover.
3. Bar folder.
4. Handy seamer.
5. Layout and development tools.
6. Tin snips.
7. Measuring instruments.
8. Soldering equipment and supplies.

Procedure

1. Calculate the size of the stretchout required as indicated by the pictorial drawing, *Figure 4*.
2. Scribe the layout lines for the bend sections of the tube.
3. Make seam allowances and mark out the bend allowances for the flanges.
4. Cut out the pattern and form the edges for the grooved lock seam.
5. Perform the bending operation, set and lock the seam. Bend the flanges.
6. Restore the work area.

Questions

1. Why are the flanges formed last?

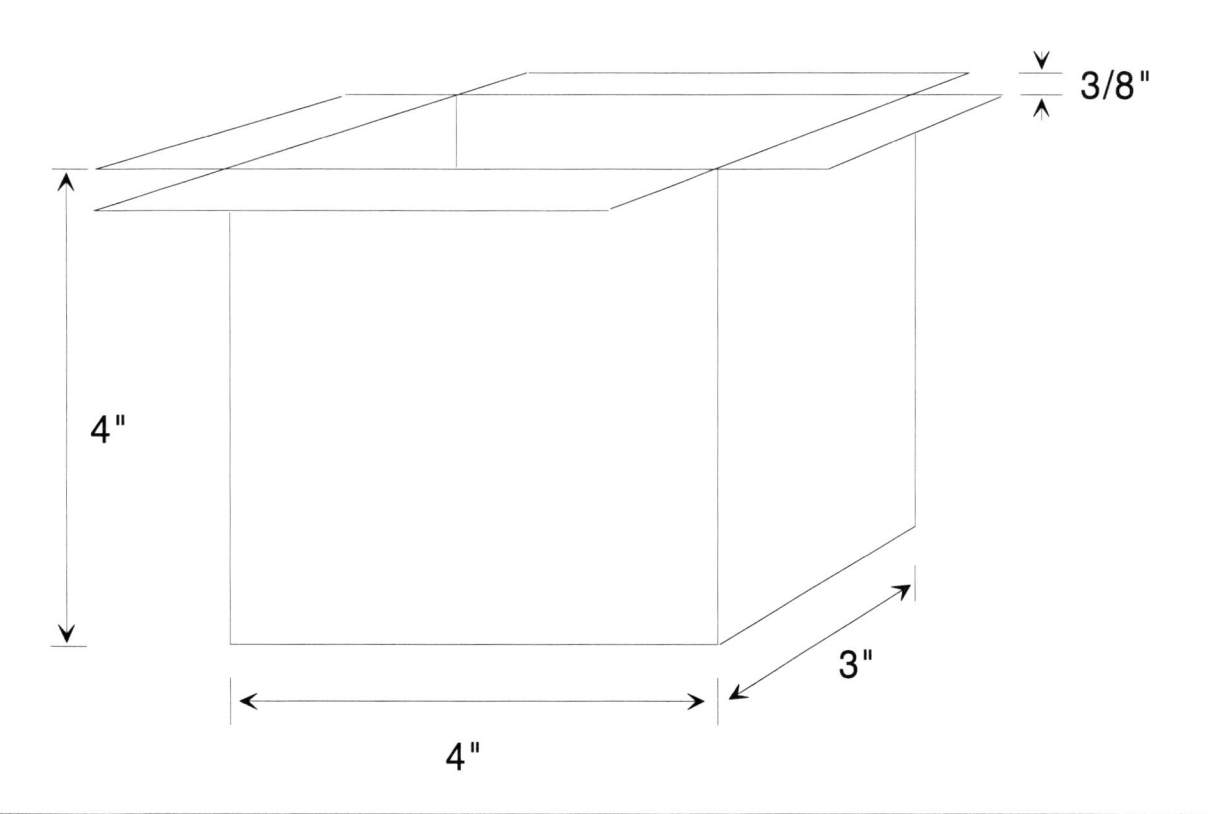

Figure 4 - Outlet Tube

GUTTERS AND DOWNSPOUTS — TRAINEE TASK MODULE 04502

TASK 4

RECTANGULAR GUTTER

Objectives

Upon completion of this task, the trainee will be able to:

1. Interpret standards as they apply to the design and construction of rectangular sections.
2. Use the specifications set forth in the module for designing a short section of rectangular gutter.
3. Design a short section of rectangular gutter style as indicated.
4. Lay out, develop, and form a short section of rectangular gutter. Gutter girth = 10".

Tools and Materials

1. One piece of appropriate gage sheet metal (galvanized steel) 12" wide (WS).
2. Box and pan brake or cornice brake.
3. Layout and development tools.
4. Squaring shear.
5. Measuring instruments.

Procedure

1. Find the gage of sheet metal required in the SMACNA Manual.
2. Establish the bend lines as implied by *Figure 5*. When forming gutter sections, it is generally accepted practice that the bend sequence begins at the shortest bend and progresses through to the longest bend.
3. Scribe the bend lines on the stretchout as calculated from the manual.
4. Bend and form the rectangular shaped gutter and check against the established standards.
5. Restore the work area.

Questions

1. What determines the gage of the sheet metal to be used for rectangular gutters?

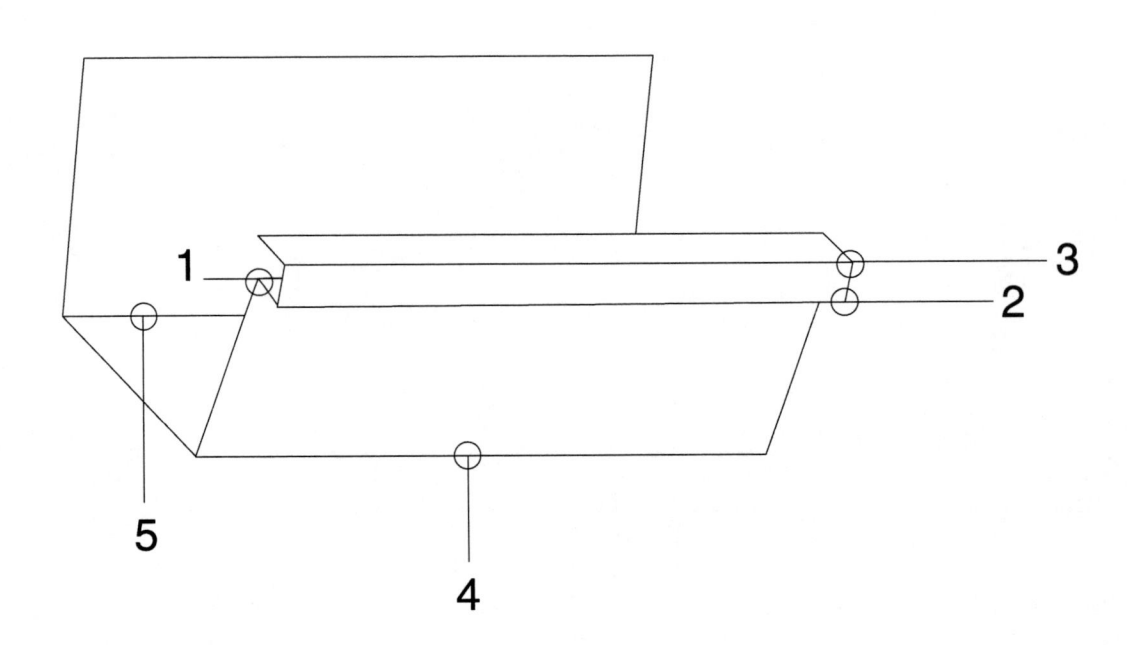

Figure 5 - Sequence of Bends

TASK 5

RECTANGULAR GUTTER

Objectives

Upon completion of this task, the trainee will be able to:

1. Design a short section of selected rectangular gutter, according to *Figure 6*.
2. Lay out, develop, and fabricate a section of selected rectangular gutter (girth = 15") per SMACNA Manual standards.

Tools and Materials

1. One piece of appropriate gage sheet metal (galvanized steel) 10" wide (WS).
2. Cornice brake.
3. Layout and development tools.
4. Squaring shears.
5. Measuring instruments.

Procedures

1. Find the gage of sheet metal required.
2. Establish the bend line sequence.
3. Establish bend line dimensions.
4. Bend and form the gutter and check against the established standards.
5. Restore the work area.

Questions

1. What impact do longitudinal breaks have on rectangular gutter design?

Figure 6 - Rectangular Gutter

GUTTERS AND DOWNSPOUTS — TRAINEE TASK MODULE 04502

TASK 6

CONICAL GUTTER OUTLET

Objectives

Upon completion of this task, the trainee will be able to:

1. Lay out and develop the pattern for a conical shaped gutter outlet.
2. Fabricate the selected gutter outlet.

In cases where the opening in the gutter will be larger than the diameter of the downspout, it is probably necessary to construct a tapering connector. The procedure for this task is based upon the radial line development process.

Tools and Materials

1. One piece of 26 gage galvanized sheet metal of the size calculated by the development process.
2. Soldering equipment and supplies.
3. Layout and development tools.
4. Squaring shear.
5. Slip roll forming machine.
6. Blowhorn stake and wooden or leather mallet.
7. Tin snips.
8. Measuring instruments.
9. Turning and burring machine.

Procedure

1. Draw the profile or elevation view of the flaring outlet which consists of a **frustum** of a cone (*Figure 7*). The upper base is defined by the horizontal line FH, the lower base is defined by the horizontal line MN. Distance RO is defined as the height of the cone.
2. Scribe the center line AB, then using the terminating points F and H on line FH locate point A by scribing a line from M through F to A, then from point N through H to A.
3. Using R as center and distance RN as radius, describe the half plan for the cone.
4. Using A as center and AN as radius, describe the stretchout arc F1.
5. Step off four times the number of spaces shown in the half plan view on the stretchout arc F1.
6. Using A as center and AH as radius describe the stretchout arc for the collar opening.
7. Make seam allowances at the top and ends.
8. Layout the collars, allowing for end and edge seams.

Note: LS of the collars is equal to the circumference plus seam allowances.

9. Cut out, form, and shape the components.
10. Solder and lock the appropriate seams.
11. Restore the work area.

Questions

1. Describe the procedure for laying out the stretchout arc for the cone.
2. How is the stretchout of the small or large collar calculated?

DOUBLE EDGE

SMALL COLLAR

SINGLE EDGE

LARGE COLLAR

FRONT PROFILE

ELEVATION

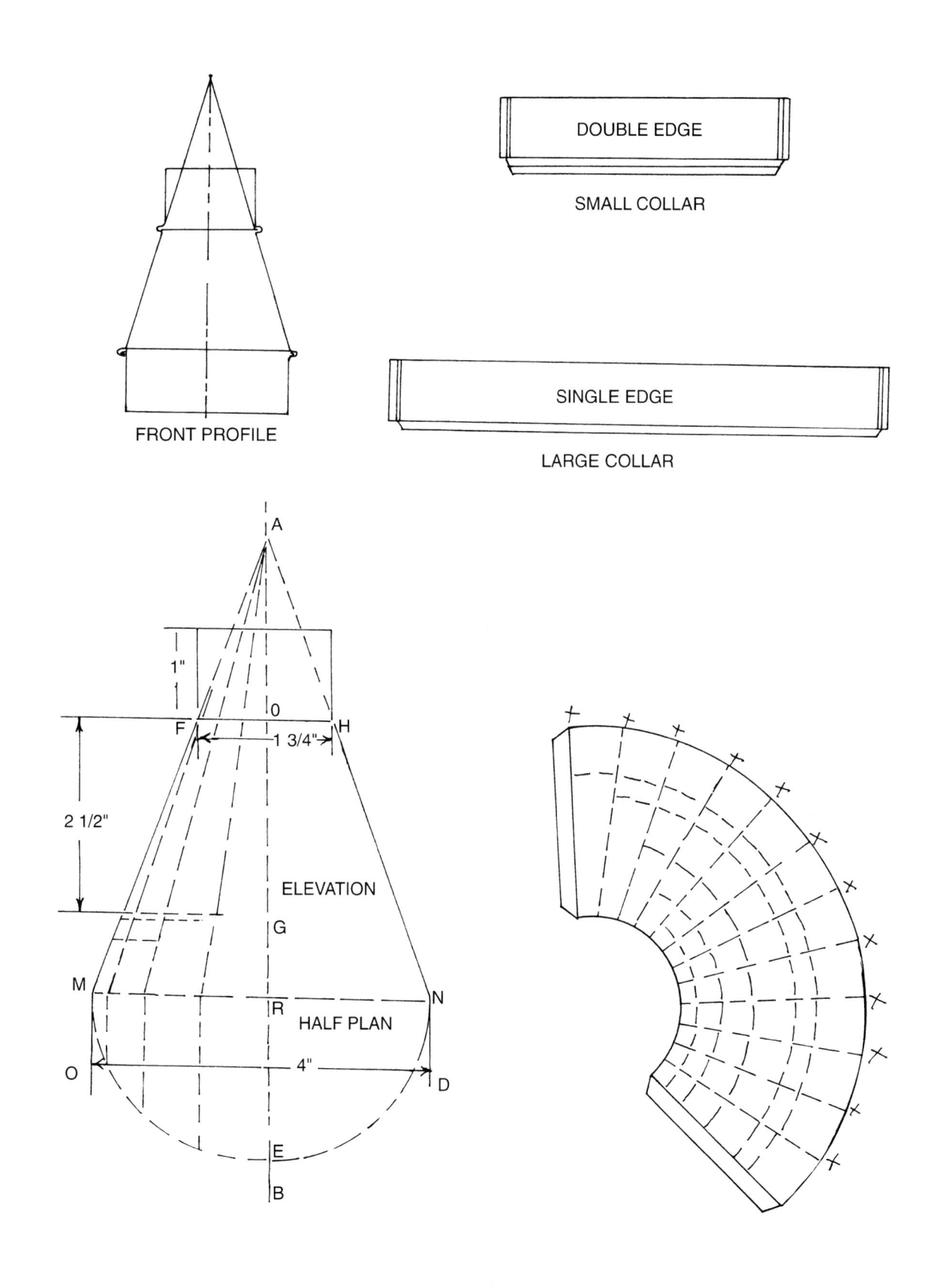

HALF PLAN

1"
1 3/4"
2 1/2"
4"

Figure 7 – Profile or Elevation View

GUTTERS AND DOWNSPOUTS — TRAINEE TASK MODULE 04502

15

TASK 7

RECTANGULAR DOWNSPOUT

Objectives

Upon completion of this task, the trainee will be able to:

1. Design a short section of selected downspout as illustrated in (*Figure 8*).
2. Lay out, develop, and fabricate a section of selected rectangular downspout designed to carry rainfall needs equivalent to 11.7 square inches.

Plain round and rectangular downspouts may be fabricated in any size necessary, but standard sizes with known cross-sectional areas may be more desirable. Some decorative downspouts may be more appropriate for particular roof drainage systems than traditional manufactured downspouts. Therefore, it may be desirable to develop skill in fabricating decorative downspout sections for particular architectural compatibility.

Tools and Materials

1. Two pieces of galvanized sheet metal of the appropriate gage and sizes required for the downspout (WS = 10").
2. Cornice brake.
3. Squaring shears.
4. Layout and development tools.
5. Measuring instruments.

Procedure

1. Find the gage and cross-sectional area for the required sheet metal; *Table 4* will yield the gage required, *Table 3* will yield the actual size for the plain rectangular gutter to match the cross sectional area.
2. Calculate the length of the stretchout.
3. Lay out and scribe the bend lines as implied by *Figure 8*.
4. Bend and shape the stretchout and form the seams.
5. Set the single lock seam.
6. Check the completed downspout section against the shape and size as implied by the manual.
7. Restore the work area.

Questions

1. Where does one find the minimum gages of standard downspouts?
2. Under what circumstances should downspouts be fabricated?

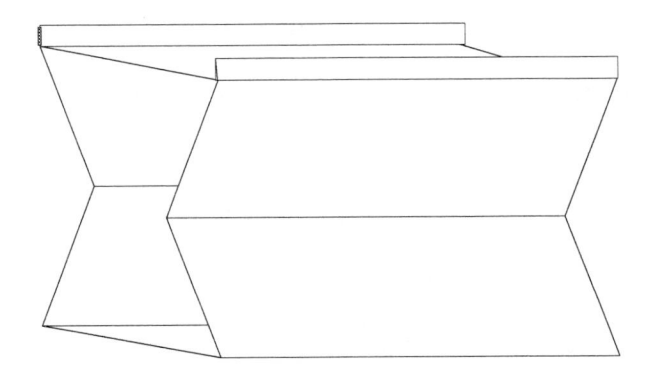

Figure 8 - Downspout

	Gutters	Downspouts
Galvanized Steel	26 gage	26 gage
Copper	16 oz.	16 oz.
Aluminum	0.025"	0.025"
Stainless Steel (Type 302)	0.020"	0.020"

Table 4 - Gages of Drainage Members

SHEET METAL — TRAINEE TASK MODULE 04502

Review Questions

1. List the charts or plates that apply to calculating roof design area.

2. What kinds of information can be found in the chart pertaining to dimensions of standard downspouts?

3. Half round gutter selection size is directly related to what other member?

4. What is the depth to width ratio for rectangular gutter design?

5. What purpose do longitudinal breaks serve in rectangular gutter design?

6. Generally speaking, how is gutter "girth" calculated?

7. What chart is used for finding the width of rectangular gutters for given roof areas and rainfall intensities?

8. How may gutter be hung in relation to the downspout? the front edge?

SUMMARY

Gutters and downspouts must be designed for the climatic region in which the structure is located. They are expected to carry water away quickly and efficiently. Generally speaking, the designs of the components are not affected by the types of materials used. Specialized components or complete systems can be fabricated and placed on architecturally selected structures to meet contemporary styles and esthetic demands.

Trade Terms

Frustum
Stretchout
LS
WS

NCCER CRAFT TRAINING USER UPDATES

The NCCER makes every effort to keep these manuals up-to-date and free of technical errors. We appreciate your help in this process. If you have an idea for improving this manual, or if you find an error, a typographical mistake, or an inaccuracy in the NCCER's Craft Training Manuals, please write us, using this form or a photocopy. Be sure to include the exact module number, page number, a description of the problem, and the correction, if possible. Your input will be brought to the attention of the Technical Review Committee. Thank you for your assistance.

Instructors – If you found that additional materials were necessary in order to teach this module effectively, please let us know so that we may include them in the Equipment/Materials list in the Instructor's Guide.

Write: Curriculum and Revision Department
National Center for Construction Education and Research
P.O. Box 141104
Gainesville, FL 32614-1104
Fax: 352-334-0932

Craft _____ Module Name _____

Module Number _____ Page Number(s) _____

Description of Problem _____

_____

_____

_____

(Optional) Correction of Problem _____

_____

_____

(Optional) Your Name and Address _____

_____

_____

notes

Roof Flashing
Module 04503

NATIONAL
CENTER FOR
CONSTRUCTION
EDUCATION AND
RESEARCH

Task Module 04503

ROOF FLASHING

Objectives

Upon completion of this task module, the trainee will be able to:

1. Demonstrate skill in understanding the principles of weather sealing as they apply to architectural sheet metal work.

2. Demonstrate skill in fabricating selected flashing components.

3. Demonstrate skill in understanding installation procedures for selected chimney flashing members.

INTRODUCTION

Built-up roofing is the weatherproofing component of a building. Flashing is an indispensable means for sealing joints at gravel stops, walls, expansion joints, vents, drains, and wherever additional accessories penetrate the roof exterior. Since sheet metal workers may install the flashing, the ultimate responsibility for providing leakproof flashing rests with the installer. Flashing leaks are said to be the common mode of roofing failure.

Copyright © 1992 National Center for Construction Education and Research, Gainesville, FL All rights reserved. No part of this work may be reproduced in any form or by any means, including photocopying, without written permission of the publisher. Updated: 1998.

PRINCIPLES OF WEATHER SEALING

Like curtain walls, structural framing, air conditioning, and other building subsystems, the roofing system is an assembly of interacting components designed for a specific function. The primary function of a roof system is, of course, the protection of the building interior, its contents, and its occupants from the weather. Built-up roofing systems (*Figure 1*) usually consist of four basic components: the structural deck, the vapor barrier, insulation and built-up membrane.

Of the four, only the structural deck and the built-up membrane are indispensable. Most modern roofs contain a third component, a layer of thermal insulation, that is normally sandwiched between the deck and the membrane. The fourth member is a vapor barrier that is usually placed between the deck and the insulation. Of interest to the sheet metal worker is the fact that each component plays a unique role in the design of a system. A systems-designed component is one of several mutually-dependent variables rather than an independent variable designed on its own in isolation.

The structural deck, for example, resists wind, dead, live, and in some cases earthquake loads. The semiflexible, waterproof membrane, a lamination of felt and bituminous mopping, weatherproofs the roof assembly. Thermal insulation reduces heating and cooling loads by impeding the transfer of heat through the roof. It may also prevent destructive condensation on interior surfaces and help to stabilize the temperature of the structural deck. The vapor barrier retards the flow of water vapor into the insulation, where condensation can harm insulation performance.

Flashing, though not a basic member of the built-up roof system, is an indispensable accessory for sealing joints at gravel stops, walls, vents, drains, expansion joints, and wherever else the membrane is interrupted or terminated. The built-up roof assembly, including the flashing, functions as a system in which each component depends upon the satisfactory performance of the other members.

Slope and rigidity are the critical factors in preventing accidental ponding of water and ensuring positive drainage of the roof's surface. Minimum roof slope is usually considered to be 1/4" per foot. The ponding of water on dead-level roofs may freeze and delaminate or split the membrane. It may also produce a warping pattern or surface thermal deformation, wrinkling the membrane.

Flashing

Flashings are classified as **base flashing**s, cap flashings, or counter flashings. Base flashings are either made of bitumen-impregnated felts or fabrics, or of sheet metal, especially when used on roof curbs, equipment stands, or objects (such as chimneys) that penetrate the roof. Base flashings form the upturned edges of the membrane where it is pierced or terminated. Cap flashings shield the exposed joints of the base flashing from above. Cap flashings are often made of sheet metal, including copper, lead, aluminum, stainless steel, or galvanized steel.

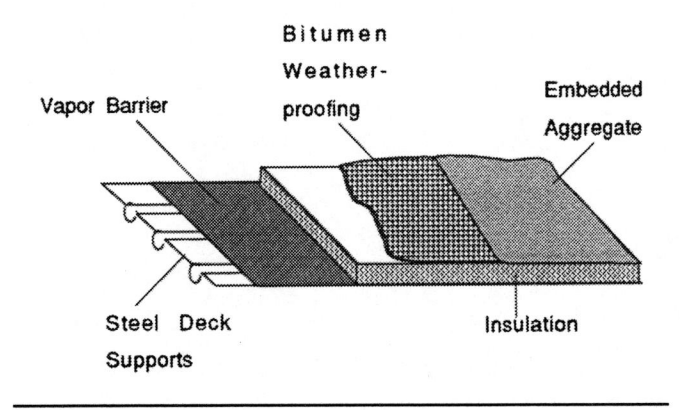

Figure 1 - Roof System

Base and **counterflashing** combinations (*Figure 2*) come in two basic types: vertical terminations and roof edges or eaves.

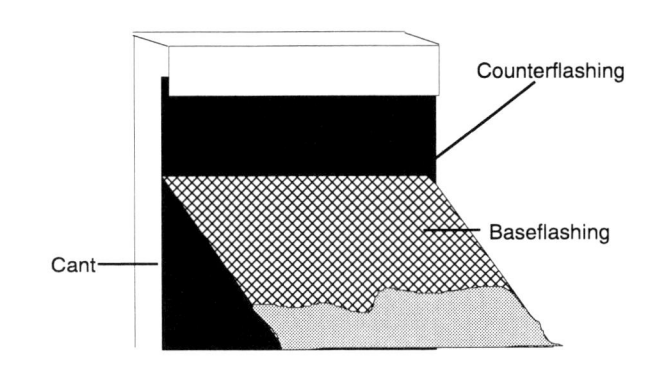

Figure 2 - Base/Counterflashing

When improperly installed, flashing may cause leaks. Flashing requires:

1. Flexibility, in order to mold to supports and accommodate thermal, wind, and structural movement.
2. Compatibility with the roofing membrane and other adjoining surfaces, particularly in coefficient of thermal expansion.
3. Resistance to slipping and sagging.
4. Durability, specifically weather and corrosion resistance (flashings should last at least as long as the built-up membrane).

Flashing materials include a wide variety of metals plus the same felt and bituminous laminations used in fabricating built-up membranes and the newer plastic elastomeric sheets. First-cost economy should be a secondary consideration in material selection and design. Quality and durability must be the prime considerations in flashing design.

Metal flashing material generally makes it unsuitable for base flashings because of its rigidity, its incompatible coefficients of thermal expansion and the difficulty of connecting it to the roof membrane. A notable exception to this rule pertains to base flashing for a roof drain where the need for stability and a bolted connection to the metal drain frame favor lead, copper, or other sheet metal. Wherever possible, skylights, ventilators, and similar roof-penetrating elements should be set on curbs to which membrane base flashings can be attached.

Edgings are usually considered to be accessories that provide a protective termination for the attached built-up composition roofing and base flashings. They must be weathertight, water-shedding, and wind-resistant. These edgings, normally made of metal, include gravel stops, **coping** covers, fascia strips, rake strips, and other similar roof-terminating devices. The flange of a metal accessory tied into a built-up roofing membrane should be at least 4 inches wide. The flange should be primed and set into place on the built-up surface in a bed of flashing cements and fastened to a nailing strip.

Counterflashings shield the exposed joints of base flashings and shed water from vertical surfaces onto the roof. Counterflashings must be rigid and durable; therefore, metal generally provides the best counterflashing material.

Good flashing design depends upon several principles:

1. Allowing for differential movement between base and cap flashings that are anchored to different parts of the structure.
2. Locating flashed joints above the highest water level on the roof.
3. Contouring flashed surfaces to avoid sharp bends.
4. Connecting flashings solidly to supports.

Anchorage for flashing is generally the same as for the built-up membrane and therefore subject to the same limitations. Secure nailing for flashings is most important because flashings are vulnerable to wind uplift and other types of physical damage. Annular ring or screw type nails are specified to prevent backout. If driven through metal flashing, nails must be compatible with the flashing material in order to avoid galvanic corrosion. Differential movement between wall and built-up roof membrane is almost inevitable. In order to isolate the vertical surface of the base flashing from the wall, upright blocking boards (*Figure 3*) are used behind the **cant** strip as a back surface for the base flashing. This blocking should be anchored to the structural deck like the cant strip. The counterflashing shields the open joint of the base flashings as illustrated in *Figure 3*.

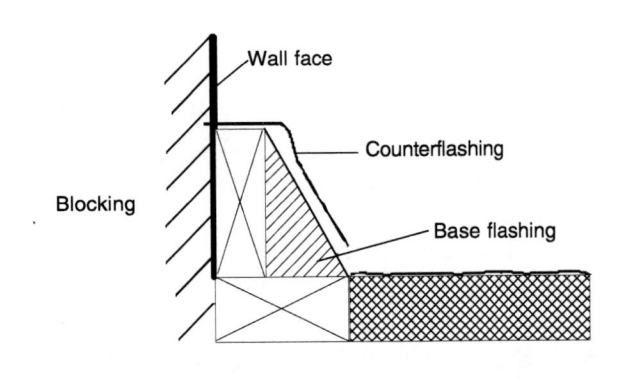

Figure 3 - Blocking Board

Water can be prevented from filtering through the core of masonry walls, by the use of through-the-wall flashing.

Parapet walls are best eliminated because of the difficulty in flashing them, unless there are compelling architectural reasons for their use.

Flashing detail at roof penetrations should follow the general rule of attaching the base flashing to the structural deck and counter flashing to the penetrating member. Pitch pockets should be avoided because they pose a constant open threat of leaks and require frequent maintenance checks and repair of bitumen embrittled by heat and cold. Whenever it is practical, pedestals should be built for roof-penetrating components and flashing should be applied.

Modern building materials may be considered to be waterproof, but they cannot be considered permanently impervious to wind-driven moisture because gradual shrinkage of some materials and the differential movement of buildings and their subsystems may eventually lead to leaks. Moisture which enters walls tends to form ponds or pockets of water and eventually finds its way into the interior of the building by gravity or capillary action. Thus, it is desirable to have permanent water barriers at all points where moisture may enter an exterior wall. Therefore, the building designer has the responsibility of designing a structure that is inherently as impervious to moisture penetration as is practical. It becomes increasingly apparent, however, that the sheet metal worker has an equally important responsibility for proper installation of quality materials and subsystems so that moisture damage to interiors and defacement of exteriors can be prevented to as great an extent as is humanly possible.

FLASHING RECOMMENDATIONS

SMACNA Manual recommendations for flashings are somewhat general in nature and include accompanying illustrations of detail flashing techniques. The manual suggests that architects should specify through-wall flashings to be furnished and cut to size by the sheet metal contractor and then to be installed by the masonry contractor. While they also inform the reader that flashings are available in metal, plastic, paper, fabric, and rubber form, they do not recommend any specific material to be used. The manual also indicates that through-wall flashing (*Figure 4*) is considered one of the most satisfactory methods permanently preventing leaks except in areas exposed to earthquakes.

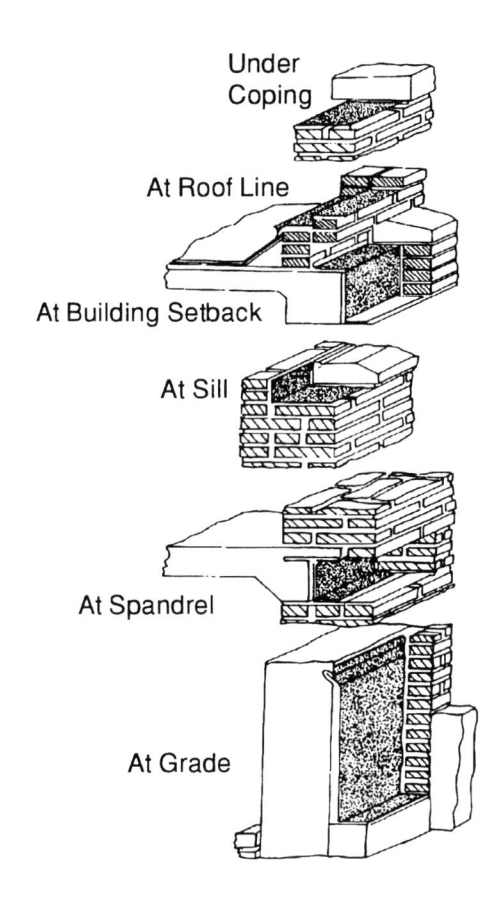

Figure 4 - Through-Wall Flashing

Flashings should be extended to within 1/2" of the exterior face and should be used wherever there is any possibility of water entering the structure.

Further recommendations include:

1. Where extreme wind and weather conditions exist, the entire wall cavity should be protected.
2. Through-wall flashings should not be used in earthquake areas.
3. Metal counter flashing should be used in conjunction with composition base flashings.
4. Composition base flashing should be applied according to the manufacturer's specification.
5. Base flashings should be applied over a cant and extended up the wall a minimum of 8" above the roof line.
6. Metal counter-flashing should be installed so that a minimum of 4 inches of the base flashing is covered.
7. Metal base-flashings (*Figure 5*) should be used with shingle or metal roofs.

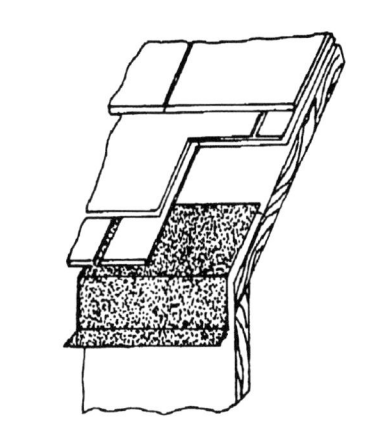

Figure 5 - Metal Base Fashing

8. Metal base-flashings should not be used in place of composition base flashing with built-up roofing membrane.
9. A metal base-flashing may be used over a composition flashing as a protective cover in areas where the base flashing may be abused by traffic.
10. The receiver and insert system (*Figure 6*) of counter flashing is recommended for masonry walls in new construction.

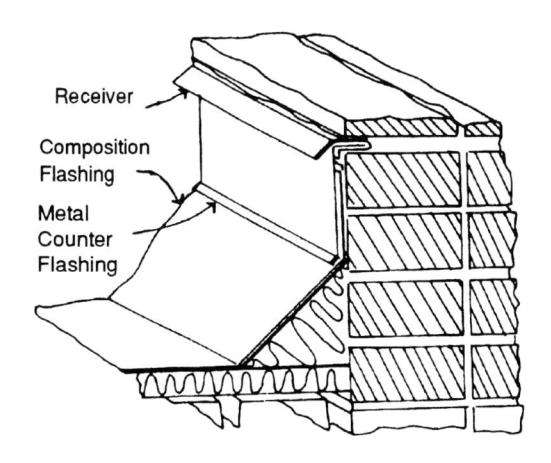

Figure 6 - Receiver and insert

11. Recommended minimum gage (ga.) for counter flashing using a receiver and insert system is 16 ounce copper, 26 gage galvanized steel, or 26 gage stainless steel. Flashing receivers should be of 16 ounce copper, 26 gage galvanized steel, or 28 gage stainless steel.

12. Where raggles are used (see Task 2), the minimum gage for counter flashing is 16 ounce copper, 26 gage stainless steel, 24 gage galvanized steel, or 0.032" aluminum. Supplemental bar or channel stiffeners need not be used if the flashing material is at least 22 gage for steel or 0.050" thickness for aluminum.

13. Where raggles are not used (*Figure 7*), the counter flashing may be held in place by a continuous length of 16 gage, 1-1/2" by 1/2" channel fastened to the wall by masonry anchors on 18" centers.

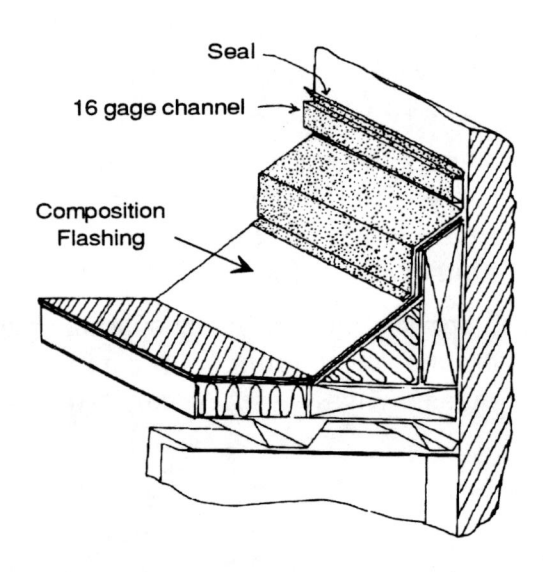

Figure 7 - Counterflashing

Specific application recommendations for identified tasks may be found in the SMACNA, or other trade manuals, by referring to the task in question. The worker need only refer to the index and select the proper title pertaining to the task at hand. Manual recommendations and specifications are based upon sound field engineering practices and should be followed unless the designer or architect specifies practices that are more stringent than the manual standards.

TASK 1

SHINGLE ROOF FLASHING

In this section, the trainee will fabricate flashing for a shingle roof.

Objectives

Upon completion of this task, the trainee should be able to:

1. Identify the recommended standards for shingle roof flashing.
2. Identify the type of flashing recommended for a selected shingle roof.
3. Select and form suitable sheet metal into a recommended shingle roof flashing (*Figure 8*).

Tools and Materials

1. One or more copies of the Sheet Metal Level 2 Module, *Blueprints and Specifications*.
2. One piece of selected sheet metal (of the proper weight, if copper; or gage, if stainless or galvanized steel) required to complete the forming and bending task – about 6" wide.
3. Cornice brake.
4. Handy seamer (elective).
5. Sheet metal scribe and other appropriate layout tools.
6. Measuring instruments.
7. Roof shape (model) to match assigned task.

Procedure

1. Consult this module for recommendations pertaining to shingle roof flashing material and gage or weight.
2. Lay out bend lines on the sheet metal to match the recommendations.
3. Form the inverted vee bend and the top and bottom hems.
4. Set the hems, and mark the position of the nails on the flashing as if it were to be fastened to a roof.

Note: The flashing is formed with an inverted V and is hemmed top and bottom. The apron portion of the flashing should cover a minimum of 4 inches of the top course of shingles. The top of the flashing is nailed to the sheathing, 1-1/2 feet on center.

5. Restore the work area.

Questions

1. What kinds of sheet metal are recommended for shingle roof flashing?
2. What gage or weight of sheet metal is recommended?
3. In consulting the manual, at what distance is the flashing nailed? How much of the top course of shingles should be covered by the flashing?

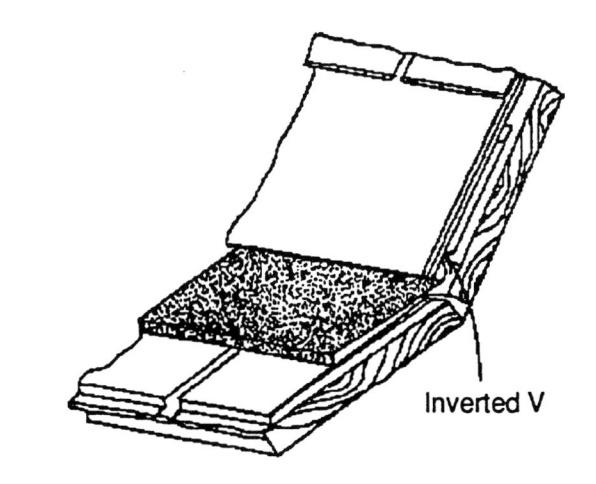

Figure 8 - Shingle Roof Flashing

ROOF FLASHING — TRAINEE TASK MODULE 04503

TASK 2

CHIMNEY FLASHING COMPONENTS

Chimney flashing consists of an apron flashing that is installed after the course of shingles immediately below the chimney is placed on the roof. The sides of the chimney are flashed with pieces of base flashing that are installed with each course of shingles. The counter flashing is installed in a raggle left by the mason. The **raggle** is an open mortar joint or groove that receives the flashing (see *Figure 10*). All other aspects of the flashing installation should conform to the following recommendations:

1. The upper edge of each piece of flashing should extend 2 inches above each course of shingles.
2. The lower edge should be 1/2 inch above the butts of the shingles forming the next course.
3. The base flashing must extend up the wall and onto the roof a minimum of 4 inches.
4. The length of each piece of counter flashing will vary with the slope of the roof but no step should be more than 3 bricks high.
5. The width will also vary but should always be wide enough to cover 4 inches of the base flashing.
6. The saddle flashing, or "cricket," must be flanged 4 inches up the wall of the chimney and 4 inches onto the roof. It is cleated to the roof deck on 12-inch centers using cleats of the same material as the saddle. The cricket may be made in two pieces or it may be formed in one piece as illustrated in *Figure 9*. All joints in the cricket must be soldered.

Objectives

Upon completion of this task, the trainee should be able to:

1. Measure, cut, form and bend apron, base, and counter flashings for a selected chimney size and roof slope (*Figure 9*).

Tools and Materials

1. One or more copies of the Sheet Metal Level 2 Module, *Blueprints and Specifications*.
2. One piece of proper weight metal for the apron flashing.
3. One piece of proper weight metal for a base flashing.
4. One piece of proper weight metal for a counter flashing.

Note: Enough pieces of base and counter flashing should be made available for team members to complete the chimney flashing procedure (two persons per team).

5. Squaring shear.
6. Cornice brake.
7. Sheet metal scribe and layout tools.
8. Measuring instruments.
9. Model of "typical" brick chimney with corresponding roof pitch.

Procedure

1. Consult the text pertaining to chimney flashing and flashing material and gage or weight per previous task.
2. Measure and mark each piece of apron, base, and counter flashing.
3. Cut to size and bend to the shapes as needed.
4. Bend and set the necessary hems and bend the receiver tabs to fit the raggle.
5. Restore the work area.

Figure 9 - Chimney Flashing

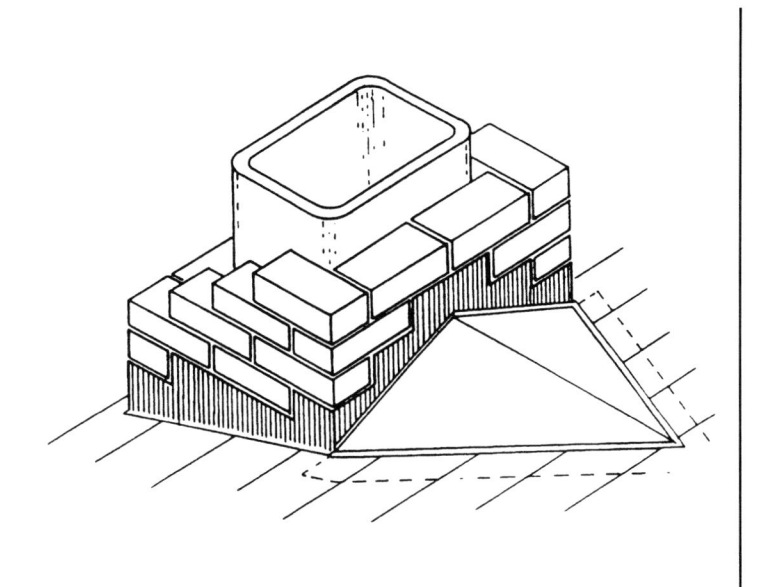

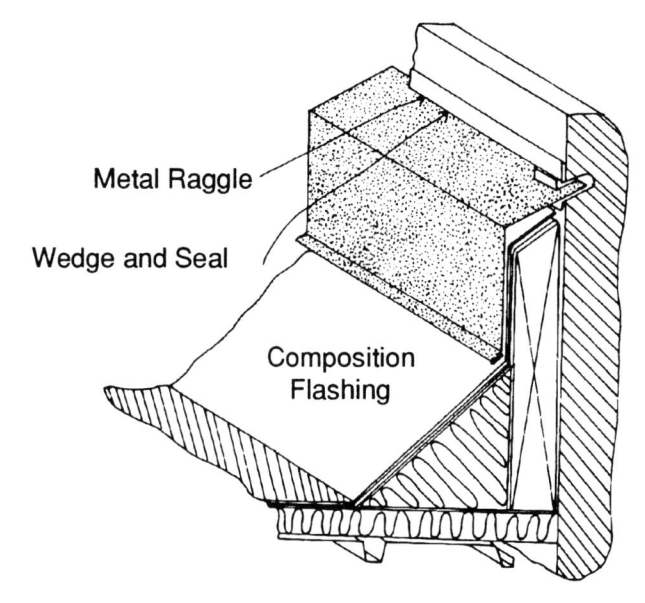

Figure 10 - Raggle Application

Questions

1. What classifications of flashing are required to "fit" a chimney roof penetration?

2. What is the purpose of the raggle as indicated in *Figure 10*?

TASK 3

METAL COPING

Objectives

Upon completion of this task, the trainee should be able to:

1. Interpret information in the module pertaining to the bending and forming process for a typical metal coping profile.

2. Measure, mark, cut, and bend an appropriate type and weight of metal to a selected metal coping shape.

3. Interpret information in the module pertaining to the types and weights of metal recommended for formed metal copings.

The horizontal top surface of a wall is the most vulnerable point for water to enter a wall or structure, particularly masonry walls. The most practical and esthetically-pleasing way to waterproof this part of a wall is to cap it with formed metal copings. Continuous wood blocking must be provided on top of the wall and covered by a layer of building paper. The coping can then be held in place by fastening to a continuous cleat anchored to the wall on the side away from the roof. Copings are fastened to the roof side by placing watertight washers on screws and securing the screws to the wood blocking through slotted holes, two feet on center. Coping is generally formed in 10 foot sections.

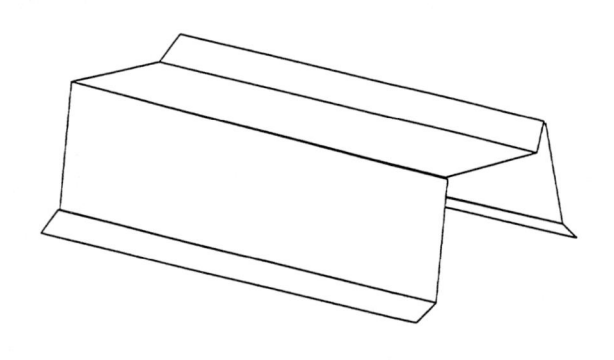

Figure 11 - Coping

Tools and Materials

1. One or more copies of the Sheet Metal Level 2 Module, *Blueprints and Specifications*.

2. One piece of proper weight and material (metal) for the coping about 6" wide, the LS is determined by the width of the "practice" wall.

3. Squaring shear.

4. Cornice brake.

5. Layout tools and measuring instruments.

6. Model section of a typical masonry wall, prepared with wood blocking and building paper.

Procedure

1. Consult the SMACNA *Architectural Sheet Metal* Manual for recommended gages for coping metal.

2. Measure the wall and transfer the dimensions to the appropriate bend lines on the coping stock, that has been correctly measured and cut to size.

3. Bend the shape as shown in *Figure 11*.

4. Check the "fitting" by placing it on the model wall.

5. Restore the work area.

Questions

1. What is the purpose of metal coping?

2. Where can one find the recommended gages and weights and thicknesses of the types of metals recommended for metal coping?

3. How is metal coping fastened on the roof side, on the side away from the roof?

TASK 4

INSTALLING CHIMNEY FLASHING

Chimney flashing might require the utilization of a raggle left by the mason when the chimney was constructed. Chimney flashing may also require the installation of several members that must be fastened in sequence. Generally, the main components of a chimney flashing system are: an apron, that is installed after the course of shingles immediately under the chimney; a base flashing, that is installed with each course of shingles; and a counter flashing, that is installed in a raggle.

Objectives

Upon completion of this task, the trainee should be able to:

1. Properly install a chimney flashing system.

Tools and Materials

1. One or more copies of the Sheet Metal Level 2 Module, *Blueprints and Specifications*.
2. The flashing members cut and formed in Task 2 of this module.
3. Lead wedges or tension forming shapes.
4. Sealant.
5. One 16 ounce carpenter's hammer and galvanized roofing nails.
6. Cornice brake, if needed.
7. Squaring shear.
8. Layout and measuring tools and instruments.

Procedure

1. Lay out the pre-fabricated members of the flashing system produced by your team.
2. Install the apron flashing.
3. Install the base flashing on the sides of the chimney. The upper edge of each piece should extend a minimum of 2 inches above each course of shingles. The lower edge should be 1/2 inch above the butts of the shingle forming the next course. It must extend up the wall and onto the roof a minimum of 4 inches.
4. Install the counter flashing in the raggle. Force the lead wedges or tension forming shape into the raggle to hold the counter flashing in place. Each piece of counter flashing should be no longer than three bricks high and should be wide enough to cover 4 inches of the base flashing.
5. Apply the sealant to the counter flashing in the raggles.
6. Install the saddle flashing if provided.
7. Restore the work area.

ROOF FLASHING — TRAINEE TASK MODULE 04503

Review Questions

1. What is the purpose of lead wedges or tension forming shapes?

2. What is the first step in installing chimney flashing?

3. What is the maximum length of a piece of counter flashing for the chimney?

SUMMARY

If moisture is allowed to enter walls, it tends to form pockets of water. The water will eventually find its way into the interior of the building either by gravity or by capillary action. Flashing is considered one of the most satisfactory methods of permanently preventing leaks. Architects usually specify the flashings to be furnished which are in some cases installed by the mason or the roofing contractor, but the sheet metal worker may prefabricate the specified components. Careful consideration must be given to flashing systems. The base flashing is expected to keep the water from entering the building and must also be designed to provide for building movement. Counter flashing is expected to turn water from a wall or other roof penetration onto the roof or base flashing. Metal base flashing may be used with shingle or metal roofs but may not be used in lieu of composition flashing on built-up roofs.

Trade Terms

Base flashing
Counterflashing
Coping
Raggle
Cant

NCCER CRAFT TRAINING USER UPDATES

The NCCER makes every effort to keep these manuals up-to-date and free of technical errors. We appreciate your help in this process. If you have an idea for improving this manual, or if you find an error, a typographical mistake, or an inaccuracy in the NCCER's Craft Training Manuals, please write us, using this form or a photocopy. Be sure to include the exact module number, page number, a description of the problem, and the correction, if possible. Your input will be brought to the attention of the Technical Review Committee. Thank you for your assistance.

Instructors – If you found that additional materials were necessary in order to teach this module effectively, please let us know so that we may include them in the Equipment/Materials list in the Instructor's Guide.

Write: Curriculum and Revision Department
National Center for Construction Education and Research
P.O. Box 141104
Gainesville, FL 32614-1104

Fax: 352-334-0932

Craft _____ Module Name _____

Module Number _____ Page Number(s) _____

Description of Problem _____

_____

_____

_____

_____

(Optional) Correction of Problem _____

_____

_____

_____

(Optional) Your Name and Address _____

_____

_____